The
BERKSHIRE
Book

A Complete Guide

Two young women await one of the biggest treats in a Berkshire summer: Inside Out at Jacob's Pillow

THE
BERKSHIRE
BOOK
A Complete Guide

SEVENTH EDITION

Lauren R. Stevens

Berkshire House
Woodstock, Vermont

On the cover:
Front: *Spring Blossoms, Bartlett's Apple Orchard, Richmond, Mass.* Photo ©
KeithEmerling.com 2000.
Back: Author photo by Judith Monachina.

The Berkshire Book: A Complete Guide
SEVENTH EDITION – 2003

ISBN: 1-58157-063-5
ISSN: 1056-7968 (series)

Editor: Dale Evva Gelfand. Managing Editor: Philip Rich. Design and composition:
Dianne Pinkowitz. Cover design and composition: Jane McWhorter. Maps: Ron
Toelke Associates. Index: Diane Brenner.

Published by Berkshire House, an imprint of The Countryman Press,
P.O. Box 748, Woodstock, VT 05091
Distributed by W. W. Norton & Company, Inc., 500 Fifth Avenue, New York, NY 10110

Manufactured in the United States of America
First printing 2003
10 9 8 7 6 5 4 3 2

*No complimentary meals or lodgings were accepted by the author or reviewers in gathering
information for this work.*

Berkshire House's
Great Destinations™ travel guidebook series

Recommended by NATIONAL GEOGRAPHIC TRAVELER and TRAVEL & LEISURE magazines.

. . . a crisp and critical approach, for travelers who want to live like locals.
USA TODAY

Great Destinations™ guidebooks are known for their comprehensive, critical coverage of regions of extraordinary cultural interest and natural beauty. The authors in this series are professional travel writers who have lived for many years in the regions they describe. Each title in this series is continuously updated with each printing, in order to insure accurate and timely information. All of the books contain over 100 photographs and maps.

Neither the publisher, the authors, the reviewers, nor other contributors accept complimentary lodgings, meals, or any other consideration (such as advertising) while gathering information for any book in this series.

Current titles available:
The Adirondack Book
The Berkshire Book
The Charleston, Savannah, & Coastal Islands Book
The Chesapeake Bay Book
The Coast of Maine Book
The Hamptons Book
The Hudson Valley Book
The Monterey Bay Big Sur & Gold Coast Wine Country Book
The Nantucket Book
The Newport & Narragansett Bay Book
The Napa & Sonoma Book
The Santa Fe & Taos Book
The Sarasota, Sanibel Island, & Naples Book
The Shenandoah Book (Fall 2003)
The Texas Hill Country Book
Touring East Coast Wine Country

If you are traveling to, moving to, residing in, or just interested in any (or all!) of these enchanting regions, a **Great Destinations™** guidebook is a superior companion. Honest and painstakingly critical, full of information only a local can provide, **Great Destinations™** guidebooks provide you with all the practical knowledge you need to enjoy the best of each region. Why not own them all?

Contents

CHAPTER ONE
From the Glaciers to the Present
HISTORY
1

CHAPTER TWO
Getting Here, Getting Around
TRANSPORTATION
17

CHAPTER THREE
The Keys to Your Room
LODGING
28

CHAPTER FOUR
Pleasing the Palate
DINING
79

CHAPTER FIVE
What to See, What to Do
ARTS & PLEASURES
145

CHAPTER SIX
Spas & the Spiritual Life
BODY & SPIRIT
205

CHAPTER SEVEN
For the Fun of It
OUTDOOR RECREATION
215

CHAPTER EIGHT
Fancy Goods
SHOPPING
259

CHAPTER NINE
Practical Matters
INFORMATION
291

Acknowledgments

The seventh edition of *The Berkshire Book,* like the sixth, has been perpetrated upon an unsuspecting public by a dubious cast of characters who have in common that they live, work, and play in Berkshire County. These include first of all the card-carrying Berkshire County Mealmen: Carol Bosco Baumann, Leslie Ceange, Jean Cowhig, Sean Cowhig, Wally Graves, Henrietta Graves, Maxene Kupperman-Guinals, Allison Lassoe, Becca MacLaren, Judith Monachina, Katherine Myers, Damon Reed, Gerard Smith, Jean J. Rousseau, Sarah Shepard, Edith Stovel, Jeffrey L. Stevens, and Lauren R. Stevens. These folks undertook to make the *Dining* chapter digestible. Never before did so few eat so much in the service of their county.

Judith Monachina, who served as photo editor, also wrote Chapter Six, *Body & Spirit.* Maryjane Fromme wrote Chapter Eight, *Shopping,* and investigated the galleries in Chapter Five. Seth Rogovoy wrote the "Nightlife" section of *Arts and Pleasures.* Thanks to them all for their wealth of knowledge and professionalism.

Mary Osak, well-versed in county matters, checked the facts. Philip Rich served as patient and diligent managing editor, while Dale Gelfand edited. Publisher Jean Rousseau kept his vigilant eye on every aspect of the book. Berkshire Book VII is more of an ensemble production than the work of any individuals. Fortunately this group worked well together. Any errors, however, should be attributed to the author. Readers could help by forwarding comments to Berkshire House.

— LRS

The Way This Book Works

ORGANIZATION

Entries are located by subject in the appropriate chapters. Among the chapters, arrangements vary to suit the needs of subject matter. Most material is arranged in three geographical groupings, with South County offerings first, followed by those in Central County, and finally North County. A few nearby listings that are located Outside the County are given, as well.

Within these geographic groupings, listings are arranged alphabetically — first by town or topic, and then by establishments' names. Some entries, such as those in *Shopping*, are arranged by type; hence all the craft shops appear together. Each chapter has its own introduction, and the specific arrangement of that chapter is spelled out there.

Factual information was researched at the latest possible time before publication, but be advised that chefs and innkeepers come and go, hours change, shops appear and disappear. When in doubt, phone ahead.

Specific information (such as address and location, telephone number, hours of business, and a summary of special features or restrictions) is presented in the lefthand column or is otherwise shown separately, adjacent to descriptions of various entries throughout the book.

PRICES

With few exceptions, specific prices are not given. Because pricing is constantly changing, generally we have noted price ranges.

Lodging prices are on a per-room rate, double occupancy, in the high season (summer, fall foliage, and ski months). Low-season rates are likely to be 20–40 percent less. We urge you always to phone ahead for updated prices and other information and for reservations.

Restaurant prices indicate the cost of an individual's meal, which includes appetizer, entrée, and dessert but does not include cocktails, wine, tax, or tip. Restaurants with a prix fixe menu are noted accordingly.

Price Codes

	Lodging	Dining
Inexpensive	Up to $100	Up to $15
Moderate	$100 to $150	$15 to $30
Expensive	$150 to $200	$30 to $50
Very Expensive	Over $200	$50 or more

Credit Cards are abbreviated as follows:
AE — American Express   DC — Diner's Club
CB — Carte Blanche   MC — Master Card
D — Discover Card   V — Visa

AREA CODE

There is one telephone area code for all of Berkshire County: **413.**

INFORMATION BOOTHS

Volunteers in several Berkshire towns staff tourist Information Booths in the summer and early fall. Often information is available at the site even when volunteers aren't. Year-round tourist information can be obtained from the *Berkshire Visitors Bureau* (413-443-9186 or 413-237-5747; Berkshire Common, Plaza Level, Pittsfield) The bureau is open Mon.–Fri., 8:30–4:30.

For a more detailed list of information sources, see "Tourist Information" at the end of Chapter Nine, *Information.*

North County
Adams (population 8,809)
Cheshire (3,401)
Clarksburg (1,686)
Florida (676)
New Ashford (247)
North Adams (14,681)
Savoy (705)
Williamstown (8,424)

Central County
Becket (1,755)
Dalton (6,892)
Hancock (721)
Hinsdale (1,872)
Lanesborough (5,989)
Lenox (5,077)
Peru (821)
Pittsfield (45,793)
Richmond (1,604)
Washington (541)
Windsor (875)

South County
Alford (399)
Egremont (1,345)
Great Barrington (7,527)
Lee (5,985)
Monterey (934)
Mount Washington (130)
New Marlborough (1,494)
Otis (1,365)
Sandisfield (824)
Sheffield (3,335)
Stockbridge (2,276)
Tyringham (350)
West Stockbridge (1,416)

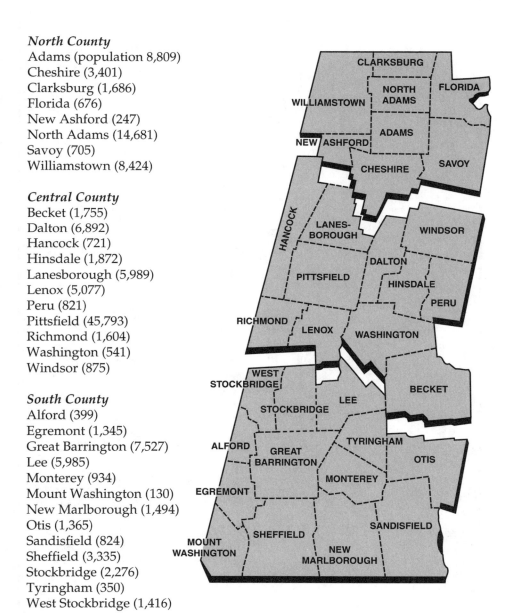

BERKSHIRE TOWNS

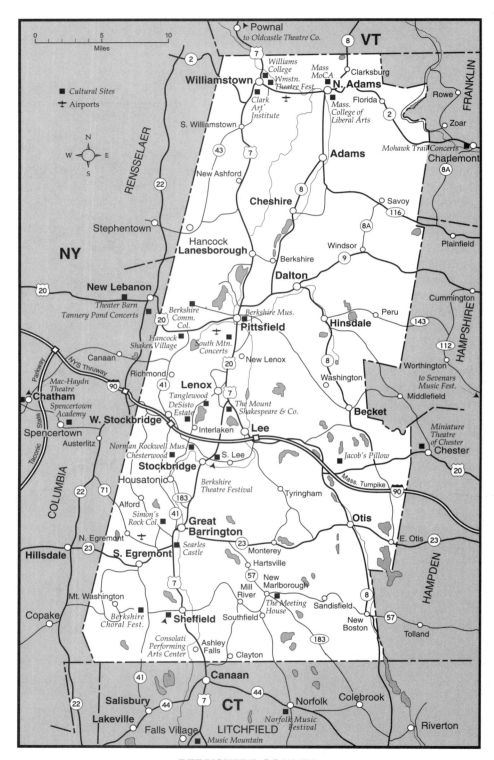

BERKSHIRE COUNTY

The
BERKSHIRE
Book
A Complete Guide

CHAPTER ONE
From the Glaciers to the Present
HISTORY

A farm house and split rail fence still grace the Tyringham Valley.

To hardworking Berkshire settlers, much of what we prize today as beauty was at the least unproductive and at the most an absolute impediment to making a living. Jeremiah Wilbur who, at age 14 in 1767, began farming on the sides of Mount Greylock, could not have had a lot of time to admire the view. This prodigious worker built a carting road over the notch between Ragged Mountain and Greylock into Adams, built a road to near the summit of Greylock that was the forerunner of today's Notch Road, cleared enough land to grow and cut 100 tons of hay in a year, tapped enough maples to produce 1,800 pounds of sugar in a year, protected his herd of free-roaming cattle from wolves, maintained the best sheep herd in the county, built a cider mill, a grist-mill, and a sawmill on Notch Brook, increased his holdings to 1,600 acres—and died in 1813 a very tired but relatively wealthy man. It may have been the promise of water power that lured this early farmer out of the valley and onto the wildest land around, but that same water was a constant threat to his road, the wildlife threatened to destroy his livelihood, and the steep terrain was hard to negotiate and tougher to plow.

We're fortunate to know a bit about this "active and industrious man" who lived in a remote part of what was still nearly frontier. In 1800 the president of Yale College, Timothy Dwight, toured the area, publishing *Travels in New England and New York* in 1822. At the time, people traveled to settle, trade furs, convert Indians, survey boundaries, or fight a war. The concept of taking a recreational spin through remote and unsettled places was unheard of. Dwight may, in fact, have been America's first native tourist. Our good fortune is that he was an intelligent, observant, literate man.

When Dwight rode his horse into Williamstown in October, he looked up the president of Williams College, Ebenezer Fitch—a fellow Yalie who had written about Wilbur's remarkable sheep—suggesting a trip up Greylock. Fitch led him to Wilbur's home, partway up the mountain. Wilbur not only allowed the men to cross his land, he "willingly accompanied" them up the road he had built to carry salt to his cattle. "We alighted from our horses within 20 feet of the summit, and found our path better than a great part of the town and country roads throughout the hill country of New England," Dwight wrote. The summit of Mount Greylock was tree covered as, of course, no one had yet built the tower that now graces it there. So to get the view, the two college presidents and the farmer each picked out a wind-battered fir tree and shinnied up.

"The view was immense and of amazing grandeur," Dwight wrote. "You will easily suppose that we felt total superiority to all the humble beings who were creeping on the footstool beneath us. The village of Williamstown shrunk to the size of a farm; and its houses, church, and colleges appeared like the habitation of martins and wrens."

Dwight recognized the Adirondacks "west of Lake Champlain," the Green Mountains, Mount Monadnock, Mount Tom, and the Catskills. He discovered the joy of the third dimension that we, who so easily drive over hills or fly

---

Berkshire, the Berkshires, the Berkshire Hills

Even residents are confused about the name of this place. The original Berkshire is in England, south of Oxford. There it's pronounced *Bark-shur*. "Shire" refers to an Anglo-Saxon administrative district.

Strictly speaking "Berkshire Hills" is the handle for south-county hills and plateau, including the adjacent Taconics in New York State and northwestern Connecticut. As time wears on, however, the term seems to be generalizing to all the high ground in and around the county.

Residents may refer to the area politically as "Berkshire County," poetically as "Berkshire" and, in relation to tourism, as "the Berkshires." This book is similarly inconsistent.

above them, take for granted. For Dwight's generation and those to follow, Mount Greylock was spectacular, as most people did not visit higher peaks—just as Bash Bish Falls, at the southwest corner of Berkshire, inspired more awe when few had been to Niagara.

Forty-four years later, when writer/naturalist Henry David Thoreau climbed past the old Wilbur homestead, Mount Greylock was still wild country, still an adventure. He exchanged a few pleasantries about reaching the summit that night with Smith Wilbur, Jeremiah's grandson. Thoreau used the trip to overcome his grief over his brother's death, his disappointment at being turned down in matrimony by a cousin, his guilt for having accidentally burned 300 acres of woodlands in Concord, and to answer his need to find his own transcendent vision. All of these things, he implies, he accomplished on his walk up Greylock, awaking the next morning to a Technicolor sunrise above the clouds. The trip was his preparation for Walden, pond and book, the next year.

Foresters examine an old-growth specimen on Mt. Greylock

Lauren R. Stevens

(Thoreau must have read Dwight, for he makes the same mistake of identifying Williamstown and its colleges from the summit. Can't be done: Mount Prospect is in the way. Thoreau admitted, in his account of the trip in *A Week on the Concord and Merrimack Rivers*, that he had only a very quick view out before the sun set.)

While Wilbur may deliberately have chosen his site for the grand view, what Dwight began (and 19th-century writers and painters continued) was to instruct hardworking, practical farmers and shopkeepers in the appreciation of the landscape. For a farmer occupied with the daily grind of growing food for his family, someone had to say (as Thoreau did more than once): Slow down, enjoy, observe the values nature maintains without any human labor.

Thus the Hudson River School of painters created large, inspiring landscapes and toured them through the towns and cities. "Look what we have here!" they exclaimed to folk who had seen little beyond the back forty. Furthermore, these artists turned around the religious view of the landscape. When the Puritans arrived, they saw the woods as dark, evil, and aligned with the devil. When Thoreau described his July sunrise on Mount Greylock or Thomas Cole painted the sun breaking through the clouds, they depicted trees, fields, and falling water as infused with heaven. Thoreau solved his own problems on Greylock, but he also taught his readers to appreciate the marvels of this godly place.

Building on this tradition, the arts in Berkshire excel and expand, still teaching residents and visitors to appreciate our surroundings.

NATURAL HISTORY

Tell me your landscape and I will tell you who you are.

—Ortega y Gasset

Artists taught us to appreciate this gentled landscape. Erosion turned jagged peaks to rolling hills in much the same way that culture has smoothed the rough edges of its people—whom Edith Wharton once called her "granite outcroppings."

Six hundred million years ago, however, the region lay flatter, covered by a shallow sea. Lapping waves built up beaches that turned to sandstone, which in turn metamorphosed into quartzite—the erosion-resistant backbone of many of the county's ridges. Shelled marine animals built coral reefs, which calcified into limestone. Deposits of this alkaline agent, which are mined on the side of Mount Greylock today, buffer the area against the worst ravages of acid precipitation. Some of the limestone recrystallized into marble, snowy chunks of which grace hiking trails and can be inspected at Natural Bridge in North Adams. Muddy, offshore sediments settled to form shales and then schists, crystalline rocks that fracture cleanly. The bands of granite that run through the southern part of the county antedate the sedimentary rock.

Then, at a speed of an inch a year over 150 million years, the land masses that would one day be North America, Africa, and Europe moved toward each other, closing the proto-Atlantic Ocean. Several arcs of offshore volcanic islands were shoved onto the continent by a series of slow but cataclysmic collisions known as the Taconic Orogeny (*orogeny* means *mountain building*). The entire continental shelf was squeezed into a series of folds, the monumental forerunners of the Appalachian Mountains. Then, slowly, the continents began to pull apart, as they are still doing.

Even as the mountains were rising to Himalayan heights, the process of erosion began. Rain fell, forming streams that raged through a landscape unrooted by vegetation. Over the eons water and wind tamed the rugged land forms, preparing them for the plants that would further soften them.

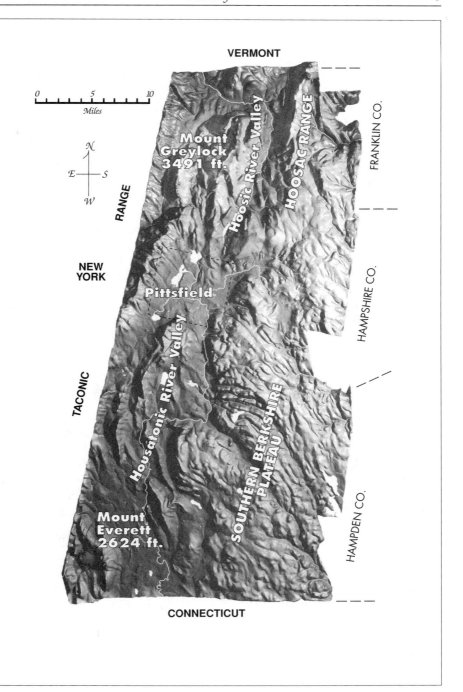

VERMONT

0   5   10
Miles

N

E —+— S

W

RANGE

NEW
YORK

TACONIC

Mount
Greylock
3491 ft.

Hoosic River Valley

HOOSAC RANGE

FRANKLIN CO.

Pittsfield

HAMPSHIRE CO.

Housatonic River Valley

SOUTHERN BERKSHIRE PLATEAU

Mount
Everett
2624 ft.

HAMPDEN CO.

CONNECTICUT

From the relief map by Bartlett Hendricks, courtesy Berkshire Museum

Less than two million years ago the first in a succession of four ice sheets ground down in response to a cooling climate. These mile-high glaciers deposited debris, gravel, and rocks around the relative nubbins of mountains that remained. Glacial lakes covered Great Barrington, Tyringham, and the valley from Williamstown to Adams, forming gravel beaches on their shorelines. But the glaciers only iced the Berkshire cake; the great work of diminution had begun—and continues—through erosion. Two great landslides on Mount Greylock in the summer of 1990 were simply more dramatic instances. The Hoosic, Housatonic, and Westfield River Valleys existed before the glaciers and remained largely the same, although glacial debris forced the Farmington River to swing north to meet the Connecticut.

As the climate warmed, as recently as 11,000 years ago, the vegetation returned and further tempered the climate. From the boggy marshland an evergreen forest moved north, lingering now only on the tops of the highest ridges. In its place, the broad-leaved deciduous forest moved in, characterized by oak and its associated species in south county and sugar maple in the north.

As the glaciers withdrew, animals returned—and perhaps a few of the earliest North American human inhabitants, whose Asian ancestors had boated the Pacific or walked across the Bering land bridge, were in Berkshire to bid farewell to the ice. The first Americans here were initially foragers, but after developing tools, they crafted weapons and became hunters. In South Egremont recently the remains of a 12,000-year-old mastodon were found; around it, arrowheads of the same age.

Seen from above, Berkshire County presents its ridges as north-to-south-running folds: the Taconics along the New York boundary, the Green Mountains protruding south from Vermont, the Hoosacs filling the northeast quadrant, and the Southern Berkshire Plateau filling the southeast quadrant. Tributaries of the two main Berkshire rivers, the Housatonic and the Hoosic, nearly meet at Brodie Mountain, flowing in opposite directions to form the extended north-south valley that US Route 7 now follows. The Greylock massif stands as a peninsula to the Taconics, as indeed it was when glacial Lake Bascom filled the Hoosac Valley to the 1,300-foot elevation. Greylock rises 3,491 feet, the highest point in southern New England, visible from most of the county. Mount Everett is the 2,264-foot sentinel of south county. It is possible to see the one from the other.

The rocky steepness of the county does not lend itself to leisurely flowing water and big lakes. With the exception of the southern reach of the Housatonic, which meanders through Sheffield, Berkshire rivers rush to their destinations. We owe the lakes we have now, excepting Stockbridge Bowl, to 19th-century industrialists who either dammed small ponds to make them larger—as with Otis, Pontoosuc, and Onota—or created reservoirs out of rivers—as with Cheshire Reservoir. They wanted a supply of water upstream they could let out in low water times to turn the mill wheels.

The two branches of the Housatonic River rise in the Greylock range and in

Washington, the northernmost part of the Southern Berkshire Plateau. They meet in Pittsfield and flow south to enter Long Island Sound at Stratford, Connecticut. The Hoosic River, flowing northward from Cheshire Reservoir (a.k.a. Hoosac Lake) through Adams, joins with its north branch in North Adams and passes through Williamstown and a corner of Vermont on its way to the Hudson River, above Albany. The Westfield forms in the Hoosac Plateau, joining the Connecticut River in Westfield, while the Farmington forms in the Southern Berkshire Plateau, mostly in Otis Reservoir —the largest recreational body of fresh water in the Commonwealth.

Although settlement and deforestation of the county once drove off the larger animals, today they are returning. One hundred years ago the county was 75 percent cleared; now, as the farms grow in, it is 75 percent wooded, providing habitat for the prolific deer, the occasional moose, black bear, red and gray fox, coyote, bobcat, beaver, and mink. Tales of eastern cougar sightings are making the rounds again; the last cougar in these parts was thought to have been shot in Vermont 100 years ago. Berkshire hosts rare salamanders that thrive only in these wetlands because the area's high lime content. Wild turkey flap about in the woods, while in 1999 a bald eagle was born in Sandisfield. Great blue heron, with wings six feet across, scurry along the streams; ruffed grouse and quail explode out of the woods.

Although formal gardens at historic homes are beautiful, so are the ephemeral spring flowers at Bartholomew's Cobble and the delicate boreal blooms on Greylock. In our postglacial melt, accelerated by global warming, a tamed Berkshire is green and welcoming.

This geology follows Lauren R. Stevens's *Hikes and Walks in the Berkshire Hills*, for which Williams College geologist Paul Karabinos consulted. The pamphlet *A Canoe Guide to the Housatonic* comments on the local ecology. Berkshire Sanctuaries Director René Laubach, in his *Guide to Natural Places in the Berkshire Hills*, invokes the flora, fauna, geology, and ecology. The Berkshire Museum, the county's center for natural-history study, displays Bartlett Hendrick's wall-sized raised relief topographic map of the county. For field trips, try any of the "Outdoor Sites" (see Chapter Six, *Recreation*).

SOCIAL HISTORY

History is to the community what memory is to the individual.

—Shaker saying

As recent archeological digs in south country have confirmed, American Indians settled and farmed in the area before the time of Europeans. The words *Housatonic* and *Hoosic* have a similar linguistic root, which may have meant "beyond place," beyond the Hudson. In prehistory, the Mahican Indians entered the area from the Hudson Valley by way of the Green, a tributary of the Housatonic, and Hoosic Rivers to hunt and farm. They fished shad, herring, and salmon in the springtime. They built weirs to trap fish in the Housatonic's tributaries and also fished with hand nets from dugout canoes on the river. They gathered mussels from the rocky river bottoms and smoke-cured them, together with their surplus fish for winter storage. They hunted duck and geese, and they maintained gardens in the river's floodplain, which were fertilized annually by the spring flood.

After the Dutch established a fur-trading outpost at Fort Orange (now Albany, New York) in 1624, the Mahicans and the neighboring Mohawk went to war over who would be gatekeepers to the valuable fur trade. By 1628 the Mahican had been driven to the east of the Hudson, some settling in Berkshire.

In 1676 the first European of record set foot in Berkshire, when Major John Talcott overtook a raiding band of about 150 Indians "neare unto Ousatunick" (Great Barrington). It was the last significant battle of King Philip's War, Major Talcott preserving both colonial security and his unbeaten battle record. Smallpox brought by the Europeans dramatically reduced Mahican ranks by the late 17th century.

As the numbers of Indians shrank, a few Dutch settlers infiltrated from the Hudson Valley to what is now the town of Mount Washington. Dutch town names, such as Van Deusenville (in Great Barrington) still exist in south county, together with traces of Dutch architecture in the stepped gable ends of old buildings.

In 1724 a small band of Mahicans led by chiefs Konkapot and Umpachenee sold their lands along the Housatonic River, including what is now Sheffield, Great Barrington, Egremont, Mount Washington, Alford, and parts of Lee, Stockbridge, and West Stockbridge. The price: "£460, 3 bbls. of cider, and 30 qts. of rum." While the first land buyers were speculators from the Massachusetts Bay Colony, the first settlers tended to come from Connecticut because it was easier to move from south to north along the river valleys than from east to west over the mountains.

English settlers moved to the Sheffield grant, building the earliest homesteads at some distance from the Housatonic, on the second river terrace. This allowed the fertile floodplain to be used for agriculture and kept the settlers away from the malarial lowlands or floods. In the mid-1730s, the Reverend John Sergeant came from Yale College to proselytize and educate the hundreds of Mahicans who lived around *W-nahk-ta-kook* ("Great Meadow"), later called Indian Town and then Stockbridge. He learned their language and won their respect.

In 1744 Berkshire was opened to cross-country travel for the first time, when the "Great Road" was laid out between Boston and Albany, crossing the county at Great Barrington. John Sergeant died in 1749. The Reverend Jonathan Edwards came to Stockbridge two years later. His zeal had offended parishioners at his previous pulpit in Northampton, and Edwards had been dismissed. Exiled, in effect, to Stockbridge, his relation to the Indians did not compare to Sargeant's. One of America's earliest philosophers of religion, Edwards published *Freedom of the Will* in 1754, Berkshire's first book. With his fiery preaching style, Edwards stirred up the "Great Awakening," a religious revival that swept New England.

When the 1759 British victory over the French at Quebec marked the conclusion of the French and Indian War, western Massachusetts was no longer as vulnerable to invading Indian attack and considered safer for settlement. On July 1, 1761, the royal governor, Sir Francis Bernard, created the county by striking off a section from the already-existing Hampshire County. He declared this one "Berkshire," after his home county in England. Although the line between New England and New York wasn't settled until the 1790s, Berkshire boundaries correspond remarkably to the mountain ridges.

In early 1773 a group of townspeople and lawyers met in the Sheffield study of Colonel John Ashley. There, in one of the earliest public assertions of American freedom, they drafted "The Sheffield Declaration," stating to Great Britain and all the world that "Mankind in a State of Nature are equal, free and independent of each other. . . ." In the following year, ferment in the county against the British intensified. In July a county convention met under the chairmanship of Colonel Ashley. From this meeting, the "Stockbridge Non-Intercourse Articles" of 1774 were drafted, complaining that "whereas the Parliament of Great Britain have of late undertaken to give and grant away our money without our knowledge or consent, . . . we will not import, purchase, or consume" any British goods. British oppression mounted. On August 16 some 1,500 people of Berkshire staged a peaceful sit-down strike around the Great Barrington Courthouse, preventing the royal judges from meeting. It was the first open resistance to British rule in America.

And in April 1775 a regiment of Berkshire Minutemen under Colonel John Paterson of Lenox started out for Cambridge to aid in the Revolutionary effort. That May former Sheffield and Connecticut resident Ethan Allen led his Green Mountain Boys, with 57 Berkshire men, in a successful surprise attack on Fort Ticonderoga on Lake Champlain. That winter (1776), General Henry Knox, Continental troops, and over 100 oxen, dragged captured Ticonderoga cannon through Berkshire on the way to General George Washington in Cambridge. Aided by this additional weaponry, Washington was able to drive the British from Boston.

In a kind of Revolutionary hangover, Daniel Shays led a revolt of western Massachusetts veterans disappointed in their lot. In 1786 they closed courthouses and released debtors from jail. Mum Bet, Colonel Ashley's slave freed by Theodore Sedgwick and then employed at the Sedgwicks, hid the family silver during the fighting. An attempt to take the Springfield arsenal the following January failed. Most of the "regulators" were killed or captured.

With peace and growing prosperity, the 1790s saw the beginnings of a number of county institutions. The Shakers established colonies in Hancock and Tyringham. Marble quarrying started in West Stockbridge. Williams College's faltering beginnings in 1793 eventually led to its position as one of the finest liberal arts colleges in the United States.

The American Indian community in Berkshire had collapsed socially and economically. As Konkapot's tribe dwindled to fewer than 400 members—including stray Indians from other tribes and rechristened "Stockbridge Indians"—in 1771, at age 94, he stepped down as chief. Beginning in 1784 the Stockbridge were forced into westward migration, leaving only their Housatonic legends—and a Bible—behind them. Their descendants returned to the Mission House for the Bible in 1984.

The farmers of Cheshire pooled the entire town's milk production for a day in 1801 producing The Great Cheshire Cheese, a 1,235 pound, barrel-shaped cheddar that was hauled by oxen to Albany and then by boat to Washington for presentation to President Jefferson.

Elkanah Watson introduced Spanish Merino sheep—and incidentally the agricultural fair—into Berkshire in 1807, tethering two of the animals on the Pittsfield common. Their wool, spun into fine worsted yarn and woven into Berkshire broadcloth in the county's state-of-the-art mills, was fashioned into President Madison's inauguration suit in 1809. Shortly thereafter, the first stage route in the county was established, running from Greenfield to North Adams, Williamstown, and Albany.

The mill on the farm became the mill in town. Plants of a new sort sprouted by the sides of Berkshire's rivers. Industry took a firm hold in Berkshire when

Judith Monachina

The paper industry has thrived in the Housatonic Valley, including Lee.

Zetas Crane began paper production in Dalton and David Estes opened the first textile mill in North Adams.

Writers and painters arrived soon after. William Cullen Bryant spent a year at Williams College and then practiced law in Great Barrington. As he attempted to divine the art of poetry while earning his living as a lawyer, his new Stockbridge friend Catherine Sedgwick published her first novel, *A New England Tale* (1820), to critical acclaim. Hudson River artist Thomas Cole painted Mount Greylock over Pontoosuc Lake, while other artists depicted the lower Housatonic and Bash Bish Falls. Alexis de Tocqueville visited the Sedgwicks by stagecoach in Stockbridge in 1831. Not long after, trains huffed into the hills, one of them bringing Henry Wadsworth Longfellow to honeymoon in Pittsfield. Dr. Oliver Wendell Holmes, the "autocrat of the breakfast table," built a home on ancestral lands at Canoe Meadows to spend his summers in Berkshire. Nathaniel Hawthorne moved from Salem to Lenox and took up residence at a property he called Tanglewood. Then in 1850 Herman Melville bought Arrowhead Farm in Pittsfield. David Dudley Field introduced Melville to Hawthorne on the occasion of a climb up Monument Mountain; the two great writers' imaginations were entwined thereafter.

Hawthorne and Thoreau

Nathaniel Hawthorne was one of 19th-century Berkshire's greatest admirers. During his year-and-a-half residency in the "Red Cottage" at Tanglewood, overlooking Stockbridge Bowl, he kept a journal, recording the fullness of his affection for the landscape.

October 16, 1850

A morning mist filling up the whole length and breadth of the valley, betwixt here and Monument Mountain; the summit of the mountain emerging. The mist reaches to perhaps a hundred yards of our house, so dense as to conceal everything, except that, near its hither boundary, a few ruddy or yellow tree-tops emerge, glorified by the early sunshine; as is likewise the whole mist cloud.

H. D. Thoreau shared Hawthorne's reverence for these hills, saying of Williams College's position at the foot of Greylock—or anyone's willingness to learn from nature:

It would be no small advantage if every college were thus located at the base of a mountain, as good at least as one well-endowed professorship. . . . Some will remember, no doubt, not only that they went to college, but that they went to the mountain.

In 1851 construction began on the Hoosac Tunnel between the Berkshire towns of Florida and North Adams, a project that was to take 195 lives. The 4.75-mile tunnel, longest in America and the one in which nitroglycerin was used for the first time, was completed in 1875.

Before those explosions were silenced, shells were fired in hate in the Civil War. Five days after the Confederate forces opened fire on Fort Sumter, Berkshire militiamen were on their way south to defend the indivisibility of the Republic. These first county recruits stayed three months and saw little action; other Berkshire regiments took their place, fighting through 1865 as far south as the state of Florida.

In 1866, after two unsuccessful attempts, Cyrus Field of Stockbridge and his engineers laid a cable across the Atlantic, connecting America with Europe. A year later in America's leading paper town, Lee, paper fabrication from wood pulp rather than rags was demonstrated for the first time in the United States.

Industry was now booming in Berkshire, with textile and paper plants lining the rivers. Fueled by the county's abundant forests, iron smelters, railroads and other heavy industries cut deep into the Berkshire woodland. It was not long before nearly 75 percent of the county's timber was gone, and the hills were nearly bald. In 1879 Crane & Co. of Dalton obtained an exclusive contract with the federal government involving a lot of money: to produce American currency.

In 1886 William Stanley installed the world's first commercial electric system, lighting 25 shops along Main Street, Great Barrington. The General Electric Company visited Stanley in his Pittsfield workshop and, soon after, moved nearby. Five years later an electric trolley system was introduced in Pittsfield, running from Park Square to Pontoosuc Lake. Soon this quiet, reliable transport would connect most of the county—and the county with the region.

The decade of the 1880s ushered in Berkshire's Gilded Age, during which millionaires came to the hills to play and build their dream "cottages." Mrs. Mary Searles had just completed her $2.5 million castle in Great Barrington; Anson Phelps Stokes had spent nearly as much in completing the largest home in America just then, his 100-room Shadowbrook in Stockbridge. A mile away, the 33-room Italianate palazzo called Wheatleigh was being finished, a gift of H. H. Cook to his daughter on the occasion of her marriage to "Count" Carlos de Heredia. The 90-plus-room Elm Court was nearby, too, in Lenox, built by rug magnate W. D. Sloane; and across town, Giraud Foster had erected his multimillion-dollar likeness of the French Petit Trianon at his estate, Bellefontaine. Also in Stockbridge was Naumkeag, Ambassador Choate's homey mansion, along with sculptor Daniel Chester French's splendid Chesterwood. Soon, in Lenox, Robert Paterson built Blantyre, and novelist Edith Wharton oversaw the design of the Mount. In all, some 75 extraordinary mansions graced the Berkshire landscape. European and urban tastes had arrived in the hills.

Yet William C. Whitney, secretary of the navy under President Grover Cleveland, acquired more land than all of these. In 1896 Whitney established an 11,000-acre game preserve in the Berkshire town of Washington, stocking it with buffalo, moose, Virginia deer, and elk. The estate later became October

Mountain State Forest, a giant reserve in the center of the county. Two years later North Adams industrialists donated 400 acres at the summit of Mount Greylock to the commonwealth, creating the first state reservation.

In North Adams a "normal school," or teachers' college, was established in 1894. Over the following century it evolved into the Massachusetts College of Liberal Arts.

David Anderson, Courtesy Edith Wharton Restoration

The Mount today, terrace side/east elevation, following recent restoration.

President James Garfield was assassinated on his way to his 25th Williams College reunion, so his vice president, Chester A. Arthur, took over. Both men had taught in the same one-room schoolhouse in Pownal, Vermont, in the 1850s. In the fall of 1902, President Roosevelt visited Berkshire, sustaining minor injury after his coach overturned near the Pittsfield Country Club. That next summer, both ex-President Grover Cleveland and humorist Mark Twain summered in Tyringham. Eight years later, on July 4, 1911, as Pittsfield observed its gala 150th anniversary, President Taft spoke before a crowd of 50,000 at the railroad station. And later that same year, Edith Wharton's novella *Ethan Frome* was published, a critical and popular success that derived many of its dramatic and scenic details from life in the Berkshires.

Twentieth-century Berkshire was marked with events principally in industry and the arts. Since 1903 General Electric has played a significant role in the county's industry. In 1914 GE established a high-voltage laboratory in Pittsfield, and seven years later the lab made electrical history by producing a million-volt flash of artificial lightning. While GE developed a large transformer business and produced naval armaments, Sprague Electric met the country's enormous need for capacitors during World War II and expanded to fill former mills in North Adams. Both manufacturers declined significantly in the second half of the century, although Commonwealth Sprague and GE Plastics remain.

In the arts, the Stockbridge Playhouse (now the Berkshire Theatre Festival) opened in 1928 with Eva LeGallienne in *Cradle Song*. Ted Shawn established his School of Dance at Jacob's Pillow in Becket in 1933. The 1930s heard the first Berkshire Symphony Festival concerts, a prelude to Tanglewood.

The Ted Shawn Theare at Jacob's Pillow.

Gary Gundersen, Courtesy Jacob's Pillow

Downhill skiing debuted in Berkshire in 1933, as Bousquet opened runs in Pittsfield and arranged for "ski trains" from New York. After the Civilian Conservation Corps carved the Thunderbolt Trail on Greylock in the 1930s, it was the scene of eastern championships before and after World War II. Soon half a dozen mountains in the county were crisscrossed by trails.

The 1950s saw the arrival of artist Norman Rockwell in Stockbridge and the creation of the Sterling and Francine Clark Art Institute in Williamstown, a collection and facility of international import. The Williamstown Theatre Festival began performances, enlivening all of Berkshire with star-studded drama. In the 1960s two more colleges joined Williams and MCLA: Berkshire Community College in Pittsfield, the first in a series of state junior colleges, and Simon's Rock Early College in Great Barrington, a progressive school that is now part of Bard College. Speaking of bards, Arlo Guthrie, scion of a folk legend and a former student at Stockbridge School, wrote a song about littering, the draft, and a community of friends in Stockbridge, "Alice's Restaurant."

The last Shaker sisters left their village in Hancock in 1960. A group of visionary citizens led by Amy Bess Miller managed to purchase their property and turn it into a living museum, today one of the county's premier attractions. And the great estates, too, have been recycled since the mid-20th century, opening Berkshire's fiefdoms to the public. In addition to uncounted B&Bs and restaurants, the arts lead in the adaptive reuse of former manors. The Mount, now owned by Edith Wharton Restorations, Inc., is open to tours in season, sponsoring lectures and other events. Shakespeare & Co. struts the stage at Springlawn. In the Glendale section of Stockbridge, the gracious Linwood estate was transformed into the new home of the Norman Rockwell Museum. Looking back toward Tanglewood from this splendid site, the visitor gets a fresh view of unspoiled 19th-century Berkshire. Tanglewood has expanded at another former estate, as well, creating a $10 million arched concert hall, where 1,200 music lovers can enjoy both acoustic intimacy and fidelity.

The Massachusetts Museum of Contemporary Art—MASS MoCA—in North Adams, resides not in an old estate but an old mill complex. It opened in the summer of 1999 to large crowds and international press coverage. Critics, even those who have reservations about individual works of art, cheer the space created and the imaginative series of film, theater, dance, and music presented.

Berkshire citizens discuss the changes in their county: condos, shopping malls, bypasses, even traffic signals. The Wal-Marting of Berkshire has begun, first in North Adams and then in Pittsfield. Some say the big box stores create jobs and bring low prices; others point out that the Berkshire Mall drained life from downtown Pittsfield, just as Prime Outlets appears to have pulled business from the Lenox shops. Once again the Berkshire barrier has been broken—this time by the nitroglycerin of mass marketing.

Environmental issues are being addressed head on. A variety of ecologically aware groups are mobilizing efforts to clean up Berkshire's principal river, the

Housatonic. And the Hoosic River appeared to be on its way to be cleansed of
PCBs for good. The Berkshire Natural Resources Council and other environmental protection groups guard and preserve the splendor of the landscape.
With the gradual shrinking of industry here and tourism among the most stable of Berkshire businesses, protecting the rolling hills makes economic and
aesthetic sense. Once the hills were decimated, shaved bald by paper and lumber mills and charcoal manufacturers. Now the hills are once more alive, fully
forested and soothing to the eye.

Tree Logic, *an installation by*
Natalie Jeremijenko, greets
visitors in the courtyard of
MASS MoCA in N. Adams.

MASS MoCA/Doug Bartow

CHAPTER TWO
Getting Here, Getting Around
TRANSPORTATION

This mural, one of many sponsored by the Berkshire Artisans, depicts Park Square in Pittsfield. Pittsfield will soon have an intermodal transportation center nearby.

Although bus lines bring some visitors to and from Berkshire County and the "B Bus" (Berkshire Regional Transit Authority) carries some through the county, most people rely on automobiles. Travel was more colorful if less comfortable in the past.

First we walked or rode horseback on county roads that were choked with dust, buried in snow, or clogged with bottomless mud, depending on the season. Then the Hudson and Connecticut Rivers carried passengers toward Berkshire aboard sailing ships, and by 1825 steamboats began regular service. Both Albany and Hartford were connected to New York City by steamboat runs, the upper Connecticut and Hudson Rivers being outfitted with an elaborate system of locks to bypass the rapids.

With the harnessing of steam for riverboat power, it wasn't long before the iron horse galloped into the Berkshire Hills. The Housatonic Railroad brought visitors from New York City and Connecticut. Two lines competed to the west: the Albany–West Stockbridge Line and the Hudson and Berkshire Line. From Boston, construction of the Western Railway up from Springfield was reportedly "delayed by competition between Stockbridge and Pittsfield for fixing of the route through their town. After surveys, Pittsfield won." During the summers of 1840–41, laborers, mostly Irish, dug deep cuts in the hills and built many bridges. When the lines were completed, Berkshire was nine hours by train from Boston and about three hours from Albany. Many who had come to work on the railroads never took the train back.

Sons of these rail workers may have labored on a remarkable system of track and overhead electric wires running from Williamstown south through North Adams and Adams, through Pittsfield, Lenox, Lee, Great Barrington, and Sheffield. Quiet and reliable, this Berkshire Street Railway grew so popular that opulent parlor cars were constructed and put into service, running till 1932. When automobiles and buses were refined, the possibilities for public transport changed; paved roads were improved, and unpaved ones were surfaced. Passenger rail and street railroad service to and within the Berkshires withered.

PRESENT POSSIBILITIES

The roads to Berkshire are smooth and scenic, so an automobile, if available, is useful to explore the back roads and byways. Buses run regularly from New York, Hartford, Boston, and Albany. Those in a hurry to get to these hills can fly in but, alas, only by private or charter plane to Great Barrington, Pittsfield, or North Adams. Closest commercial air service is to Bradley International, north of Hartford and the Albany International Airport; from there, car rentals or limousine and bus service are available. The future of Amtrak's once-a-day service to Pittsfield is questionable. For convenience, a host of details about Berkshire transportation follows—none of it as up-to-date as a telephone call, however.

GETTING TO THESE HILLS

BY CAR

From Manhattan: Take the Major Deegan Expressway or the Henry Hudson Parkway to the Saw Mill River Parkway, and then proceed north on one of the most beautiful roadways in the world, the Taconic State Parkway. For the southern Berkshire, exit the Taconic at "Hillsdale, Claverack, Route 23," and follow Route 23 east, toward Hillsdale and on to Great Barrington. For Stockbridge, Lee, and Lenox, proceed up Route 7. For Pittsfield and northern Berkshire, exit the Taconic at Route 295 and head east to Route 22, following Route 22 north to Route 20 for Pittsfield or to Route 43 through Hancock to Williamstown and North Adams.

From New Jersey, Pennsylvania and south: take the New York Thruway to I-84 east; at the Taconic Parkway exit, turn north, following "From Manhattan"

BERKSHIRE ACCESS

Using Tanglewood (on the Stockbridge-Lenox line) as the Berkshire reference point, the following cities are this close. (Newly increased speeds on the interstates bring Berkshire somewhat closer to the rest of the world than this table indicates.)

CITY	TIME	MILES
Albany	1 hr	50
Boston	2.5 hrs	135
Bridgeport	2 hrs	110
Danbury	1.75 hrs	85
Hartford	1.5 hrs	70
New Haven	2.5 hrs	115
Montreal	5 hrs	275
New York City	3 hrs	150
Philadelphia	4.5 hrs	230
Providence	2.5 hrs	125
Springfield	.75 hr	35
Waterbury	1.5 hrs	75
Washington, DC	7 hrs	350
Worcester	1.75 hrs	90

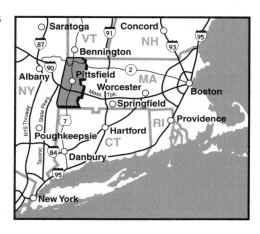

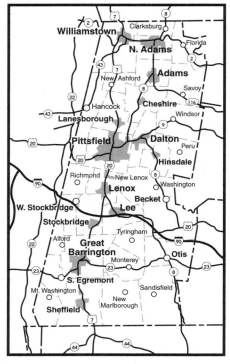

Berkshire County is 56 miles in length from Sheffield to Williamstown, and, depending on the season and the weather, it normally takes 1.5 hours to drive along Rte. 7. Because of the mountain ranges that also run north to south, east-west travel across the county remains more difficult. All of the county's east-west routes (2 in the north, 9 midcounty, and 23 in the south) are tricky drives in freezing or snowy weather. Back roads in particular vary tremendously in condition and type, ranging from smooth macadam to rough dirt. On these back roads especially, drivers should keep an eye out for bicyclists, horseback riders, hikers, joggers, rollerbladers — and deer, bear, moose, and bobcat.

instructions. If local color is high on your list, or you'd rather ramble than scurry northward, Route 22 north is a good choice, and you can pick it up as far south as Armonk or Bedford in Westchester County, New York. Route 22 is a road still proud of its diners: of particular note is the Red Rooster in Pawling, just north of I-684's end. Farther upstate on Route 22, turn right at Hillsdale on Route 23 east toward Great Barrington, on Route 20 to Pittsfield, or on Route 43 to Williamstown.

From Connecticut and/or the New York Metro Area: Route 7 north was an early stagecoach thoroughfare to Berkshire, and you join the same trail at Danbury, via I-684 and I-84. Driving up Route 7, you'll wend your way along the beautiful Housatonic River, north through New Milford, Kent, and Canaan and into Massachusetts through Ashley Falls (an especially good ride for picnics and antiques). To arrive in southeastern Berkshire, Route 8 is a quick and scenic drive as it follows the Farmington River north.

From Boston and east: The scenic Massachusetts Turnpike (MassPike, I-90) is the quickest, easiest route west to south Berkshire and Pittsfield, and from Boston there's no better bet, especially as tolls at the western end have been dropped. West of the Connecticut River, you can get off the turnpike at exit 3, and take Route 202 south to Route 20 west, and pick up Route 23 west at Woronoco for the best route to Otis Ridge, Butternut Basin, and Catamount ski areas. Most people stay on the turnpike right into the Berkshires, exiting either at Lee or West Stockbridge.

A less rapid but more colorful route westward from Boston is Route 20, which cuts across southern Massachusetts, connecting with Lee. If you're coming west to the Berkshires from more northern latitudes, Route 9 from Northampton is a splendid drive, a high road, with long lovely vistas and few towns. Still farther to the north, eastern entry to Berkshire County can be gained by driving the Mohawk Trail, originally an Indian byway. Also known as Route 2, this is the most direct way to North Adams, Williamstown, and north Berkshire ski areas.

From Hartford: The quickest route is I-91 north to the Massachusetts Turnpike west. Then proceed as in directions for Massachusetts Turnpike travel from Boston. A slower but more pleasant drive is Route 44 west, up through Avon, Norfolk, and Canaan, where you take Route 8 or Route 7 north into Berkshire County.

From Montreal or Albany: Leaving Canada, take I-87 (known as "the Northway") south to Albany, and exit at Route 7 to Route 2 toward Williamstown, Route 20 to Pittsfield, or continue on I-87 south to I-90 east, connecting then to the Massachusetts Turnpike, which is the continuation of I-90 east. Exit at either Canaan, New York, or Lee.

BY BUS

From Manhattan (3.5 hours): *Bonanza* (800-556-3815) serves the Berkshires out of New York City's *Port Authority Bus Terminal* (212-564-8484) at 40th

Street between 8th and 9th Avenues. Tickets may be purchased at the *Greyhound* ticket windows (212-971-6363), near 8th Avenue. Several buses a day. Boarding is down the escalators at the center of the terminal, and then to the right, usually at Gate 13. Berkshire locales marked with an asterisk are Flag Stops, where you must wave to the bus driver in order to be picked up.

Berkshire Phone Numbers for New York Buses

Canaan, CT	Canaan Pharmacy, Main St.	203-824-5481
Gt. Barrington	Bill's Pharmacy, 362 Main St.	413-528-1590
Hillsdale, NY	*Junction Rtes. 22 & 23	800-556-3815
Lee	McClelland Drugs, 43 Main St.	413-243-0135
Lenox	Lenox News & Variety, 39 Housatonic St.	413-637-2815
New Ashford	*Entrance to Brodie Mt. Ski Area, Rte. 7	800-556-3815
Pittsfield	Bus Terminal, 57 S. Church St.	413-442-4451
Sheffield	Rte. 7, *Bank of Boston	800-556-3815
S. Egremont	*Gaslight Store	800-556-3815
Stockbridge	Chamber of Commerce Booth, Main St.	413-298-3344
Williamstown	The Williams Inn, Main St.	413-458-2665

From Boston (3.5 hours): *Peter Pan/Trailways* runs daily to Pittsfield and Lee-Lenox out of the Trailways Terminal at South Station. Change to *Bonanza* in Springfield for North Adams–Williamstown. Contact 800-343-9999 or www.peterpanbus.com for prices and schedules.

Under construction in Pittsfield is an intermodal center that will bring local and long-distance buses together with Amtrak on Columbus Avenue between North and Center Streets.

Berkshire Phone Numbers for Boston Buses

Lee	McClelland Drugs, 43 Main St.	413-243-0135
Lenox	Lenox News & Variety, 39 Housatonic St.	413-637-2815
Pittsfield	Bus Terminal, 57 S. Church St.	413-442-4451
Williamstown	The Williams Inn, 1090 Main St.	413-458-9371

From Hartford (1.75 hours): The *Greyhound Line* (800-231-2222) runs two buses to Pittsfield daily, with a transfer at Springfield, from the *Greyhound Terminal* at 1 Union Place (in the train station), Hartford.

From Montreal (6 hours): *Greyhound* runs south to the Albany Greyhound Terminal. Connect to Pittsfield as noted below.

From Albany (1 hour): *Bonanza* runs two buses daily from Albany to Pittsfield. *Greyhound* runs one bus daily.

BY TRAIN

From Manhattan: Commuters ride at a fraction of the regular rate if they take *Metro North* out of Grand Central Station and get off at Wassaic, New York (on Route 22 near Sharon, Connecticut). *Amtrak* (800-USA-RAIL, 413-872-7245) can also help you get to the Berkshires. Their Turboliner from Pennsylvania Station runs frequently and smoothly along the Hudson River, a splendid ride. For southern Berkshire, stay aboard till Hudson, a river town recently restored; for northern Berkshire, stay on to Rensselaer. For travel connections from Wassaic, Hudson, or Rensselaer to the Berkshires, see "By Taxi or Limousine."

From Boston: *Amtrak may* continue to run a single train daily through the Berkshires, starting from Boston's South Station, although the run is threatened. To find the Pittsfield shelter: Take West Street westward past the Crowne Plaza hotel; at the first light, turn right onto Center Street; take the next right onto Depot Street; the shelter is on the left. Anyone boarding the train in Pittsfield must purchase tickets on the train. The round-trip ticket prices vary, depending on time of travel and seat availability. Private compartments are available. Under construction in Pittsfield is an intermodal center that will bring local and long distance buses together with Amtrak on Columbus Avenue between North and Center Streets.

From Montreal: *Amtrak* runs one train daily from Montreal through Albany. There is no same-day train connection from this run to the Berkshires; see "By Limousine or Taxi"; or see "By Bus."

From Albany: *Amtrak* may continue a single Pittsfield-bound (same Depot Street shed) train daily from the Albany/Rensselaer Depot on East Street (2 miles from downtown Albany).

BY PLANE

If you own a small airplane or decide to charter one, you can fly directly to the Berkshires, landing at Great Barrington, Pittsfield, or North Adams airports.

From New York City: Feeling rich, traveling high with some friends, or riding on the corporate account? There are several charter air companies in the metropolitan New York area that will fly you from La Guardia, JFK, or other New York metropolitan airports near to any of the Berkshire airports. Charters currently flying these routes include:

Business Air Services, Oxford, CT	800-226-6022
Chester Air, Chester, CT	800-752-6371
Executive Airlines & Aviation,	800-645-9572
First Flight, Horseheads, NY	800-221-1802

And from Westchester County:

Panorama (White Plains airport)   914-328-9800
Richmor Aviation   800-331-6101, 518-828-9461

From Boston: Numerous charter flight companies fly from Beantown to Berkshire.

From Hartford: **Bradley Airport** in Hartford handles numerous domestic and international airlines, so you can fly to Bradley from nearly anywhere. From there, charter air service to the Berkshires is available through any of the companies from Boston or through the Berkshire County companies listed below.

From Albany: Albany is terminus for a substantial volume of domestic jet traffic and, being under an hour from the Berkshires by car, is the closest you can get to these hills by big plane. Charter connector flights are available from Albany to the Berkshires, based at the Albany International Airport or through the Berkshire County companies listed below.

In Berkshire County: Three aviation companies in Berkshire County operate air taxi service to just about any other northeastern airport:

Berkshire Aviation	Great Barrington Airport	413-528-1010, 528-1061
Lyon Aviation	Pittsfield Airport	413-443-6700
Esposito Flying Service	Harriman & West Airport,	
	North Adams	413-663-3330

BY LIMOUSINE OR TAXI

If you're with a group or want to pamper yourself, a limousine direct to Berkshire is the smoothest approach. Many limousine services will whisk you away from urban gridlock to the spaciousness of this hill country.

From New York City and its Airports:
    Carey   212-935-9700
    Kabot   718-545-2400

From Boston and Logan Airport:
    Cooper   617-482-1000, 800-343-2123

From Hartford and Bradley Airport:
    Carey Elite Limousine   860-666-9051, 800-RELIMOS
    Ambassador   203-633-7300, 800-395-LIMO

From Albany, Albany Airport, and Rensselaer:
    See **By Taxi or Limousine** below.

From Hudson, New York, and its Amtrak Station:
    Star City Taxi   518-828-3355

GETTING AROUND THE BERKSHIRES

Route 7 is Berkshire County's main roadway, connecting cities and towns from south to north. Driving in winter, you'll certainly need snow tires. In summer the cruising is easy, but on certain weekends during Tanglewood and fall foliage seasons, temporary traffic delays in popular villages are likely. Whenever possible, park and walk. Friendly but firm traffic police will suggest outlying parking areas. And motorists beware: State law requires a full stop for pedestrians in crosswalks.

Note: Individual town maps of Great Barrington, Stockbridge, Lenox, Pittsfield, North Adams, and Williamstown can be found at the back of the book.

BY BUS

Berkshire County is no longer served by the electrified Berkshire Street Railway, but the *"B,"* a public bus system, has in some ways filled the gap. The buses run from early morning to early evening. Information can be obtained from the **Berkshire Regional Transit Authority** (413-499-2782; from Massachusetts phones 800-292-2782). Fares vary by distance. If you're visiting without a car, the *B* will provide plenty of access to other communities, but Sunday service is not available. Under construction in Pittsfield is an intermodal center that will bring local and long-distance buses together with Amtrak on Columbus Avenue between North and Center Streets.

BY RENTED CAR

Car rental agencies abound in Berkshire. Most will not deliver cars—you must first go to their place of business to do the paperwork. Berkshire car rentals are available through the following agencies:

Adams	Enterprise Rent-A-Car	413-743-7805
Gt. Barrington	Affordable	413-526-0848
	Enterprise Rent-A-Car	413-644-9644
	Larkins Car Store	
	(used only)	413-528-2156
	Pete's Ford	413-528-0848,
		800-698-0848
Lee	R.W.'s, Inc.	413-243-0946
Pittsfield	Affordable	413-445-5795
	Hertz	413-499-4153,
		800-654-3131
	National	413-442-4200

	Pete's Leasing	413-445-5795
	Rent-A-Wreck	413-447-8117,
		800-499-8117
North Adams	Affordable	413-663-3777
	Hertz	413-664-4734
	Rent-A-Wreck	413-664-1000

BY TAXI OR LIMOUSINE

Numerous taxi and limo companies serve Berkshire County. The following is a listing by town, with notations indicating if they have only taxis (T), only limos (L), or both (B).

Dalton	Jenkins Livery	413-684-1893 (T)
Great Barrington	Taxico	413-528-0911,
		413-528-0567 (T)
Lee	Abbott's Limousine & Livery	413-243-1645 (L)
	Park Taxi	413-243-0020 (T)
Lenox	Alston's	413-637-3676 (L)
	Tobi's Limousine Service	413-637-1224 (L)
North Adams	Berkshire Livery Service	413-662-2609,
		800-298-2609 (L)
	Norm's Limousine Service	413-663-8300,
		663-6284 (B)
Pittsfield	Arrow Taxi	413-499-4860 (B)
	Airport & Limousine	413-443-7111 (L)
	Berkshire Limousine	413-499-3232,
		800-543-6776
	Rainbow Taxi	413-499-4300 (T)
Stockbridge	Stockbridge Livery	413-298-4848 (T)

BY BICYCLE

Bicycling in the Berkshires gives an exciting intimacy with the rolling landscape. Depending on your willingness to bundle up, biking from town to town is possible nearly year-round. Bike rental prices vary widely, with bikes available through:

Canaan, Connecticut	The Bike Doctor	860-824-5577
Great Barrington	Berkshire Bike & Blade	413-528-5555
Lenox	Arcadian Shop	413-637-3010
	Mean Wheels	413-637-0644
North Adams	Sports Corner	413-664-8654

| Pittsfield | Plaine's Bike & Ski Center | 413-499-0294 |
| Williamstown | The Mountain Goat | 413-458-8445 |

ON FOOT

For those with the time, we've got the trail. The Appalachian Trail enters southern Berkshire in the town of Mount Washington and runs over hill and dale, past Great Barrington, through Monterey, down into Tyringham Valley, then up near the town of Washington, through Dalton and Cheshire, over Mount Greylock, and toward Vermont. See "Walking, Hiking, Camping, X-C Skiing" in Chapter Seven, *Outdoor Recreation*.

Many Berkshire towns are small enough for walking exploration. Four in particular are well suited to visiting without a vehicle: Lee, Lenox, Stockbridge, and Williamstown. All are lovely villages, with good accommodations, fine dining, interesting shopping, and first-rate cultural attractions within easy walking distance.

NEIGHBORS ALL AROUND

Just as the name "Berkshire" has spread to adjacent areas, the county and its people frequently have close ties with neighboring communities, counties, and states. Travelers will want to connect with the neighbors, too, for Berkshire is surrounded by areas of extensive natural beauty. Certain nearby towns are loaded with good restaurants, old inns, and cultural attractions.

TO THE SOUTH

The Litchfield Hills of northwest Connecticut are gentler than the Berkshire Hills but still make for good hiking. There is lovely architecture in this area, with many stately homes in Salisbury, Lakeville, Sharon, Litchfield, and Norfolk. And there are music festivals, as well, such as the ones at Norfolk and at Music Mountain in Falls Village. See "Music" in Chapter Five, *Arts & Pleasures*.

TO THE EAST

Halfway over the Berkshire highlands between the Housatonic River Valley and the Connecticut River lies the jagged eastern county border, shared with Franklin County up north and Hamden and Hampshire Counties. Besides this eastern area's natural splendor, an attractive array of cultural possibilities is located here. The "Five College Area" of Amherst, South Hadley, and Northampton (a cultural mecca all by itself) offers all the aesthetic and academic action anyone could want with the presence of Amherst, Hampshire, Mt. Holyoke, and Smith Colleges, and the University of Massachusetts.

TO THE NORTH

The Green Mountains of Vermont offer great skiing, hiking, and camping. The town of Bennington makes an interesting stopover, with its museum (featuring Grandma Moses paintings), a fine college (Bennington), and Robert Frost's grave behind the historic Old Bennington Church. There is also the extraordinary Bennington Pottery, where a visitor can both buy and dine on handsome stoneware. Route 7 up here continues to architecturally stunning Manchester: well worth the time, even dawdling along Historic Route 7-A.

TO THE WEST

The farms and small towns of Columbia County, in New York State, hold treasures for antiques and "untiques" hunters. Berkshire is not far from the Hudson Valley, an area rich with history and vineyards worth visiting. And then there's Albany, which offers big-city cultural entertainment such as the touring New York Metropolitan Opera, performing at the capital city's structurally unique theater, the Egg. A bit farther north is Saratoga with its spas, its springs, its own summer arts festival (Saratoga Performing Arts Center, known as SPAC), and its elegant and justly famous racecourse.

CHAPTER THREE
The Keys to Your Room
LODGING

The gracious front porch of the Red Lion Inn.

As stagecoach travel through Berkshire developed in the 18th century, the need for roadside lodgings grew. The *New Boston Inn* in Sandisfield, still welcoming travelers, was likely the first. Built in 1737, this restored inn is about as authentic an early-American lodging experience as can be found in New England. Close in age and attention to period detail is the *Old Inn on the Green* (1760), in New Marlborough. This inn served as a tavern, a store, and later as post office. Today it comforts travelers with a small number of authentically colonial rooms (more in various outbuildings) and a superlative restaurant. In 1770 Colonel Benjamin Simonds established *Riverbend Farm* in Williamstown, now a B&B meticulously restored by David and Judy Loomis. Next came the *Red Lion Inn* (1773) in Stockbridge, which provided not only housing for sojourners but also a meeting place for pre-Revolutionary political activists eager to communicate their grievances to Britain. More than 225 years later, distinguished guests still communicate from the Red Lion . . . around the world.

Many other 18th-century Berkshire inns continue to offer warmth, hospitality, and a good night's sleep, often in a four-poster bed—among them, the *Vil-*

lage Inn in Lenox, built as a farmhouse in 1771; the *Egremont Inn* (1780) and the *Weathervane Inn* (1785) in South Egremont; the *Elm Court Inn* (1790) in North Egremont; and the *Williamsville Inn* in West Stockbridge, originally a farmhouse dating from 1797.

Or if the 19th century's sumptuous Gilded Age stirs our stirrup cup, Berkshire offers, among other possibilities, an Italian palazzo called *Wheatleigh* and a Tudor castle called *Blantyre,* both in Lenox. Strikingly different in style, these palatial estates-turned-hotels share the ability to satisfy even the most refined of tastes and to do so with panache.

About 300 Berkshire lodgings exist today, some shorter perhaps on romance but more reasonably priced than others. Berkshire Visitors Bureau executive director William R. Wilson Jr., estimates 4,000 "heads in beds" capacity for the county. There are an ever-growing number of guesthouses, both in town and out, many offering bed and breakfast ("B&B"); there are simple inns where precious quiet is an everyday experience; and there are modern hotels and all grades of motels.

We present a representative sampling, in terms of price, geography, and architecture. To include lodgings, we place a high value on hospitality, the personal attention and sincere care that can turn a visit into an unforgettable sojourn. We also assign value and significance to the architectural qualities of a property, to its history and traditions and care in furnishing and use of antiques or other art, and to the views and the natural beauty right at its doorstep. As always, we would appreciate hearing about disappointments—or pleasant surprises.

BERKSHIRE LODGING NOTES

Rates

Rate cards are generally printed in the spring and will change slightly from year to year. Reminder: Price codes are based on a per-room rate, double occupancy, during the high seasons (summer, fall foliage, skiing). Off-season rates are usually lower. Many establishments adjust for midweek, as well.

Inexpensive	Up to $100	Expensive	$150 to $200
Moderate	$100 to $150	Very Expensive	Over $200

These rates exclude required room taxes or service charges, which may be added to your bill.

Minimum Stay

Many lodgings require a minimum stay of two, three, or even four nights in summer and autumn. For a single night's stay in Berkshire at such times, motels are the best bet. During the off season, minimum-stay requirements relax.

Deposit/Cancellation

Deposits are usually required for a confirmed reservation. Policies regarding deposits, cancellations, and refunds vary. It is always wise to inquire about these in advance. In the high season, including college graduation weekends in late May and early June, lodging demand occasionally exceeds supply, so reservations for the more popular places need to be made months or even years ahead.

Special Features

Wherever pertinent, we mention special features of lodgings, along with any caveats. Few establishments allow smoking indoors. Many limit pets or ages of children. This information is intended as a general guide only, and it is always best to call and inquire as policies may be flexible.

Other Options

We include Web sites. We do not list e-mail addresses as these are usually available on Web sites. Visitors may also want to browse general lodging or community sites, such as www.berkshirelodging.com, leelodging.org, berkshireweb.com, or greatbarrington.org.

For last-minute or emergency lodging arrangements in Berkshire, here are some numbers to phone.

Berkshire Bed and Breakfast Reservation Service: 413-731-8785
Berkshire Lodgings Association: 413-298-4760, 800-298-4760
Berkshire Visitors Bureau: 413-443-9186

For single-night stays in the high season or spur-of-the-moment arrangements at other times, visit any of the **tourist information booths** listed in the Introduction.

INNS AND B&BS SOUTH COUNTY

Egremont

North Egremont

BALDWIN GRANGE B&B INN
Innkeepers: Heather and Holly Dobbins.
413-528-2808, 888-770-8350; fax 413-528-0653.

What fun to stay in an 1803 grange, posts and beams exposed. Eight bedrooms are redolent of the era, with eclectic furnishings. All have full baths, and all are air conditioned. A comfortably furnished living room provides a base for expedi-

www.baldwingrangeinn.com.
Mailing Address: PO Box
47, N. Egremont, MA
01252.
On Rte. 71, Prospect Lake
Rd.
Price: Expensive.
Credit Cards: AE, D, MC, V.
Special Features: Hiking;
near distinguished
restaurant.

South Egremont

**BALDWIN HILL FARM
B&B**
Owners: Richard and
Priscilla Burdsall.
413-528-4092, 888-528-4092;
fax 413-528-6365.
www.baldwinhillfarm.com.
121 Baldwin Hill Rd. N-S,
Gt. Barrington, MA
01230.
N. on Baldwin Hill Rd. (off
Rte. 23 & 41) to S.
Egremont, 1.5 mi. to inn
on left.
Price: Moderate.
Credit Cards: AE, D, MC, V.
Special Features: View;
pool; no smoking; no
pets; children over 10
welcome.

THE EGREMONT INN
Owners: Steven and Karen
Waller.
413-528-2111, 800-859-1780;
fax 413-528-3284.
www.egremontinn.com.
10 Old Sheffield Rd., PO
Box 418, S. Egremont,
MA 01258.
Side street off Rte. 23 in
village center.
Price: Moderate.
Credit Cards: AE, D, MC, V.
Special Features: Pool, 2
tennis courts.

tions into the inviting countryside that surrounds
this piece of Americana.

The Dobbins do their own baking, make their
own jam, and put together unusual breakfasts,
including apple or peach French toast, rice pudding, and crème brûlée. Tea is served afternoons
and evenings.

Baldwin Hill provides a 360-degree view of its
magnificent surroundings. The establishment
includes an 1820s farmhouse-turned-B&B and
barns galore. It provides an opportunity for guests
to stay at what they think farms were like. Peace,
quiet, and tranquility abound on 300 acres perfect
for hiking, cross-country skiing, or simply observ-
ing the wildlife. Guests enjoy reading by the fieldstone fireplace in winter or on the screened porch
in summer. Four rooms, two with private bath,
have views across fields to the mountains beyond.
Full breakfast, from a menu with numerous
choices, is served by friendly innkeepers. They take
pride in this farm that has been in the family since
1910.

Coziness, low ceilings, five—count 'em, five—fireplaces downstairs, broad porches, 20 delightful
rooms furnished with antiques: These set the tone for
this historic 1780 stagecoach inn nestled on a quiet
side street in the heart of a classic village. All rooms
have private baths and central air-conditioning. Both
two-room suites have fold-out sofas. Scenery ranges
from lovely to gorgeous. Tavern and fine restaurant
located on main floor. Live music two nights a
week.

**THE WEATHERVANE
INN**
Owners: Maxine and
Jeffrey Lome.
413-528-9580, 800-528-9580;
fax 413-528-1713.
www.weathervaneinn.com.
Box 388, S. Egremont, MA
01258.
Rte. 23 just E. of the village.
Closed: Thanksgiving and
Christmas.
Price: Expensive to Very
Expensive.
Credit Cards: AE, MC, V.
Handicap Access: Limited.
Special Features: Pool; no
pets; children welcome.

This is a comfortable, clean, and well-run operation set within a 1785 farmhouse. The 10 rooms and two suites all have private baths and air-conditioning. The hosts are skilled at their trade and provide their version of colonial lodging and catered fine dining for groups of 10 or more. The Weathervane's location is convenient to some of the best antiques shopping in the Berkshires, including one shop just behind the inn. Weekends in July and August have a three-night minimum stay.

Great Barrington

**COFFING-BOSTWICK
HOUSE**
Proprietors: Diana and
William Harwood.
413-528-4511;
fax 413-528-9054.
98 Division St., Gt.
Barrington, MA 01230.
Corner of Rte. 41, 2 mi. N.
of town.
Price: Moderate.
Credit Cards: None.
Special Features: No pets.

The sleepy village of Van Deusenville was once a bustling town with mills, factories, and a train station. Little remains except Isaac Van Deusen's large 1825 mansion, now a six-room bed and breakfast. The guest rooms are spacious and well appointed, as are the public rooms. Local caterer Diana Harwood prepares a sumptuous full breakfast. Just down the street is the church, now owned by Arlo Guthrie, where Alice of "Alice's Restaurant" lived.

GREENMEADOWS
Owners: Frank Gioia and
Susie Kaufman.
413-528-3897;
fax 413-528-6334.
www.gmeadows.com.
117 Division St., Gt.
Barrington, MA 01230.
1.5 mi. N. of town, 0.25 mi.
W. of Rte. 41.
Open: May–Oct.
Price: Moderate.
Credit Cards: AE, MC, V.
Special Features: No
smoking; no pets.

This inn fronts a quiet, country road in a rural setting—in what is still a farming area—although close to the center of Great Barrington. The four rooms include private baths, cable TV, and air-conditioning. The owners serve a full breakfast on a sunny, glass-enclosed porch.

SEEKONK PINES INN B&B
Owners/Innkeepers: Lefkowitz Family.
413-528-4192, 800-292-4192.
www.seekonkpines.com.
142 Seekonk Crossroad, Gt. Barrington, MA 01230.
Rte. 23 between S. Egremont and Gt. Barrington.
Price: Moderate to Expensive.
Credit Cards: MC, V.
Special Features: Pool; bicycles; no smoking; no pets.

Originally the main house for a large estate, this 170-year-old house surrounded by meadows and well-groomed acreage keeps getting better and better. Furnished in country antiques and collectibles, the six guest rooms, all with private baths, are filled with personal touches. A guest pantry has a refrigerator, hot-water dispenser, and sink, with complimentary beverages available. Guests can dip in the swimming pool on hot summer days and walk or read in the formal gardens. A hearty breakfast is served.

THORNEWOOD INN
Owners/Innkeepers: Terry and David Thorne.
413-528-3828, 800-854-1008; fax 413-528-3307.
www.thornewood.com.
453 Stockbridge Rd., Gt. Barrington, MA 01230.
Rte. 7 just N. of Gt. Barrington.
Price: Expensive to Very Expensive.
Credit Cards: AE, MC, V.
Special Features: Pool; no smoking; no pets; children over 11; packages include dinner.

Creativity and imagination are evident throughout this inn. Having purchased an old rundown but handsome Dutch colonial, the Thornes restored and expanded it to create 15 guest rooms, all with private bath, and four public rooms—picturesque right down to the uneven floors. The antiques used throughout include canopy beds, pier mirrors, and original sinks. The three-room carriage house, refurbished in 1992, is convenient for families. (Spencer's Restaurant may be moved to a new building by the time this appears.) The full breakfast might include strawberry-stuffed French toast or apple pancakes. The inn enjoys hosting banquets and weddings.

TURNING POINT INN
Owners: Dennis, Rachel, and Tava O'Rourke.
413-528-4777.
www.turningptinn.com.
3 Lake Buel Rd., Gt. Barrington, MA 01230.
Jct. of Rte. 23 E. of Gt. Barrington.
Price: Inexpensive to Moderate.
Credit Cards: None.
Special Features: Children welcome.

Turning Point is a well-regarded lodging in a handsome brick-and-clapboard former stagecoach inn that's 200 years old. An informal atmosphere prevails. Full breakfast served; Saturday-evening dinner can be arranged (Rachel is a chef and Tava a pastry chef who also cater). Stay in one of six inn rooms (four with private baths); a separate two-bedroom cottage is perfect for families. The popular Butternut Basin ski area is a third of a mile down the road.

WAINWRIGHT INN
Innkeeper: Marja Tepper
  Grader.
413-528-2062;
  fax 413-644-6410.
www.wainwrightinn.com.
518 S. Main St., Gt.
  Barrington, MA 01230.
Rte. 7, 1 block S. of jct. with
  Rte. 23.
Price: Expensive to Very
  Expensive.
Credit Cards: MC, V.
Handicap Access: Yes.
Special Features: No smoking;
  dining room reserved for
  guests; no pets; inquire
  about children.

This beautiful gabled house built by Peter Ingersoll in 1766 was the Tory Tavern and Inn until David Wainwright purchased it in 1790, and then it passed down through his descendants as a family home. The present owners purchased it in 2000, keeping it open year-round with nine guest rooms/ suites with private baths, some with fireplaces. One guest room has been renovated to be entirely wheelchair accessible. Full breakfast served.

WINDFLOWER INN
Owners: Liebert and Ryan
  Families.
413-528-2720, 800-992-1993.
www.windflowerinn.com.
684 S. Egremont Rd., Gt.
  Barrington, MA 01230.
Rte. 23 just E. of S.
  Egremont.
Price: Expensive.
Credit Card: AE.
Handicap Access: Limited.
Special Features: Pool; no pets.

One of the prettiest settings in South Berkshire complements the soothing, comfortable interior of this gracious and respected inn. Antiques furnish the common rooms as well as the bedrooms. All 13 rooms have private bath, and 6 have fireplaces. Full breakfast and afternoon tea and cookies served. The inn and its restaurant are available for special catered occasions. The inn is across from the country club, which is open to the public.

Housatonic

**CHRISTINE'S B&B AND
  TEA ROOM**
Innkeepers: Steve and
  Christine Kelsey.
413-274-6149, 800-536-1186;
  fax 413-274-6296.
www.christinesinn.com.
325 N. Plain Rd.,
  Housatonic, MA 01236.
Rte. 41, 4 mi. N. of Gt.
  Barrington.
Price: Expensive.
Credit Cards: MC, V.
Special Features: No
  smoking; no pets;
  children over 11;
  business-traveler
  discount.

A little jewel (three rooms, all with private bath) off the beaten path between Great Barrington and West Stockbridge. The rooms and the innkeepers are delightful. Two rooms have queen canopy beds, and the third has a high-poster. All are filled with antiques and are air-conditioned. Table-served breakfast. Afternoon tea.

Lee

(See also *South Lee*)

APPLEGATE INN
Owners: Len and Gloria
  Freedman.
413-243-4451, 800-691-9012.
www.applegateinn.com.
279 West Park St., Lee, MA
  01238.
Off Rte. 7, between
  Stockbridge and Lenox.
Price: Expensive to Very
  Expensive.
Credit Cards: MC, V.
Special Features: Heated
  pool; no pets; children
  over 12.

This magnificent white-pillared colonial is special in every way, and a stay at Applegate will be cherished. Public rooms are large, with fireplaces and bay windows. The puppets that appear to be part of the decor are also for playing. Guests are greeted in their room with fresh flowers, a crystal decanter of brandy, and Godiva chocolates. The main house has six large guest rooms; all have private baths and fireplaces. The carriage house has two suites with private patios, whirlpool tubs, and wet bars. The house has central air-conditioning. From the screened-in porch filled with wicker furniture, a tranquil view across the pool reveals six landscaped acres. If anyone wishes to go farther afield, the Friedmans have four bicycles to loan.

**AUNTI M'S BED &
  BREAKFAST**
Owners: Michelle and Phil
  Celentano.
413-243-3201.
www.auntimsbnb.com.
60 Laurel St., Lee, MA 01238.
On Rte 20.
Price: Inexpensive to
  Expensive.
Credit Cards: None.
Special Features: No smoking;
  no pets; children over 15.

Aunti M's is a restored Victorian within walking distance of a historic downtown. All five comfortable rooms—named for nieces and nephews of the owners—have period furnishings, floral wallpapers and borders, and oak floors. One has a private bath, and the others share two baths. The homey feeling is exemplified as Michelle Celentano says of her guests, "Whatever is ours is theirs." An elegant full breakfast is served; the piano in the foyer is the focal point for after-breakfast camaraderie.

**BEST WESTERN BLACK
  SWAN INN**
Owner: Shatish Desai.
413-243-2700,
  800-876-SWAN (7926).
435 Laurel St., Lee, MA 01238.
Rte. 20 on Laurel Lake N. of
  town.
Price: Very Expensive.
Credit Cards: AE, D, DC, MC,
  V.
Handicap Access: Yes.
Special Features: Pool;
  exercise room and sauna;
  no pets.

From the outside, this 52-room inn looks decidedly like a motel, but its location on placid Laurel Lake, its private balconies, colonial decor, and hospitality provide an innlike atmosphere. Lovely restaurant, swimming pool, and exercise room with sauna. There are boat rentals for boating on the lake. Close to Tanglewood, hiking trails, countless other Berkshire amenities. Conference facilities are available. In the summer, meals are not included; in winter a continental breakfast is served.

CHAMBÉRY INN
Owners: Joe and Lynn
  Toole.
413-243-2221, 800-537-4321.
www.berkshireinns.com/
  chambery.hmtl.
199 Main St., Lee, MA
  01238.
On Rte. 20.
Price: Moderate to Very
  Expensive.
Credit Cards: AE, D, MC, V.
Handicap Access: Yes.
Special Features: No
  smoking; no pets;
  children over 15.

The Chambéry Inn began life as a schoolhouse in 1885, when five nuns arrived from France to teach the youngsters of St. Mary's Parish in Lee. Joe Toole's grandfather was in the first class. Concerned that it was scheduled for the wrecker's ball and enchanted by its history, Joe moved the schoolhouse to its present location. He left the proportion of the rooms as they were, which is *big*, with 13-foot ceilings and massive windows. There are nine rooms, including three schoolhouse suites and three deluxe suites; all king or queen beds and large private baths with whirlpools. The furniture, including canopy beds, is Amish handcrafted cherry. A charming feature of the suites is the original blackboards. All the rooms have central air-conditioning, telephones, and cable TV (including HBO). Breakfast is delivered to the room.

Tea time at Crabtree Cottage, in Lee. Many small inns and B&Bs have tea time or offer early evening snacks or place chocolates on guests' pillows.

Judith Monachina

CRABTREE COTTAGE
Owner: Janis Monachina.
413-243-1780.
www.crabtree cottage.com.
65 Franklin St., Lee, MA
  01238.
Off Main St.
Price: Moderate.
Credit Cards: None.
Special Features: Pool;
  children over 12.

This lovely Greek Revival home on a quiet residential street is handsomely garbed in Victorian furnishings. The single room, one-room suite, and efficiency suite all have private baths, air-conditioning, and television with VCR. The option of a kitchen goes with the suite. Guests have access to a common room, deck and swimming pool. Janis's husband, contractor Jeffrey Keenan, who grew up in the home, has done much of the extensive refurbishing. Cordials and treats in the afternoon; full candlelit breakfast.

DEVONFIELD B&B
Owners/Managers: Jim
and Pam Loring.
413-243-329, 800-664-0880;
fax 413-243-1360.
www.devonfield.com.
85 Stockbridge Rd., Lee,
MA 01238.
Off Rte. 20 just outside
village.
Price: Expensive to Very
Expensive.
Credit Cards: AE, D, MC, V.
Special Features: Heated
pool; tennis; bicycles;
Jacuzzis and fireplaces.

No expense was spared in renovating this 1800s house, built by a Revolutionary War soldier and initially restored by George Westinghouse in the early 1900s. The small estate became the 1942 summer sanctuary for Queen Wilhelmina of the Netherlands, her daughter Princess Juliana, and granddaughters Beatrix and Irene. The house is secluded, with 10 air-conditioned rooms, all with private bath. Full breakfast.

INN ON LAUREL LAKE
Innkeeper: Thomas Fusco.
413-243-1436, 413-243-9749;
fax 413-243-2936.
www.laurellakeinn.com.
615 Laurel St., Lee, MA
01238.
Rte. 20, 2 mi. N. of
MassPike exit 2.
Price: Expensive to Very
Expensive.
Credit Cards: AE, D, MC, V.
Handicap Access: Limited.
Special Features: Private
beach with canoes,
paddleboats; tennis; no
smoking.

On the shore of Laurel Lake, this 120-year-old country property has attracted a loyal following with its 19 comfortable bedrooms (17 with private baths) and 2 sitting rooms filled with an impressive collection of record albums, books, and games. The tennis court and private beach add to guests' playtime possibilities. Full breakfast buffet served.

THE MORGAN HOUSE INN
Owners: Wesley and
Kimberly Bookstaver.
413-243-3661;
fax 413-243-3103.
www.morganhouseinn.com.
33 Main St., Lee, MA 01238.
On Rte. 20, 0.8 mi. N. of
MassPike exit 2.
Price: Expensive.
Credit Cards: AE, MC, V.
Special Features: No pets;
children welcome.

The Morgan House, built in 1817 and a stage-coach stop beginning in 1853, has a bustling and convenient in-town location. This full-service inn, totally refurbished in 1999, offers 12 comfortable rooms in a variety of shapes and sizes, 7 with private bath. The dining room has also been spruced up; light fare is available in the tavern. While the old hotel registers that once served as wallpaper in the lobby could not be saved, the spirit of former guests remains to provide a patina for a modern inn. Lunch and dinner served seven days a week.

PARSONAGE ON THE GREEN

Innkeepers: Barbara and Don Mahony.
413-243-4364.
www.bbhost.com/parsonageonthegreen.
20 Park Pl., Lee, MA 01238.
On the green, adjacent to church.
Price: Expensive.
Credit Cards: None; checks accepted.
Special Features: Access to Laurel Lake beach; no smoking; no pets; children over 12.

This 1851 colonial, originally the parsonage for the church next door, was entirely refurbished by the present owners, who have run it since 1997. Four sunny rooms upstairs, each with private bath, have comfortable four-poster beds, family memorabilia, and other nice touches. Coffee and tea are available upstairs after 7:00 in the morning; a formal three-course breakfast is served in the dining room downstairs. Also downstairs are a parlor and a library (with games and TV), both filled with pictures of the Mahony family and early occupants of the house. Although the inn sits in the middle of Lee, it is on the opposite side of the green from the main drag, so visitors enjoy quiet as much as easy access to the town.

South Lee

THE FEDERAL HOUSE

Owners: Dick and Sue Cody.
413-243-1824, 800-243-1824; fax 413-243-1828.
www.federalhouseinn.com.
1560 Pleasant St., PO Box 248, S. Lee, MA 01260.
On Rte. 102 just E. of Stockbridge.
Price: Moderate to Very Expensive.
Credit Cards: AE, D, MC, V.
Special Features: No smoking; no pets; children 12 and older.

Thomas Hurlburt built this house in 1824, when he came to South Lee to operate the paper mill on the Housatonic River. In this historic property, which has been beautifully restored, the 10 graceful and charming guest rooms feature antique furnishings. Some rooms have fireplaces; all have private bath and air-conditioning. Guest pantry. Full breakfast included.

HISTORIC MERRELL INN

Innkeepers: George and Joanne Crockett.
413-243-1794, 800-243-1794; fax 413-243-2669.
www.merrell-inn.com.
1565 Pleasant St., S. Lee, MA 01260.
On Rte. 102 just E. of Stockbridge.
Closed: Christmas and week preceding.

Those who walk through the massive door of this striking 1794 brick inn will find themselves transported back in time. For years it served as a stagecoach stop on the busy Boston-Albany Pike. It lay idle and boarded up for over 100 years until late 1980. Now lovingly and carefully restored, the inn is listed on the National Register of Historic Places. Of the nine bedrooms and one suite, some are furnished with four-poster and canopy beds, and all have private baths, air-conditioning, and telephones; four have fireplaces. The Old Tavern Room features the original circular colonial bar. A

Price: Moderate to
  Expensive.
Credit Cards: MC, V.
Special Features: No
  smoking; no pets.

New Marlborough

groomed lawn in back leads through old founda-
tions to a screened gazebo on the banks of the
Housatonic River. A full breakfast is served from a
menu.

Judith Monachina

The rustic ambience at Gedney Farm in New Marlborough belies the elegance one finds inside.

**THE OLD INN ON THE
GREEN AND GEDNEY
FARM**
Innkeepers: Bradford
  Wagstaff and Leslie Miller.
413-229-3131, 800-286-3139;
  fax 413-229-8236.
www.oldinn.com.
Mailing Address: Star Rte.
  70, New Marlborough,
  MA 01230.
On Rte. 57, center of village.
Price: Expensive to Very
  Expensive.

A beautiful village rich in unaffected nostalgia is
the setting for this 18th-century inn. The 5
rooms in the inn, each with private bath, have been
lovingly restored and furnished in a simple Ameri-
can-country style. Gedney Farm, a short walk from
the inn, has 16 guest rooms with 4 suites, carved
out of a Normandy-style barn, which was built
around 1900 as a showplace for Percheron stallions
and Jersey cattle. All suites feature fireplaces in the
living rooms, large bedrooms, and whirlpool tubs
in the master baths. Gedney Manor, 12 rooms all
with private baths, is 0.5 mile and the most deluxe.

Credit Cards: AE, MC, V.
Special Features: Restaurant.

Thayer House has an additional 5 rooms with Jacuzzis, while Stebbins House can be leased by the week or longer. The restored second horse barn serves as space for weddings, parties, meetings, and concerts. The restaurant in the inn is one of the finest in the Berkshires.

THE RED BIRD INN
Managers: Barbara and
   Doug Newman.
413-229-2349;
   fax 413-229-2433.
16 Adsit Crosby Rd., New
   Marlborough; mail: Rte.
   57, Gt. Barrington, MA
   01230.
From Gt. Barrington, Rte.
   23 E. to Rte. 57.
Price: Expensive to Very
   Expensive.
Credit Cards: AE, MC, V.
Handicap Access: Limited.
Special Features: No
   smoking; no pets.

A former stagecoach stop, the 1791 Red Bird Inn is a classic New England colonial with Greek Revival trim. The inn, located on 10 acres on a quiet country road, has seven rooms, all with private baths. The rooms are furnished with antiques and retain their original wide-plank floors, fireplaces, and old ironwork. Luxurious linens and bathrobes are laid out. A separate cottage suite has one huge room with a queen-sized bed, two twins, a sitting area, and private bath. The large screened porch is a popular feature with warm-weather guests. Doug, a chef, prepares a full country breakfast.

Sandisfield

NEW BOSTON INN
Innkeeper: Susan and
   Conrad Ringeisen.
413-258-4477, 888-776-7774;
   fax 413-258-4234.
www.newbostoninn.com.
PO Box 601, Sandisfield,
   MA 01255.
Jct. Rtes. 8 and 57 in village
   of New Boston.
Price: Inexpensive.
Credit Cards: AE, MC, V.
Special Features: 1737 pub
   and full-service
   restaurant.

The owners of this remarkable old stagecoach inn, built in 1737 and listed on the National Register of Historic Places, continue to make improvements. The six guest rooms are—true to the period—snug. Low ceilings, wide-board floors, and multipaned windows hark back to the 18th century and, in most cases, are original. All rooms feature private baths and are decorated with early pine furniture and stenciling. All closets are cedar lined.

After wandering through the cozy bedrooms on the second floor, we enter the spacious ballroom— now called the Gathering Room—complete with an antique billiards table and a barrel-vaulted ceiling. The matching fireplaces at either end accent the sense of openness and grace. Another historic delight is the taproom, now open as a pub, that adjoins the low-ceilinged dining room. The 22-inch-wide pine boards on the wall are called "king's wood." The trees were cut by the colonists in spite of being reserved for masts for the royal navy. In this room as throughout the inn, the wooden moldings, plaster walls, slanted floors, venerable windows and doorways (there is hardly a right angle in the place) provide a powerful charm and sense of history.

What's more, the New Boston Inn has a resident ghost. She is real enough to have been reported in *Yankee* magazine: an Irish maiden, dressed in bridal black, who was shot by a scorned suitor in an upstairs room.

Breakfast included.

Sheffield

BIRCH HILL BED & BREAKFAST
Owners: Michael and Wendy Advocate.
413-229-2143, 800-359-3969; fax 413-229-3405.
www.birchhillbb.com.
254 S. Undermountain Rd., Sheffield, MA 01257.
On Rte. 41, 4 mi. S. of Rte. 23.
Price: Expensive to Very Expensive.
Credit Cards: None.
Special Features: Pool; dogs welcome; children over 9.

Set along one of the most scenic roads of South Berkshire, Birch Hill (formerly Ivanhoe Country House) provides seven comfortable rooms, all with private bath and refrigerator, some with fireplaces. Guests may take a dip in the pool before dinner, play the piano, enjoy the fire in the chestnut-paneled room, and select from the many fine area restaurants for an evening meal. At the base of Race Mountain, traversed by the Appalachian Trail, 20 wooded acres hug this 1780-vintage country house. "Out of the ordinary" breakfast served.

BROKEN HILL MANOR
Owners:Michael Farmer and Gaetan Lachance.
413-528-6159, 877-535-6159; fax 413-644-8872.
www.brokenhillmanor.com.
771 West Rd., Sheffield, MA 01257.
From Rte. 7, W. on Lime Kiln Rd. to N. on West Rd.
Price: Moderate to Expensive.
Credit Cards: All major.
Special Features: No smoking; no pets; children over 14.

A long drive leads to the top of the world: Broken Hill Manor rests with its 12 acres atop a hill, totally surrounded by woods—a fine place to view the stars. And perhaps hear them, in the quiet. Stars there are: Each of the eight rooms is named for an opera heroine, from Aida to Violetta. The rooms are air-conditioned and contain CD players, with an ample supply of disks. The 100-year-old rambling house, wood and peanut-brittle stone, was inhabited by two playwrights until 1997. Now it offers seclusion, comfortable beds, and a full cooked breakfast, served either inside or on the terrace.

ORCHARD SHADE
Owners: Debbie and Henry Thornton.
413-229-8463, 877-672-4233; fax 413-229-2711.
www.orchardshade.com.

The Thorntons' small B&B, built in 1850, is truly set in the trees—and located a bit farther from Route 7 than expected. They furnished their three bedrooms with antiques, and one room has a private bath. The fireplace in the common room wards

999 Hewins St., Sheffield,
  MA 01257.
E. side of the Housatonic,
  between County Rd. and
  Rte. 7.
Price: Inexpensive to
  Moderate.
Credit Cards: AE, D, MC, V.
Special Features: No
  smoking; no pets;
  children welcome.

off the chill on cooler evenings. The large porch is
perfect for relaxing after a busy day of Sheffield
antiquing, as are the two acres and gardens.

RACE BROOK LODGE
Innkeeper: Allegra
  Graham.
413-229-2916, 888-725-6343.
www.rblodge.com.
864 S. Undermountain Rd.,
  Sheffield, MA 01257.
On Rte. 41, 2 miles S. of
  Berkshire School.
Price: Moderate to
  Expensive.
Open: Year-round.
Credit Cards: AE, MC, V.
Handicap Access: Ground-
  level entry to many rooms.
Special Features: No
  smoking; well-behaved
  dogs accepted; children
  welcome.

This rustic lodge beside Race Brook has its own
trail leading to a state forest with waterfall,
ravine, and the Appalachian Trail. A large rambling
barn, dating from the 1790s, embraces rooms and
suites in what were once haylofts, with exposed
original beams, stenciling, nooks and alcoves, and
windows and stairs in unexpected places. The variety of bedroom, bathroom, and entrance arrangements can work for couples, family groups, or
friends traveling together. Having converted a
garage into the Meeting House and built a new
post-and-beam barn, the lodge emphasizes team-
building retreats.

The interiors have been specifically designated a
"chintz-free zone" to maximize informality. The
rooms are also smoke free, phone free, and TV free.
More rooms and suites, 32 in all, are in nearby cottages. In the lofty common rooms at the heart of the
barn is the well-stocked, always-open Horseshoe Wine Bar—run on the honor system—along with tables and a TV corner, and a horseshoe bar. The lodge will produce lunch and suppers for groups on request. A hearty breakfast buffet is served.

RAMBLEWOOD INN
Owners: Cliff and Nadine
  Hawver.
413-229-3363, 800-854-1862;
  fax 413-229-5942.
www.ramblewoodinn.com.
400 S. Undermountain Rd.,
  Box 729, Sheffield, MA
  01257.
On Rte. 41.
Price: Expensive.
Credit Cards: MC, V.

Up a short hill off scenic Route 41, this Alpine
structure at the edge of the woods has an attractive rustic look, with all the comforts of home, including central air-conditioning. The Hawvers offer six
guest rooms (four with private bath) and a ground-
floor suite with full kitchen, bedroom, living room,
and bath. The inn owns pond-front property across
the road, where guests may swim, canoe, and fish.

A full gourmet breakfast is served. The Berkshire
School, site of the Berkshire Choral Institute (see
the "Music" section in Chapter Five, *Arts & Pleasures*), is a mile down the road.

STAVELEIGH HOUSE B&B

Innkeeper: Ali A. Winston.
413-229-2129.
www.staveleigh.com.
59 Main St., Sheffield, MA 01257.
On Rte. 7 just S. of village center.
Price: Moderate.
Credit Cards: All major.
Handicap Access: Limited.
Special Features: No smoking; no pets; inquire about children.

The Reverend Bradford, minister of the oldest church in Berkshire, built his lovely house in 1817 in the heart of Sheffield. The Staveleigh family acquired the property at the turn of the 20th century. *House & Garden Magazine* has documented Ali's old-fashioned welcome: "The hospitality at Staveleigh House is deeper and more thoughtful than any you will find elsewhere." All eight guest rooms are air-conditioned; terry-cloth robes are provided. The grounds feature perennial beds, an herb garden, and a place to sit under the trees. Ali serves a splendid breakfast and afternoon tea.

Stockbridge

ARBOR ROSE BED & BREAKFAST

Owner: Christina Alsop.
413-298-4744, 877-298-4744.
www.arborrose.com.
8 Yale Hill Rd., Box 114, Stockbridge, MA 01262.
Off E. Main St. (Rte. 102).
Price: Moderate to Expensive.
Credit Cards: MC, V.
Special Features: No smoking; no pets; children welcome.

The first thing one hears on entering the driveway to Arbor Rose is the soothing sound of rushing water. The large white house sits on a hill overlooking an early 1800s sawmill and millpond. The house has six guest rooms and one efficiency that sleeps four, all with private bath and air-conditioning. Four rooms are in the mill. The decor is highlighted by colorful paintings by the owner's mother, Suzette Alsop, a noted local artist.

Full breakfast includes magnificent muffins (continental breakfast midweek).

BLUE WILLOW

Owners: Lila and Joseph Ruggio.
413-298-3018;
fax 413-298-0009.
www.bluewillowbb.com.
2 Lincoln Lane, PO Box 843, Stockbridge 01262.
Off Rte. 102, 0.5 mi. E. of Red Lion Inn.
Price: Moderate to Expensive.
Credit Cards: None
Special Features: Secluded road; on Housatonic River across from Laura's Tower.

The Ruggios purchased an abandoned house 19 years ago, gutted it, redid it, added to it, and opened it seasonally for guests. Recently they began hosting visitors year-round in their tidy B&B. The theme: a collection of blue willow china they began many years ago and have been adding to that depicts the daughter falling in love with the gardener, which angers the father, who kills them both; but they fly off as birds. The three rooms (one with deck, one in the carriage barn) have television, air-conditioning, and private baths. They are furnished with antiques, including brass beds. Full breakfast.

BERKSHIRE THISTLE B&B
Owners: Gene and Diane Elling.
413-298-3188;
    fax 413-298-3549.
www.berkshirethistle.com.
19 East St., Box 1227,
    Stockbridge, MA 01262.
On Rte. 7, N. of village.
Price: Moderate to Expensive.
Credit Cards: None.
Special Features: Pool; no smoking; no pets; children 12 and older.

The owners of one of the truly impressive homes on Route 7, well-seasoned innkeepers, have had years of training in the bed and breakfast business. This location, midway between Lenox and Stockbridge, is unbeatable. The house, a recently built colonial, it is comfortable and beautifully sited, with a wraparound deck to take advantage of the views. All five rooms have private baths and air-conditioning. Easy access to theater, Tanglewood, and great hiking trails. Swimming pool and picturesque pasture with grazing horses on five acres.

CONROY'S B&B
Owners: James and Joanne Conroy.
413-298-4990;
    fax 413-298-4990.
www.conroysinn.com.
11 East St., Box 191,
    Stockbridge, MA 01262.
On Rte. 7 about 1.5 mi. N. of village.
Price: Expensive.
Credit Cards: AE, D, MC, V.
Special Features: No smoking; no pets; families welcome; special-events catering; two week's notice of cancellation.

Located just north of Stockbridge in a handsome 1830s Federal-style house, Conroy's B&B is well situated for cultural attractions. The Conroys offer five double rooms year-round in various configurations, some with private baths, some shared, all air-conditioned. Two rooms have working fireplaces. Three seasonal rooms and an apartment/ suite are located in an air-conditioned detached barn. In busy summer and fall months, dining is extended from tables in the great room in the front house into a wonderfully renovated, equally old attached barn section in its rear. Period charm is not compromised. Full breakfast is included. Families with well-behaved children are welcome.

THE INN AT STOCKBRIDGE
Innkeepers: Alice and Len Schiller.
413-298-3337, 888-466-7865;
    fax 413-298-3406.
www.stockbridgeinn.com.
Box 618, Stockbridge, MA 01262.
On Rte. 7 about 1 mi. N. of village.
Price: Expensive to Very Expensive.
Credit Cards: AE, D, MC, V.
Handicap Access: Limited.
Special Features: Pool; no smoking; no pets; children over 12.

A marvelous, secluded inn run by friendly, professional people. The large, white-columned, 1906 house is decorated with impeccable taste, featuring priceless antiques and many thoughtful touches. All eight rooms in the main house have private baths and are air-conditioned. Barn and cottage contain eight suites with fireplaces; seven have whirlpool baths. Exercise and fitness equipment is available as is a massage room.

Wine and cheese are served in the living room— warmed by a fire in chilly weather—and breakfast in the formal dining room includes homemade pastries, with croissants, French toast, and cinnamon buns possible offerings. Special private dinners can be arranged on request.

THE RED LION INN
Director of Operations:
  Dennis Barquinero.
413-298-5545;
  fax 413-298-5130.
www.redlioninn.com.
30 Main St., PO Box 954,
  Stockbridge, MA 01262.
Village center, jct. Rtes. 7 &
  102.
Price: Expensive to Very
  Expensive.
Credit Cards: AE, D, DC,
  MC, V.
Handicap Access: Yes.
Special Features: Pool; new
  fitness room; massage
  therapist.

In 1773 (or so) the Red Lion Inn first opened its doors to travelers on the stagecoach route linking Albany, Hartford, and Boston. Two hundred thirty years later, the Red Lion still welcomes visitors and locals, with consummate colonial charm. The present inn, rebuilt in 1897 after a fire, is an icon of the Berkshires, representing graceful country lodging at its best.

Antique furniture and a fine collection of china teapots adorn the lobby. Each of the 108 private rooms (including 25 suites) is decorated with unique period appointments, carefully coordinated by the inn's owners, the Fitzpatrick family, who also own Country Curtains. Recent improvements have concentrated on refurbishing the rooms. Throughout the inn, the loving attention to detail is evident in every aspect of its operation. It's easy to feel at home here because all the inn's top-quality services are offered by a vibrant, eager-to-please staff. In summer, one's porch or courtyard company may be an actor or actress of note who spends evenings nearby on the boards of the Berkshire Theatre Festival.

The atmosphere is faithful to the rhythms of a simpler, slower time while providing all contemporary comforts. Sipping a cool drink on a hot summer's day on the Red Lion's famous porch or meeting a companion in front of the cheery fireplace in the lobby in winter is to beat to the heart of the Berkshires. The Red Lion Inn is not, however, a particularly tranquil place. The main building is full of activity and people, and the streets outside are sometimes noisy with traffic. There's a conviviality and gaiety about the lobby that some folks love. Others might prefer the cottages that form a complex around the inn: Stafford House, O'Brien House, Meadowlark (at Chesterwood), Yellow Cottage, Stevens House, Fire House, McGregor House, and Two Maple Street.

Reservations should be made in advance, especially in the summer. The rooms are complemented by an excellent formal dining room; casual or informal dining in the Widow Bingham Tavern; nightly entertainment in the Lion's Den, a pub; a courtyard for summer meals under the trees, surrounded by bushels of impatiens; the Red Lion Inn Gift Shop; and a Country Curtains retail store.

SEASONS ON MAIN
  B&B
Innkeepers: Pat and Greg
  O'Neill.
413-298-5419, 888-955-4747;
  fax 413-298-0092.
www.seasonsonmain.com

This gracious house is within an easy walk of Stockbridge shops, restaurants and Berkshire Theatre Festival. Downstairs, the inn offers three sitting rooms with Victorian-inspired furnishings and wallpaper and a dining room with a Duncan Phyfe-style dining table and Larkin sideboards.

47 Main St., Box 634,
  Stockbridge, MA 01262.
On Rte.7 E. end of town
  center.
Price: Expensive to Very
  Expensive.
Credit Cards: AE, MC, V.
Special Features: No
  smoking; no pets or
  children; 3-night
  minimum during
  Tanglewood season.

Upstairs, the four air-conditioned guest rooms follow a seasonal motif; one has a king-sized sleigh bed, fireplace, TV, and large bath. Guests have the use of a comfortable, west-facing porch that affords a view of Main Street and handsome gardens.

**STOCKBRIDGE
COUNTRY INN**
Innkeepers: Vernon and
  Diane Reuss.
413-298-4015;
  fax 413-298-3413.
www.stockbridgecountry
  inn.com.
26 Glendale Rd, PO Box
  525, Stockbridge, MA
  01262.
On Rte.183, 0.5 mile S. of
  Norman Rockwell
  Museum.
Price: Expensive to Very
  Expensive.
Credit Cards: AE, D, MC, V.
Special Features: Heated
  pool; no smoking; no
  pets or children.

Formerly Roeder House, this delightful hideaway, in a small village far from the crowds but close to summer attractions, is just three-quarters of a mile from the new Norman Rockwell Museum. Awaiting house guests are seven large, exquisitely furnished air-conditioned rooms, all with private bath and filled with antiques and four-poster queen-sized beds. The entire house reflects the impeccable taste of the owners, who also run an antiques shop. A full breakfast is served on tables set with china, silver, and crystal on the charming screened-in porch, weather permitting.

TAGGART HOUSE B&B
Owners: Hinckley and
  Susan Waitt.
413-298-4303.
www.taggarthouse.com.
18 Main St., Stockbridge,
  MA 01262.
Price: Very Expensive.
Credit Cards: AB, MC, V.
Special Features: No
  smoking; no pets; inquire
  about children; golf and
  tennis available.

A stunning array of art and antiques in the richly detailed architectural setting of a 19th-century mansion, with a fireplace around just about every corner, a billiards room, a paneled library, a music room, and three acres of secluded gardens and field: the description of a romantic country manor house in a Victorian novel. Actually, the Taggart House is right on Main Street in Stockbridge, where the resident owners have transformed fiction into reality. Their personal collection of antique furnishings and artwork, with dramatic choices of color and texture, artfully blend elegance and whimsy, opulence and coziness.

Throughout the downstairs living rooms and the upstairs bedrooms are a variety of fabulous faux effects painted on walls and ceilings, including bois and tortoiseshell finishes. In the butler's pantry, trompe l'oeil painting merges a real garden scene with an illusory one. The abundance of imaginative details also includes fabrics and wallpaper with William Morris designs, a birch-bark canoe suspended from a frescoed ceiling over the billiards table, curtains drawn back with antlers, a collection of Native American artifacts in the library, and a pillowed nook halfway up the stairs. The cavernous music room has hosted chamber concerts from Bach to Gershwin—and an 18-foot Christmas tree. Four bedrooms feature rich and restful color themes, fireplaces, and luxurious antique beds; each room's private bath is equally sumptuous, with antique furnishings, heated towel racks, and even bath salts. Morning brings gourmet breakfasts, and there are some self-serve options, too. Afternoon tea can be provided as well as early-evening hors d'oeuvres.

Tyringham

COBBLEVIEW B&B
Owners: Lynn Bertelli and Alan Wilcox.
413-243-2463, 800-914-7945; fax 413-243-1299.
www.cobbleviewbandb. com.
123 Main Rd., Tyringham, MA 01264.
Across from Town Hall.
Price: Expensive to Very Expensive.
Credit Cards: MC, V.
Special Features: Hiking and cross-country skiing; no smoking; no pets; call ahead about children under 12.

This attractive B&B, formerly the Golden Goose, is set smack in one of the most scenic landscapes in the commonwealth. Its six newly refurbished rooms—whose decor could be defined as "elegant country"—include a loft that holds four and a studio with bedroom, bath, and kitchen. All rooms have private bath and air-conditioning. For breakfast, Lynn serves a Continental buffet, always including something she's baked fresh, to be eaten at the huge dining-room table or on the deck. The six acres of land are coming alive with gardens.

West Stockbridge

THE CARD LAKE COUNTRY INN
Owners: Ed and Lisa Robbins.
413-232-0272; fax 240-376-2174.
www.cardlakeinn.com.
29 Main St., Box 38, W. Stockbridge, MA 01266.
Price: Moderate to Expensive.
Credit Cards: MC, V.
Special Features: No pets.

The inn offers 14 guest rooms featuring brass and iron beds. All have private bath. Village shops across street are artsy-craftsy. Guests may want to ask for a room at the back of the inn to avoid traffic noise. Restaurant and tavern on the premises.

SHAKER MILL INN
Innkeepers/Owners: Lori
  Bashour and Michael
  Lee.
413-232-4600;
  fax 413-232-4601.
www.shakermillinn.com.
2 Oak St. Box 61, W.
  Stockbridge, MA 01266.
On Rte. 102.
Price: Expensive to Very
  Expensive.
Credit Cards: AE, MC, V.
Special Features: Children
  and pets welcome.

The inn offers nine enormous modern, deluxe rooms, some with patio or balcony, with queen-sized beds and complete with small kitchens and living rooms. The Berkshire Suite has two full bedrooms, two full baths, a large fully equipped kitchen, living room; three TVs, laundry, and just about anything else anyone might want. All accommodations are in a converted barn. Continental breakfast is served.

Yoga (Phoenix Rising) offered next door (See Chapter Six, *Body & Spirit*).

INNS AND B&BS CENTRAL COUNTY

Becket

LONG HOUSE B&B
Owners: Roy and Joan
  Simmons.
413-623-8360.
www.the-longhouse.com.
155 High St., PO Box 271,
  Becket, MA 01223.
Off Rte. 8.
Open: Year-round.
Price: Moderate.
Credit Cards: MC, V.
Special Features: No
  smoking; no pets.

The Simmonses have been welcoming bed-and-breakfast guests since 1966. Their 1820 country home, listed on the National Register of Historic Places, has four cozy rooms, one with private bath. Convenient to Jacob's Pillow, hiking, and the Appalachian Trail. Full breakfast offered. In summer, a weekly plan can be arranged.

Dalton

THE DALTON HOUSE
Hosts: Gary and Bernice
  Turetsky.
413-684-3854;
  fax 413-684-0203.
www.thedaltonhouse.com.
955 Main St., Dalton, MA
  01226.
Price: Moderate to
  Expensive.
Credit Cards: AE, MC, V.
Special Features: Pool; no
  smoking; no pets;
  children over 10.

Set in a small New England village, this inn offers 11 rooms in the main house and carriage house. All have private baths, telephones, and televisions. The house has been partially furnished with antiques. Summer guests enjoy air-conditioning, a pool, extensively landscaped lawn and flower gardens, and a picnic area. Breakfast is served, with blueberry pancakes when in season.

Hancock

HANCOCK INN
Owners: Joe and Gail
   Mullady.
413-738-5873;
   fax 413-738-5758.
www.thehancockinn.com.
102 Main St., Hancock, MA
   01237.
On Rte. 43 between
   Williamstown and
   Stephentown, NY.
Price: Moderate.
Credit Cards: D, MC, V.
Special Features: No
   smoking; no pets;
   children under 5 free.

This cozy Victorian inn is set in a village that seems unaware of the 21st century's arrival. A tastefully furnished family-run establishment, the inn has the charm of a delightful, forgotten keepsake discovered one day in grandmother's attic. Six comfortable rooms, all with private bath and air-conditioning. A full breakfast is included; dinners, at extra cost, at the guests' request. The dining room is open to guests of the inn only.

Hinsdale

MAPLEWOOD B&B
Innkeepers: Charlotte and
   Bob Baillargeon.
413-655-8167.
435 Maple St., PO Box 477,
   Hinsdale, MA 01235.
On Rte. 143.
Price: Inexpensive to
   Moderate.
Credit Cards: None.
Special Features: No
   smoking; no pets.

Country setting, country style. Set on six acres with a small pond, this antiques-filled house has two rooms with private baths and a two-bedroom suite with private bath. Guests have a common room, with library, dining room, and separate entrance. Full breakfast might feature fresh trout or corn pancakes with fresh, locally made maple syrup; special diets can be accommodated.

Lanesborough

**THE TUCKERED
   TURKEY**
Managers: Dan and
   Marianne Sullivan.
413-442-0260.
30 Old Cheshire Rd., PO
   Box 638, Lanesborough,
   MA 01237.
From Rte. 7, turn E. on
   Summer St., then N.on
   Old Cheshire Rd.
Price: Moderate.
Credit Cards: None.
Special Features: No
   smoking; no pets.

A restored 19th-century colonial farmhouse set on four acres with spacious views. Three antiques-furnished rooms share baths. Guests are welcome to bring their children to play with the owner's children. Full breakfast served.

Lenox

THE APPLE TREE INN & RESTAURANT
Owners: Sharon Walker and Joel Catalano.
413-637-1477;
    fax 413-637-2528.
www.appletree-inn.com.
10 Richmond Mtn. Rd., PO Box 699, Lenox, MA 01240.
Just S.of Tanglewood main gate.
Price: Expensive to Very Expensive.
Credit Cards: AE, D, MC, V.
Special Features: Pool; tennis; no pets.

Magically set, the Apple Tree Inn is indisputably the lodging that lies closest to the main gate of Tanglewood. The 13 guest rooms in the main house are down-comforter dainty, some with antique brass beds and fireplaces, all with private bath. The Lodge, with 21 additional rooms— bringing the total number of units to 34—is less charming, though the rooms are convenient and clean.

The Apple Tree would be worth a visit for the views alone: a magnificent Berkshire panorama from the south-facing rooms, from poolside, or from the gazebo, which serves as a restaurant (see Chapter Four, *Dining*). There is also dining on the deck. The downstairs parlor is thoughtfully appointed and very comfortable; the bar has rich wood paneling, stained-glass windows, and a huge hearth. A crowning touch is the landscaping, boasting hundreds of varieties of roses set among the apple trees—truly a visual feast throughout late spring and summer. Continental breakfast included.

BIRCHWOOD INN
Owner: Ellen Chenaux.
413-637-2600, 800-524-1646.
www.birchwood-inn.com.
7 Hubbard St., Box 2020, Lenox, MA 01240.
Corner of Main St.
Price: Moderate to Very Expensive.
Credit Cards: AE, D, MC, V.
Special Features: No smoking; no pets; children over 12.

The oldest house in Lenox, this elegant 1767 mansion high on the hill overlooking a storybook town continues renovations. Nine rooms in the main house, all with private bath, and two rooms in the carriage house. All rooms are air-conditioned. A magnificent library extends along one side of the house, with books, magazines, and games galore. The wicker-furnished front porch is a popular spot in summer. A full gourmet breakfast is included. Tea is served (weather permitting) on the porch.

BLANTYRE
Manager: Katja Henke.
413-637-3556;
    fax 413-637-4282.
www.blantyre.com.
16 Blantyre Rd., Lenox, MA 01240.
Off Rte. 20, 3 mi. N. of MassPike exit 2.
Closed: Early Nov. to early May.

Regally set amid over 100 conscientiously groomed acres of lawns, trees, and hedges, Blantyre offers its guests attentive and even ingenious service, great natural and architectural beauty, palatial furnishings, and magnificent vistas. Built by New York City businessman Robert Paterson in 1902 as a replica of his wife's ancestral home in the Scottish village of Blantyre—east of Glasgow— Blantyre went through several hands in the mid-

Price: Very Expensive.
Credit Cards: AE, DC, MC, V.
Handicap Access: Limited.
Special Features: Pool; tennis; croquet; exercise room; sauna; hot tub; no pets; children over 12.

20th century and fell into disrepair. In 1980 Jack and Jane Fitzpatrick bought the property (which has now passed to their daughter Ann), restored it to its present excellent condition: a baronial yet hospitable place—massive but comfortable, grand yet delicately appointed.

A member of the prestigious Relais et Châteaux, Blantyre has also been awarded four stars in the Mobil Travel Guide. The five original suite-sized bedrooms—with four-poster beds, fireplaces, and magnificent bathrooms—are the true "jewels" in Blantyre's crown. Three other rooms are on the same floor, created in the "nanny's wing" on a different scale—smaller but just as elegant. Twelve more rooms are neatly tucked away in the original carriage house. There are also three cottages on the grounds: cozy, endearingly whimsical, and brilliantly situated.

In addition to its superb accommodations, Blantyre has a magnificent gourmet dining room, which AAA recognized with four diamonds. The hotel maintains four Har-Tru tennis courts and two tournament-sized bent-grass croquet courts. A delightful exercise room fashioned out of a former potting shed provides a sauna and hot tub. Nearby is a lovely, landscaped swimming pool. Tanglewood is a mere 3 miles to the west. Conferences and small meetings are welcome. (The grounds and buildings are *not* open to the public for casual viewing.)

BROOK FARM INN
Owners/Innkeepers: Linda and Phil Halpern.
413-637-3013, 800-285-7638.
www.brookfarm.com.
15 Hawthorne St., Lenox, MA 01240.
Just off Old Stockbridge Rd.
Price: Expensive to Very Expensive.
Credit Cards: AE, D, MC, V (checks only in summer).
Special Features: Heated pool; no smoking; no pets; children 15 and over.

The Halperns bought this inn in March 2001. Twelve antique-furnished rooms—all with private bath, air-conditioning and telephones—are offered in this large Victorian home, close to many Berkshire attractions. Several of the rooms have been renovated, with special attention lavished on the two large rooms at the front of the house, both with four-posters, sitting areas, and new bathrooms. A third-floor room offers a queen-sized bed and two twins. Plans are in place to build a carriage house—handicap accessible—to open May 2003. A unique attraction to this inn: Each day has it own poem, displayed in the 1,400-volume library and supplemented by 75 poets on tape. Occasional readings and storytellings (Linda is a storyteller) take place, accompanied by tea and scones. A buffet breakfast and afternoon tea are served daily to guests.

CANDLELIGHT INN
Owner/Innkeeper: Rebecca
  Hedgecock.
413-637-1555, 800-428-0580;
  fax 413-637-1594.
www.candlelightinn-
  lenox.com.
35 Walker St., Lenox, MA
  01240.
Corner of Church St.
Price: Moderate to Expen-
  sive.
Credit Cards: AE, D, MC, V.
Special Features: No pets;
  children over 10.

This comfortable, antiques-furnished inn has eight large guest rooms, all with private bath, some retaining their original fixtures. Like the rooms, a small upstairs lounge is furnished in period style. Centrally located in the heart of Historic Lenox Village, the inn features a charming restaurant on the main floor. Beside that is a storied wooden bar, once part of the former Curtis Hotel and, prior to that, a famous old Boston hotel that was destroyed in a fire (the bar itself was scorched). Continental breakfast is included.

CLIFFWOOD INN
Owners: Scottie and Joy
  Farrelly.
413-637-3330, 800-789-3331;
  fax 413-637-0221.
www.cliffwood.com.
25 Cliffwood St., Lenox, MA
  01240.
Just off Main St. in the
  village.
Price: Expensive to Very
  Expensive.
Credit Cards: None.
Special Features: Indoor and
  outdoor pools, putting
  green; no smoking; no
  pets; children over 11.

This special inn, on a quiet, residential street, was built for a French diplomat in 1889. The elegant public rooms have tall ceilings, polished inlaid hardwood floors, and grand fireplaces. The seven guest rooms have private baths and air-conditioning; six come with their own fireplaces. The inn features an outdoor pool, an indoor counter-current pool, and a putting green. The spacious veranda overlooks the gardens, pool, and putting green. We move in winter to the warming fire in the oval dining room, with its ornate wood-carved fireplace mantel. Wine, hors d'oeuvres, and friendly conversation are served early evening; coffee and juice in the morning.

CORNELL INN
Owners: Billie and Doug
  McLoughlin.
413-637-0562, 800-637-0562;
  fax 413-737-0927.
www.cornellinn.com.
203 Main St., Lenox, MA
  01240.
Rte. 7A just N. of center of
  town.
Price: Expensive to Very
  Expensive.
Credit Cards: AE, CB, D,
  DC, MC, V.
Handicap Access: Two
  rooms.
Special Features: Pub; no
  smoking, no pets; children
  13 and over.

Written in the guest book at the Cornell Inn: "Charming home. The pancakes were delicious." The home began life in 1888 as a large, well-built Victorian, and the owners keep making all the right improvements. Each of the 13 bedrooms in the main house has its own bath and is furnished with brass or four-poster beds; several have fireplaces. Eight additional rooms are in the converted carriage house and 10 in the adjacent 223-year-old McDonald House. The McDonald House rooms have fireplaces and whirlpool tubs. Phone, color TV in all rooms. Extended continental breakfast; full breakfast Sunday.

THE GABLES INN

Owners: Frank and Mary
  Newton.
413-637-3416, 800-382-9401;
  fax 413-637-3416.
www.gableslenox.com.
81 Walker St., Lenox, MA
  01240.
On Rte. 183 in center of
  village.
Price: Moderate to Very
  Expensive.
Credit Cards: D, MC, V.
Special Features: Pool; tennis;
  no pets; children over 12.

This charming, handsome 1885 home is where Edith Wharton summered while her "cottage," the Mount, was being built. Visitors can sleep in her room or in that of her husband, Teddy. He stayed there until 1928, long after she'd taken off. Frank Newton discusses the Whartons knowledgeably. The inn is fully air-conditioned, with TV and VCR. The 17 bedrooms all have private baths; nine have fireplaces. Full breakfast. A sister inn, called the Summer White House, is at 17 Main Street, Lenox.

GARDEN GABLES INN

Owners: Mario and Lynn
  Mekinda.
413-637-0193.
www.lenoxinn.com.
135 Main St., PO Box 52,
  Lenox, MA 01240.
Price: Expensive to Very
  Expensive.
Credit Cards: AE, D, MC, V.
Special Features: Pool; no
  pets; children over 13.

The Mekinda family has brought new life to this inn since purchasing it in 1987. All 18 rooms have been upgraded to include air-conditioning and private bath (three have whirlpools), all have telephones and answering machines, eight have fireplaces; some have private porches, and some have TV. The five acres of landscaped grounds include the largest outdoor pool in Berkshire County. Walking distance to shops and restaurants—even to Tanglewood for the hardy. The breakfast buffets are special.

GATEWAYS INN

Owners: Fabrizio and
  Rosemary Chiariello.
413-637-2532, 888-492-9466;
  fax 413-637-1432.
www.gatewaysinn.com.
51 Walker St., Lenox, MA
  01240.
Just off Main St.
Price: Expensive to Very
  Expensive.
Credit Cards: AE, D, DC,
  MC, V.
Special Features: Restaurant;
  no smoking; no pets; call
  about children.

Built in 1912 by Harley Procter of Procter and Gamble, this Berkshire "cottage" continues to receive extensive upgrading. Up a graceful, sky-lighted mahogany staircase from an award-winning restaurant are 11 spacious, elegant rooms, each with bath, eight with fireplaces, a four-poster here, a canopy bed there, and peace and quiet everywhere. A guest library has everything from a computer terminal to old-fashioned games. Arthur Fiedler, who stayed here when performing at Tanglewood, gave his name to the lovely "Fiedler Suite." Television and telephone in each room; air-conditioned throughout; a Jacuzzi in the suite.

HAMPTON TERRACE

Owners: Stan and Susan
  Rosen.
413-637-1773 (phone/fax),
  800-203-0656.

The Rosens have thoroughly renovated and refurbished this lovely property, which consists of the Main House and the Carriage House, both dating from 1897. The Main House, renovated in 2001, has six rooms with private baths and air-con-

www.hamptonterrace.com.
91 Walker St., Lenox, MA
  01240.
Price: Expensive to Very
  Expensive.
Credit Cards: AE, D, DC,
  MC, V.
Special Features: No pets;
  children 10 and over.

HARRISON HOUSE
Owner: Andrew Fishbein.
413-637-1746;
  fax 413-637-9957.
www.harrison-house.com.
174 Main St., Lenox, MA
  01240.
Across from Kennedy Park.
Price: Expensive to Very
  Expensive.
Credit Cards: AE, D, MC, V.
Handicap Access: Limited.
Special Features: No pets.

ditioning; some rooms have fireplaces, some have spa tubs or claw-foot tubs. Period furnishings preserve the 19th-century flavor. The Carriage House, refurbished in 2000, features six additional rooms with king- or queen-sized beds, private baths, fireplaces, Jacuzzis, air-conditioning, and television/VCRs—but likewise has vintage furniture, drapes, and decorations. The property is listed at www.luxurylink.com. A full breakfast is served.

Acharming country inn offering seven elegant guest rooms and splendid public areas is at home in an attractive Victorian, at the crest of Main Street. It has a wraparound porch and a handsome sitting/breakfast room overlooking the back lawn. The bedrooms are air-conditioned, each with a private bath and period fixtures and décor. There are fireplaces—many with the original Victorian tiles—in every room as well as cable TV. Duvets and cutwork linens add a romantic touch. The Norman Rockwell suite has a canopy bed, a sitting room with sofa bed, and an especially splendid bathroom. Full buffet breakfast served.

Judith Monachina

The Kemble Inn, seen from Trinity Church, Lenox.

THE KEMBLE INN

Owners/Innkeepers:
Richard and Linda
Reardon.
413-637-4113, 800-353-4113.
www.kembleinn.com.
2 Kemble St., Lenox, MA
01240.
On Rte. 7A.
Price: Expensive to Very
Expensive.
Credit Cards: MC, V.
Handicap Access: Yes.
Special Features: No
smoking; no pets;
children 12 and over.

This luxury bed-and-breakfast inn in Lenox is named for the actress Fanny Kemble, who once lived on the street named for her. It occupies yet another Berkshire "cottage"—this one the Georgian mansion built in 1881 by President Chester A. Arthur's secretary of state, Frederick T. Frelinghuysen. Richard Reardon, a contractor, has supervised the complete renovation of the house, which included adding several bathrooms. Each of the 15 guest rooms has a private bath and air-conditioning. The furnishings throughout the house are period reproductions. The master suite has a bedroom with fireplace and a bathroom with Jacuzzi— and another fireplace. The most impressive features inside the inn are the elegant and spacious common spaces on the ground floor—foyer, reception room, dining room—all with magnificent Adams-style paneling. Also magnificent are the views of the mountains to the back and historic Trinity Church to the front. Continental breakfast is included in the summer.

ROOKWOOD INN

Owner/Innkeeper: Amy
Lindner-Lesser.
413-637-9750, 800-223-9750;
fax 413-637-1352.
www.rookwoodinn.com.
11 Old Stockbridge Rd., PO
Box 1717, Lenox, MA
01240.
Just off Main St. in center of
town.
Price: Expensive to Very
Expensive.
Credit Cards: AE, D, DC,
MC, V.
Handicap Access: Limited.
Special Features: No
smoking; no pets;
children welcome.

The Lessers purchased the inn in the fall of 1996. This grand 1825 Victorian lady sits on a quiet street behind the Town Hall. All 20 rooms and the two-room suite have private bath, and 8 include fireplaces. The two-level turret room is a marvelous secluded aerie, and the 3 rooms in the back of the house can be considered small suites. *New York Magazine* and Target stores have named Rookwood as a top B&B in New England.

A gourmet chef prepares innovative and low-fat breakfasts. Special dietary needs can be accommodated. Children are welcome as guests, and babysitting can be arranged.

SEVEN HILLS INN

Owners: Jim and Patty
Eder.
413-637-0060, 800-869-6518.
www.sevenhillsinn.com.
40 Plunkett St., Lenox, MA
01240.
Just beyond the Mount.

In 1993, after years in the financial world, the Eders purchased this Berkshire cottage. Formerly belonging to Emily Spencer, it had been a summer house on 27 well-landscaped acres. The Eders kept the lovely main building largely intact, gutted and redid the Terrace House to make it more useful as an inn, and more recently added a carriage house.

Price: Expensive to Very
  Expensive.
Credit cards: AE, D, DC,
  MC, V.
Handicapped Access: Yes.
Special Features: Fireplaces
  in many rooms; pool;
  pets accepted.

All 58 rooms have private baths. Each comfortable and welcoming room is imaginatively decorated in a different style, and all look out on the wooded scene that surrounds Edith Wharton's the Mount. Patty Eder kept much of the original furnishings and traveled to auctions to pick up the rest.

While the tone is less formal than Wheatleigh or Blantyre, the inn aims at conferences and weddings. As well as the attractive dining room on the first floor of the main building, public spaces include a banquet room and other functions and a bar from which music wafts on summer evenings. A full breakfast is included in the room rate for a night's stay, or guests may choose other combinations of meals and lodgings.

STONOVER FARM
Owners: Tom and Suky
  Werman.
413-637-9100;
  fax 413-637-1717.
www.stonoverfarm.com.
169 Undermountain Rd.,
  Lenox, MA 01240.
Closed: Jan.–Apr.
Price: Very Expensive.
Credit Cards: All major.
Special Features: On a
  scenic road 0.7 mi from
  Tanglewood.

Tom Werman, returning to Massachusetts after a career as a record producer in Los Angeles, opened his refurbished 1890's stone farmhouse, a stone's throw from Tanglewood, in 2002, by hosting Linda Ronstadt. He has created three suites in the main house as well as a four-room cottage. He serves wine and cheese in the afternoons and a full breakfast.

Luxurious, elegant, all details attended to, plus all the hi-tech electronics anyone could desire, Stonover is a platinum disk of a B&B.

THE VILLAGE INN
Proprietors: Clifford
  Rudisill and Ray Wilson.
413-637-0020, 800-253-0917;
  fax 413-637-9756.
www.villageinn-lenox.com.
16 Church St., PO Box 1810,
  Lenox, MA 01240.
Off Walker St. in center of
  town.
Price: Expensive to Very
  Expensive.
Credit Cards: AE, D, DC,
  MC, V.
Handicap Access: Yes.
Special Features: No
  smoking; no pets;
  children over 6.

Innkeepers Cliff Rudisill and Ray Wilson are cultivated, hospitable hosts whose personal warmth complements this old, highly respected hostelry. Their pride in restoration and furnishings is evident. Of the 32 guest rooms, all with private bath and telephone, six have fireplaces. The suite has a kitchenette. The smoking ban includes the public rooms.

The inn was built in 1771 as a farmhouse; four years later, its original owner started to put up weary travelers arriving by horse-drawn coach. By 1815 he had sold his surrounding land, presumably to continue exclusively an innkeeper.

Full breakfasts are served in season on the sunny porch as is a weekend English-afternoon tea for which the Village Inn is justly famous (breakfast is included in the room rate). The full-scale restaurant as well as a downstairs tavern feature English ales.

WALKER HOUSE INN
Innkeepers: Peggy and
  Richard Houdek.
413-637-1271, 800-235-3098;
  fax 413-637-2387.
www.walkerhouse.com.
64 Walker St., Lenox, MA
  01240.
On Rte. 183.
Price: Moderate to Very
  Expensive.
Credit Cards: None.
Handicap Access: Limited.
Special Features: No
  smoking; well-mannered
  pets with prior approval.

Attractive, well-furnished 1804-vintage Federal house operated by two friendly people. The three acres of garden and woods behind the house are gorgeous. Eight rooms all have private baths; five have fireplaces. The decor in each is an impression of the composer for whom the room is named, the Houdaks will explain. Sitting rooms offer an impressive collection of music and books, and a 12-foot video screen enhances the Library Theatre—wonderful for watching opera, films, and sporting events. Generous continental breakfast. Within walking distance of Tanglewood, Lenox shops, and restaurants.

Judith Monachina

The Italianate entrance to Wheatleigh.

WHEATLEIGH
Owners: Susan and Linfield
  Simon; Manager:
  Francois Thomas.
413-637-0610;
  fax 413-637-4507.
www.wheatleigh.com.
Hawthorne Rd., PO Box
  824, Lenox, MA 01240.

Wheatleigh is pure romance. An estate built for heiress Georgie Bruce Cook, wife of "Count" Carlos de Heredia, it encourages flights of imagination. The grounds and setting captivate. From the broad terrace, the manicured lawns slope down to a grassy stairway and then to a fountain. Straight ahead is a view of the Stockbridge Bowl with the

From Rte. 183 in Lenox, L.
on Hawthorne Rd. to
Wheatleigh sign.
Price: Very Expensive.
Credit Cards: AE, DC, MC,
V.
Special Features: Pool;
tennis; fitness room; no
pets; children over 9.

Berkshire hills in the distance. The heated pool is hidden away in a knoll surrounded by trees, and the tennis court is off in another direction.

Owners Linfield and Susan Simon have preserved the expansive luxury of the interior space and decorative details in this turn-of-the-20th-century mansion. The approach is by way of a winding driveway, then through an enclosed courtyard with a circular drive—reminiscent of a 16th-century private palazzo in the hills outside Florence. Once inside, the Great Hall is impressive with its magnificent Tiffany windows lining the grand staircase, antique furnishings, and original brass chandelier. The dark-wooded Conservatory with its cooling breezes is perfect for summer dining.

The 19 guest rooms, newly renovated, are baronial in size. Nine have working fireplaces. All have television, VCR, and personal portable telephones. The bathrooms are splendid, several with original fixtures. Wheatleigh contains an award-winning prix-fixe restaurant, whose food is complemented by an award-winning wine list. The premises are available for business meetings, weddings, and parties.

WHISTLER'S INN
Managers: Richard and
Joan Mears.
413-637-0975;
fax 413-637-2190.
www.whistlersinnlenox
.com.
5 Greenwood St., Lenox,
MA 01240.
Cor. Rte.7A.
Price: Expensive to Very
Expensive.
Credit Cards: AE, D, MC, V.
Special Features: No pets.

Charming, much-admired guesthouse created within a seven-acre 1820s English Tudor summer estate. Cultivated, accommodating hosts (Richard is an author; Joan is an artist) put us at ease. The inn is furnished with antiques, chandeliers, and Persian rugs, resulting in an Old-World Victorian atmosphere. The 14 bedrooms, all with private bath, are quaint and cozy. A seasonal suite features an African motif. The interior is full of pleasant surprises, including an extensive library. From the stone-walled terrace you can walk among seven gardens and woodland—or wind through the kudzu maze. Full breakfast is provided.

Pittsfield

**THADDEUS CLAPP
HOUSE**
Innkeeper: Becky Smith.
413-499-6840, 888-499-6840;
fax 413-499-6942.
www.clapphouse.com.
74 Wendell Ave., Pittsfield,
MA 01201.

This recently renovated Victorian house has eight suites (one wheelchair friendly), which include all communications media, catering to both the business traveler and recreational tourist. The wood furnishings are Victorian, the upholstered pieces more contemporary. A large front porch provides a view of passing events. Clapp House is

The Thaddeus Clapp House in Pittsfield, a comfortable and elegant Victorian B&B.

S. of Berkshire Athenaeum.
Price: Moderate to Very
Expensive.
Credit Cards: AE, D, MC, V.
Handicap Accessible: Yes

WHITE HORSE INN
Innkeepers: Joe and Linda
Kaltsz.
413-442-2512;
fax 413-443-0490.
www.whitehorsebb.com.
378 South St., Pittsfield, MA
01201.
On Rte. 7 & 20, S. of town
center.
Price: Moderate to
Expensive.
Credit Cards: All major.
Special Features: No
smoking; no pets.

close to the Berkshire Museum, downtown restaurants, and the shuttered Colonial Theater—which may soon be resuscitated.

An attractive 1907 Colonial Revival—set back from the busy main street, south of the center of Pittsfield—offers eight rooms with private bath, air-conditioning, phone, and TV (and fax and computer capability). The rooms have been redecorated with charming linens and wallpapers. Guests may use a kitchenette and a small sitting room on the second floor. A full breakfast is served in the dining room, where guests have individual tables, or on the deck in summer. Perennial gardens and a picnic table complete the picture.

*The White Horse Inn,
Pittsfield.*

Judith Monachina

Richmond

**BERKSHIRE HILLS
COUNTRY INN**
Owner: Ann Meyer.
413-698-3379.
673 Dean Hill Rd.,
  Richmond, MA 01254.
Near W. Stockbridge sign on
  Rte. 41, turn on Baker St.,
  then Dean.
Closed: Nov.–May.
Price: Inexpensive.
Credit Cards: None.
Special Features: No smoking;
  no pets; children over 17.

Enjoy a great view of the Berkshires from this 147-acre hilltop property. "It's really marvelous," Ann says. Three comfortable rooms share a bath. Another has a private bath. Continental breakfast served. Tanglewood and Hancock Shaker Village are just a hop, skimp, and a jump . . . such as the resident chicken and sheep might make.

**ECHEZEAUX, A
COUNTRY BED &
BREAKFAST**
Proprietors: Ronald Barron
  and Ina Wilhelm.
413-698-2802;
  winter: 617-965-3957.
180 Cheever Rd., Richmond,
  MA 01254.
N. on Swamp Rd. 2.25 mi.
  from W. Stockbridge, then
  R. on Cheever.
Closed: Labor Day–last
  weekend in June.
Price: Moderate.
Credit Cards: None.
Special Features: Pool; no
  smoking; no pets.

Delightful country retreat, owned by a member of the Boston Symphony Orchestra and frequently rented to other BSO members, this house often fills the surrounding hills with music. Just 2 miles from the front gate of Tanglewood, the main house has three, antiques-furnished rooms that share a bath. A fourth room in a separate building is available for weekends or weekly rental. An elegant continental breakfast is served.

**THE INN AT
RICHMOND**
Owners: Dan and Jerri
Buehler.
413-698-2566, 888-968-4748;
fax 413-698-2100.
www.innatrichmond.com.
802 State Rd., Richmond,
MA 01254.
On Rte. 41.
Price: Expensive to Very
expensive.
Credit Cards: V, MC.
Special Features: 27 acres
available to guests; no
pets; no smoking; inquire
about children; member,
Berkshire Grown.

This 230-year-old house, former dairy farm, and former Morgan horse farm welcomes guests to three rooms (including two suites) in the main house, plus three fully equipped apartments and an additional suite in cottages adjacent to the house. All rooms have room phones, air-conditioning, king- or queen-sized beds, and private baths; also cable television with VCRs available from the house library. The cottage suites have sleep sofas. Gourmet breakfasts feature locally grown berries, shiitake mushrooms, coffee from Barrington Coffee Roasters, and Berkshire Mountain Bakery bread,

This lovely property with a 360-degree view of farms and hills has its own walking trails and leases land to the Richmond Stables. In season, minimum length-of-stay applies.

INNS AND B&BS NORTH COUNTY

Adams

BASCOM LODGE
Managed: Nature's
Classroom.
413-743-1591.
Summit Road, Adams, MA
01220.
From Rte. 7 take N. Main
St., Lanesborough, to
Rockwell Rd.; from Rte.
2, N. Adams, Notch Rd.;
to the summit of Mt.
Greylock.
Closed: Mid-Oct.–mid-May.
Price: Inexpensive.
Credit Cards: MC, V.
Handicap Access: Yes.
Special Features: Rustic
lodge; extraordinary
view.

Bascom Lodge atop Mount Greylock reveals a marvel of dramatic beauty. Operated by Nature's Classroom and owned by the Massachusetts Department of Environmental Management, the lodge at the 3,491-foot summit of the state's highest peak was built of stone and wood by the commonwealth and Civilian Conservation Corps during the Depression. Generations of hikers, birders, and canny travelers have celebrated the accommodations, returning often.

The stone fireplace and hand-cut oak beams cultivate a sense of adventure, which the magnificent hills and trails confirm. This is lodging for the hearty—or at least the sporting. Although linens are supplied, travelers might want to bring a sleeping bag or extra blanket. The guest rooms are private or dormitory style, with bathrooms down the hall. Breakfast and dinner are served family style at a set time. Reservations are required for rooms or meals.

HARBOUR HOUSE INN
Owners: Eva and Samuel
  Amuso.
413-743-8959.
www.harbourhouseinn
  .com.
725 N. State Rd., Cheshire,
  MA 01225.
On Rte. 8.
Price: Moderate to
  Expensive.
Credit Cards: AE, D, MC, V.
Special Features: No
  smoking; full breakfast.

Cheshire

The main farmhouse for Rolling Acres Farm was converted to a B&B in 1998, with six guest rooms, four with private baths and one with working fireplace. A third-floor two-room suite overlooks Mount Greylock. The rooms, which are artfully decorated with curtains, wall coverings, and canopies, all have names such as "Field of Dreams" for the bridal room, "Country Sunshine," and "Garden View"—a family-sized room. Guests have the use of a spacious common room, music room, and formal dining room, where a full breakfast is served.

The house has a colorful history, from its 18th-century origins through massive 1903 additions, having served as a tavern, stagecoach stop, and possibly a stop on the Underground Railway—for which it is named. Set on an eminence among sweeping fields, its views of Mount Greylock and the Hoosac Valley are immense.

North Adams

BLACKINTON MANOR
Hosts: Dan Epstein and
  Betsey Peters-Epstein.
413-663-5795, 800-795-8613.
www.blackinton-
  manor.com.
1391 Massachusetts Ave.,
  N. Adams, MA 01247.
One block off Rte. 2,
  minutes from
  Williamstown.
Price: Expensive.
Credit Cards: MC, V.
Special Features: Pool;
  chamber music; hiking;
  no smoking; no pets;
  children over 7.

This handsome Federal-style mansion offers the most elegant and romantic bed and breakfast experience in northern Berkshire County. Reopened in 1993 after a complete renovation by new owners, the 1849 house is notable for its Italianate features—including intricate wrought-iron balconies, floor-to-ceiling pocket windows, and a spacious bay window. The five bedrooms, all now with private baths, have furnishings, fabrics, and wallpaper appropriate to the period, but all are comfortably air-conditioned. A full gourmet breakfast is served in the formal dining room or, in summer, on the screened porch.

Dan is pianist for the Raphael Trio, and Betsy is an opera singer and invested cantor, so house concerts and chamber music workshops are a regular part of life at Blackinton Manor. Hiking weekends are also a specialty since the Appalachian Trail is out the back door.

JAE'S INN
Owner: Jae H. Chung.
413-663-6933.
1111 S. State St., Box 193, N.
  Adams, MA 01247.
Rte. 8, 2 mi. S. of N. Adams
  City Hall.

Jae Inn's owner, who also owns the Miss Adams Diner in Adams and a restaurant chain in the Boston area, has invested $500,000 to turn the Twin Sisters into the upscale Jae's Inn, including 10 rooms, a 45-seat restaurant and bar, a health club and spa in the basement; tennis courts and swimming pool.

THE PORCHES INN
Manager: Olivier
  Glattfelder.
413-664-0400;
  fax 413-664-0401.
www.porches.com.
231 River St., North Adams,
  MA 01247.
Across from MASS MoCA.
Price: Expensive to Very
  Expensive.
Credit Cards: AE, DC, MC,
  V.
Special Features: Packages
  include MoCA
  admission.

This 52-room all-convenience inn—including DVD players, hot tub, heated lap pool, fitness center, sauna, cordless telephones, and high-speed internet access—results from the miraculous transformation of six refurbished Victorian-era row houses. Untransformed row houses and small businesses flank the inn, whose rooms and suites are a synthesis of retro and contemporary design, described as "industrial-granny chic"—including long verandas, bold inside/outside spaces, and striking, colorful interiors. Named one of the hottest new inns nationwide; also named one of the coolest hotels in the world by *Condé Nast* (UK).

A European-style breakfast is offered in the dining room or delivered to guests' rooms. Cocktails are available. Management is under the same careful eyes as the Red Lion Inn, in Stockbridge.

Williamstown

BUXTON BROOK FARM
Innkeeper: Nancy B. Alden.
413-458-3621;
  fax 413-458-3640.
www.buxtonbrookfarm
  .com.
91 Northwest Hill Rd.,
  Williamstown, MA
  01267.
Between W. end of Main
  and Bulkley Sts.
Price: Expensive.
Credit Cards: AE, D, MC, V.
Special Features: No
  smoking; no pets; no
  small children.

Situated on 70 country acres adjacent to 2,500-acre Hopkins Memorial Forest, Buxton Brook Farm is one of the most gracious B&Bs in these pages. The spacious Federal-style house has one suite and several combinations of rooms and bathrooms. The rooms are somewhat smaller in the former servants' wing. The furnishings and appointments, although related to individuals in the family, are of the 1820s—tasteful without being fussy.

Common space on the first floor focuses on three fireplaces and a wood stove. The grounds include a pool. Nancy serves a homemade breakfast, either in the stylish dinning room or on the terrace in the summer. Buxton Brook Farm is within two scenic miles of the Williamstown Theatre Festival, the Clark Art Institute and the Williams College Museum of Art. Miles of the best hiking and cross-country skiing trails in town are out the back door.

This restaurant and two motels make up the 1896 Motel complex in Williamstown.

Judith Monachina

1896 HOUSE COUNTRY INN & MOTELS
Owners: Sue Morell and
    Denise Richer.
413-458-1896, 888-999-1896.
www.1896house.com.
910 Cold Spring Rd.,
    Williamstown, MA
    01267.
On Rte. 7 & 2.
Price: Moderate to Very
    Expensive.
Credit Cards: AE, D, DC,
    MC,V.
Handicap Accessible: Yes.
Special Features: Pond,
    brooks; pool; restaurant
    on premises.

The buildings that comprise the 1896 House now include Barnside, a country inn with 6 luxury suites located in the large barn that also accommodates Col. Bullock's Tavern; 12 rooms at the Pondside Motel, including an apartment and a small "Sweetheart" room; and 16 rooms at the Brookside Motel. (These are all within a few hundred feet of one another along US Routes 7 & 2.) Owners Sue and Denise have excellent taste in decor and a keen eye for upkeep so that each unit of this extensive property, ranging in amenities from suites to pondside, has its own charms and is immaculately cared for. Each of the suites has an historical decorating theme (all appear on the Web site). TVs are stowed in handsome furniture, bathrooms have Jacuzzis, and one suite has its own kitchen. A three-course candlelit breakfast is served in a breakfast room. The motel units, too, have their own distinctive personalities and accessories. Breakfast is also served. A pool is available to all guests. Adirondack chairs grace the grounds.

Packages are available with dinner at Col. Bullock's.

FIELD FARM GUEST HOUSE
Innkeeper: Seamas Nassar; Assistant: Deidre Nassar.
413-458-3135.
www.thetrustees.org.
554 Sloan Rd., Williamstown, MA 01267.
From jct. of Rtes. 43 and 7, 1 mi. on R.
Price: Expensive to Very Expensive.
Credit Cards: AE, D, MC, V.
Special Features: Pool; tennis; hiking/skiing trails; no pets.

A property of the Trustees of Reservations, Field Farm comprises 254 acres, excellent for hiking and cross-country skiing, and a house built in 1948 in the American Modern style (for comparison, see the Frelinghuysen-Morris House under *Arts & Pleasures*). Five guest rooms all have private bath, two have working fireplaces, and three have sun decks. A swimming pool and tennis courts are available. Country living, with views of Mount Greylock and the Taconic Range, just minutes from the attractions of Williamstown, with a full breakfast.

GOLDBERRY'S
Host: Mary Terio.
413-458-3935.
www.goldberrys.com.
39 Cold Spring Rd, Williamstown, MA 01267.
On Rte. 7 & 2.
Near the Williams Inn.
Price: Moderate.
Credit Cards: None.
Special Features: No smoking; no pets.

J.R.R. Tolkien fans will recognize the name. Hobbits are welcome. This bed and breakfast opened in 1991 within three blocks of the Williams College campus, the Williamstown Theatre Festival, and the Clark Art Institute and just a short drive to MASS MoCA. The 1830s Georgian house is comfortably furnished with antiques and appropriate companion pieces, and guests are invited to use the living room, dining room, and back porch overlooking the perennial gardens. The three bedrooms have private baths. Mary's breakfast might include baked-apple French toast or crumb pancakes, or omelets and fresh fruit. She serves tea with pastries at 4:00 in the afternoon and sometimes a late-night snack.

THE HOUSE ON MAIN STREET
Innkeepers: Timothy Hamilton and Donna Riley
413-458-3031; fax 413-458-2254.
www.houseonmainstreet. com
1120 Main St., Williamstown, MA 01267.
W. of the Williams Inn.
Price: Moderate.
Credit Cards: AE, MC, V.
Handicap Access: Limited.
Special Features: No smoking; no pets; children welcome.

Known as the Victorian Tourist and Antiques House in former times, this bed and breakfast has been receiving guests since the 1930s. In 1991 Bud and Phyllis Riley bought the B&B, changing it from a seasonal to a year-round concern. In July 2000 their daughter, Donna Riley, and son-in-law, Timothy Hamilton, moved from Manhattan to carry on the family tradition of innkeeping.

This home began in the 18th century, with a major Victorian addition in 1860. The six guest rooms are light and spacious, with accents of antique furnishings, pretty country prints, and braided rugs. The 21st century is represented by high-speed Internet access.

A healthful and hearty breakfast—seasonal fruits; various organic cereals with low-fat milk, soy or rice beverages; French toast, or light whole-wheat pancakes—is served in the country kitchen. The innkeepers are happy to provide vegetarian, vegan, or other dietary changes, as requested by health-conscious guests. Guests can enjoy the fireplace in the parlor or the wicker-furnished screened porch in warmer months. The innkeepers are well versed in the attractions of Williamstown, all within walking distance.

THE ORCHARDS HOTEL
Owner: Sayed M. Saleh.
413-458-9611, 800-225-1517; fax 413-458-3273.
www.orchardshotel.com.
222 Adams Rd., Williamstown, MA 01267.
On Rte. 2, E. of town center.
Price: Expensive to Very Expensive.
Credit Cards: AE, CB, DC, MC, V.
Handicap Access: Yes.
Special Features: Pool; exercise center with sauna, environmental chamber, and whirlpool; no pets; private conference and meeting rooms.

This small luxury hotel—a member of Preferred Hotels & Resorts Worldwide—is reminiscent of an English country inn. Antique furnishings, complimentary afternoon tea, and 47 enormous guest rooms—newly renovated and featuring four-poster beds with down pillows—are just a few of the amenities. Many rooms have wood-burning fireplaces and bay windows. The Orchards's award-winning restaurant, the Yasmin, features a menu that reflects New England's heritage and the chef's distinctive international talents. In summer al fresco patio dining is available overlooking the pond in the nicely landscaped inner courtyard. Chocolate chip cookies are a regular bedtime treat.

RIVER BEND FARM
Owners: David and Judy Loomis.
413-458-3121.
643 Simonds Rd., Williamstown, MA 01267.
On Rte. 7, 1 mi. N. of town green.
Price: Moderate.
Credit Cards: None.
Closed: Nov.–Mar.
Special Features: Restored 1770 tavern.

A stay at River Bend Farm, an authentic 1770 tavern listed on the National Register of Historic Places and featured on PBS's *This Old House*, comes as close to an 18th-century lodging experience as one can have—but with heat and running water. Colonel Benjamin Simonds built the house as a tavern. Thanks to painstaking work by the Loomises, original features are intact: wide-pine floorboards, magnificent paneling, corner cupboards, and a central chimney containing five separate fireplaces, three ovens, and an attic smoking chamber. Furnishings, accessories, and fabrics used throughout the house are from the period or appropriate to it. Four guest rooms share two very large bathrooms (one was the buttery of the house, and its walls are lined with crocks, paddles, and other implements). Breakfast (homemade breads, jams, and granola, with River Bend's own honey) is served in the keeping room at the back of the house, and the former taproom is a guest parlor. In summer, lawn furniture and a hammock are placed among the perennial and herb gardens, which feature a variety of 18th-century plants.

STEEP ACRES FARM
Owners: Mary and Marvin Gangemi, Daniel Gangemi.
413-458-3774.
520 White Oaks Rd., Williamstown, MA 01267.
From Rte. 7, E. on Sand Springs Rd., N. on White Oaks Rd.
Price: Inexpensive to Moderate.
Credit Cards: None.
Special Features: Pond for swimming, boating, and fishing; hiking trails; no smoking; no pets; children 5 and over.

Two miles from the center of Williamstown, Steep Acres offers country lodging up a long, gravel drive. The 1900 stone-and-shingle house sits on a hilltop on the Vermont state line, overlooking Mount Greylock. The property's 50 acres include a 1.5-acre pond for canoeing, trout fishing, and swimming (there is a diving board and raft), plus trails for hiking and cross-country skiing. A patio off the sun porch—great for summer breakfasts or reading—seems to be perched at the top of the world. The house features an attractive decor combining late-Victorian oak, wicker, and handsome fabrics. Two of four possible guest rooms available, depending on the preference of the party; three baths. Next door, in a contemporary house, the Birches at Steep Acres offers three more rooms— twin, queen, and king with Jacuzzi and fireplace. A full gourmet breakfast and afternoon refreshments are included.

STRATTON INN
Owners: Linda and Shaun Buckler
413-458-1303;
fax 413-458-1304.
www.strattoninn.com.
62 Stratton Rd., Williamstown, MA 01267.
Price: Moderate.
Credit Cards: None.
Special Features: Fireplace in dining- and common rooms; breakfast porch.

In 1830, as a result of barter, a mason added an imposing brick front to an 1790s home, which has been put to many uses since—recently as headquarters for one of the J. Paul Getty art enterprises. Now it is back to a home again, in which three spacious rooms with attached baths are available. In this gracious setting, a mile from Williams College and the Williamstown Theatre Festival, Linda offers a full homemade breakfast, with high tea available. Breakfast is either by candlelight in the high-ceilinged dining room or on a sunny porch. The Bucklers, their children in school, are realizing a longtime dream of hosting the public at a bed and breakfast.

WILLIAMS INN
Owners: Carl and Marilyn Faulkner.

The generous Faulkners are much respected for making their inn a hub of town activities.

Judith Monachina

The Williams Inn greets travelers by bus or automobile.

413-458-9371.
www.williamsinn.com.
Main St., Williamstown,
  MA 01267.
On the green, jct. Rtes. 7 &
  2.
Price: Expensive.
Credit Cards: All major.
Handicap Access: Yes.
Special Features: Indoor
  pool, sauna, whirlpool;
  full-service dining room;
  banquet facilities; no
  pets.

Although its architecture ain't quaint, the Williams Inn and its staff please a great many North County travelers—and take the hassle of being an interstate bus stop, as well. Vast and modern, the facility offers 120 rooms, each with a telephone and TV. Sunday brunch is highly regarded. The Faulkners are energetic about organizing special events, such as horse-drawn wagon rides. On Friday evenings a guitarist provides entertainment in the Tavern; on Saturday evenings, jazz. Nearby are two of America's fine art museums and the renowned Williamstown Theatre Festival. There is no charge for children under 14 in parents' room.

**THE WILLIAMSTOWN
  BED AND BREAKFAST**
Owners: Kim Rozell and
  Lucinda Edmonds.
413-458-9202.
www.williamstownbandb.
  com.
30 Cold Spring Rd.,
  Williamstown, MA
  01267.
Rte. 7 just S. of town library.
Price: Moderate.
Credit Cards: None.
Special Features: No
  smoking; no pets;
  children over 12.

Open for business since 1989, the Williamstown Bed & Breakfast credits its success to a central in-town location and a high proportion of returning guests. This spacious and airy Victorian has been completely renovated, including central air-conditioning, and is tastefully furnished with a mixture of antiques and comfortable sofas and chairs. Each of the four guest rooms has its own bath and is individually decorated in period oak, maple, or mahogany furniture. Guests have exclusive use of the living room, dining room, and broad front porch. Lingering around the table after one of the inn's popular breakfasts—featuring homemade breads, muffins, scones, and always a hot entrée—

is standard operating procedure at Williamstown B&B. Summer guests enjoy the perennial gardens and hammocks for lazy afternoons.

INNS AND B&BS OUTSIDE THE COUNTY

Salisbury, Connecticut

THE WHITE HART INN
Owners: Scott and Roxanne Bok; Manager: Kendra Tobin.
860-435-0030, 800-832-0041; fax 860-435-0040.
www.whitehartinn.com.
The Village Green, Box 545, Salisbury, CT 06068.
Jct. of Rtes. 41 & 44 in center of town.
Price: Expensive to Very Expensive.
Credit Cards: AE, CB, D, DC, MC, V.
Handicap Access: Yes.
Special Features: Pets in some rooms; children welcome; senior discount weekdays.

The oldest portions of the inn were built prior to 1810, when records indicate that the farmhouse was converted to a tavern. The public spaces display an air of country elegance and comfort. Twenty-three charming guest rooms plus three suites all offer private baths, air-conditioning, phones, and cable TV. Meals are not included in the rate, but breakfast, lunch, and dinner are served on the premises.

Averill Park, New York

LaPERLA AT GREGORY HOUSE
Owners: Alfonso and Anna Maria Acampora
518-674-3774; fax 518-674-8916.
www.gregoryhouse.com.
Box 401, Averill Park, NY 12018.
On Rte. 43.
Price: Moderate to Expensive.
Credit Cards: AE, D, MC, V.
Handicap Access: Limited.
Special Features: Pool; no smoking; no pets.

LaPerla at Gregory House has a clean, sophisticated country look. Twelve guest rooms, all with air-conditioning, television, and private baths, have stenciled walls and attractive country furnishings. A continental breakfast is served to guests, and the cozy bar and the restaurant are open for dinner Wednesday through Monday. Averill Park is convenient to Williamstown attractions and North County ski areas as well as to the Saratoga Performing Arts Center.

Berlin, New York

THE SEDGWICK INN
Innkeepers: Chet and Diane
  Niedzwiecki.
518-658-2334;
  fax 518-658-3998.
www.sedgwickinn.com.
17971 State Route 22, PO
  Box 250, Berlin, NY
  12022.
Price: Moderate to
  Expensive.
Credit Cards: AE, D, MC, V.
Special Features: Jacuzzi;
  pets and children in
  annex only.

A 1791 house with restaurant and small motel unit (the Annex) attached, set on 12 acres in the country. Privately owned and operated, this quaint, well-kept property offers 11 comfortable rooms and proximity to Berkshire attractions. Rooms in the main house are preferred.

Hillsdale, New York

**SWISS HÜTTE
  COUNTRY INN**
Managers: Gert and Cindy
  Alper.
518-325-3333; 413-528-6200.
www.swisshutte.com.
PO Box 357, Hillsdale, NY
  12529.
Rte. 23, 2 mi. E. of Hillsdale
  on MA–NY border.
Price: Moderate.
Credit Cards: MC, V.
Handicap Access: Limited.
Special Features: Pool;
  tennis.

L ocated at the entrance to the popular South County ski area Catamount, this property boasts several tennis courts, a pool, lovely gardens, and, of course, an inviting downhill slope in its front yard. Fourteen comfortable, well-furnished rooms are split between the original wooden chalet and a newer building. An award-winning restaurant completes the picture. A modified American plan is available. Breakfast is not included with the basic room rate.

New Lebanon, New York

**CHURCHILL HOUSE
  BED & BREAKFAST**
Owners: Michele and
  Michael Arthur.
518-766-5852, 800-532-2702.
www.churchillhousebb
  .com.
228 Churchill Rd., New
  Lebanon, NY 12125.
Rte. 22, 0.25 mi. S. of Rte.
  20.
Price: Moderate to
  Expensive.
Credit Cards: AE, D, MC, V.

C hurchill House was built in 1830 for the Reverend Silas Churchill and remained in the Churchill family until 1965. The Arthurs bought the property, which includes 18 acres of land, in 1991. Churchill House has four guest rooms with private baths; two can have an additional bed in the room. There is air-conditioning, cable TV, and one room has a private phone line. A charming room under the eaves has morning glories stenciled by Michele. Each room has bathrobes, and the beds are mounded high with comforters. The liv-

Special Features: Hiking trails; no smoking; no pets; children over 6 welcome.

SHAKER MEADOWS
Owners: Jean and Sean Cowhig.
518-794-9385; fax 518-794-9381.
www.shakermeadows.com.
14209 Rte. 22, Canaan, NY 12029.
Price: Inexpensive to Expensive.
Credit Cards: AE, D, MC, V.
Special Features: 50 acres for hiking, function room, children welcome, rentals by the week accepted.

ing room and wraparound front porch with views of the Taconic Hills are for the guests' use. A full breakfast is served on weekends, a continental breakfast on weekdays. Away from the madding crowds but handy to all Berkshire attractions.

Guests have their choice of three rooms with private baths plus two small rooms in the 1821 farmhouse, or three suites in the creamery that was renovated in 1993. The common area in the farmhouse has full kitchen facilities but, thankfully, no phones or TV. The suites, which can sleep four to six each, have king- or queen-sized beds, kitchens, private decks or lawn space, phones, TVs, VCRs. Room rent includes beach privileges at nearby Quechee Lake. The property was the Palmer House B&B until 1999 and, before that, Sleepy Hollow Dairy, which processed the produce of local cows.

A breakfast room serves all the guests a hot meal—guaranteed tasty as both Jean and Sean have extensive experience in lodging and cooking. The function room accommodates 50 for parties of meetings. Tents on the adjacent lawn can increase the number of guests to 150, with food provided by the owners or a caterer. Twelve miles to Tanglewood and 12 miles to Jiminy Peak.

Stephentown, New York

MILL HOUSE INN
Innkeepers: Frank Tallet and Family.
413-738-5348, 800-563-8645; fax 518-733-6025.
www.themillhouseinn.com.
Mailing Address: Box 1079, Hancock, MA 01237.
On Rte 43, Stephentown, NY.
Price: Moderate to Expensive.
Credit Cards: AE, MC, V.
Handicap Access: 1 unit.
Closed: Mar. 15–May 15; Sept. 1–Oct. 1.
Special Features: Pool; no smoking; no pets.

Old-World touches in a former sawmill enhance this cozy, well-regarded country inn, with refurbishing ongoing. Furnished with antiques, the rooms are warm and whimsical. A living room with fireplace offers warm comfort. Seven rooms and five suites, several with fireplaces of their own, all have private baths, air-conditioning, and telephones. Set on three peaceful, rural acres with formal gardens, stone walls, garden paths, and a pool, it's the perfect romantic escape—a touch of country with a European flair. Afternoon tea and continental breakfast are served; a full breakfast is available à la carte.

HOTELS & RESORTS

BUCKSTEEP MANOR (413-623-5535, 800-645-BUCK; www.bucksteep manor .com; 885 Washington Mtn. Rd., Washington, MA 01223; off Rte. 8 N. from Becket) Price: Moderate. Credit Cards: AE, MC, V. Handicap Access: Limited. Special Features: X-C ski center; pool; no pets; children welcome.

Deep in the Washington woods, a cross-country skier's paradise. Of the eight rooms in the manor, all share baths and are comfortably furnished. Fourteen rooms in the lodge have private baths. In the summer nine cabins plus campground ($10 for adults) increase the number of accommodations and add to the rustic feeling of the property. Hiking, biking, and birding opportunities abound. Pool and tennis. Great dancing. Rock, country, bluegrass, and reggae concerts in the barn and on the lawn on summer weekends. Good vibes, funky buildings, and a mellow, laid-back feeling predominates.

CRANWELL RESORT SPA AND GOLF CLUB (413-637-1364, 800-272-6935; www.cranwell.com; 55 Lee Road, Lenox, MA 01240; Rte. 20, S. of Lenox center, 3.5 mi. from exit 2 Mass. Pike) Price: Expensive to Very Expensive. Credit Cards: AE, D, DC, MC, V. Handicap Access: Yes. Special Features: Pool, tennis, golf, spa; no pets.

Cranwell is a 380-acre estate high on a hill with one of the finest views of the Berkshire Hills. The 1893 Tudor Mansion is surrounded by lawns, gardens, and a par-71 championship golf course. Guest rooms are in the Mansion, Beecher's Cottage, the Carriage House, Founder's Cottage; and a group of one-bedroom cottages (totaling 105 units). The most luxurious bedrooms in the Mansion are spacious and individually decorated in the Victorian style, with private marble baths. In the various outbuildings, accommodations are slightly simpler and more contemporary, but some have the advantages of wet bar, refrigerator, and/or galley kitchens. Two dining rooms, Sloane's Tavern, and numerous conference rooms complete the full-service offerings of this property.

CROWNE PLAZA HOTEL (413-499-2000; www.crowneplaza.com; Berkshire Common, One West St., Pittsfield, MA 01201; off Park Square) Price: Expensive to Very Expensive. Credit Cards: All major. Handicap Access: 8 units. Special Features: Exercise room, indoor pool; sauna; Jacuzzi.

The Crowne Plaza crowns downtown Pittsfield—a big hotel with all the comforts. Located within striking distance of central, north, and south Berkshire, it is a good choice for travelers who prefer modern amenities over rustic charm.

Children appreciate the Sony Play Stations (video games) in each room, and the television channels are beyond counting. Rooms, rugs, and drapes are fancy; the beds spacious and comfortable. Rockwell's, the formal dining room, should reopen by the time this book appears. Other amenities include Dewey's, the lounge adjacent to the indoor pool, and Muddy McGee's, a sports bar. From a grand ballroom to small meeting rooms, the Crowne Plaza is prepared for business needs.

EASTOVER RESORT AND CONFERENCE CENTER (413-637-0625, 800-822-2386; www.eastover.com.; 430 East St., Lenox, MA 01240; from Rte. 7 in Lenox, take Housatonic St. E., then L. onto East St. for a little over 1 mi.) Price: Moderate. Credit Cards: AE, D, MC, V. Special Features: Indoor & outdoor pools; tennis; exercise room; sauna; driving range; miniature golf; horseback riding; X-C skiing; toboggan run; no pets.

Eastover is a picturesque, amiable place, admirably free of pretension. Another of the celebrated Lenox "cottages," this grand Gilded Age house is obviously living out of character but seems to be thriving. The sprawling grounds present tennis, swimming, biking, volleyball, horseback riding, and all sorts of winter activities, including cross-country skiing, and the longest tobogganing run in New England.

Inspired by the remarkable spirit of the late founder, George Bisacca, the staff is up for anything as long as it's fun. To add to the festivities, there is dancing to live music during happy hour and again later in the evening. No liquor license here, so it's BYOB, but the band can play into the wee morning hours. Special weekends are organized for couples, singles, and families. Prospective guests should call ahead. While wandering the grounds, guests may catch a glimpse the American bison, geese, and other pets. The founder's collection of Civil War artifacts and the museum in the Heritage Room will fascinate boys of all ages. The 165 guest rooms are large in the main house and of various sorts elsewhere.

HOLIDAY INN BERKSHIRES (413-663-6500, 800-465-4329; www.holiday innberkshires.com; 40 Main St., N. Adams, MA 01247) Price: Moderate. Credit Cards: All major. Handicap Access: Yes. Special Features: Indoor pool; sauna and steam room; Jacuzzi; full fitness center; no pets.

The 86 air-conditioned rooms—all with private bath, color TV, and telephones—are large and decorated in soft tones of red and blue. The Steeples, a full-service restaurant, serves breakfast, lunch, and dinner. Conference and meeting facilities are available, tours are welcome, and the gymnasium is available to local membership as well as guests.

JIMINY PEAK, THE MOUNTAIN RESORT (413-738-5500, 800-882-8859 [outside Mass.]; www.jiminypeak.com.; Brodie Mountain/Corey Rd., Hancock, MA 01237; bet. Rtes. 7 & 43, 10 mi. N. of Pittsfield). Price: Very Expensive. Credit Cards: AE, D, DC, MC, V. Handicap Access: Yes. Special Features: Pool; tennis; health club; trout fishing; Alpine Slide; downhill skiing; no pets.

This full-service resort has it all. In the Country Inn, all 105 suites feature kitchen, living room with queen-sized sofa bed, bath with powder room, and a master bedroom with king-sized bed. Most of the units can be rented for one night on weekdays or two nights on weekends. There are also one-, two-, and three-bedroom condominiums for rent. Add to that the Founders' Grille, Christiansen's Tavern, and two cafeterias during ski season; tennis, swimming, trout fishing, an Alpine Slide for summer, and—best of all— great downhill skiing, totaling one of the Berkshire's most complete resorts. Conference facilities are available. Meals are not included. Several package plans.

MOTELS

South County

Barrington Court Motel (413-528-2340; 400 Stockbridge Rd., Gt. Barrington, MA 01230; on Rte. 7, N. of town) Price: Expensive to Very Expensive. AE, D, MC, V. Handicap access. 21 motel units with refrigerator; 4 suites with kitchenettes, Jacuzzi; pool.

Best Value Inn (413-243-0501, 800-329-7466; Rte. 102, 980 Pleasant St., Box 426, Lee, MA 01238; between Stockbridge and Lee) Price: Moderate to Expensive. AE, D, DC, MC, V. 26 units convenient to Tanglewood, Berkshire Theatre Festival, Jacob's Pillow, and other South County attractions. Cable TV; AC.

Briarcliff Inn (413-528-3000; 506 Stockbridge Rd., Gt. Barrington, MA 01230; on Rte 7, N. of town) Price: Inexpensive to Moderate. AE, D, DC, MC, V. 16 units. Spacious landscaped grounds with view of Monument Mountain.

Days Inn, Gt. Barrington (413-528-3150; 372 Main St., Gt. Barrington 01230) Price: Moderate to Expensive. AE, CB, D, DC, MC, V. Handicapped access. 62 units.

Holiday Inn Express Hotel & Suites (413-528-1810; 415 Stockbridge Rd., Gt. Barrington, MA 01230; on Rte. 7, N. of town) Price: Inexpensive to Very

Expensive. AE, D, DC, MC, V. 58 units, including 20 suites. Cable TV, AC. Pool, exercise room. Continental breakfast.

Lantern House Motel (413-528-2350, 800-959-2350; 256 Stockbridge Rd., Box 97, Gt. Barrington, MA 01230; Rte. 7, 1 mi. N. of town) Price: Moderate. (3-night weekend min. in summer). D, MC, V. 14 rooms. Refrigerators, cable TV, pool.

Laurel Hill Motel (413-243-0813; 200 Laurel St., Box 285, Lee, MA 01238; on Rte. 20) Price: Moderate to Expensive. AE, D, DC, MC, V. 23 units, 2 efficiencies. Pool, view.

Monument Mountain Motel (413-528-3272; 249 Stockbridge Rd., Gt. Barrington, MA 01230; Rte. 7, N. of town) Price: Moderate to Expensive. AE, D, DC, MC, V. Cable TV, heated pool, lit tennis courts, picnic tables, 20 acres bordering Housatonic River, flower gardens.

Mountain View Motel (413-528-0250; 304 State Rd., Gt. Barrington, MA 01230; Rte. 23E., E. of town) Price: Moderate to expensive. AE, D, MC, V. 17 units. Cable TV, pets allowed; 1 mi. to Butternut.

Pilgrim Inn (413-243-1328; 165 Housatonic St., Lee, MA 01238; Rte. 20, E. of town) Price: Expensive. AE, D, DC, MC, V. 34 units. Cable TV, pool.

Pleasant Valley Motel (413-232-8511; Rte. 102, W. Stockbridge, MA 01266; sandwiched between Exit 1, Mass. Pike & Rte. 102) Price: Inexpensive to Expensive. AE, D, MC, V. Handicap access. Cable TV, pool. Continental breakfast included summer weekends.

Sunset Motel (413-243-0302; 150 Housatonic St., Rte. 20, Lee, MA 01238) Price: Inexpensive to Expensive. AE, CB, D, DC, MC, V. 22 units with AC, cable TV, pool. Convenient to MassPike Exit 2.

Super 8 Motel (413-243-0143; 170 Housatonic St., Lee, MA 01238; Rte. 20, just off MassPike) Price: Inexpensive to Moderate. AE, D, DC, MC, V. Handicap access. 49 rooms, including nonsmoking. Free coffee and paper. Cable TV

Central County

Berkshire Inn (413-443-3000; 150 W. Housatonic St., Pittsfield, MA 01201; Rte. 20, W. of town) Price: Moderate to Expensive. AE, MC, V. 38 units, 9 with refrigerator; cable TV, AC. Pool. Continental breakfast.

Colonial Motor Lodge (413-442-2633; Housatonic St., Pittsfield, MA 01201; Rte. 20 , W. of town) Price: Inexpensive to Moderate. AE, D, MC, V. 24 units. Cable TV, AC, phones.

Comfort Inn (413-443-4714; 1055 South St., Pittsfield, MA 01201; at Rtes. 7 & 20) Price: Moderate to Very Expensive. AE, D, DC, MC, V. 58 units. Cable TV, AC, exercise room; discount pass to Berkshire West. Pool. Deluxe continental breakfast.

Heart of the Berkshires Motel (413-443-1255; 970 W. Housatonic St., Pittsfield, MA 01201; Rte. 20, W. of town) Price: Inexpensive to Moderate. AE, MC, V. 17 units. Cable TV, AC.

Howard Johnson Motel (413-442-4000, 800-446-4656; 462 Pittsfield Rd., Lenox,

MA 01240; Rte. 7 & 20, N. of town) Price: Moderate to Very Expensive. AE, D, MC, V. 44 units, some with Jacuzzis. Cable TV, AC. Pool.

Lampost Motel (413-443-2979; Box 335, Lanesborough, MA 01237; Rte. 7, N. of Pittsfield) Price: Inexpensive to Moderate. AE, D, MC, V. 10 units, all with efficiency kitchens. Cable TV. Pool available.

Lanesborough Mountain Motel (413-442-6717; Rte. 7, Box 335, Lanesborough, MA 01237) Price: Inexpensive to Moderate (special midweek rates). AE, D, MC, V. 10 rooms.

Lenox Inn (413-499-0324; Rte. 7 & 20, Box 713, Lenox, MA 01240; N. of town) Price: Moderate to Expensive. AE, D, MC, V. 17 units. Cable TV, AC. Pool.

Mayflower Motor Inn (413-443-4468; 474 Pittsfield-Lenox Rd., PO Box 116, Lenox, MA 01240; Rte. 7 & 20, N. of town) Price: Inexpensive to Expensive. AE, D, MC, V. 20 rooms. Cable TV. Pool, views.

Mt. View Motel (413-442-1009; 499 S. Main St., Lanesborough, MA 01237) Price: Moderate to Expensive. AE, D, MC, V. 13 rooms in motel; 3 efficiency cottages available year-round. Cable TV.

Pittsfield Travelodge (413-443-5661, 800-578-7878; 16 Cheshire Rd., Pittsfield, MA 01201; jct. of Rtes. 8 & 9) Price: Inexpensive to Expensive. AE, D, DC, MC, V. Handicap access. 47 units. Cable TV.

Quality Inn (413-637-4244; 130 Pittsfield Rd., Rte. 7, Lenox, MA 01240) Price: Inexpensive to Very Expensive. AE, D, DC, JCB, MC, V. 120 rooms. Cable TV, AC, refrigerators, in-room coffee. Outdoor pool and tennis courts. Continental breakfast included. Cocktail lounge, banquet facilities.

Ramada Inn & Suites (413-442-8714; 1350 W. Housatonic St., Pittsfield, MA 01201; Rte. 20, W. of town) Price: Moderate to Very Expensive. AE, D, DC, MC, V. 59 units; 10 two-bedroom suites, 9 executive suites.

Shamrock Village Inn (413-684-0860; 645 Main St., Dalton, MA 01226) Price: Moderate. AE, D, MC, V. 15 units. Cable TV, restaurant.

Super Eight Motel (413-637-3560, 800-800-8000; 194 Pittsfield Rd., Lenox, MA 01240; Rte. 7 & 20, N. of town) Price: Expensive. AE, D, DC, MC, V. 59 units. Cable T; pool.

Wagon Wheel Motel (413-445-4532; 484 Pittsfield Rd., PO Box 808, Lenox, MA 01240; Rte. 7 & 20, 3 mi. N. of town) Price: Inexpensive to Expensive. AE, D, MC, V. 18 units, 2 Jacuzzi rooms. Cable TV, refrigerators in rooms.

The Weathervane Motel (413-443-3230; 475 S. Main St., Lanesborough, MA 01237; Rte. 7, S. of town) Price: Moderate. AE, CB, D, MC, V. 17 units.

Yankee Inn (413-499-3700, 800-835-2364; 461 Pittsfield Rd., Lenox, MA 01240; Rte. 7 & 20, near Pittsfield line) Price: Moderate to Very Expensive. AE, D, DC, MC, V. Handicap access. 106 units; 22 rooms with fireplaces; some rooms with Jacuzzis, and manicured grounds. Cable TV, indoor pool, spa. Three-night minimum in summer.

North County

Berkshire Hills Motel (413-458-3950; 1146 Cold Spring Rd., Williamstown, MA 01267; on Rte. 7 & 2, 2 mi. S. of town) Price: Moderate to Expensive. AE, D, MC, V. 21 rooms. King-sized beds available, cable TV, no smoking, cable TV. Heated pool, landscaped grounds. Cold breakfast buffet.

Carriage House Motel (413-458-5359; PO Box 925, Lanesborough, MA 01237; on Rte. 7) Price: Inexpensive. AE, CB, D, DC, MC, V. Partial handicap access. 14 units. Pool.

Chimney Mirror Motel (413-458-5202; 295 Main St., Williamstown, MA 01267; Rte. 2, E. of town) Price: Moderate. AE, MC, V. 18 units. Cable TV; continental breakfast included on summer weekends.

Cozy Corner Motel (413-458-8006; 784 Sand Springs Rd., Williamstown, MA 01267; at Rte. 7, N. of town center) Price: Moderate. AE, D, MC, V.12 units across from convenience store at gateway to Vermont.

Dug Out Motel (413-743-9737; 99 Howland Ave., Adams, MA 01220; Rte. 8, N. of town) Price: Inexpensive. AE, DC, MC, V. 14 rooms, 2 efficiencies. Handicap access on first floor. Cable TV.

Econo Lodge Springs Motor Inn (413-458-5945; Rte. 7, New Ashford, MA 01237) Price: Moderate to Expensive. AE, D, DC, MC, V. 40 motel rooms; 2 small chalets with fireplaces. Cable TV, in-room coffee. Pool, tennis court.

Four Acres Motel (413-458-8158; 213 Main St., Williamstown, MA 01267; Rte. 2) Price: Moderate to Expensive. AE, D, DC, MC, V. Handicap access. 31 units. Cable TV; garden area with pool. Continental breakfast.

Green Valley Motel (413-458-3864; 1214 Simonds Rd., Williamstown, MA 01267; Rte. 7N, N. of town) Price: Moderate. AE, MC, V. 18 units. Cable TV; pool. Continental breakfast.

Jericho Valley Inn (413-458-9511, 800-537-4246; 2541 Hancock Rd., Williamstown, MA 01267; Rte. 43) Price: Moderate. AE, MC, V. 25 units; suites, cottages available. Satellite TV. Heated pool. 350 mountain acres with spectacular views, fireplace lounge. Pets allowed in cottages.

Maple Terrace Motel (413-458-9677; www.mapleterracehotel; 555 Main St., Williamstown, MA 01267; Rte. 2, 0.5 mi. from Williams College) Price: Moderate. AE, D, DC, MC, V. 17 units, 2 efficiencies. Cable TV, VCR in all rooms. Heated pool; mountain views.

New Ashford Motor Inn (413-458-8041; 259 Rte. 7, New Ashford, MA 01237; 1 mi. N. of Brodie Mtn.) Price: Inexpensive to Moderate. AE, D, MC, V. 16 units, Direct TV, air-conditioning, telephones.

Northside Motel (413-458-8107; 45 N. St., Rte. 7, Williamstown, MA 01267; N. of Inn) Price: Inexpensive. AE, D, MC, V. Handicap access. 32 units. Cable TV; pool. Coffee shop for breakfast.

Villager Motel (413-458-4046; 953 Simonds Rd., Williamstown, MA 01267; Rte.

7, N. of town) Price: Inexpensive. AE, MC, V. 13 rooms. Cable TV, AC. Expanded continental breakfast.

Wigwam & Western Summit Cottages (413-663-3205; 2850 Mohawk Trail, PO Box 7, North Adams, MA 01247; Rte. 2, E and above town) Price: Inexpensive to Moderate. AE, D, MC, V. Five cottages. TV. Porch with fantastic view of Mount Greylock. Gift shop. Open late May to mid-Oct.

The Willows Motel (413-458-5768; 480 Main St., Williamstown, MA 01267; Rte. 2, E. of town) Price: Inexpensive to Moderate. AE, MC, V. 17 rooms. Cable TV; heated pool.

CHAPTER FOUR
Pleasing the Palate
DINING

Some of the county's showiest restaurants are found in the "cottages" of the Gilded Age: at Orleton, now called the Gateways, and at Blantyre and Wheatleigh. Yet a great table is set as well in more humble Berkshire settings, such as pre-Revolutionary farmhouses, old mills, and inns.

The fare is no longer just American, with a dash of the continental, but has become abundant in many other cuisines, including Japanese, Chinese, Indian, Vietnamese, even Finnish.

The number of restaurants in the county is vast: more than 225—nearly 40 in Great Barrington alone! —and they keep popping up. To cover all of them would require a book twice this size. Diners should be guided by what we suggest but follow their own hunches, as well. (We

Judith Monachina

One of the newest additions to Railroad Street in Great Barrington, Pearl's has one of the best views of the street.

would be pleased to hear of discoveries for a future edition.) We have grouped the best of the breakfast/lunch eateries in a section of their own (pages 128 to 130). There are dozens of specialty food suppliers, too, engaging alternatives to supermarkets.

We have concentrated on those establishments that we've found most interesting and most successful, risking critical judgments. A dining experience has many dimensions. The food, of course, is primary, but we have also based our judgments on factors such as the range of the menu, the decor and ambiance of the restaurant, the quality of service, and value for price. We also note that a restaurant participates in the Berkshire Grown Restaurant Certification Program, which restaurateurs are invited to join if they "pledge to buy and utilize locally grown food and food products to they extent that [they] are able, thus supporting local farmers and food producers who preserve and sustain the beauty and the bounty of the Berkshire region." Patrons who dine at Berkshire Grown restaurants enjoy their fine meals knowing that they are also supporting the local agricultural way of life. Berkshire Grown also hosts a wonderful opportunity to sample local produce as skillfully prepared by local chefs at the Beautiful Bountiful Berkshires tasting in the early autumn.

Reviews are organized first by section of the county, then alphabetically by town, then by restaurant name. Food purveyors are grouped alphabetically by type, then by name of establishment. Every entry appears in the general index, too. While the information is as up-to-date as we can make it, it is still wise to call ahead.

We designate each restaurant with a price code, signifying the approximate cost of a meal, including appetizer, entrée, and dessert, but *not* cocktails, wine, tax, or tip. Restaurants with a prix-fixe menu are noted accordingly.

For further gustatory experiences, sample "A Taste of the Berkshires" or "Taste of Williamstown" or any of several another town-sponsored annual extravaganzas that celebrate the bounty of our region. Books of Berkshire recipes are also available. *As You Like It* is the Williamstown Theatre Festival's prize-winning compilation of the favorite recipes of the festival's stars, directors, writers, and associates. For the Berkshire County Historical Society's *Berkshire Victuals*, editor Janet Cook researched county cooks, both dead and alive, and came up with scores of delicious local recipes. *The New Red Lion Inn Cookbook* (a revision of the original edition) honors the cuisine of the county's best-known inn, while *Best Recipes of Berkshire Chefs* by Miriam Jacobs demonstrates the culinary specialties of a range of fine contemporary county chefs. *The Kripalu Cookbook* by Atma Jo Ann Levitt features vegetarian recipes from the kitchen of the Kripalu Center in Lenox, suitably scaled down for home use.

Dining Price Codes

Inexpensive	Up to $15	Expensive	$30 to $50
Moderate	$15 to $30	Very Expensive	$50 or more

Credit Cards

AE – American Express	DC – Diner's Club
CB – Carte Blanche	MC – MasterCard
D – Discover	V – Visa

Meals:

B – Breakfast   SB – Sunday Brunch
L – Lunch   D – Dinner

RESTAURANTS IN SOUTH COUNTY

North Egremont

ELM COURT INN
413-528-0325.
http://www.elmcourtinn
.com.
227 Rte. 71, N. Egremont,
MA 01252.
Closed: Mon. and Tues. in
winter; Mon., July–Aug.
Price: Expensive.
Cuisine: Continental.
Serving: D.
Credit Cards: AE, MC, V.
Reservations:
Recommended.
Special Features:
Fireplaces.

We were treated with such honor that we felt as if we were ambassadors, as the Elm Court's hosts Glee Bieri and her chef husband, Urs Bieri—a former executive chef at the United Nations—maintain the Swiss tradition in Berkshire County. The staff in the dining room is knowledgeable and friendly. Our servers knew the ingredients and tastes of the dishes, and could recommend with aplomb. With a fire crackling on a cool evening, the comfort level is high and relaxing.

The wine list includes a good variety—the house pinot grigio was excellent—and the concise menu is filled with choices hard to make. Our Asian duck salad was rich with delicious slivers of well-prepared duck in a brown sauce. The flavorful escargot compelled us to mop up the butter sauce with chunks of rustic bread. The crisp baby-spinach salad was large enough to share. The veal Suisse comes in a generous portion with wild mushrooms. The flame-seared tuna, although rich and meaty as a beefsteak, came in rare, tender slices, beautifully served. Family-style side dishes of buttery Brussels sprouts and sweet baby carrots were hearty and crisp. Roesti potatoes, a specialty of the house, accompanied our entrées.

Our just desserts? Apple tart and pecan Kahlua pie, a perfect ending to an excellent meal.

South Egremont

THE EGREMONT INN
413-528-2111.
www.egremontinn.com.
10 Old Sheffield Rd., S.
Egremont, MA 01252.
Off Rte. 23 in center of
village.
Closed: Mon. and Tues.
Price: Moderate to
Expensive.

Proprietors Steve and Karen Waller have created a charming dining experience at their inn. One or the other greets all visitors, welcoming them to what is indeed the Wallers' home.

The appetizers are generous and tasty. The salad is wonderfully textured with many flavors and ingredients. The sauce on the side of the crab cakes is worth repeated visits. The steak was tender and the salmon luxurious.

Cuisine: American and
Continental.
Serving: D.
Credit Cards: AE, MC, V.
Special Features: Fireplaces;
live entertainment Thurs.
and Sat.

Steve asked us if we wanted to see the short or the long wine list. The complete one runs perhaps 50 pages, with wines from all over the world. *Wine Spectator* has cited the Egremont Inn for its cellar. Desserts are rich and fabulous. We had a chocolate mousse that defied description. Specialties include Berkshire products and excellent coffee.

JOHN ANDREW'S
413-528-3469.
www.jarestaurant.com.
Rte. 23, S. Egremont, MA
01252.
2.5 mi. west of village.
Closed: Wed., Sept.–June.
Price: Moderate to
Expensive.
Cuisine: American.
Serving: D.
Credit Cards: MC, V.
Reservations:
Recommended
(necessary in summer).
Special Features: Glassed-in
back porch, fireplace,
outdoor deck and terrace
in-season; member,
Berkshire Grown.

John Andrew's Restaurant continues to stand in the first rank of restaurants in the Berkshires and is certainly one of the best bargains in that category. The subtly decorated dining rooms are perfectly in tune with the excellent, understated New American cuisine. Service is attentive, professional, and discreet. The delicious breads are fresh baked on premises. The grilled, roasted, and braised entrées emphasize marvelous natural flavors, enhanced with perfectly executed vegetable accompaniments. The wine list has been chosen with sufficient care and taste to bring John Andrew's a *Wine Spectator* magazine Award of Excellence.

Proprietors Susan and Danny Smith are true professionals and excellent hosts. Susan creates an enviable combination of efficiency and serenity in the dining rooms, while Danny is the hands-on executive chef.

OLD MILL
413-528-1421.
Rte. 23, S. Egremont, MA
01252.
Center of village.
Closed: Mon. in winter.
Price: Moderate to
Expensive.
Cuisine: American and
Continental.
Serving: D.
Credit Cards: AE, DC, MC,
V.
Reservations:
Recommended for
parties of five or more.
Special Features: Private
dining room; fireplace;
member, Berkshire
Grown.

An understated interior of warm, glowing antique walls and floors gives this renovated 1797 gristmill a particularly welcoming air. The colonial atmosphere creates the feeling of stepping back in time. Owner/host Terry Moore has presided here for a quarter century, making the Old Mill if not actually colonial, certainly a venerable institution among Berkshire restaurants. It is also an enduring favorite among residents and second-home owners who wouldn't think of stopping anywhere else on Friday night after escaping New York. The unobtrusive, pleasant, timely service contributes greatly to the soothing atmosphere.

The regular menu is an eclectic blend of generally Continental offerings, always supplemented with several specials of the day, both appetizers and entrées, conveniently described in a supple-

Many restaurants throughout North, South, and Central Berkshire make a pledge to buy locally produced foods when possible, entitling them to display the Berkshire Grown logo.

mental note rather than recited by the waitperson. Maine crab cakes and the house-cured gravlax are delicious regular appetizers. Grilled fish, chops and steaks, pan-seared calf's liver, several vegetarian dishes, and other offerings provide a fine range of entrées. The wine list is extensive, mostly French, American, and Italian, with offerings from $18 to $75. Desserts tend toward the rich and sinful—for example, Grand Marnier chocolate mousse in a chocolate cake crust. Delicious!

Always welcoming, reliable but not predictable, the Old Mill continues to reward its loyal following and new arrivals, too.

Great Barrington

AEGEAN BREEZE
413-528-4001.
327 Stockbridge Rd., Gt.
 Barrington, MA 01230.
Price: Moderate to
 Expensive.
Cuisine: Greek.
Serving: L, D.
Credit Cards: AE, D, MC, V.
Handicap Access: Yes.
Reservations:
 Recommended.

Although a new entrant to the burgeoning Great Barrington restaurant scene, Aegean Breeze is just too good to keep waiting, as this publication generally does with brand-new ventures. Proprietor George Neophitidis and manager Minos Psihudakis have created a light and pleasant atmosphere as evocative of Greek-island dining as one can imagine on Route 7. The staff is young, well trained, quietly attentive, and good. The kitchen produces classic Greek specialties from *mezes*— "more than just appetizers"—to dessert. An assortment of the generously proportioned hot and cold *mezedes* can be combined into a delicious tasting meal if desired. But the crowning glory of the cuisine is the *thalasina* (from the sea) offerings, four marvelous grilled or broiled whole-fish entrées and a dozen other fish and shellfish specialties. Grilled lamb shish kebab and moussaka, too, of course, plus excellent steaks and chops. Aegean Breeze has deservedly become very popular, so potential diners should be sure to call ahead and plan to enjoy a great meal.

BARRINGTON BREWERY & RESTAURANT
413-528-8282.
www.barringtonbrewery
.com.
420 Stockbridge Rd., Gt.
Barrington, MA 01230.
At Jenifer House
Commons.
Price: Inexpensive to
Moderate.
Cuisine: American.
Serving: L, D.
Credit Cards: AE, D, MC, V.
Special Features: Outdoor
patio in summer; pool
tables and dart board;
member, Berkshire
Grown.

Sizzling streaks and burgers, sandwiches, and salads may seem like the backbone of the extensive Barrington Brewery and Restaurant menu, but a closer look reveals the real star: That's right, beer. Barrington brews its own on the premises, including a very good Black Bear Stout and Barrington Brown Ale. But beer isn't only found in pint-sized glasses here: Beer battered fries, onion rings, and mozzarella sticks; a cheddar ale soup; even a steak and stout: sliced sirloin marinated in stout, open faced on garlic bread. Vegetarians don't fare badly here, either: vegetarian burgers, nachos, salads, and soups, of course, but also veggie pockets, tortellini salad, and more.

The atmosphere is cozy and lively, with some large tables that always seem filled with groups and families. Small tables and tucked away booths are also available.

A special kids' menu includes the standards: PB&J, pizza, grilled cheese, burgers, and spaghetti (with butter or red sauce). This is a real kid-friendly place: The back page of the menu is games and crossword puzzles.

BIZEN
413-528-4343.
17 Railroad St., Gt.
Barrington, MA 01230.
Price: Moderate to
Expensive.
Cuisine: Japanese.
Serving: L, D.
Credit Cards: AE, D, MC,
V.
Handicap Access: Yes.
Reservations:
Recommended.
Special Features: Sushi bar;
Japanese grill; private
room available, tatami
booth; full bar; member,
Berkshire Grown.

Bizen was the first of the fine sushi bars that Great Barrington now enjoys. New York City–based second-home owners and numerous sophisticated locals keep them all deservedly busy, but Bizen still stands first. Proprietor Michael Marcus learned the classic Japanese arts of both sushi making and fine pottery in Japan. He brings intensity, creativity, and high standards to both. Bizen is furnished with ceramic tableware all from Michael's own Joyous Spring Pottery. It complements the authentic-seeming décor, which especially features a traditional tatami booth for the cross-legged set. The tables are close together and the ambience somewhat bustling. There is a full bar and a Japanese grill. The menu covers the full array of traditional Japanese cuisine, from sushi and sashimi by

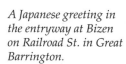

A Japanese greeting in the entryway at Bizen on Railroad St. in Great Barrington.

Judith Monachina

the piece, to varied and delicious hand rolls, excellent cooked and grilled dishes, soups, and salads. A perfect Japanese *bistrot.*

CASTLE STREET CAFÉ
413-528-5244;
  fax 413-528-8863.
www.castlestreetcafe.
10 Castle St., Gt.
  Barrington, MA 01230.
Closed: Tues.
Price: Moderate to
  Expensive.
Cuisine: Continental–
  Contemporary American
Serving: D.
Credit Cards: AE, D, MC, V.
Special Features: Wine by
  the glass; live jazz (daily,
  summer; weekends,
  winter); member,
  Berkshire Grown.

Michael Ballon's Castle Street Café continues to charm, fully deserving its legion of loyal followers as well as its new devotees. The bistro atmosphere of exposed brick walls, frequently changing hangings of contemporary paintings, white-linen tablecloths, and fresh flowers never fails to please the eye. The eclectic menu is always a mixture of classic favorites (steak au poivre, grilled Cornish game hen) and new features (saffron shellfish quartet over basmati rice, sautéed breast of duck with braised apples and pears and black currant sauce) Michael proudly features—and prepares himself—locally grown and produced foods, from goat cheese to French bread to fresh produce. The *Wine Spectator* award-winning wine list features many moderately priced French and American wines that complement the fine food without breaking the bank. The veteran and accomplished wait staff know their business and do it to perfection. One always feels welcome—well attended to but perfectly undisturbed.

The adjoining Celestial Bar and Jazz Club does not obtrude on the dining-only crowd. Offering jazz (soloists weeknights, combos on weekends) and a lighter menu six nights a week, it provides a welcome atmosphere for both the pure jazz aficionado and the more casual diner.

THE EAST
413-528-8850.
305 Stockbridge Rd., Gt.
  Barrington, MA 01230.
Open: Daily.
Price: Moderate
Cuisine: Chinese and
  Japanese.
Serving: L, D.
Credit Cards: AE, MC, V.
Reservations:
  Recommended for
  weekend dinners.

For those who delight in Chinese food, The East is a welcome and attractive addition to South County. It serves Chinese food from Hunan, Szechwan, and Canton, and makes fresh sushi, sashimi, and other Japanese dishes. The tuna maki is fresh and tasty—we watched the chef roll the maki, standing before his work area to see how efficiently he moved—with a varied texture of fish and rice. Other specialty fillings are cucumber, salmon, octopus, eel, and avocet; not to mention the sweetened squash maki and sea urchin sushi. The crispy tofu, under the vegetarian menu, is quite good. The dim sum list will probably grow.

Although Chinese selections can be pedestrian, here they are served with generosity and attention. Substitutions are cheerfully made, such as tofu for chicken and bok choy for broccoli.

Luncheon specialties, served from 11 to 3, are in large portions but smaller than the dinner servings. We recommend the roast pork with Chinese vegetables. The vegetables are crisp, the pork not too salty.

HELSINKI TEA ROOM (See under "Nightlife," Chapter 5)

HUDSON'S RESTAURANT
413-528-2002.
www.hudsonsrestaurant.
  com.
50 Stockbridge Rd.), Gt.
  Barrington, MA 01230.
Rte. 7.
Closed: Sun. night. and
  Mon.
Price: Moderate to
  Expensive.
Cuisine: Eclectic
  contemporary American.
Serving: L, D, SB.
Credit Cards: AE, D, DC,
  MC, V.
Special Features: Member,
  Berkshire Grown.

Hudson's continues to appeal to discerning South County diners. Proprietors Cindy and Geoffrey Brown, both trained at the prestigious Culinary Institute of America, offer quite varied, original, and generally excellent luncheon, dinner, and brunch menus. While they compete ably in the crowded Great Barrington dinnertime market, they have staked out the upscale luncheon market every day except Monday as their own. The luncheon menu offers extensive selections in the soup and salad category, a mouthwatering array of gourmet sandwich plates, and four entrées (onion tart to a vegetarian Mediterranean platter).

Dinner every night features entrées seemingly representing every region of the land, from pan-seared Maine crab cakes to grilled Chipolte pork tenderloin. Among the appetizers, the roasted corn and red pepper polenta stack with black beans, melted cheddar, and salsa is a delicious favorite. The Sunday brunch menu offers the customary array of eggs, omelets, pancakes, and waffles, albeit in mouthwatering variations but also country fried chicken and New Orleans gumbo with shrimp, crab, and Andouille sausage for the heartier appetite.

By the way, Hudson's website is among the best, showing their full brunch, lunch, and dinner menus, hours of operation, directions, and more. Try it—and the real thing, too.

PEARLS
413-528-7767.
www.pearlsrestaurant.com.
47 Railroad Street, Gt.
   Barrington, MA 01230.
Price: Expensive.
Cuisine: Continental.
Serving: L, D, SB.
Credit Cards: AE, MC, V.
Handicap Access: Yes.
Reservations:
   Recommended (no
   reservations in bar).
Special Features:
   Handsome dine-in bar.

Another bit of New York sophistication come to the Berkshires, Pearl's is handsome in a contemporary vein, elegant without demanding formal wear of its patrons, and a significant addition to the upscale end of the local dining scene. Having begun with a special tilt toward steaks and chops, Pearl's now also features game dishes in a generally Continental cuisine. Its few critics assert that the décor is a bit superior to the food, and some remark on the New York air of the prices, but it is a success and a well deserved one. The handsome bar—its glass wall making it seemingly open to a lively vista down Railroad Street—offers excellent (and reasonably priced) drinks and a more casual setting to enjoy a light repast or full dinner—without a reservation.

SHIRO RESTAURANT
413-528-1898.
105 Stockbridge Rd., Gt.
   Barrington, MA 01230.
Open seven days.
Price: Moderate.
Cuisine: Japanese.
Serving: L, D.
Credit Cards: V, MC, AE

Shiro is a fantastic Japanese culinary experience and avoids the frustration of trying to park in downtown Great Barrington. Shiro, north of the intersection of Routes 7 and 23, is a compact haven of muted greens and tans in a space emanating tempting aromas that lure us in as soon as we open the stocky wooden doors. From the inside, it is hard to believe that this used to house Burger King!

The simple, immaculate wooden tables are each nestled against a wall, affording a sense of privacy even though the tables are not far apart. An efficient waitperson seats us and shortly thereafter greets us with a plush, hot towel—a soothing courtesy. Our questions are patiently and thoroughly answered, and we are encouraged to try something unusual, rather than the more standard (but delicious!) tempura and teriyaki dishes. The wine list includes an excellent array of sake, of course, and a mix of domestic and imported wines (carefully selected to complement the menu).

We tried a mixture of appetizers and entrées, beginning with the oshi tashi horenso, spinach sautéed and finished with garlic sauce. The dish arrived hot from the pan, the sauce a fine balance between sesame and garlic. (It was fresh and fabulous! We could have eaten three more orders.) The misoshiru (soybean broth with tofu, seaweed, and scallion) was rich and complex in taste but light enough to whet the appetite. The gyoza—pan-fried pork-and-vegetable dumplings—were very tasty and not at all greasy.

Shiro offers all the usual types of sushi, but we opted to try the special crispy, spicy, white fish roll: Large, with delicate cooked white fish wrapped with rice and seaweed and topped with a spicy, caviar-filled mayonnaise (we could have done with less of the topping, but it was an interesting balance of cool and spicy). We tried the seafood kushiyaki combo: Grilled shrimp, scallop, salmon, and vegetables on skewers. It was perfect. This dish is served on a bed of braised onions in a tantalizing sauce, with mung bean sprouts, broccoli, and green peppers. Shiro also has a hibachi area where the whole family will enjoy watching the chef exhibit his flair for chopping and flipping the food atop tiny bursts of fire.

SPENCER'S RESTAURANT AT THE THORNEWOOD INN
413-528-3828, 800-854-1008.
www.thornewood.com.
453 Stockbridge Rd., Gt. Barrington, MA 01230.
Jct. 183.
Closed: Mon., Tues., Wed (summer); Sun.–Thurs. (winter).
Price: Moderate to Expensive.
Cuisine: Country Continental.
Serving: D, SB (seasonal).
Credit Cards: AE, D, MC, V.
Reservations: Preferred.
Special Features: View from terrace.

Although plans are afoot for an addition to the porch that would create a new dining room, Spencer's Restaurant in the Dutch-colonial Thornewood Inn currently welcomes diners in the formal, candlelit room with dance floor, and in the publike atmosphere of the library. On Saturday evenings and during summer's Sunday brunch, innkeeper David Thorne leads his trio in mellow jazz and blues selections.

Dinner is gracefully placed on crisp white table linens. Chef Terry Thorne presents a brief, creative menu, with much thought given to how subtle flavors relate. Although three salads were offered, we began with cheddar, bacon, and chive tomato soup and bruschetta with brie over a beefsteak tomato (which could have been heated a bit to make the cheese melt). A rack of lamb served with rosemary, garlic, and walnuts was delicious both inside and out. The duck was tasty in a sauce of plum and molasses. Both were accompanied by mashed potatoes, green beans, and baby carrots, artfully arranged. An Australian white wine and an Australian red brought out the flavor of the food and the thoughts of the diners. The smooth lemon tart, contrasting sweet and sour, had a delightful crumb shell.

Dreams of an autumn evening included returning in the summer to sit on the deck, overlooking Taft Farm, and sampling other delightful offerings such as the fish of the day or vegetable pie with a French-bread crust or salmon stuffed with scallop mousse. And, of course, others of those fresh homemade desserts prepared on the premises.

20 RAILROAD STREET
413-528-9345.
20 Railroad St., Gt.
  Barrington, MA 01230.
Price: Inexpensive.
Cuisine: American.
Serving: L, D, SB.
Credit Cards: MC, V.
Handicap Access: Yes.
Special Features: Open late;
  member, Berkshire
  Grown.

20 Railroad Street is the restaurant granddaddy of the Railroad Street revival. In the warm high-ceilinged brick dining room, always convivial, we shared dining space with jovial families, couples young and old, as well as softball teams and ski patrol squadrons. We heard about divorces and deals, patients and quarterbacks. In story or in person, most of southern Berkshire has been in 20 Railroad. The 28-foot-long mahogany bar and back bar, built in New York City in 1883, arrived in Great Barrington in 1919. It served one of the area's speakeasies during Prohibition, referred to as "Mahogany Ridge" by those who explained to their spouses just where they were hunting.

But good food is what makes 20 Railroad chug along. For lunch, dinner, or whenever, 20 Railroad's starters, salads, sandwiches, and burgers are legendary. Unusual starters include the Plowman's Snack, a combination of brie, soprassata sausage, and French bread. Pocket sandwiches are outstanding, with the vegetarian side pocket being among our favorites. The restaurant also nurtures a whole Rueben family (available in halves), with ham (Mama Rueben), turkey (Rebecca Rueben), and roast beef (Rolland Rueben). More than a dozen different burgers and an equal number of sandwiches fill out Railroad Street's printed menu.

UNION BAR AND GRILL
413-528-6228.
293 Main St., Gt.
  Barrington, MA 01230.
Open: Daily
Price: Moderate to
  Expensive
Cuisine: New American.
Serving: L Saturday, SB; D
  daily.
Credit Cards: MC, V.
Handicap Access: Yes.
Reservations: Only for
  parties of 10 or more
Special Features: 40-foot
  bar; Kids' menu; Food
  served to 11pm winter,
  12pm summer; member,
  Berkshire Grown.

Susan and Dan Smith passed the Union Bar and Grill torch to New York restaurateur Gianfranco Sorrentino in January 2002 and returned to full-time management of John Andrew's. Sorrentino has kept up the high standards the Smiths set from the beginning. Lunch is served on Saturdays, brunch on Sundays, and dinner seven nights of the week year-round. A good kids' menu for the early set and a lively bar scene and dining until midnight combine to make the Union one of the most popular bistros in all of Berkshire County.

The menu changes often, keeping a few regulars like the grilled flank steak sandwich with grilled red onion, smoked Gouda, and an Asian barbecue sauce on flatbread. Steaks and hamburgers served with excellent fries satisfy the meat-and-potatoes crowd, while a variety of seafood appetizers and entrées appeal to subtler tastes. Desserts are delicious, and they all cost $7. The apple tart specialty is made from a homemade flaky, crisp, buttery, golden puff pastry round topped with micro-thin sliced apples and a dollop of homemade vanilla-y! ice cream.

The Union is a great place for a leisurely weekend lunch, a sophisticated dinner, or a late-night supper or bite. The food is consistently good and innovative.

**VERDURA CUCINA
RUSTICA**
413-528-8969.
44 Railroad St., Gt.
  Barrington, MA 01230.
Closed: Wednesday.
Price: Expensive.
Cuisine: Italian.
Serving: D.
Credit Cards: MC, V.
Reservations:
  Recommended.
Special Features: Member,
  Berkshire Grown.

"Creative" is the key word for Verdura's operation. The atmosphere is self-consciously sophisticated; with low lighting, comfortable tables, and a large tree growing out of the corner of the bar, it strives for the feeling of an upscale city restaurant. Food is intended to excite the palate; no substitutions is the policy—allowing the chef to put together his combinations of flavors. Verdura makes extensive use of local products.

The warm duck confit salad was beautifully presented, although inhabited more by fingerling potatoes than duck. We slowed and savored the flavors and textures. The grilled tenderloin was tender—and rich. The bruschetta with smoked goose breast and goat cheese was crunchy and smooth. The crisp-crusted pizzas come with unusual toppings, such as leek, chevre and white truffle oil.

The menu, although brief, is varied, with good choices for vegetarians. Desserts are creative as well.

"Creativity" included a benevolent attitude toward toddlers, who wandered freely among the diners, some of whom may have preferred not to socialize with the under-five set. And the staff is young and eager if not particularly experienced.

VIVIANI'S
413-528-3843.
177 Main St., Gt.
  Barrington, MA 01230.
N. end of Main.
Closed: Wed.
Price: Moderate.
Cuisine: Italian.
Serving: D, B, L Sat. and
  Sun.
Credit Cards: MC, V.
Reservations:
  Recommended.

Italian dining in Gt. Barrington? Not really—until now. Owner/chef Nancy Pecorelli has established it with Viviani's, a small and bustling trattoria in a very modest storefront setting. At the "wrong" end of Main Street, it is the real thing, worth the few blocks' trip. Parking is a breeze compared to Railroad Street. The décor is simple and attractive, featuring a wall full of fascinating period family pictures that seem familiar even if not sprigs of the viewer's family tree. While there are only about a dozen tables in the main floor dining room, Viviani's offers full bar service: An all Italian wine list with about 18 well-chosen and well-described offerings, many available by the glass. Complimentary special appetizers are offered with pre-dinner drinks. The menu has a full range of regular plus daily special antipasti, pastas, *primi e secondi* entrées and desserts, all prepared to order by Nancy herself and served by a small but attentive and well trained staff.

Breakfast and lunch are offered on weekend mornings. A worthy addition to the Barrington dining scene—and at a good bargain price, too. And we will all watch for the dining space Nancy plans to create downstairs: a glassed-in dining room and outdoor terrace to be open in-season on the Housatonic Riverwalk—a first for Great Barrington.

Housatonic

JACKS GRILL
413-274-1000.
www.jacksgrill.com.
1063 Main St., Housatonic, MA 01236.
Closed: Halloween to Mothers Day.
Price: Moderate.
Cuisine: American.
Credit Cards: AE, MC, V.
Reservations: Suggested.
Special Features: Kid's menu; electric train overhead; genuine comfort food

Jacks Grill. No apostrophe, no *e*. "Honest Food; Satisfaction Guaranteed," is Jacks' motto. And Jacks delivers. With well-made drinks, user-friendly wines, and Jacks' regular daily specials— from corned beef and cabbage (Tuesday) to roast pork, cornbread, and applesauce (Sunday), satisfaction is the theme, and it is pervasive. The menu selections, the setting in a former hardware store in an old mill town, and the decor (the original store shelves are full of endlessly varied collections of stuff, and an operating electric train hangs from the ceiling) all say: "comfort" loud and clear. Families are welcome, of course. There is nice selection of kids' stuff on the menu to satisfy the younger set while parents enjoy more adult fare.

The Fitzpatrick family knows hospitality. The food is seriously well prepared. Guinness and Harp are on tap. Every wine on the very serviceable wine list is available by the glass or the bottle. The wait staffers are eager and attentive. It's a great, simple evening out—and at a painless price, as well.

Lee

CORK 'N HEARTH
413-243-0535.
635 Laurel St., Lee, MA 01238
Rte. 20, on Laurel Lake N. of Lee.
Closed: Mon.
Price: Moderate.
Cuisine: New England contemporary.
Serving: D.
Credit Cards: AE, MC, V.
Special Features: Fireside ambiance, view of lake; member, Berkshire Grown.

Owner/chef Christopher Ryan maintains the charm and warm hospitality of Cork 'N' Hearth, on the shores of lovely Laurel Lake. While not overflowing with ambiance, amenities include antique quilts on the walls, a profusion of flowers and plants, and attentive wait staff.

The food is dependably good, from an extensive menu or prepared to order. Our choice of Atlantic scrod with seasoned bread crumbs, lemon wine, and butter was baked to perfection and served with a delicious green salad, baked potato, and chilled sorbet.

FROM KETCHUP TO CAVIAR

413-243 6397.
www.fromketchuptocaviar.com.
150 Main Street, Lee, MA 01238.
Closed: March.
Price: Moderate to Expensive.
Serving: D daily, summer; closed Tues., winter.
Cuisine: American.
Credit Cards: AE, MC, V.
Reservations: Required in summer, suggested other seasons.
Special Features: Catering.

They're back! And a mighty good thing, too! It was a great loss to Berkshire dining when Lynne and Christian Urbain passed Once Upon a Table to other hands a few years ago to concentrate on catering. But luckily for us they couldn't stand normal living and From Ketchup to Caviar is the result. Downtown Lee has other good dining options, but K2C tops the chart, and since it is appreciably larger that Once Upon a Table, more of us can enjoy the great dining experience. Divided into three dining rooms, the atmosphere is intimate throughout. Summer dining begins at 5pm to accommodate the Tanglewood, Jacob's Pillow, and theater audiences. Lynne presides graciously in front while Christian sparks a kitchen team of superior skills.

The menu changes with each season. Both appetizers and entrées run from classics (escargots with garlic tarragon butter; coq au vin) to quite contemporary (terrine of leek and goat cheese; crisp skin seared salmon over lobster bread pudding with carrot coriander sauce). Portions are generous but not staggering. All are delicious. The wine list offers perhaps the best selection of moderately priced, well-described wines we've encountered anywhere. Wines from France, California, Chile, New Zealand, and South Africa, among others, are thoughtfully selected to complement every meal and taste. Not inexpensive but excellent values throughout. Desserts are rich and succulent. Enjoy!

JOE'S DINER

413-243-9756.
85 Center St., Lee, MA 01238.
Cor. Center (Rte. 20) and Main Sts.
Closed: Sun.
Price: Inexpensive.
Cuisine: American.
Serving: B, L, D.

The owner might like to sell, but he's baaack, which is good news for the dining public. Joe's: the little diner that time forgot but history honors, where things are just as they were. Still bustling with the vigor of the 1940s, Joe's stocks packets of Red Man Chewing Tobacco right next to buckets of lifetime-guarantee combs; artichokes are practically free, and a real New York egg cream runs only a few cents more. A politician wouldn't think of breezing through Berkshire without a photo op and a plate of meat loaf at Joe's.

But the secret of success is that Joe Sorrentino and his family serve good food. This ex-army cook will happily serve "breakfast at dinner or dinner at breakfast." Joe creates a special each day. "We'll go through a whole hip of beef every Monday, 120 pounds of corned beef every Thursday," says Joe. Those serious about taking in one of Joe's specials (like a roast beef dinner with vegetable, potato, and bread) had better arrive early. We came on corned beef night recently and watched the last of the 120 pounds disappear quickly, leaving disappointed latecomers. Not for long. They soon wrapped their tongues around something even better that they just hadn't thought of.

PARADISE OF INDIA
413-243-0500.
5 Railroad St., Lee, MA 01238.
Price: Moderate.
Cuisine: Indian.
Serving: L, D.
Credit Cards: AE, D, MC, V.

A cheerful, casual restaurant tucked off the main street in Lee, Paradise of India is the place in South County for those who enjoy Indian cuisine (the same owners run Glory of India in Great Barrington, offering a similar menu in a warm, comfortable space on that town's main street). A bright, sunny spot for lunch and warm and cozy for dinner, this restaurant offers a wide variety of meat and meatless dishes, from tandoori specialties (marinated meats, poultry, and seafood cooked in a traditional clay charcoal-burning oven) to masala to curries. The mixed platter for two presents a savory assortment of Indian appetizers—specify if you prefer vegetarian items. It's a nice way to try a little of everything! The Indian breads (naan, roti, etc.) are fantastic and practically a lunch in themselves. The gobhi paratha, fine flour bread stuffed with fresh cauliflower, ginger, and cilantro, is delicious and unusual. Some of the meals come with naan; diners should order one of the specialty breads as a treat for the table.

Our flavorful tandoori dishes arrived at the table sizzling. The shrimp was a bit overcooked. The aloo tikka with chana masala, a combination of potatoes and garbanzo beans cooked in a medium spiced sauce, is not to be missed. Another excellent meatless item is the traditional daal makhani—a rich, fragrant black lentil stew that is delicate, complex, and creamy, not at all grainy as some lentil stews are. A wide variety of chicken, seafood, and lamb dishes are offered in addition to the many fine vegetarian options. Soft traditional Indian music and Indian pop tunes round out this delightful dining experience.

SALMON RUN FISH HOUSE
413-243 3900.
78 Main St., Lee, MA 01238.
Price: Inexpensive to Moderate.
Cuisine: Seafood.
Serving: L, D.
Credit Cards: D, MC, V.
Reservations: Recommended for four or more.
Special Features: Private dining room for up to 40; monthly seasonal specials; kids' menu.

O pened in 1999 by Dawn and Paul Face, Salmon Run has made itself a well-loved member of the Lee family in a short time. Occupying a storefront on Main Street, it may be short on elaborate décor but conveys both its nautical theme and a friendly air.

The menu offers a wide range of seafood and other (buffalo wings!) appetizers. Otherwise, except for a few token main-course offerings for meat eaters, Salmon Run is a fish house. The house specialty is (surprise!) salmon—offered six different ways—or the Salmon Sampler of three of them. Other fish and shellfish offerings are available, singly or in numerous combinations. Overstuffed, mostly seafood, sandwiches are served all day. There is a full-service bar and a fairly brief beer and wine list.

For very good food, a welcoming atmosphere, and generous servings, Salmon Run is a great spot for a full meal on a moderate budget.

South Lee

THE SWEET BASIL GRILLE
413-243-1114.
1575 Pleasant St., S. Lee, 01260.
Rte. 102.
Closed: Mon. in winter.
Price: Moderate.
Cuisine: Italian.
Serving: L (summer), D.
Credit Cards: AE, DC, MC, V.
Reservations: Recommended.

Owners Rick and Lynn Penna make certain that the service is friendly and knowledgeable in spite of numerous trips up and down the stairs, the prices reasonable, and the food tasty. Sweet Basil, settled in a comfortable house in South Lee near the Stockbridge border, is dependable and occasionally outstanding. The cream of garlic soup and salads of crisp, fresh greens are an excellent start. The bread, however: a bit ho-hum and could have come from the supermarket. Of the specials, the tuna steak was not overdone, while the pork with onions in a white sauce was exceptional. The penne pasta and sauce, on the other hand, was a touch watery, needing more stove time. The lemon lush, a featured dessert, was uninspired, with ingredients perhaps left over from baking a lemon meringue pie.

The house wines—from a specific Italian community and available by the glass, half carafe, or carafe—were a pleasant accompaniment to an enjoyable evening.

New Marlborough

THE HILLSIDE
413-528-3123.
Rte. 57, New Marlborough, MA 01230.
Closed: Mon.; Mon. and Tues. in winter.
Price: Moderate.
Cuisine: Continental.
Credit Cards: AE, MC, V.
Serving: Sun. lunch 12–2; D.
Reservations: Recommended.
Special Features: Catering for parties up to 75 people.

The Hillside, celebrating its 30th year in 2002, continues to excel in traditional Continental cuisine. No "nouvelle" dishes for owner/chef Giuseppe (Joe) Chighine. He knows how to cook classical dishes, and what a pleasure they are.

A modest but satisfactory wine list is available. We enjoyed a marvelous French onion soup and an avocado stuffed with *real* crab meat. A fresh green salad accompanied the entrées, with a choice of dressing: Roquefort (creamy and delicious), Russian, Italian, or French. When a fine chef offers five different veal dishes, they are a sure bet. Our veal picatta was the best we've had in recent years. The filet of sole meunière was done to perfection. Other entrées included rigatoni puttanesca, entrecote au poivre, chicken (or veal or filet of sole) Oscar, and roast duckling flambé.

The crème caramel was fine, but the coconut cream pie was insufficiently moist. Espresso, cappuccino, and a wide selection of international coffees were available. Well prepared food, good service, and an attractive setting put the Hillside on our "to repeat" list.

The Old Inn on the Green in New Marlborough is lit entirely by candlelight.

Judith Monachina

OLD INN ON THE GREEN AND GEDNEY FARM
413-229-3131, 800-286-3139; fax 413-229-8236.
www.oldinn.com.
Mail: Star Route 70, New Marlborough, MA 01230.
Rte. 57, on the Green, 6 mi. E. Rte. 23.
Closed: Mon.–Wed.; open six days in summer.
Price: Weekdays: Moderate to Expensive; Saturdays: Very Expensive, prix fixe.
Cuisine: French, American.
Serving: D.
Credit Cards: AE, MC, V.
Reservations: Required.
Special Features: Intimate candlelight dining; outdoor patio dining in summer; member, Berkshire Grown.

We can almost hear the stagecoach coming as we sit in the candlelit dining room. It can't possibly be more romantic. We wish we lived farther away, so we would have an excuse to stay the night. Clippety clop to a 240-year-old inn.

Nothing outdated about the food, however. Our dinner on a Saturday was from a prix fixe menu (à la carte during the week) that changes monthly. Appetizers included chilled green pea and truffle soup; a salad with pears, figs, and Berkshire blue cheese; Maryland-style crab cake with Maui onions; and red pepper aioli. Entrées included a choice of beef tenderloin with bacon-wrapped Blue Point oysters, rare Ahi tuna with salad à la niçoise, or a cassoulet of veal medallions with sweetbreads and braised Belgian endive.

On the chef's recommendation we enjoyed a 1996 Cabernet Sauvignon Chateau Montelena that perfectly matched our beef and cassoulet. We were delighted that the dessert menu included a cheese course, uncommon in Berkshire County. It was Pecorino Tuscano with roasted red bell pepper mousse and arugula purée.

It is no surprise that *Food and Wine* magazine lists this inn as one of America's 50 best hotel restaurants.

Sandisfield

NEW BOSTON INN
413-258-4477.
www.newbostoninn.com.
Rte. 57, Sandisfield, MA
   01255.
At Rte. 8.
Price: Inexpensive to
   Moderate.   .
Cuisine: American.
Serving: L, D; SB June–Sept.
Credit Cards: AE, MC, V.
Reservations:
   Recommended for
   dinner.

Proudly situated at a crossroad somewhat removed, the New Boston Inn is cheerful, accommodating, and friendly. This 1737 landmark with seven rooms up steep stairs is the oldest continually operating inn in the county. The several dining rooms have been carefully restored, its walls still stenciled. Some of the original wide boards remain in the bar.

The staff is knowledgeable about the cuisine and the area, local people congregate, and the atmosphere is homey and familial. The food is comforting, not surprising: Burgers, fries, Philly steak sandwiches, fresh fish dishes, and pasta are made to order. When asked about the potato salad, the server brought out a generous sample to try before deciding. It was delicious. We said yes. Desserts change with the season and the whims of the competent chef.

Sheffield

STAGECOACH HILL INN
413-229-8585.
854 S. Undermountain Rd.,
   Sheffield, MA 01257.
Rte. 41, N. of Lakeville, CT.
Closed: Mon., Tues.
Price: Moderate.
Cuisine: American.
Serving: D.
Credit Cards: AE, MC, V.
Reservations:
   Recommended.
Special Features: Candlelit
   dining; catering for
   groups & wedding
   receptions.

Chef/owner David Essenfeld holds forth in a picturesque building redolent of serving food and spirits since 1829. Diners may eat at rustic tables in the bar or in the more formal dining room. The menu is short but engaging; the food good if not outstanding. Anyone for spinach gnocchi, shrimp provençal, duck breast over port wine reduction, or house-smoked pork chops? We enjoyed the chicken special and rack of lamb, both served with light and lovely herb biscuits and a house salad of mixed greens and baby lettuces in lemon-garlic vinaigrette. Garlic potatoes and a mixture of diced squashes completed the entrée. We might have chosen to begin with steamed mussels, house-cured gravlax, or quesadilla, among others. Vegetarian appetizers and entrées are also available.

We chose the house wine, a chardonnay, from a short but varied wine list. Usually a number of excellent beers and ales are on tap, as well. Our meal ended with a chocolate Kahlúa mousse and a highly satisfactory apple crisp à la mode.

Stockbridge

GLENDALE RIVER GRILL
413-298-4711;
fax 413-298-4711.
www.ggrill.com.
14 Glendale Rd., Glendale, MA 01229.
Rte. 183.
Serving: D daily; 5–9.30 weekdays, 5–11 weekends
Price: Moderate to Expensive
Cuisine: American-Continental.
Credit Cards: AE, MC, V.
Reservations: Appreciated.
Special Features: Custom catering; "Tuesdays" tavern section.

Veteran Berkshire restaurateur Al Weinman presides over the hottest (800 degrees) grill hereabouts, and produces from it excellent steaks, chops, fish, and fowl, all with their own delicious juices sealed in. A bit secluded on the banks of the Housatonic just down the road from the Norman Rockwell Museum, the Glendale River Grill is a fine exemplar of the classic (and disappearing) country highway steakhouse. The grilled offerings are accompanied by choices of a dozen or so excellent sauces and condiments, all homemade and delicious. The balance of the menu offers Continental selections, including several hearty and tasty vegetarian entrées. The lamb specialties feature delicious local Berkshire lamb. The simple and moderately priced wine list is predominantly American and has a good selection of the increasingly appreciated wines of the eastern United States. Al has redesigned the tavern section as "Tuesdays" (a nod to the legendary Mundays that once occupied these premises) for those in search of well-made potables and lighter fare.

ONCE UPON A TABLE
413-298-3870.
36 Main St., PO Box 1428, Stockbridge, MA 01262.
The Mews.
Price: Moderate to Expensive.
Cuisine: American.
Serving: L daily, D Wed.–Mon.
Credit Cards: AE, MC, V.
Reservations: Recommended.
Special Features: Member, Berkshire Grown.

Once Upon a Table fits nicely—and literally—between the Red Lion Inn and the Stockbridge General Store or the Elm Street Market in the Stockbridge dining scene. Small, secluded in the Mews, informal and attractive, it offers tasty full lunches and dinners, well served in a pleasant setting. Neither as formal as the Red Lion nor as casual as the above-mentioned diners, it fills its niche very well, as attested by its frequently full tables and very good reputation. Mussels in white wine broth are a tasty specialty appetizer, which can do as a lighter main course, as well. Another five or six appetizers, three salad options and a half dozen entrées—somewhat lighter at lunch, more substantial at dinner, provide choices for all. Moderately priced wines by the glass or bottle further enhance a pleasant, low-key dining experience.

Early Fall brings rare quiet moments to the courtyard at the Red Lion Inn, where lunch and dinner are served, weather permitting.

THE RED LION INN
413-298-5545.
www.redlioninn.com.
30 Main St., Stockbridge,
  MA 01262.
Rte. 7.
Price: Expensive.
Cuisine: Traditional
  American.
Serving: B, L, D.
Credit Cards: AE, DC, MC,
  V.
Reservations:
  Recommended.
Handicap Access: Yes.
Special Features: Member,
  Berkshire Grown.

The Red Lion Inn is almost everyone's idea of a classic New England inn. Not surprising, as that is just what it has been since 1773 (or thereabouts; local historians differ on the exact date). A hotbed of pre-Revolutionary fever then, it has been the focal point of the Stockbridge community ever since. Owned and operated by the Fitzpatrick family since 1968, the inn has grown and evolved with the times. Many things about the inn seem changeless—the wonderful collections of antiques, the festive holiday decorations, the 19th-century wirecage elevator, the enormous and eclectic artwork. The cuisine, on the other hand, has made real advances in recent years. The classic favorites remain, from Red Lion clam chowder to carved native turkey to old-fashioned apple pie, but there are numerous contemporary New American style selections, as well, designed to tempt the palate of the more demanding diner. Complementing the newer menu selections, the inn has developed one of the most extensive and interesting wine lists in the region and has earned a *Wine Spectator* magazine Award of Excellence for its efforts.

Both the handsome 19th-century main dining room and the adjoining Widow Bingham's Tavern offer the full menu. During the balmy days of summer (late spring and early autumn, too), so do the back porch and courtyard. Jackets are required at dinner in the dining room. The tavern, which has a wonderful rustic air, and the porch and courtyard are informal. A prime, and famous, place for cocktails or tea is the sweeping front porch, complete with wicker rocking chairs. The Lion's Den, in the basement of the inn, is a lion of a different color. Live music, a menu running to soups and sandwiches, and a busy bar make this one of the livelier nightspots in this quiet community. The Red Lion Inn is, deservedly, a very busy and popular place, especially during the summer months and the autumn leaf-peeping season, so reservations are always a good idea—and a day or two in advance during those times.

West Stockbridge

Judith Monachina

Rouge, a French restaurant and bistro in West Stockbridge, decorates for Halloween.

ROUGE
413-232-4111
3 Center St., W.
  Stockbridge, MA 01266.

William and Maggie Merelle have put their hearts and souls into their intimate restaurant in West Stockbridge. Colorful, with pretty

Open: Wed.–Sun.
Price: Moderate.
Cuisine: French.
Serving: L Fri.–Sun, D
    Wed.–Sun.
Credit Cards: MC, V.
Reservations: For parties of
    six or more.
Special Feature: Member,
    Berkshire Grown.

place settings and a bar that William crafted himself, this French bistro is a delightful addition to the small village that hosts more than its fair share of good food and pretty views. Rouge is tucked into a side street, somehow making it feel like a surprise, a secret find.

We sampled the torte vegetarian, sautéed salmon encrusted with pistachios and plantains, and New York strip steak. Everything was delicious, pleasantly presented and served. This new spot is delightful.

TRUC ORIENT EXPRESS
413-232-4204.
3 Harris St., W. Stockbridge,
    MA 01266.
One block off Main St. (Rte.
    102), over the Williams
    River.
Closed: Tues. Sept. to May.
Price: Moderate to
    Expensive.
Cuisine: Vietnamese.
Serving: D.
Credit Cards: AE, DC, MC,
    V.
Reservations:
    Recommended.
Special Features: Vegetarian
    dishes; outdoor dining;
    Vietnamese gift shop.

Truc was earning converts to Vietnamese cuisine long before one could find it in every major city in the USA. This West Stockbridge fixture and favorite, set behind Main Street and the Williams River, was founded in 1979 by the husband-and-wife team of Luy Nguyen and Drai Duong. The family has been beguiling Berkshire residents and visitors ever since with the flavors of classic Vietnamese fare tailored to American tastes, a complex and sophisticated blend of sweet and sour, mellow and piquant.

Special shrimp rolls, a crisp-fried, rice-paper pocket filled with crabmeat, pork, shrimp, and cabbage, and jumbo battered honeycomb shrimp, coated in cellophane noodles, quick-fried and served with a thick soy-peanut sauce, are favorite appetizers. The summer rolls are a cool, fresh summertime must starter. Barbecued pork on rice noodles—very flavorful, well marinated, and tender— is an excellent entrée as is the deep-fried whole flounder in a sweet-sour sauce with chilies. Also recommended is the happy pancake (a rice-flour crêpe studded with lots of meat and fresh vegetables). Vegetarian offerings abound throughout the menu, as well. At lunch, everything is at least one-third off the evening price.

The interior is light and spacious, with wide wooden floorboards, a plant-filled balcony, Vietnamese art on the walls, and attractive bamboo curtains, all signs of the owner's dedication to a quality dining experience. The adjoining shop has been very handsomely expanded to become an attraction in its own right, filled with imported Asian gift and decorative items.

RESTAURANTS IN CENTRAL COUNTY

Becket

DREAMAWAY LODGE (See under "Nightlife" in Chapter Five)

Hancock

**FOUNDERS'
RESTAURANT**
413-738-5500.
37 Corey Rd., Hancock, MA
 01237.
Btw. Rtes 7 and 43.
At the Country Inn, Jiminy
 Peak.
Price: Moderate.
Cuisine: American.
Serving: B, D.
Credit Cards: AE, D, DC,
 MC, V.
Special Feature: Member,
 Berkshire Green.

On the top floor of the Country Inn at Jiminy Peak, Founders' Restaurant functions as a convenience and amenity for the 96-room inn, Jiminy Peak condos, numerous other condos springing up like mushrooms across the road, and the ski clientele. A polished bar and a row of wooden booths dominate the cavernous main dining room, decorated with iron chandeliers, wooden carts, a canoe, and sleighs hung by chains from a cathedral ceiling. Dim lighting, dark-green carpeting, exposed wood—a barn, in fact. Many barns do a good business in Berkshire County on a summer Friday evening. This restaurant should be the centerpiece of a considerable upscale clientele: So why is it nearly empty?

The answer may be the food. The simple menu is limited to grilled or sautéed steaks, chops, fish, and game. Our lamb and our pork were tough, although the sea bass was nicely cooked. The melange of vegetables was acceptable but not exciting. When the entrées are disappointing, we look toward the accompaniments. Our appetizers—a trout and some chicken fingers, both with appropriate dips—were fun but not memorable. A freshly baked, delicious loaf of sunflower seed bread arrived first, followed by an acceptable house salad with lots of veggies. It says something, though, that the highlight of the meal was a piece of organic apple pie with granola crust.

We appreciated that wine was served by the glass, but we were not impressed by the selection.

**POWDER HOUNDS
RESTAURANT AND
TAVERN**
413-738-5660.
137 Brodie Mountain Rd.,
 Hancock, MA 01237.
Price: Moderate
Closed: Tues.
Cuisine: American
Serving: D.

Located at the foot of Jiminy Peak ski area and in the midst of burgeoning Hancock condominiums, Powder Hounds—named for the dogs Fred and Lisa Kruger keep out back—is a bar and grill in an American roadhouse building. Still, the chef has aspirations, preparing dishes of interest and presenting them with flair. Our meat loaf, nestled beside sculptured scoops of mashed potatoes, was covered with wild mushrooms. The string beans

Credit Cards: AE, MC, V.
Special Feature: Entire
menu available to go.

were cooked the right amount and fresh—as were
the carefully arranged different textures of lettuce
and tomatoes in the house salad. A peach pie,
while not made in-house, provided decorative and
tasty nuts around the shell.

Several varieties of beer are on tap.

Lenox

APPLE TREE INN
413-637-1477;
　fax 413-637-2528.
www.appletreeinn.com.
10 Richmond Mountain
　Rd., Lenox, MA 01240.
Off Rte. 183, S. of
　Tanglewood main gate.
Closed: Mon.–Wed.
　off-season.
Price: Moderate to
　Expensive.
Cuisine: Continental.
Serving: SB, D.
Credit Cards: AE, D, DC,
　MC, V.
Reservations:
　Recommended.
Special Features: Member,
　Berkshire Grown.

An enchanting 19th-century house, high on a
hill overlooking the Stockbridge Bowl and the
grounds of Tanglewood, provides an entryway to
the Apple Tree Restaurant. We begin with a drink
in the cozy, paneled Victorian bar and move to
either the spacious porch or delightful octagonal
carousel room, both with spectacular views, for a
well-prepared meal from the interesting menu. A
luscious list of appetizers offers a meal in itself,
beginning with the crispy-crusted homemade pizza,
the caramelized onion bisque, or grilled chicken
quesadilla. The tasty black bean soup du jour left us
wishing for more. Breads are homemade and memorable.

For entrées, tempting offerings included black
and white sesame-encrusted salmon, wild- mushroom ravioli, pistachio-crusted lamb loin with
couscous and fresh vegetables, garlic chicken
breast with boursin risotto, and a tri-pepper filet
mignon. Desserts are homemade, seasonal, and also include the favorite combination of chocolate mousse with raspberry sauce.

To facilitate the lively Tanglewood crowd: No separate checks, and an 18 percent gratuity is added to parties over five. Begin a wonderful summer evening
at this delightful spot, and end it by listening to a symphony under the stars.

BLANTYRE
413-637-3556;
　fax 413-637-4282.
www.blantyre.com.
16 Blantyre Rd., Lenox, MA
　01240.
Off Rte. 20, NW of Lee.
Closed: Early Nov.–early
　May.
Price: Very Expensive (prix
　fixe).
Cuisine: French, country
　house.

Blantyre, a member of the world-renowned
Relais & Châteaux association, is one of the
very best dining venues in the region, some say
the best. Built as one of the grandest and most
impressive of the Berkshire "cottages" of the
Gilded Age, Blantyre was rescued and restored
inside and out over two decades by the Fitzpatrick family. It has been developed to a high
state of period excellence and offers a true taste of
the life of its original time. Manager (since 2000)
Katja Henke presides with a sure and graceful

Serving: L (July and Aug.)
by reservation, D (jacket
and tie required at
dinner).
Credit Cards: AE, MC, V.
Reservations: Required.
Handicap Access: Yes.
Special Features: Fireplaces;
private dining room;
excellent wine cellar;
member, Berkshire
Grown.

hand, sustaining an atmosphere of formal elegance without stiffness.

Before dinner, drinks are offered in the parlor from a handsome rolling bar. Champagne seems almost obligatory in these surroundings. Chef de cuisine Chris Brooks generally offers six to eight appetizers and the same number of entrées on the prix-fixe menu. The cuisine is characterized as "country house"—utilizing contemporary French techniques to combine local, regional, and New England products. Offerings change seasonally. The food is exquisite—absolutely worth the lofty price—and the wine list is what one would expect from such an establishment, a *Wine Spectator* Award of Excellence winner, of course. Desserts are varied, generally rich, and worth the extra indulgence. The luncheon menu is a bit lighter but still a major dining experience. Blantyre is the perfect setting for one of those "memorable occasion" celebrations. Though as many as a half dozen restaurants may have their adherents for "the best dining in the Berkshires," Blantyre and neighboring Wheatleigh stand alone in their combination of superlative dining with truly regal surroundings.

BISTRO ZINC
413-637-8800.
www.zincbistro.com.
56 Church St., Lenox, MA
01240.
Price: Moderate to
Expensive.
Cuisine: French Bistro.
Serving: L, D.
Credit Cards: AE, MC, V.
Reservations:
Recommended for dinner
(necessary in summer).
Special Features: Smoking
permitted in separate bar
area.

Bistro Zinc is a popular favorite for both lunch and dinner in the southern Berkshire dining scene. Both the dining room and the commodious separate bar/dining room convey a welcoming atmosphere. The dining room features perimeter banquettes and closely ranked tables in true bistro manner. It is separated from the handsome, more open, bar/dining area by a glass wall, permitting everyone to see everything but allowing the non-smokers in the dining room to breathe undisturbed by the exhalations of the tobacco slaves in the bar.

The dinner menu is classic bistro: mussels marinière, charcuterie; a number of delicious green salads; ten different grilled, roasted, or sautéed entrées; and desserts from selected cheeses to tarte tatin. The wine list is almost all French, moderately priced, and very well chosen. The lunch menu is a bit simpler and lighter and one of the good dining bargains of the Berkshires. As a nice additional touch—not in the bistro tradition—Zinc offers a short but very good kids' menu, complete with kids' drinks and classic birthday cake with ice cream for dessert (adults can order it, too). Everything is served—pleasantly and efficiently—in both dining rooms.

CAFÉ LUCIA
413-637-2640.
90 Church St., Lenox, MA 01240.
Closed: Sun., Mon.
Price: Expensive.
Cuisine: Italian.
Serving: D.
Credit Cards: AE, CB, DC, MC, V.
Reservations: Recommended.
Special Features: Outdoor dining; member, Berkshire Grown.

Café owners Jim and Nadine Lucie preside over this sophisticated but informal restaurant, where Tony May and John Klostermyer serve as chefs. The many regular clients expect and get their popular dishes of Italian pasta and osso buco. Lucia has a fine wine cellar, with an excellent selection of half bottles, which we found useful with one fish and one osso buco between us. Our waitress was friendly, experienced, and very knowledgeable concerning the wine selection.

As is becoming the norm, the antipasti and insalata were substantial—ample for sharing, especially for those who hope to make it to dessert. The roasted baby beet and sugar-snap pea salad was crisp and delicious, and the unbreaded grilled calamari the best we've ever tasted. The only disappointment was the linguine con Melanzane. The sauce was light and fresh, but the slices of eggplant could have been a thicker—a minor complaint considering the delicious other pasta choices such as fresh sea scallops and orrechiette or fettuccine with fresh lobster and peas.

For dessert we recommend egg custard and tarta della Nonna ("grandmother's lemon tart"). *Food and Wine* magazine deservedly recommends Café Lucia, which is a regular stop for local residents and visitors.

THE CANDLELIGHT INN
413-637-1555, 800-428-0580.
www.candlelightinn-lenox.com.
35 Walker St., Lenox, MA 01240.
Rte. 183.
Closed: Wed.
Price: Moderate.
Cuisine: Continental, American.
Serving: L (late June-Labor Day), D.
Credit Cards: AE, MC, V.
Reservations: Recommended.
Special Features: Fireplaces.

The wood-beam ceiling, fireplace, lace-covered French doors, Victorian-style windows, mirrored wall, flickering candles, and soft background music of the Candlelight Inn provide an amiable atmosphere in which to enjoy its pleasing food. With seasoned chef Aggie Ziemek on board, we can be assured that the food will satisfy. For instance, she puts her duck through a lengthy process to remove the fat, leading to a remarkably flavorful but not overwhelming duck confit. This was served, on one visit, with an artistic arrangement of shoestring mixed vegetables and shaped rice. The duck itself was a sculpture on the plate, some pieces sliced, some still on the bone and rising into the air. The corn chowder with bacon was outstanding and an apple-pear crisp with a dab of ice cream a perfect finish—all complemented by the pinot grigio house wine. Furthermore, diners at other tables on the porch were highly complimentary of their entrées. The service was professional, the details well thought through.

In warmer weather, the Candlelight Inn offers dining al fresco in its lovely backyard garden. This leaf-shaded glade is the catbird seat of Lenox. From this perch, diners can watch passersby on Church Street and music pilgrims on their way along Route 183 to Tanglewood.

Judith Monachina

A serious discussion over lunch at the Church Street Cafe in Lenox.

CHURCH STREET CAFÉ
413-637-2745,
    fax 413-637-2050.
65 Church St., Lenox, MA
    01240.
Closed: Sun. and Mon.,
    Oct.–May.
Price: Moderate.
Cuisine: American,
    Regional Eclectic.
Serving: L, D.
Credit Cards: MC, V.
Reservations:
    Recommended.
Special Features: Outdoor
    dining; member,
    Berkshire Grown.

We walk by the Church Street Café in summer to catch the smells wafting over the lively diners on the spacious, shaded deck. In fall, the deck abandoned, we are drawn into one of the three bright dining rooms warmed with desert hues, local art, and, of course, those good smells. The mood is informal, the menu interesting, and the food delicious. The seasonal fall menu featured a luscious, velvety butternut squash soup, sweetened with apple, and finished with a hint of cheddar. A luncheon delight was early autumn chicken stew, richly flavored with roasted chicken breast and garlic, butternut squash, greens, mushrooms, and sage. A favorite of midday diners is "The Real Deal"—a pulled-pork sandwich with homemade barbecue sauce or North Carolina spicy vinegar, with excellent coleslaw and homemade fries.

Dinner entrées range from a classic coq au vin to autumn yam and roasted-onion ravioli with wild mushrooms, glazed shallots, and sautéed greens to seared Japanese sea bass with shrimp raviolis, dashi broth, and steamed greens — and on to a grilled dry-aged top sirloin steak with mashed potatoes and crispy fried onions.

The wine list is interesting. Dessert could be a meal by itself. How about a pumpkin marble brownie sundae with walnut toffee and cinnamon ice cream? Or perhaps a mocha ice cream torte with dark-chocolate sauce? A nice selection of local farmhouse cheeses could also provide a proper ending to a meal well prepared and beautifully presented.

CRANWELL
413-637-1364, 800-272-6935;
    fax 413-637-4364.
www.cranwell.com.
55 Lee Rd., Lenox, MA
    01240.
Rte. 20.
Price: Expensive.
Cuisine: New American,
    French with Asian
    accents.
Serving: B, L, SB, D.
Credit Cards: AE, D, DC,
    MC, V.
Reservations:
    Recommended for SB, D.
Special Features: Member,
    Berkshire Grown.

In the last few minutes of a Technicolor late-autumn sunset, where else to be than at Wyndhurst—the "cottage" of John Sloane, a formal Tudor estate, with gardens by Frederick Law Olmsted—now known as Cranwell. The restaurant serves the condominium resort but also the rest of us in its main dining room, with its cream-colored oval relief ceiling and damask curtains. The fresh flowers and fireplace, together with luxurious seasonal decorations, focus our attention as dusk settles.

Executive chef Carl DeLuce and chef de cuisine Christopher Bonniver know what they are about. Chilled Chilean sea bass with a citrus glaze swam tenderly down the gullet, and a lemon pepper tagliardi pasta dish, with tomatoes, olives, and fresh parmesan cheese—and could it be a hint of garlic?—was just as satisfying. The food was presented neatly but not ostentatiously. Service, as always, was impeccable without being stuffy.

The menu makes the rounds from fish to steak to rack of lamb. Chef concentrates on the artistry of a few selections rather than squandering his talent on a multitude. Appetizers are imaginative, adding significantly to the variety of the menu. Although the elegant wine list is lengthy, a limited selection goes by the glass. *Wine Spectator* magazine praised Cranwell's wine list in 2002. Desserts meet the basic, biological imperative for chocolate or cream. We recommend the chocolate mousse to meet the daily minimum sweetness requirement in a delightful way.

GATEWAYS INN
413-637-2532.
www.gatewaysinn.com.
51 Walker St., Lenox, MA
    01240.

Pearly praise and glittering awards don't always guarantee a good meal. So it is fair to wonder if the Gateways Inn could possibly live up to the accolades it has received from *Gourmet*, *Wine Spec-*

Closed: Mon. off-season.
Price: Expensive.
Cuisine: American.
Serving: B, D.
Credit Cards: AE, CB, D,
   DC, MC, V.
Reservations:
   Recommended.
Special Features: Vegetarian
dishes; outdoor dining;
private dining room; La
Terrazza bar and lounge
serves light meals,
desserts, cocktails;
member, Berkshire
Grown.

tator, and other salivating critics. However, with its graceful service and menu stocked full of Continental knockouts, Gateways more than justifies the acclaim.

Tucked in the front of soap magnate Harley Procter's Victorian cottage, the restaurant blends classic appointments with bright flourishes. Chef Tyson Podolski achieves a similar balance, serving up European-accented dishes sparkling with fresh, seasonal flavors. Fall starters included gnocchi laced with wild mushrooms and pumpkin ravioli garnished with white truffles. A sumptuous slice of foie gras might have lost its way under a glaze of pomegranate honey and scattering of apple chutney, but the sweet and savory tones were delicately balanced.

Main courses tend toward pan-seared meats and fishes as well as the stray pasta. The New York sirloin steak was a modest disappointment, failed mainly by an uninspired béarnaise sauce. However, the inn's trademark rack of lamb was a delight: succulent medallions of lamb served atop a rich mix of cannellini beans and Swiss chard. The justifiably lauded wine list offers an international selection to compliment any dish. Desserts, including a homey apple-cherry crisp, were a fitting end to a meal that balanced sophistication with elegant simplicity.

Despite its fine china and tuxedo-clad wait staff, Gateways betrays nary a bit of stiffness. The meal comes with a healthy dollop of small-town charm: Portions are generous—the gnocchi could easily pass as a main course at some restaurants—and the servers, warm and attentive. The result is a meal that delivers that rare combination of Continental class and country comfort.

LENOX 218
413-637-4218,
   fax 413-232-4205.
www.lenox218.com.
218 Main St., Lenox, MA
   01240.
Rte. 7A.
Price: Moderate.
Cuisine: New American,
   Continental, Northern
   Italian.
Serving: L, D.
Credit Cards: AE, D, DC,
   MC, V.
Handicap Access: Yes.

From the crackling fire, sleek bar, framed prints, spacious room, comfortable chairs, and art deco decor, Lenox 218 is a feast for the eyes as well as the palate. The basket of breads and warm muffins were so irresistibly light and flavorful, they could have been meals in themselves. Wines are varied; service and presentation are attentive and gracious.

Recent entrées by chef Jimmy DeMayo included delectable salmon fillets with red roasted pepper sauce, chicken Parmesan with penne pasta, and an interesting assortment of veal, chicken, duck, and fish. Several vegetarian selections are available, as well.

Desserts such as the toll house nut pie with

chocolate sauce and ice cream and deep dish fruit pies are delectable. Lenox 218 meets expectations.

PANDA HOUSE
413-499-0660.
506 Pittsfield-Lenox Rd.,
  Lenox, MA 01240.
On Rte. 7 and 20, N. of
  town.
Price: Inexpensive to
  Moderate.
Cuisine: Chinese.
Serving: L, D.
Credit Cards: AE, D, MC, V.

This Panda House, not affiliated with other Pandas in the area, is the best Chinese restaurant in the Berkshires. The décor at Panda House may be lackluster, but its Szechuan, Mandarin, and Hunan food is not!

In the previous edition of this book, we suggested trying scallion cakes, should they be offered as a special. A second time around confirms that wisdom—light, crispy, and not too greasy, pan-fried scallion-filled pancakes dipped in a garlic and ginger sauce. Sheer perfection. This time around we tried the house-special vegetables crepes, delicate and airy bean-curd crepes wrapped around an earthy mixture of matchstick vegetables, including shitake mushrooms, jicama, and bamboo shoots. The hot and sour seafood soup—another favorite of ours—was chock full of lobster, shrimp, scallops, an assortment of Chinese mushrooms, crisp sweet snow peas, and silken tofu. The soup goes down smoothly and left us with the perfect afterbite of heat.

All the usual old-time favorites are offered here: The chow mein is full of taste and not the pasty, bland concoction one encounters elsewhere. The sweet and sour chicken is, indeed, quite sweet, but the tender morsels are lightly fried to perfection. For seafood, the crispy sesame shrimp offers giant prawns dredged in lotus flower, fried (not overcooked), and finished with a delicate, pleasingly sweet and very light sesame sauce, all surrounded by steamed broccoli. Also flanked by fresh broccoli, the jumbo chef's special shrimp is topped with a fluffy secret sauce that betrays its origins in orange.

The host is cheerful, the service is friendly and good, and the kitchen puts out meals in a timely fashion—no worries about being late for Tanglewood. There are also plenty of choices for vegetarians. Take-out is always an excellent option.

SPIGALINA
413-637-4455.
80 Main St., Lenox, MA
  01240.
Closed: Tues.
Price: Moderate.
Cuisine: Italian.
Serving: D.
Credit Cards: All major.
Special Features: Member,
  Berkshire Grown.

Those who subscribe to the adage that the three most important factors in determining the success of a business are location, location, and location, will jump to invest in Spigalina. With its Main Street Lenox location and a spacious porch over looking the main drag, Spigalina is easy to find and a perfect vantage point. Though appearing small, the restaurant is actually a series of connected rooms. The exposed beams, tile floor, and ochre walls create a pleasant Mediterranean feeling throughout, while fashionable tourists carrying Prada and Gucci bags add to European ambiance.

The restaurant also promotes its menu as "cuisine reflecting the flavors of the sunny Mediterranean"; while a bit uneven, it succeeds in offering fresh flavors in some eclectic and exciting combinations. A delicious salad of goat cheese wrapped in a bird's nest of shredded phyllolike dough on a bed of spring greens with dried cranberries and nuts was memorable. Monkfish— which seems nearly impossible to find in the Berkshires—was wonderfully prepared, sweet and spicy, on a bed of orzo and fennel. Other entrées included osso buco, pancetta wrapped tenderloin, and a number of pastas, including one with limoncello—an odd liqueur that is ubiquitous in Italy but rarely seen in the States. For dessert we recommend the panna cotta, slightly sweet, melt-in-the-mouth creamy, loaded with vanilla, and topped with fruit.

The wine list is long and well balanced, although not particularly well priced. A fine selection of sherries and ports is also available.

TRATTORIA IL VESUVIO
413-637-4904.
242 Pittsfield Rd., Lenox, MA 01240.
Rte. 7 and 20.
Closed: Mon. in winter.
Price: Moderate to Expensive.
Cuisine: Italian.
Serving: D.
Credit Cards: AE, D, MC, V.
Special Features: Member, Berkshire Grown.

It has been seven years since Anna Arace and her brother Davidé Manzo opened Trattoria Il Vesuvio in a handsomely refurbished barn on the Pittsfield-Lenox Road. When they did, they raised the bar considerably for Italian cuisine in the Berkshires. Brother Davidé has since left to open his own Trattoria Rustica in downtown Pittsfield (hurray for that!), but Il Vesuvio has lost none of its polish and excellence under Anna's solo ownership. It is slightly tricky to find if driving north on Route 7, being partially obscured by earthen bank and foliage on a long downgrade, but well worth looking for. Its high ceilings, wood beams, and warm wood walls create a comfortable, country atmosphere, while Diretorre Rino Coppola's friendly staff and the savory aromas of northern Italian cooking at its finest further conspire to make the diner welcome.

The menu offerings are the usual for a good Italian restaurant: Several excellent antipasti, a dozen pasta offerings (some available as half orders for a first course), and an array of fish, fowl, and meat main courses. Two items constitute house trademarks: delicious, chewy, homemade bread, baked fresh every day by Anna's mother; and the arrosto di vitello, a rolled breast of veal, stuffed with prosciutto and spinach and slow-roasted for several hours until wonderfully tender and flavorful. There are many other excellent options. The frutti di mare—a delectable combination of seafood in a pinot grigio — garlic-tomato broth — begs for a refill of grandma's bread to get every last drop of the fine fish broth. Entrées come with a choice of pasta, creamy and corny homemade polenta, or mashed potatoes. For dessert, the homemade tiramisú is as good as one will find anywhere.

THE VILLAGE INN

413-637-0020, 800-253-0917.
www.villageinn-lenox.com.
16 Church St., Lenox, MA
  01240.
Open: Sat. and Sun. only,
  winter and spring.
Closed: Mon. for dinner,
  summer and fall.
Price: Moderate.
Cuisine: American.
Serving: B, SB, D.
Credit Cards: AE, DC, MC,
  V.
Reservations:
  Recommended.
Special Features: English
  tea Sat. afternoon.

Nestled in the quaint heart of Lenox, the Village Inn offers classic American fare in colonial quarters. Built in 1771, the inn certainly has a cozy charm. Meals are served either in a simply appointed dining room or the warmly lit, glass-enclosed porch.

However, chef John Goslin doesn't get bogged down by history. He enlivens his roster of regional dishes with modest modern twists and bold flavors. Broiled Maine crab cakes were served speckled with chives, while a salad of poached pear and mixed baby field greens was sparked by tangy Stilton cheese and spiced pecans. The requisite pear, however, had the syrupy taste and mushy consistency of canned fruit. The inn's main courses suffered from similarly erratic preparation—their "famous" pecan-breaded breast of chicken arrived smothered in a zesty pile of pecans and Dijon mustard, but the dry chicken nearly spoiled the dish. Portions are also unpredictable: The jumbo shrimp sauté came with a generous bowl of lemony pasta but a mere smattering of shrimp.

Friendly service and an extensive wine list help mitigate these shortcomings, although the small dessert menu, including a perfunctory blueberry torte, ended the meal on a flat note. Only time will tell if the Village Inn can live up to its rich history.

Elegance at Wheatleigh.

Judith Monachina

WHEATLEIGH

413-637-0610.
www.wheatleigh.com.

Proprietors Linfield and Susan Simon are uncompromising perfectionists. Wheatleigh is the product of their quarter-century drive for excel-

Hawthorne Rd., Lenox, MA 01240.
Price: Very Expensive (prix fixe).
Cuisine: Contemporary French.
Serving: L (guests only winter), D.
Credit Cards: AE, DC, MC, V.
Reservations: Required.
Special Features: Fireplaces; private dining room; member, Berkshire Grown. The Library has limited menu, somewhat more moderate pricing.

lence. A complete renovation of the interior over the past three years by distinguished architects Calvin Tsao and Zack McKown has been universally praised for its elegant but unobtrusive blending of the Beaux Arts architecture of the building with clean, modern effects. The reactions of rapturous critics, and much else, can be viewed on Wheatleigh's informative website.

Executive chef Bryce Whittlesey succeeded longtime occupant Peter Platt in 2002 and he has sustained the restaurant's well-deserved reputation as one of the finest anywhere. It can truly be said that Wheatleigh competes on the world, not merely the U.S. or Berkshire, dining scene. The prix-fixe menu changes nightly, but the structure is constant. Dinner is served in four courses, supplemented with several delicious small entremets between courses. There are generally three choices for each course. To this admiring reviewer, the cuisine evokes the best of classic French. Not given to heavy sauces, it relies on the development of natural flavors and is full of imaginative and varied choices. The service is faultless and literally Continental, as the young staff are all European, trained in the rigorous schools of restaurant service there. The wine list has earned Wheatleigh a *Wine Spectator* Award of Excellence every year since 1989—perhaps the longest run for that prestigious honor of any Berkshire restaurant. The wine selections are varied, running toward the finer and more expensive that such food deserves.

For those days and evenings when something less opulent appeals, Wheatleigh has created the Library. Offering a simpler but still beautifully prepared three-course à la carte menu for lunch and dinner with the same array of wines and faultless service, the Library is one of the area's best fine dining options—not inexpensive but wonderful value.

Pittsfield

DAKOTA
413-499-7900,
    fax 413-499-8610.
www.dakotarestaurant.com.
1035 South St. Pittsfield,
    MA 01201
On Rtes. 7 and 20.
Price: Moderate.
Cuisine: American.
Serving: D, SB.
Credit Cards: AE, DC, MC, V.

With its pine walls, raised fieldstone fireplaces, mounted deer and moose heads, and overhanging birch-bark canoes, the Dakota successfully communicates the feeling of a grand hunting lodge. In addition, the restaurant fills its odd spaces and some of its walls with Native American artifacts, all of museum quality. (Some, in fact, come from Andy Warhol's collection.) Spacious and comfortable, well managed and conceived, the Dakota is one of the county's most popular restaurants.

Reservations: Strongly recommended.
Special Features: Fireplaces; member, Berkshire Grown.

With good reason. The restaurant usually operates with clockwork precision, serving an array of steak and seafood dishes that are simply prepared—mesquite-grilled, broiled, or baked—and simply presented. We chose from sirloin steak, pork and lamb chops, prime rib, shrimp, salmon, scallops, and chicken teriyaki, among others. A lobster tank up front offers lobster lovers their pick, with the day's price per pound clearly posted above. The copious salad bar features fresh greens, bean and grain salads, and a variety of marinated vegetables.

All meals come with huge slabs of good, freshly baked whole-grain bread and unlimited salad bar privileges. The wine list offers two dozen popular varieties. Desserts are unabashedly rich and sure to please any chocolate lover (we recommend the chocolate falling cake). In all, with its relaxed atmosphere, moderate prices, and all-you-can-eat Sunday brunch—which includes delicious omelets made to order with an array of ingredients—it's easy to see why the Dakota remains a Berkshire roadside favorite.

DRAGON RESTAURANT
413-442-5594.
1231 W. Housatonic St., Pittsfield, MA 01201.
Rte. 20.
Closed Monday.
Price: Moderate.
Cuisine: Vietnamese.
Serving: D.
Credit Cards: MC, V.
Reservations: Not accepted.

To meet the East, it may be necessary to go west—to Kim Van Huynh's restaurant, nearly as far west on Housatonic Street as Hancock Shaker Village. Offering a variety of delicious Vietnamese and other far-Eastern cuisine, fragrant with lemon grass and filled with delicious contrasts, Dragon is a great place to initiate a novice into the wonderful world of this French-inspired fare. The menu is in English, with clear descriptions of each dish. Portions are generous: A doggie bag will yield not just lunch for the next day but probably dinner, as well.

We began with the requisite spring rolls, offered both vegetarian and not, and a truly mellow lemon grass soup, full of vegetables and chicken. Our favorites entrées include exquisite fried fish; pat Thai (either vegetarian or shrimp), which is loaded with crispy vegetables; vegetable curry, a surprisingly spicy melange of vegetables in red curry sauce; and Shaken beef served on a bed of watercress and tomatoes.

Elegance, no—the tables are covered in plastic cloths—just great food. Kim urges that we allow an hour to eat since he is preparing food to order. Just relax, enjoy some Vietnamese beer, and savor the flavors of this one-of-a-kind cuisine.

ELIZABETH'S CAFE PIZZERIA
413-448-8244.
1264 East St., Pittsfield, MA 01201.

Elizabeth's Borderland Café has added space upstairs yet remains just as good as ever: Good news to those who like pizza, pasta, and enormous salads. Elizabeth's still stands like a tiny beacon

Across from "the G.E."
Price: Inexpensive.
Credit Cards: None.
Special Features: Specialty pizzas; no smoking.

across from the enormous sprawl of the old GE complex. (If heading out from Pittsfield, drivers need to stay on East Street, without being beguiled onto the new bridge.) Elizabeth's accepts "American money, personal checks, and IOUs" but no credit cards. The sentiments expressed on the menu are free.

We started with smooth tomato soup, enlivened by a bit of spice. The salads are superior—for example, the insulata mista is chunked with delicious feta cheese, studded with old world olives, striped with roasted pepper, crowned with slices of kiwi, and supported by a bed of the freshest, youngest, most tender baby salad greens from the heart of the lettuce. The bread is also among the best available hereabouts.

The baked cavatapi Alfredo was in the family of, but a several generations removed from, noodles and cheese: cream, parmesan, mozzarella, and sweet peas under a lovely crust. The pasta cacciatore, this time with a bit of chicken in the sauce, just slides down the gullet until we can't believe how much we ate. We did draw the line at desserts, though, either cheesecake or a chocolate confection.

Chef Tom presides with his accustomed verve. While not obnoxious, he enjoys interaction—especially with those who reveal it is their first visit and choose to sit downstairs.

FRAZIER'S
413-442-0313.
17 Wendell Ave., Pittsfield, MA 01201.
Closed: Mon. and Tues.
Price: Expensive.
Cuisine: New American.
Serving: D.
Credit Cards: MC, V.
Reservations: Recommended.
Special Features: Live music downstairs.

An intimate (30-seat) bistro has opened in the first floor of the old Allen Hotel, further evidence that the words "taste" and "Pittsfield" can be swallowed in one bite. Whoever created the understated decor of wood paneling, fireplace, and pastel appointments has exhibited considerable taste, in fact—which chef/owner Gordy Hebler more than matches with his culinary creations. We enjoyed a succulent portabello Florentine and bowl of light but not exciting mushroom soup; a plentiful, fresh garden salad easily split two ways. The succulent sea bass entrée rested comfortably on a cushion of cannellini beans, spinach, and minced tomatoes, nestled beside a dollop of potato and squash. Hebler likes cooking fish, and they seem to like his treatment. Gourmet turf and surf is the specialty of the house: We had a fine steak and shrimp, in the same environment as the bass. Of the two desserts offered, the linzertorte was delectable, the dark chocolate cake a bit dry.

Frazier's offers many and unusual wines. The house by-the-glass selections of white and red were a fine match for a distinguished meal.

HOUSE OF INDIA
413-443-3262.
122 North St., Pittsfield,
   MA 01201.
Open: Daily.
Price: Inexpensive.
Cuisine: Indian.
Serving: L, D.
Credit Cards: MC, V.

Sitting in the window of this storefront restaurant in Pittsfield, we feel we may have left the Berkshires. A decidedly urban environment replaces the usual bucolic scenery and beautiful vistas. The view out the window and the no-frills decor belie a quite good meal. For an elegant or romantic ambiance other restaurants are a better choice; for a really good meal at a really good price, the House of India is a really good place to dine.

The service is attentive without being fawning, the beer is cold, and, most importantly, the food is perfectly spiced. We are constantly amazed at how the chef reads our minds when it comes to the level of spiciness. At House of India, medium is indeed medium, just hot enough to make us appreciate a bite of cooling raita but not so hot that we must dive for the water pitcher.

While we love to watch the action on North Street, for those not in a mood to speculate on Pittsfield's peculiar blend of characters, take-out is available.

SANGEET
413-445-6700;
   fax 413-445-6789.
26 Cheshire Rd., Pittsfield,
   MA 01201.
Jct. Rtes. 8 and 9, at the
   Pittsfield Travelodge.
Closed: Mon.
Price: Moderate.
Cuisine: Indian.
Serving: L, D.
Credit Cards: AE, D, DC,
   MC, V.
Reservations:
   Recommended for D.
Special Features: Off-
   premises catering.

Sangeet offers the best Indian cuisine in the Berkshires in a most unlikely setting: The former I-Hop (International House of Pancakes) in the Coltsville section of Pittsfield.

A cheerful waitperson brings crispy, peppery pappadums (lentil wafers) to begin the meal and will gladly describe and recommend menu items. We have never been steered wrong. The chef will adjust the spiciness of our meal to our preference.

In the spirit of a masala (a mixture of spices), we like to try a little of this and a little of that. The Sangeet Milan is an ample assortment of vegetable pakoras (fritters) and samosas (cripsy pastry stuffed with potatoes and peas) with a tangy dipping sauce. Any of the breads are an excellent choice, but we favor garlic naan or roti (roasted whole wheat), perfect for offsetting the spiciness of the food. We like the fabulous thali vegetarian sampler, usually featuring aloo gobi palak (potatoes, cauliflower, and spinach, pureed and delicately spiced), baigan bharta (mashed barbecued eggplant cooked with tomatoes, onion and green peas), and an outrageous daal makhani (lentil stew). Fear not: Sangeet also offers samplers for meat-eating folks. The tandoor (clay) oven turns out authentic kababs and tikkas, and the shrimp Madras is excellent—shrimp cooked in a coconut sauce "tempered with mustard and curry leaves." Indian and domestic beers are on the menu, and French wine by the glass.

Our favorite meal is the Sunday buffet—a beautiful, aromatic arrangement of tasty vegetarian, chicken, and lamb dishes—from appetizers to dessert. For a late lunch we settle into a Naugahyde booth, relax to the pulsating sounds of the sitar and tablas, and eat enough for the rest of the day!

SOUTH MOUNTAIN GRILLE
413-499-2075.
1015 South St., Pittsfield, MA 01201.
Price: Moderate.
Serving: SB, D.
Cuisine: American.
Credit Cards: AE, MC, V.

This sprawling, busy restaurant on the east side of Route 7, south of Pittsfield center, seems to be a favorite for regulars, families, and special events (birthday folks can convert their age into a percentage subtracted from their bill). Early-bird specials, before 6pm, also allow for substantial savings. However, the price for such a large-scale operation is generally not cheap.

Yet our experience suggested that the kitchen had little regard for the food. The lettuce in the extensive salad bar appeared to have stayed up too late the night before, the garlic potatoes appeared to have been tossed at the plate from a considerable distance, and the various parts of the chicken cordon bleu, including an unidentifiable sauce, were indistinguishable from one another in flavor. Although the service staff were friendly and efficient, they seemed to have little respect for what they were placing before customers—perhaps rightly so. The roast beef survived preparation and presentation somewhat better. It may be the diner should stick with the grill items.

The bread came in the standard small loaves. South Mountain Grille had a good variety of beer on tap. Desserts included the predictable cheesecake, chocolate cake, and apple turnover. Although we were able to look out a window, the view was of a weed-infested and eroding hillside.

All in all, South Mountain Grille is the closest thing to chain food available in a local independent entity.

TEO'S HOT DOGS
413-447-9592.
1410 East St., Pittsfield, MA 01201.
Price: Inexpensive.
Serving: L, D.
Cuisine: American.
Credit Cards: None.

Teo's is an institution and a local tradition—and home to the tastiest miniature (4 inch) hot dogs smothered in chili sauce we've ever eaten. Friendly controversy rages as to who invented the sauce and when. We don't care; it is enough to know that Teo's is at its present home. We drop by for "the works" (chili sauce, chopped onions, and mustard), washing them down with Genesee Cream Ale or Rolling Rock on tap. Then we stop at the take-out window for a bagful for the crowd at home, who love 'em.

The building that houses this cantina Americana also houses an Italian restaurant, Trattoria Rustica, and a bakery, Daily Bread, in the Central Block on North Street, Pittsfield.

TRATTORIA RUSTICA
413-499-1192.
75 North St., Pittsfield, MA
   01201.
Entrance on McKay St.
Closed: Tues.
Price: Moderate.
Cuisine: Italian.
Serving: D.
Credit Cards: Major.
Reservations:
   Recommended on
   weekends.

Who knew that the basement of the Central Block had been fashioned into a *cave*—stone and brick walls, with lanterns and candles. Not the casual passerby because signs are scarce, and the doors at 75 North are locked at night (enter from McKay Street). Here chef/owner Davidé Manzo, having built his wood-fired oven, serves food prepared with a vast assortment of herbs and inspiring skill. Each thinly sliced zucchini, carrot, and eggplant in the appetizer we shared carried its delicate freight of seasoning, individual and unforgettable. The basciale, a pasta entrée, mated with mushrooms, leeks, and prosciutto before our eyes, while the pollo a la rustica, tender chicken apparently raised on a tasty assortment of cheeses, was less salacious but equally salubrious. Out of the oven in its own dish, by itself it took the chill of a windy evening off the entire corner of one of two dining areas. While the menu carried ample variety, the young waitress recited a dozen specials that were not only enticing but a good test of her Italian. She passed with aplomb.

The homemade bread dipped in olive oil, a fine assortment of desserts—some made on the premises and some imported from Italy—and an intriguing wine list of Italian extraction, including ample selections by the glass for those who want to explore—all of these are features of a new and intriguing restaurant in, of all places, downtown Pittsfield. Summer brings an opportunity for al fresco dining in an adjacent courtyard.

RESTAURANTS IN NORTH COUNTY

Adams

The Silvia Inn in Adams.

Judith Monachina

THE SILVIA INN
413-749-0004.
17 Commercial St., Adams,
  MA 01220.
Rte. 8.
Closed: Mon.
Price: Moderate.
Cuisine: American.
Serving: L, D, SB.
Credit Cards: Major.
Reservations: Appreciated.
Special Features:
  Handicapped accessible;
  accommodations;
  member, Berkshire
  Grown.

What a treat for the town of Adams. What serendipity. Silvia Biurrun visited MASS MoCA, decided the area needed an inn, and found a former mill owner's home/nursing home in Adams that had been unoccupied for several years. Silvia is now a gracious and enthusiastic hostess. The staircase is worthy of Scarlett O'Hara; several fireplaces are large enough to hide a 10-year-old. Silvia has redone her namesake inn tastefully and serves as a chef, presenting excellent, moderately priced food. Furthermore, she has trained her wait staff to be friendly and attentive without being overbearing. The only concerns the night we ate in the library was a draft that crawled along the floor and up our ankles, plus a minimal use of anything to dampen the sound.

The food may not be adventurous, yet crostini—

delectable toast, cheese, and olives—arrived with the menu; French bread later. The soup of the evening was spinach, creamy but not cloying. The salad, which comes with all meals, was leafy green and fresh, with a balsamic vinaigrette dressing. The swordfish steak and the pork were perfectly done, swimming in colorful young carrots and new potatoes. Silvia claims the use of rock salt from Argentina imparts a special flavor. So be it! For dessert, the flan was delectable, as was the berry compote. The wine list departs into Spain and Argentina from the normal France and California; we liked a house Chardonnay from Argentina that admirably seconded the flavor of the food.

New Ashford

MILL ON THE FLOSS
413-458-9123.
342 Rte. 7, New Ashford,
  MA 01267.
Closed: Mon.
Price: Moderate to
  Expensive.
Cuisine: French.
Serving: D.
Credit Cards: AE, MC, V.
Reservations:
  Recommended.
Special Features: Member,
  Berkshire Grown.

The Mill on the Floss provides elegant dining and service in an informal French country style. An open kitchen adorned with hanging copper pots over a country-tile counter is part of the cozy atmosphere also created by massive exposed beams, a large stone fireplace, and blue-and-white patterned rustic china. In winter, a table by the fire fits a romantic event.

Suzanne, daughter of the late chef/owner Maurice Champang, maintains a classic French menu that delights regular diners who love coq au vin and braised sweetbreads in beurre noir. Specialties change with the seasons. Other staples include a starter of richly flavored onion soup baked with lusciously browned Swiss and Parmesan cheeses on top or a delicate crab cake adorned with a Dijon mayonnaise (also an entrée). Several lightly dressed salads of the freshest greens provide additional appetizers. For dinner a sumptuously delicious duck à l'orange with a darkly glazed crackling skin was one choice; another, tornados of beef tenderloin, perfectly cooked and lovingly arranged.

The extensive wine list includes selections from France, Italy, and California. The dessert cart beckoned with la gateau de maison, a densely delicious chocolate cake; tasty apples bursting from puff pastry in the deep-dish apple pie; and creamy crème caramel. Still, the simple sundae of intense coffee ice cream with wonderfully gooey butterscotch sauce attracted us.

North Adams

ELEVEN
413-662-2004.
1111 MASS MoCA Way, N.
  Adams, MA 01247.
Building 11, MASS MoCA.
Serving: L, D.

Nancy Thomas, the successful restaurateur behind Williamstown's Mezze Bistro and Bar, opened Eleven on August 31, 2001, just two weeks after Mezze burned. The happy result of the disaster was that Mezze's talented wait staff were able

Open: Daily, summer, fall;
closed Sun., winter,
spring.
Price: Moderate.
Cuisine: International.
Reservations:
Recommended.
Handicapped Accessible:
Yes.
Special Features: Member,
Berkshire Grown.

to join Eleven. Thomas has a love and talent for design. Eleven is as beautiful as was old Mezze. Thomas describes the decor as "on Prozac." With mint-green flooring, white walls, low gray chairs, a fabulous modulated ceiling that serves to break up the open dining room, plus some soft neons, it is an extremely relaxing environment.

For Eleven, Thomas has continued the tradition of creating combinations of flavors never before imaged, inspired by the bounty of the Berkshires. Firmly committed to using local products, the restaurant is at its peak in summer and fall, when it receives a constant stream of the best vegetables from local farmers. Yet even when there is not a fresh tomato within 1,000 miles, Eleven's chef manages to find great local produce to transform into memorable meals. When in doubt, a visitor can always follow the advice of patty connoisseurs that Eleven serves "the best burger ever eaten." The wine list is reasonable, and for those not interested in an entire bottle, Eleven has a large a good selection of wines by the glass.

GRAMERCY BISTRO
413-663-5300.
24 Marshall St., N. Adams,
MA 01247.
Across from MASS MoCA
parking lot.
Closed: Tues.
Price: Moderate.
Cuisine: International.
Serving: BR, D.
Credit Cards: AE, MC, V.
Reservations: Suggested.

"Gramercy"—that is, "Thank you very much," for providing an unadorned, short-menu bistro with interesting choices and an extensive wine list. One soup, three salads, a few small-helping dishes that might be called meals, and eight or so entrées, ranging from vegetarian to fish to beef and lamb. The basics, with interesting treatments. The house salad was sprinkled with bachelor's buttons. The vegetable with the entrées was spinach. Herbs informed all flavors. Yes, a predictable New York cheesecake for dessert but also apple brown Betty—resurrected from our childhood and served with panache.

MILAN AT 55 MAIN
413-664-9995.
55 Main St., N. Adams, MA
01247.
Closed: Tues.
Price: Moderate.
Cuisine: Italian.
Serving: L, D.
Credit Cards: AE, MC, V.
Reservations:
Recommended.

Having taken the old 55 Main restaurant and softened the ambiance with pastel colors, chef Jack Carlow has created a decidedly upscale venue that nevertheless appeals to local residents. It is another sign of the North Adams renaissance, and, like the other new restaurants, it will have to compete for its market share until either the clientele increases or restaurants fall by the wayside.

Warm bread arrived early on, with oil and a tasty garlic dip. The menu carries almost as many insulata dishes as entrées. They enjoyed a variety of textures, and we enjoyed them. Pasta, meat (mostly veal), and a couple of fish dishes are all tastefully prepared and well presented, based on our own and what we could see on other tables. A well-flavored veal picatta rested on polenta. The nicely prepared beans, carrots, and asparagus were stacked like a snake fence. We shared three good desserts, of which the key-lime cheesecake was most distinctive. The wine selection was varied but not extensive. The wait staff were anxious to please and helpful, even on an unexpectedly busy evening.

Williamstown

CAPTAIN'S TABLE
413-458-2400.
505 Cold Spring Rd.,
  Williamstown, MA
  01267.
Rtes. 2 and 7.
Closed: Tues.
Price: Moderate to
  Expensive.
Cuisine: American.
Serving: D.
Credit cards: AE, D, MC, V.
Reservations:
  Recommended.

For consistently good family dining, we drag our chairs up to the Captain's Table. The generous salad bar, with perfectly cooked shrimp, makes appetizers seem unnecessary, although the selection includes escargot in mushroom caps, clams casino, and steamed little necks. Tots-in-tow keep busy with the salad course until dinner arrives (ordered from a children's menu).

Specializing in seafood and steak, the Captain serves the freshest and dare we say the largest lobsters 120 miles from the ocean. A 14-pounder looked big enough to take on Jabba the Hutt. We enjoyed making a mess cracking the claws and sucking on the legs of some smaller ones. As for the "small" serving of prime rib, the Captain is generous to a fault. (The staff routinely packages leftovers for at-home consumption.) Sirloin (including sirloin teriyaki), chicken parmigiana, baked scrod and halibut, shrimp scampi, fried oysters and clams, and various surf and turf combos—what's not to like?

For those whose stomachs have a chocolate compartment, the mud pie or fudge brownie à la mode should suffice.

**COL. BULLOCK'S
  TAVERN**
413-458-1781.
910 Cold Spring Rd.,
  Williamstown, MA
  01267.
Rte. 7, at the 1896 House.
Price: Moderate.
Cuisine: American.
Closed: Mon.
Serving: D.
Credit Cards: AE, D, MC,
  Transmedia, V.
Special Features: Tavern
  fare

Chef Robert Andrews, formerly chef at the 1896 House Restaurant, now leases Col. Bullock's Tavern, at the same location, tightening up the operation by inserting various members of his family. The service—which was flaky under the previous ownership—is now organized and efficient. The dining room, still featuring the homey, overstuffed chairs, is heavy on atmosphere if a bit noisy; a table by the window or the fireplace is a relaxing and comfortable seat for a pleasant evening.

Col. Bullock's aims to be straightforward and filling, with comfort food and some more adven-

plus main dining room; terrace dining in summer; member, Berkshire Grown.

turesome fare as Chef Andrews expands his menu. Early-to-arrive corn fritters were warm, the salad simple but colorful, beef and lamb entrées adequate. Chicken, veal, tuna, other seafood, and mushroom entrées were also available. The wine list includes a half-dozen options by the glass for mixing and matching. Desserts were tasty if predictable. Groups have begun seeking out the barn's recesses for outings. Reportedly a high point is the summer Friday evening terrace menu—just for the halibut!

HOBSON'S CHOICE
413-458-9101.
159 Water St., Williamstown, MA 01267.
Rte. 43.
Price: Moderate.
Serving: D.
Credit Cards: MC, V.
Reservations:
  Recommended.

Locals know making Hobson's Choice is a good one in Williamstown for a quiet drink, dinner, or a late-evening snack. Dark wooden booths line the walls of the restaurant, creating a sense of intimacy. Hobson's is a comfortable place to linger—especially with the expansion, which now provides an entrance door that doesn't blow cold air on diners.

With owner Dan Campbell playfully holding court from the open kitchen behind the salad bar—one of the tastiest in northern Berkshire—the patron is likely to get a meal custom-cooked just the way she likes it. We were delighted with the chicken Santa Fe, nicely presented with fresh asparagus and seasoned just so. Hobson's offers a wide variety of chicken (grilled, blackened, barbecued, teriyaki, and Santa Fe style), beef, fish, pasta, and vegetarian specialties, all flavorfully prepared. It makes its own soups: An onion soup gratiné is especially good. The desserts are also excellent, especially the mud pie.

A comfortable, well-stocked bar includes a nice selection of imported beers and ales, plus a modest wine list. Espresso and cappuccino provide warmth and cheer for the abstemious.

MEZZE
413-458-0123.
16 Water St., Williamstown, MA 01267.
Rte. 43, jct. Rte. 2 (Main St.).
Price: Expensive.
Cuisine: Fusion.
Serving: D.
Credit Cards: AE, MC, V.
Reservations:
  Recommended.
Special Features: In former general store; member, Berkshire Grown.

It was a sad day in Williamstown when Nancy Thomas's original Mezze suffered a devastating fire in August 2000. Thomas had established a restaurant known for great food and great hospitality. Flowers were left outside the door, and a Website was established devoted to peoples' Mezze memories. While Mezze loyalists were thrilled that Thomas opened a new restaurant, Eleven at MASS MoCA, just 10 days later, they were doubly happy when their old favorite reopened in May 2002, just up the hill from its original Water Street location.

The new Mezze is bigger, but the food, warm greeting, and chic ambiance are welcome holdovers. Thomas and chef Todd Clements emphasize the freshest ingredients and buy locally so that their vegetables glow. Even sophisticated diners find new ingredients and new combinations on the Mezze menu. A peekytoe crab appetizer was beautifully presented as a tower, with layers of tomato, crab, and avocado; while another fish starter was a very tasty hamachi (yellow tail) with jicama. Entrées range from tenderloin to goat cheese stuffed ravioli; or a tasting dish is available ($58 per person), with a morsel of everything on the menu. Desserts are equally sophisticated. The Brillat Savarin (a salty, creamy cheese) with candied pecans and honeyed grapes was worthy of the high recommendation it received from the staff.

The wine list, filled with interesting varieties and excellent values, is large enough to offer diversity but not overwhelming. A surprising number of wines are available by the half bottle.

In the summer Mezze caters to the Williamstown Theatre Festival patrons, so come after they have left for an 8pm curtain.

THE ORCHARDS
413-458-9611.
222 Adams Rd.,
   Williamstown, MA
   01267.
Price: Moderate to
   Expensive.
Cuisine: Eclectic
Serving: B, SB, L, D.
Credit Cards: AE, DC, MC,
   V.
Reservations:
   Recommended.
Special Features: Table
   settings and linens;
   member, Berkshire
   Grown.

Sayed Saleh's Orchards in Williamstown is truly a place to dine for a special night out. The physical setting is elegant and uncrowded. If possible we arrive a little early to enjoy a walk in the garden, which includes a koi pond (with children, this visit is a must). It is such an attractive, quiet setting that it's almost hard to go back indoors for dinner. Sayed usually hires his wait staff from European countries, and the young ladies can be very engaging to talk with. Our server recently was from Bosnia.

For starters we had lomi-lomi (raw tuna) and mint-pickled eggplant, both delicious. For those with a light appetite, either could have been a meal. Since mixed greens were included on the plates, we chose not to order separate, additional salads. Both appetizers were very original in composition and presentation. As main courses we had the Vermont free-range chicken supreme with open faced ravioli, morels, and sugar-snap peas and the yellow tail snapper with a mango-asparagus confit coriander crepe. We especially like a chef who matches individual accompaniments to each main course and does not overwhelm the diner with volume. For a finish we highly recommend the lemon tart.

Prices are on the high side for dinner; however, the wine list includes some good, reasonably priced bottles and includes domestics and imports that span the globe. Wines by the glass are no higher than we have found at most restaurants. Diners with a Williams College connection might want to try a selection from the list of vineyards operated by Williams graduates—maybe even someone you know.

The Orchards is an elegant gem set in north Berkshire County, having won the Five Star Diamond Award from the American Academy of Hospitality Sciences.

Judith Monachina

Pappa Charlie's is a popular place for students and others in Williamstown.

PAPPA CHARLIE'S DELI SANDWICH SHOP
413-458-5969.
28 Spring St.,
Williamstown, MA
01267.
Price: Inexpensive.
Cuisine: American.
Serving: B, L, D.
Special Features: Open late.

Pappa Charlie's reigns supreme as a people's place and local hangout, convenient to Images Cinema and the Williams College gymnasium. It serves sandwiches, chili, and mulled cider. The delicious overstuffed sandwiches—and elaborately adorned, well-stuffed bagels—are mostly named for actors at the Williamstown Theatre Festival, politicians, and other well-known local folks. Anyone for a bite of Blythe Danner? Richard Chamberlain? Kate Burton? James Naughton—or a taste of Zonker Harris for that matter? Or how about an Avocado Smoothie—bagel of choice, spread of cream cheese, slices of avocado—all zapped in the steamer? The philosophical issue is whether or not the dishes are a commentary on the named.

The fresh cider, root beer that traces its roots to the A&W where Charlie Nikitas began, exotic fruit juice combos like strawberry-banana OJ—these are the potable Pappa. The cooler holds one of North County's better arrays of domestic and imported cheeses. The ambiance is created by the friendly service and plain wooden booths. The benches in the small park to the north are a fine alternative; however, the basement has all the charm of a middle-school lunchroom.

TACONIC RESTAURANT
413-458-9499.
1161 Cold Spring Rd.,
 Williamstown, MA
 01267.
Jct. Rtes. 7 and 2.
Price: Moderate.
Cuisine: New England.
Serving: L (Sun. only), D.
Credit Cards: AE, D, MC, V.
Reservations:
 Recommended.
Special Features: Also home
 of Jimmy Dean's
 Catering; member,
 Berkshire Grown.

Deborah Guiden, James Guiden, and Dean Grimes's restaurant provides gracious space for banquets and dependably good food for the wayfarer. The menu, which features a half-dozen veal dishes, revels in its New England environment, serving locally grown produce (Jimmy Guiden's brother farms). Dependable, fun, not exotic: a place to get a good baked potato with sour cream and string beans still crunchy. The main dining room provides an uninspiring view of the Route 7 traffic, but there's a large fireplace to ward off a cool evening. The restaurant attracts local people, drive-bys, and groups.

The soup du jour recently was a savory cream of mushroom. The "original Vermont chicken" was a playful concoction with cinnamon apples and a maple brown sauce. Among the other desserts, the "Taconic pie" is an extraordinarily confection that tests even a chocolate-lover's capacity. The Taconic carries an adequate variety of wines and beer.

THAI GARDEN
413-458-0004;
 fax 413-458-2220.
27 Spring St.,
 Williamstown, MA
 01267.
Price: Inexpensive.
Cuisine: Thai.
Serving: L, D.
Credit Cards: All Major.
Special Features: Take-out.

Aside from the protective Buddha behind the counter and the food served to the guests, Thai Garden makes no attempt to reproduce Thai culture: The decor is solidly in the American diner tradition. The helpful menu, in English, signals the degree of heat of a dish by one, two, or three chili peppers in the margin. The only chili trifecta is the "Drunken Squid."

Our pad Thai—rice noodles, chicken, and shrimp with peanut sauce—was a large helping of tastiness, while the Thai pepper beef (one chili) luxuriated in "the chef's special sauce." Owner Bob Khun explains that, although Thai food is known for its heat, the goal is harmony. We will come back another time to learn how the sweet coconut milk dishes, for example, bring out the more delicate ingredients.

Some Thai desserts, beer, and wine are available.

WATER STREET GRILL
413-458-2175.
123 Water St., Williams-
 town, MA 01267.

The owners of the Freight Yard Pub in North Adams also own Water Street Grill as an upscale outlet. The Tavern side is more like the Freight Yard, with nachos, fajitas, burgers, and sea-

Rte. 43.
Price: Inexpensive to
  Moderate.
Cuisine: Contemporary
  American.
Serving: L, D.
Credit Cards: AE, MC, V.
Reservations:
  Recommended.
Handicap Access: Yes.
Special Features: Tavern;
  expanded menu in Grill,
  with fireplace.

food; open lunch and dinner. (A buffet is a lunch option.) In the Grill (open dinner only) we enjoyed Absolut (vodka) chicken and the special, sirloin tips with mushrooms. The house Chardonnay was above average. The house salad offered a great variety of dressings, and the bread sticks received a bonus for being served warm. Our wait person seemed interested without hovering. All in all, a fine night out for the price.

One caution—or maybe it's an enticement: Overly live acoustics in this all-wood room can turn innocent diners into eavesdroppers.

RESTAURANTS OUTSIDE THE COUNTY

Hillsdale, New York

AUBERGINE
518-325-3412.
www.aubergine.com.
Mail: PO Box 387, Hillsdale,
  NY 12529.
Jct. Rtes. 22 and 23.
Closed: Mon., Tues.
Price: Moderate to Very
  Expensive.
Cuisine: American with a
  French twist.
Serving: D.
Credit Cards: AE, MC, V.
Reservations:
  Recommended.
Special Features: Vegetarian
  dishes; member,
  Berkshire Grown.

Chef/owner David Lawson and his wife, Stacy, preside over Aubergine, offering fine food and lodging in a venue long renowned for both. Trained at London's legendary Gavroche, David is a both a classic hands-on executive chef and a charming and affable host who offers "French-inspired country cooking" and hospitality to a devoted clientele. Aubergine is housed in a handsome 1783 Dutch Colonial mansion in Hillsdale, New York, just outside Berkshire County proper but close enough for easy access—and well worth the trip. The atmosphere is not terribly formal; "high casual" is the suggested standard for attire, although most of the clients seem inclined to put on at least a jacket if not a tie out of respect for the food, the fine wine, and the warm atmosphere that the Lawsons offer.

Like many of Berkshire's finest restaurants, Aubergine incorporates the best of locally produced foods into its menu. Selections are largely in the traditional French vein, imaginatively adapted by David to incorporate more cosmopolitan and contemporary elements, a couscous, a polenta, gnocchi, or shiitake mushrooms. The wine list draws on a cellar that has been there for many years and is one of the deepest and best in the region, featuring mostly fine French and California offerings. Desserts are rich and worth the calories. David's classic soufflés are a signature feature of the restaurant. They must (and should) be ordered at the outset of the meal and are themselves worth the visit.

SWISS HÜTTE
413-528-6200, 518-325-3333;
  fax 413-528-6201.
www.swisshutte.com.
Rte. 23, Hillsdale, NY
  12529.
On Mass. line.
Price: Expensive.
Cuisine: Continental.
Serving: D.
Credit Cards: MC, V.
Reservations:
  Recommended.
Special Features: View of
  ski slopes; seasonal
  outdoor dining; member,
  Berkshire Grown.

We turn sharply back toward Massachusetts at the Catamount ski slopes to dine in something like a chalet, with a lovely deck for warm weather. Swiss Hütte is a comfortable, friendly spot that seems to attract an older clientele—regulars, perhaps. The staff is especially well trained and gracious, good at judging just how far we want to take the discussion of wine—not far—or desserts—at length. Precision and reliability describe Swiss Hütte.

The French onion soup was perfect, down to the cheese cooked to the ceramic pot. The chicken liver pâté was also tasty, including the small onions that accompanied it. About the salad course that followed, let it be said that we got our money's worth in paying $1.50 extra for blue cheese. The pork chops, smothered in delectable toasted-onion flakes, while resting sublimely on Granny Smith apple slices, dreamed of earlier days feasting on apple drops. The halibut, beautifully served on a bed of spinach, delicate tomatoes, and herbs, was tasty and moist—and good for weight watchers. All dishes at the Hütte are beautifully presented.

Management brought in a bard to recite the dessert menu, an extended paean to pleasure. We chose crème brûlée, done to perfection, and a tiramisù with the added touch of a thin layer of chocolate icing.

New Lebanon, New York

**THE PILLARS
  CARRIAGE HOUSE
  RESTAURANT**
518-794-8007;
  fax 518-766-5141.
860 Rte. 20, New Lebanon,
  NY 12125.
Price: Moderate.
Cuisine: Continental.
Serving: D.
Closed: Mon., Tues.
Credit Cards: AE, MC, V.
Reservations:
  Recommended.

The Pillars is a Lebanon Valley institution. Owned and operated by Paul and Patti Bock since 1987, it occupies the former carriage house of the 1834 Abner Haight estate and evokes a strong sense of continuity with the past.

This is a restaurant for a special occasion. From the entrance, flanked by stone pillars, the driveway leads through landscaped grounds decorated with whimsical sculpture and small trees glowing with miniature white lights. The entry hall—with a wood floor, high ceiling, elaborate moldings, and impressive staircase—feels like an inn, which the building was in the 1970s. The many small dining rooms, floral padded-fabric wall coverings, and scent of polished wood create an ambiance of genteel civility. The decoration at Christmas is elaborate, with cheerful figures of carolers grouped in the hall and marching up the stairs.

Dinner begins with a variety of unusual breads, followed by hot popovers served with the first course. The wine cellar, well suited to the menu, stocks New York wines, varietals, and other regionals. Each dish is imaginatively presented and impeccably prepared. The menu blends Continental tradition and international fusion. Oysters Mornay, tournedos Charlemagne, frogs legs provençal or fines herbs, veal Oscar, and chateaubriand maison for two—carved tableside—share the page with grilled sea bass—in a sauce of miso, sake, and nurin, with wasabi and sweet soy—and shrimp fritters in honey and horseradish. Accompaniments, which on a recent occasion included zucchini provençal and potato croquettes with applesauce, are served family style.

Desserts here are a frequent subject of local legends and longings. Chef displays his special creations of spun sugar and chocolate in the entry, including a piano, molded in dark chocolate with white chocolate keys, its top propped up to reveal a creamy, slightly tart raspberry mousse filling—something to think about while enjoying the rest of the meal.

The news that one year (in November) the Pillars was booked for the next eight weekends prompts us all to call *well* ahead for reservations.

Charlemont, Mass.

WARFIELD HOUSE
413-339-6600.
www.warfieldhouseinn
    .com.
200 Warfield Rd.,
    Charlemont, MA 01339.
N. off Rte. 2, E. of the
    Charlemont Inn.
Price: Moderate.
Cuisine: Austrian.
Serving: B (for guests), L, D.
Closed: Mon.–Wed.
Credit Cards: AE, D, MC, V.
Reservations:
    Recommended.
Special Features: View;
    function room.

Good news: After being closed and put up for sale, the Warfield House, with its spacious dining rooms and 20-mile view, is again open for business. Windows in the main dining room look out on the Deerfield Valley and the slopes of Berkshire East Ski area, while a stone fire place arises on another wall. The farm has been in owner John Warfield Glaze's family since 1868. Going east on Route 2, it is hard to find the road until driving by it once.

We admit a bias for a barn with a view, a half hour or so from Berkshire. The affable executive chef, Jonathan Krock, has tilted the menu toward his family's Austria, with a trace of other European flavors. We enjoyed an Alsatian cassoulet, based on white beans, with sausage, duck, and lamb, and a tasty veal with onions and mushrooms. The food was arranged on the plate with an eye to color and variety. Appetizers included Camembert, smoked trout, and baked onion soup with Muenster. Diners choose desserts Viennese style, from a tray: no shortage of chocolate and an intriguing marzipan cake. While the wine list is not extensive, a carafe of merlot was appropriate to the occasion.

BREAKFAST & LUNCH

Of the many Berkshire eateries designed to gladden morning and noon, we have selected a handful. As is appropriate, almost all are on the inexpensive end of the scale.

BLUEBERRIES (405 Stockbridge Rd., Gt. Barrington, MA 01230)

Open from 7am to 2pm except Tuesdays, Blueberries offers all-American breakfasts, including bakery treats, with plenty of cholesterol options for bacon, ham, sausage, home fries, and, of course, eggs.

BREWHAHA! (413-664-2020; 20 Marshall St., North Adams, MA 01247)

Brewhaha! presents a menu of coffees, muffins, wraps, soups, grilled sandwiches, and desserts that is changeable to "maintain the brouhaha in Brewhaha!" At this coffee bar and café, within walking distance of MASS MoCA, small groups munch pannini while singles sip coffee as they work their laptops. Others dash in for a take-out latte and bagel. Chef/owner Barry Garton wraps fluffy eggs, ham, cheese, and tomato in a large tortilla as his wife, Nancy, bakes fresh, tasty muffins. Member, Berkshire Grown (closed Wednesday).

CAFFE POMO D'ORO (413-232-4616; 6 Depot St., W. Stockbridge, MA 01266)

A bit more upscale (and expensive) than others in this section, Caffe is dining proof that good things come in small packages: eight small tables in a portion of an old train station. Tough to find a seat on a Sunday morning (closed Tuesday and Wednesday in winter).

CAROL'S (413-637-8948; Franklin St., Lenox, MA 01240)

Serving in what was formerly an elder services center, Carol's offers scant ambiance but good and popular down-home food, especially including Carol's own homemade seven grain and sourdough breads baked daily and offered for breakfast toast and sandwich wrappers. Breakfast is served all day, highlighted by imaginative pancake and omelet options and justly famous home fries. Lunch features big and tasty sandwiches, plus a good number of hearty vegetarian selections.

CHEF'S HAT (413-458-5120; 905 Simonds Rd., Williamstown, MA 01267; Rte. 7, N. of town center)

Packed every lunch, serving breakfast early enough for hunters, serving occasional weekend dinners, the Chef's Hat has a formula that clearly works. From truck drivers to Williams College academics, it has a true, eclectic clientele. Booths, tables, and counter, Chef's Hat serves solid, reliable, inexpensive breakfast and luncheon foods to regulars and even outsiders, without making them feel conspicuous.

COURT SQUARE BREAKFAST & DELI (413-442-9896; 95 East St., Pittsfield, MA 01201)

Lawyers, judges, and politicians in the county seat mostly turn up at the Court Square for breakfast. And it's a good breakfast, too: eggs, French toast, omelets—just about anything these folks need before sitting through a long day of weighty matters. They may get to be a bit more weighty, too, but satisfied.

ELM STREET MARKET (413-298-3040; 4 Elm St., Stockbridge, MA 01262)

Now owned by the Red Lion Inn, ESM continues to offer a classic lunch counter, much favored by Stockbridge locals. It serves a tasty chili and two good soups daily. The sandwiches are as filled as a hungry person wants them to be, including the hearty special.

THE GASLIGHT CAFÉ (413-528-0870; Rte. 23, S. Egremont, MA 01258)

Yankee magazine loves the Gaslight. So do parents with kids and sentimental- ists of all ages. The food is always fun—well-prepared sandwiches, burgers, omelets, and pancakes. The ambiance overflows to the patio and brook below. Member, Berkshire Grown.

JACK'S HOT DOGS (413-664-9006; 12 Eagle St., N. Adams, MA 01247)

Jack's Hot Dogs holds its historic position as *the* place to get hot dogs in north county. Continuing a 70-year family tradition, owner Jeff Levanos and man- ager Maria Carmain provide a continuous flow of hot dogs, plain and fancy, with rapid-fire conversation accompanying the bustle behind the counter. Whether pressed against the wall waiting for an order to go or wedged on one of the 12 stools along the counter munching hot dogs and fries, customers are experiencing a lively bit of history.

JUICE N' JAVA (413-243-3131, 60 Main St. Lee; 413-499-6130, 216 Elm St., Pitts- field, MA 01201; 413-684-5080, 661 Main St., Dalton, MA 01226)

Coffee, juices, plus salads and sandwiches to eat in or take out.

MAIN STREET CAFÉ (413-298-5465; 40 Main St., Stockbridge, MA 01262)

Theresa offers a full and diverse breakfast menu, from ham and eggs to break- fast burritos, and an extensive selection of luncheon choices. The roomy, rustic dining area with a large window onto Main Street is a pleasant setting for tasty fare. Member, Berkshire Grown.

MARTIN'S (413-528-5455; 49 Railroad St., Gt. Barrington, MA 01230)

Martin's is bright and light, serving breakfast all day. Omelets are varied and outstanding. Pancakes come standard plus the daily special, such as pumpkin. For lunch, burger styles include the Berkshire cheeseburger (mushrooms, onion, tomatoes, and peppers), sandwiches, salads, soups, and specials. Beer plus the usual. Crayons at every table so that artists can illustrate on their placemats, with true talent ending up on the wall. Member, Berkshire Grown.

DINING IN

From the freshest sweet corn at the farm stand, raced from purchase to pot, to the latest imported gourmet specialty appearing by candlelight on a Tanglewood picnic blanket, Berkshire supplies food that ranges from pure and simple to sophisticated and innovative. The food and beverage purveyors listed below are sources for baked goods, coffee and ice cream, produce and other farm products, picnic provisions, and health and gourmet food. The surprising array of unique food specialties created and produced in the Berkshires is listed at the end of the chapter.

BAKERIES

European pastries, New York bagels, French baguettes, and grandma's pies: Breads and baked goods from Berkshire bakeries offer the staff of life and all its variations. Many of these bakeries also provide dining areas.

Bagel Smith (413-243-4041; 33 Park St., Lee, MA 01238) Tucked in the plaza behind Dunkin' Donuts, this spot offers bagels, sit-down breakfast and lunch, and more.

Bagels Too (413-499-0119; 166 North St., Pittsfield, MA 01201) Huge assortment of bagels and pastries; coffee to go or drink in. This place bustles on a weekday morning as folks head to work.

Clarksburg Bakery, Inc. (413-458-2251; 37 Spring St., Williamstown) Heather's bread is the staff of life; eschewing the most fancy, gooey stuff, she provides sustenance plus cookies and sticky buns. Member, Berkshire Grown (closed Monday in winter).

Cakewalk Bakery & Café (413-243-2806; 56 Main St. Lee, MA 01238) For a gourmet sweet or a light lunch, Lee rejoices in this new arrival.

Daily Bread (413-528-9610, 17 Railroad St., Gt. Barrington, MA 01230; also 413-298-0272, 31 Main St., Stockbridge, MA 01262; also 413-499-3441, 75 North St., Pittsfield, MA 01201) Give us our daily bread: real crusty sourdough French baguettes fresh out of the oven plus almond crescent cookies, hazelnut torte, sticky buns, and other necessities of life (closed Sunday).

Neville's Donut Shop (413-663-5855; 149 Eagle St., N. Adams, MA 01247) This bakery exists to show that real doughnuts taste much better than simulated confections of national chains. Early hours; closed during parts of the day. Worth a call ahead.

Judith Monachina

Suchèle Bakery in Lenox provides welcome tastes and smells.

Suchèle Bakers (413-637-0939; 27 Housatonic St., Lenox, MA 01240) Geraniums in the window, Victorian accouterments inside, and tarts and tortes, sticky buns, muffins, wholesome bread, pastries, cakes, fresh fruit pies, and more, baked daily (closed Monday off-season).

Sweet Pea & Petunia (413-528-7786; 325 Stockbridge Rd., Gt. Barrington, MA 01230) Baked goods, sandwiches and wraps made to order, and quiche. Also serves sit-down meals and homemade ice cream.

COFFEE SPECIALISTS

A sunny spot in front of the Appalachian Bean in North Adams.

Judith Monachina

Appalachian Bean (413-663-7543; 67 Main St., N. Adams, MA 01247) A pleasant spot for a quick sip or leisurely drink, the chairs in and tables out provide for ideal people-watching.

Barrington Coffee Roasting Co., Inc. (413-528-0998; 955 S. Main St., Gt. Barrington, MA 01230) Coffees from all over the world, available at the touch of a faucet.

Berkshire Bistro (413-442-4226; 44 West St., Pittsfield, MA 01201) Offers coffee (Seattle's best) and light breakfast fare Monday–Friday from 7am; Saturday from 9am. Lunch is the main meal served Monday–Saturday, plus specialty sandwiches and desserts until 9pm. Take-out service and gourmet coffees to serve at home.

Berkshire Coffee Roasting Company (413-528-5505, 286 Main St., Great Barrington, MA 01230; also 413-637-1606, 52 Main St., Lenox, MA 01240) A top choice for exceptional coffee in an unpretentiously funky setting, conducive to the related activities of conversation, relaxing, people-watching, reading, or admiring the latest art exhibit on the walls. Choose from a selection of coffee flavors plus cappuccino, espresso, hot chocolate, cookies, muffins, and biscotti (try the chocolate-covered variety). Bags of coffee beans are for sale. The popular coffee take-out setup thoughtfully provides raised lids for preserving the foam on the cappuccino.

Cold Spring Coffee Roasters, Ltd. (413-458-5010; 47 Spring St., Williamstown, MA 01267) More than 60 varieties of specialty coffees are roasted on the premises here (and there are 25 varieties of loose teas). Cappuccino, latte, or espresso can be accompanied by ice cream and baked goodies in a café atmosphere—or take out.

Roasting their own beans and serving a loyal clientele, the Berkshire Coffee Roasting Company is a popular Main Street spot in Great Barrington for locals and tourists.

Judith Monachina

Sip of Seattle (413-528-6913; 343 Main St., Gt. Barrington, MA 01230) Shares space with the deli, offers coffee and espresso drinks, and great pannini (hot sandwiches made in a press).

FARM, ORCHARD, AND PRODUCE MARKETS

Fresh tomatoes right off the vine, crisp and juicy apples, enormous heads of organically grown lettuce—bounty from Berkshire fields and hills is available at area produce markets, farm and orchard outlets, seasonal farm stands, and farmers' markets, where area growers truck in their harvests to a central outdoor location one or two days a week. Homegrown is potent, as in the restaurants that have enrolled in the Berkshire Grown program. Sources of non-Berkshire produce throughout the county—for those occasions when only kiwi fruit or bok choy will do—are listed, as well.

The *Berkshire County Extension Service* (413-448-8285; 44 Bank Row, Pittsfield, MA 01201) and *Berkshire Grown* (413-528-0041; 22 Railroad St., Gt. Barrington, MA 01230) can provide up-to-date information on seasonal farm stands and farmers' markets.

Bartlett's Orchard (413-698-2559; Swamp Rd., Richmond, MA 01254) "Buy 'em where they grow 'em." Apple varieties throughout the season include Empire, Macs, Delicious (Red and Golden), Cortland, Northern Spy, Macoun, Ida Red, Jonagold, and more. Each variety is labeled with a

---

Farmers' Markets

Farmers' markets, where local growers set up temporarily to offer this week's freshest harvest, have sprung up throughout the county. Held from June to the first frost, for the markets' days, times, and locations check a newspaper or the extension service (413-448-8285). In *Pittsfield*, the Allendale Shopping Center hosts a market on Wednesday and Saturday mornings, and downtown Pittsfield sets up an open-air market on Columbus Avenue on Friday. In *Great Barrington*, the Farmer's Market is Saturday from 8:30am to 12:30pm in the yard of the old train station, with vegetables plus local cheeses and hand-crafted products related to farming. In *Lee*, Friday 12-6, next to the post office, find fresh seafood (Vic's), herbs, veggies, flowers, and more. In *Williamstown*, on Saturday morning July through September, local farmers set up in the parking lot at the foot of Spring Street.

---

description of its distinct flavor and best use. Bartlett's own cider is all natural and preservative free. The shop also stocks an array of apple products and other country-gourmet condiments and preserves; the bakery offers doughnuts, turnovers, and pies.

Burgner's Farm Products (413-445-4704; Dalton Division Rd., Pittsfield, MA 01201) The turkey farm is a neighborhood gathering place for fresh produce, including "Burgner's own," especially its corn in-season, plus other fruits and vegetables from local farms and farther afield. Eggs, chicken, and turkey products are a specialty.

Chenail's Farmstand (413-458-4910; Luce Rd., Williamstown, MA 01267) Not easy to find since corn huskers must follow Luce Road partway up to Mt. Greylock, but the corn and other vegetables Chenail's puts out are tastefully fresher than those at stands not on the farm. The farm stand should not be confused with **Chenail's Farm Fresh Products** (413-458-4737; 903 Simonds Rd., Williamstown, MA 01267; Rte. 7), which offers corn, plants, crafts, and seasonal decorations.

Corn Crib (413-528-4947; Rte. 7, Sheffield, MA 01257) Farm-raised produce plus that of other local farmers—fresh fruit, veggies, plants, perennials. **Carol's Cookery** has homemade pastries, soup, and bread; **Dolls & Dwellings** offers dolls, supplies, doll houses, miniatures, dried flowers.

Green River Produce & Stables (413-458-2470; 2480 Green River Rd., Williamstown, MA 01267; at the Five Corners) Lovely new farm stand with attractively displayed local produce, pick-your-own strawberries, and apple trees coming along.

Guido's Fresh Marketplace (413-442-9909; 1020 South St., Pittsfield, MA 01201; Rte. 7; also 413-528-9255; 760 S. Main St., Gt. Barrington, MA 01230) A fine place to buy vegetables and fruit in the county, with local produce in-season and a multicultural array of standards and exotics from all over the world year-round—baby carrots, cilantro, radicchio, endive, fresh herbs, oriental vegetables, tropical fruits, mushrooms. A true marketplace ambiance with distinct Guido touches: the signs posted at the carefully arranged but overflowing produce bins are polite and informative, and help carrying bags out to the car is available. Also at Guido's Pittsfield are **Berger's Bakery and Deli, Mazzeo's Meat Center, Masse's Seafood,** and **Pasta Prima** (described in the appropriate categories below) plus all sorts of cooking supplies, health foods, earth-conscious cosmetics, gourmet items, candles, baskets, Guido's T-shirts. Also at Guido's Gt. Barrington, **Masse's** (including sushi), **Mazzeo's, Bella Flora** florist, and **The Kitchen Store.**

Jaeschke's Brothers Farms (413-743-3896; West Rd., Adams, MA 01220) In spite of a fire at the orchard on West Road, do-it-yourselfers can pick apples and pears at the orchard after the pro pickers have been through, or pick up apples and cider any time. The farm store is in Pittsfield, 736 Crane Ave., near Allendale (413-443-7180).

Taft Farms in Great Barrington draws customers to its fresh produce.

Judith Monachina

Taft Farms (413-528-1515; Rte. 183 & Division St., Gt. Barrington, MA 01230) Taft Farms's own delicious produce in-season, including potatoes, tomatoes, peppers, broccoli, cucumbers, and their famous just-picked sweet corn. It's all grown according to the Integrated Pest Management system, which minimizes or eliminates the use of pesticides. Taft also offers fruit and vegetables from other climes, such as radicchio, kiwi fruit, or pomegranates. Pasture-raised chicken, baked goods, jams and jellies, cider, Taft salsa, and seafood from the fish market (Thursday–Saturday); flowers and plants from the greenhouse, too.

GOURMET & DELI MARKETS & CATERERS

The small grocery markets and specialty food shops and caterers of the Berkshires will please the palates of just about everyone, from the classicist to the experimenter. These markets and food specialists combine the latest culinary styles with ethnic traditions and personal service, and also magnificently

Picking Your Own Fruit

A berry or apple picking expedition is a great way to enjoy the Berkshire country-side, while gathering the makings for a special dessert, muffin, or pancake breakfast. Blueberries in particular are available wild throughout these hills, but few natives will reveal their special picking spots. Call ahead at the following farms and orchards for picking conditions.

Blueberries abound at **Blueberry Hill Farm,** which offers 320 acres for family picking from late July until frost (East Street, 7 miles up the Mount Washington ridge; call 413-528-1479 for a recorded message about the status of picking). At **Strawberry Acres** (413-655-2672; off Route 8, Hinsdale) there are blueberries and Christmas trees, too. Three acres of **strawberries** are at **Crooked Row Farm** (413-698-2608; Dublin Rd., Richmond, MA 01254). Strawberries can also be picked at **Ioka Valley Farm** (413-738-5915; 3475 Hancock Rd., Hancock, MA 01237; Rte. 43) and **Green River Produce** (413-458-3112; 2480 Green River Rd., Williamstown, MA 01267). **Apples** at **Windy Hill Farm** (413-298-3217; Rte. 7, Gt. Barrington, MA 01230) are waiting to be picked in-season; there's also a garden shop and nursery (open April–October).

Maple Sugar and Syrup

Turner Farms Maple Syrup in Egremont.

Judith Monachina

Maple sugaring and syrup making is a Berkshire tradition. Watch the process, or participate at the following places during the season (usually March), or just pick up some of the final product at any time of year. Williams College's **Hopkins Forest** (413-458-3080; Northwest Hill Rd., Williamstown, MA 01267) usually demonstrates sugaring off. **Sunset Farm Maple Products** (413-243-3229; Tyringham Rd., Tyringham, MA 01264) has an open sugar house. **Turner Farms Maple Syrup** (413-528-9956; Phillips Rd., S. Egremont, MA 01258): The sugar shack operation is open to the public; groups of 15 or more should make appointment for a tour. Other sources of local maple products include **Gould Farm's Roadside Store and Café** (413-528-2633; Rte, 23, Monterey, MA 01245); **Holiday Farm** (413-684-0444; Rte. 9, Windsor, MA 01270); and **Mill Brook Sugar House** (413-637-0474; 317 New Lenox Rd., Lenox, MA 01240).

maintain the celebrated Berkshire custom of the gourmet picnic. There's an old-time country store or two thrown in, too.

A Mano Café (413-698-8698; 2089 State Rd., Richmond, MA 01254) An upscale café underneath the Richmond Store (both have fine cheeses): Pannini, roasted chicken, sandwiches, salads; fancy baked goods; eat in or take out, 8am–6pm except Tuesday.

Arugula (414-458-2152; 25 Spring St., Williamstown, MA 01267) Argentinean tasty take-out.

Kate Baldwin (413-698-2885; 630 Dublin Rd., Richmond, MA 01254) Those in the know, know that Kate provides for some of the best catered events.

Berger's Specialty Foods (413-442-1898; 1020 South St., Pittsfield, MA 01201; at Guido's) Some assert that the best baguettes to be found in the Berkshires are here; others avoid the controversy by selecting from the abundant variety of cheeses, crackers, condiments, pasta and other salads, and gourmet items from far and wide. Berger's also caters and does gift baskets.

La Bruschetta (413-232-7141; 1 Harris St., W. Stockbridge, MA 01262) Offers gourmet catering.

Caffe Pomo d'Oro (413-232-4616; 6 Depot St., W. Stockbridge, MA 01266) Gourmet provisions and a café in a sunny room in West Stockbridge's small-scale downtown. Cheese and deli items, bread, imported gourmet foods, even their own gourmet vinegar. Catering. Member, Berkshire Grown.

Canteen (413-664-4415; 139 Ashland St., N. Adams, MA 01247) A restaurant known for simple, tasty food also caters.

Cheesecake Charlie's (413-528-7790; 271 Main St., Gt. Barrington, MA 01230) Toasted Almond, Creamsicle, Piña Colada, Peppermint Patty—these are only a few of the cheesecake flavors that you can get here. Available in different sizes, and the store ships, too. Breakfast, lunch, dinner, or a break for a cappuccino or a healthy, refreshing blast from the well-stocked juice bar. Member, Berkshire Grown.

Chez Vous Catering (413-298-4278; Box 1162, Stockbridge, MA 01262) Elegant food beautifully presented, including Oriental roast beef, Madeira chicken, lentil-salad plates, and desserts.

Gorham & Norton (413-528-0900; 278 Main St., Gt. Barrington, MA 01230) This authentically old-fashioned market has up-to-the-minute good things: groceries, gourmet items, imported cheese, an excellent wine selection.

Helen's Place (413-458-1360; 60 Spring St., Williamstown, MA 01267) Specialty food, restaurant, some catering, take-out—with a juice bar, fresh fish, poultry, Helen's is ready for almost anything.

Hickory Bill's Bar-B-Que (413-663-6665; 20 Holden St., N. Adams, MA 01247) Bill offers the best ribs for the best price in Berkshire.

The Marketplace (413-528-5775; 760 S. Main St., Gt. Barrington, MA 01230; at Guido's) Take out a complete fine restaurant meal, lunch or dinner. A variety of salads, hot and cold, fish, cold cuts, and more are also take-out ready. All explained and served up with enthusiasm and panache.

Monterey General Store (413-528-4437; Rte. 23, Monterey, MA 01245) Not necessarily a gourmet shop but an established oasis in southeastern Berkshire, this old-time general store stocks fresh vegetables, cold cuts, preserves, and locally made maple syrup. It offers fresh-baked goods daily. With a lunch room in the back and a front porch for people-watching, this spot is a perennial gathering place.

Picnic Provisions

The Berkshires are ideal picnic territory, whether the context for al fresco dining is a hike, an all-day canoe trip, or the prelude to an outdoor performance at the Mount or Tanglewood. The picnic may start with turkey and end with ice cream, but the picnic specialists listed here also offer many other options. And, of course, the picnickers can provision the picnic themselves at any of the markets and gourmet shops described above.

Cheesecake Charlie's makes a special New England Clambake Picnic for Two, which includes lobster, mussels, clams, shrimp, corn on the cob, melon, and bread. *Moore Fine Food* (see under "Gourmet & Deli Markets & Caterers") will provide an unforgettable picnic. *Perfect Picnics* (413-637-315; 72 Church St., Lenox, MA 01240) offers gourmet dishes and will deliver to Tanglewood. *The Marketplace* (see under "Gourmet & Deli Markets & Caterers") will customize a gourmet picnic, with 24 hours' notice. *The Red Lion Inn* (413-298-5545; 30 Main St., Stockbridge, MA 01262) offers pick-up picnics, too. *Samel's Deli & Catering* (see under "Gourmet & Deli Markets & Caterers") has boxed meals ideal for portable dining. *The Store at Five Corners* (see under "Gourmet & Deli Markets & Caterers") will pack a picnic from its deli.

Moore Fine Food (413-637-0336; PO Box 85,Lenox, MA 01240; also 413-528-4500; 148 Main St., Gt. Barrington, MA 01230) Some say the best in the county for catering; she also does elegant take out.

Samel's Deli and Catering (413-442-5927; 115 Elm St., Pittsfield, MA 01201) Bread, chicken, wine, cheese, pepperoni, legendary pickles, and much more in the deli and gourmet line. It delivers in the Pittsfield area.

Store At Five Corners (413-458-3176; 6 New Ashford Rd., Williamstown, MA 01267; jct. Rtes. 7 and 43) Upscale country store, with well-chosen wine and beer selections, juices and waters, imported and domestic cheeses, fresh-baked breads and treats. Also homemade fudge, picnic and gift baskets, gifts, fresh produce, deli items such as sandwiches and salads, fancy preserves, gourmet coffee and ice cream, and various international offerings. Breakfast and light fare on the deck or inside. It will ship and cater.

Other area restaurants or markets with catering services include the *Castle Street Cafe, Harry's Supermarket, Michael's Restaurant, The Silver Screen*, and the *Sweet Basil Grille.*

A Place for Pasta

Pasta Prima (413-499-7478; 1020 South St., Pittsfield, MA 01201; at Guido's; also: 413-528-3755; 740 Main St., Gt. Barrington, MA 01230) Fresh pasta made on the premises. Cut to order or purchased in sheets for cutting at home. Selection of other pastas of the dried variety, sauces, and Parmesan and Romano cheese for grating.

HEALTH/NATURAL FOOD STORES

Berkshire Co-op Market (413-528-9697; 37 Rosseter St., Gt. Barrington, MA 01230) Open to the public, but co-op members get a 2 percent discount. Ingredients for healthy eating and living, including organic produce, much of it grown locally, and baked goods, macrobiotic foods, bulk pasta, beans, grains, and herbal remedies.

Clearwater Natural Foods (413-637-2721; 11 Housatonic St., Lenox, MA 01240) Fresh bread, sandwiches, a wide range of groceries, including macrobiotic and allergy-free selections; organic produce, non-dairy and dairy ice cream. Look for monthly specials.

Locke, Stock, and Barrel (413-528-0800; 265 Stockbridge Rd., Gt. Barrington, MA 01230; Rte. 7) Where health food meets gourmet food, artfully and abundantly arranged: a large selection of cheeses, and cold cuts, fish, honey, teas, yogurt, juices, fresh tofu, flours, grains, rices, and soy and tamari sauces. There's a wall-length case of frozen health foods, and vitamins, mineral supplements, and natural cosmetics.

Sprout House (413-528-5200; 284 Main St., PO Box 1100, Gt. Barrington, MA 01230) Steve Meyerowitz, the "Sproutman," has sprouting kits and books, indoor vegetable kits and organic seeds; via mail order and wholesale.

Sunflowers Natural Foods (413-243-1775; 42 Park St., Lee, MA 01238) Organic and natural items include bread, coffee, fat-free snacks, and natural personal-care items; products are available here that are wheat-free, gluten-free, sugar-free. Vitamins, books, health video club.

Wild Oats Community Market (413-458-8060; Rte. 2, Colonial Shopping Center, Williamstown, MA 01267) Organic and local produce, whole foods, gourmet and specialty items, vitamins, natural cosmetics along with food and health books and magazines. Members get discounts, but the public is welcome; the offerings appeal to a wide audience.

ICE CREAM

Berkshire-made ice cream, plus that of those two guys from Vermont, can be found in strategic locations throughout the county. Reliably delicious, Massachusetts' own *Friendly's* ice cream, in cones, containers, and sundaes, is also available at one of the many Friendly's restaurants in the county.

Ben & Jerry's Ice Cream (413-448-2250; 179 South St., Pittsfield, MA 01201; also 50 Water St., Lee, MA 01238) Vermont's famous ice cream, in cones, cakes, sundaes, and containers; also frozen yogurt. Worth standing in line for.

Berkshire Ice Cream (413-232-4111; 4 Albany Rd., W. Stockbridge, MA 01266) High Lawn Jersey cows produce the county's own premium ice cream, sold in specialty shops.

Bev's Homemade Ice Cream (413-637-0371; 38 Housatonic St., Lenox, MA 01240; also 413-528-6645; 5 Railroad St., Gt. Barrington, MA 01230) Bev's is made daily on the premises and comes in traditional to exotic flavors; ice cream sodas and sundaes, malteds, and egg creams, plus coffee and baked treats.

Jilly's Ice Cream (413-499-2961; 119 Elm St., Pittsfield, MA 01201) We can enjoy our ice cream, working it off at Jilly's miniature golf.

Lickety Split, an ice cream shop in Williamstown, is a restaurant in the Massachusetts Museum of Contemporary Art. Also at MASS MoCA is a stylish bistro, Eleven.

Judith Monachina

Lickety Split (413-458-1818; 69 Spring St., Williamstown, MA 01267) With Herrell's Famous Ice Cream from Northampton, Lickety Split is a great day or evening; hot soup in the winter. Also serves light fare at MASS MoCA. Member, Berkshire Grown.

Rita Marie's Ice Cream (413-448-2742; 685 S. Main St., Lanesborough, MA 01237) Rita Marie's is the colorful shack across from the north end of Lake Pontoosuc.

Utter Delight (413-644-9100; 684 Main St., Gt. Barrington, MA 01230) Featuring Berkshire Ice Cream and other brands.

MEAT, FISH, & POULTRY MARKETS

Burgner's Poultry Farm (413-445-4704; Dalton Division Rd., Pittsfield, MA 01201) Burgner's raises and sells turkeys and chickens; order them uncooked, roasted, or stuffed and roasted, in all sizes. Burgner's turkey pot pies are local favorites. The farm store also carries eggs, produce, and store-made bakery items and fresh homemade potato salad and Cole slaw.

Masse's Seafood (413-528-4913, 760 S. Main St., Gt. Barrington, MA 01230; also 413-499-3474; 1020 South St., Pittsfield, MA 01201; at Guido's) A variety of fresh and frozen former denizens of the sea.

Mazzeo's Meat Center (413-528-4488; 760 S. Main St., Gt. Barrington, MA 01230; also 413-442-2222; 1020 South St., Pittsfield, MA 01201). Meat concessions at both Guido's. Carnivores need seek no further.

Otis Poultry Farm (413-269-4438; Rte. 8, Otis, MA 01253) CUSTOM LAID EGGS says the sign— eggs and chickens, geese, ducks, and capons, too. Their excellent frozen chicken and turkey pies are a staple of well-stocked Berkshire refrigerators. Various homemade goodies join sheepskin gloves and slippers and so forth in the country store.

Pizza

Pizza cravings will be easily satisfied anywhere throughout Berkshire County, but all pizzas are not created equal. Top choices or choices of toppings) include the following:

Babalouie's Sour Dough Pizza Co. (413-528-8100; 286 Main St., Gt. Barrington, MA 01230) offers Italian-style pizzas (thin-crust, organic sourdough, or wheat-free crusts), cooked in a wood-fired oven with super fresh toppings and a full menu, too (member, Berkshire Grown*). Manhattan Pizza Company* (413-528-2550; 490 Main St., Gt. Barrington,. MA 01230) Pizzas here are big, flat, oozing, and delicious. They reheat well and are available by the slice. The *East Side Café* (413-447-9405; 278 Newell St., Pittsfield, MA 01201), essentially a bar, makes pizza only on Thursday–Sunday evenings from 5pm on; it's small, thin, crisp, and tasty. *Elizabeth's Borderland Café* on East St., Pittsfield (see under "Restaurants") offers signature "white pies" with abundant toppings and fresh, innovative ingredients. The unbeatable taste of a wood-fired brick-oven pizza is somewhere *Over the Rainbow* (413-445-6836; 109 First St., Pittsfield, MA 01201); generous toppings and imaginative combinations include chicken pesto, spinach and broccoli, or the "primavera"— eggplant, black olives, broccoli, and more. Take-out or eat in and watch the flames in the oven. *Pasta's Wood-Fired Pizzas* (413-499-5562; 660 Cheshire Rd., Lanesborough, MA 01237) likewise offers the wood-fired flavor. *Hot Tomatoes* (413-458-2722; 100 Water St., Williamstown, MA 01267) may be the best in town for those who prefer the thinner crust.

Additional options for meat and fish include **Harry's Supermarket** (413-442-9084; 290 Wahconah St., Pittsfield, MA 01201; also 413-443-7247; 37 Elm St., Pittsfield, MA 01201), **Vic's Seafood** at the Lee Farmer's Market, Friday 12–6. **The Other Brother Darryl's** (413-269-4235, 800-6FLOPPIN; Rte. 8, Otis, MA 01253) and **Other Brother Darryl's Too** (413-528-8088; 760 S. Main St., Gt. Barrington, MA 01230; at Guido's). They offer wholesale seafood to retail customers and promise "still-floppin'" freshness.

WINE & LIQUOR

L iquor stores in Massachusetts are closed Sundays, except those within 10 miles of the Vermont or New Hampshire borders.

Domaney's Discount Liquors (413-528-0024; 66 Main St., Gt. Barrington, MA 01230) An excellent selection, and Ed is knowledgeable.

Gorham and Norton (413-528-0900; 278 Main St., Gt. Barrington, MA 01230)

Liquors Inc. (413-443-4466; 485 Dalton Ave., Pittsfield, MA 01201) The biggest and best for discount wine, beer, and spirits.

Liquor Mart (413-663-3910; State Rd., Adams, MA 01220)

Locke, Stock & Barrel (413-528-0800; 265 Stockbridge Rd., Gt. Barrington, MA 01230; Rte. 7) A great wine selection.

Nejaime's Wine & Liquor (413-448-2274; 598 Pittsfield-Lenox Rd., Lenox, MA 01240), **Nejaime's Stockbridge Wine Cellar** (413-298-3454; 3 Elm St., Stockbridge, MA 01262), and **Lenox Wine Cellar and Cheese Shop** (413-637-2221; 33 Church St, Lenox, MA 01240.) In addition to wines, beers, and spirits, they offer gourmet and deli items, and helpful, knowledgeable assistance.

Queensborough Spirits (413-232-8522; 20 Main St., W. Stockbridge) Beer, liquor, and wine.

South Egremont Spirit Shoppe (413-528-1490; 71 Main St., S. Egremont, MA 01258; Rte. 23) "The wine shop of The Berkshires." Also a good selection of cigars.

Spirit Shop and Deli Station (413-458-3704; 280 Cole Ave., Williamstown, MA 01267) Beer, liquor, wine,and a deli.

Trotta's Discount Liquors (529-3490; 490 Main St., Gt. Barrington, MA 01230; Rtes. 23 and 7) Beer, liquor, wine, and fine cigars.

Val's Pipe & Package Store (413-743-0962; 5 Columbia St., Adams, MA 01220) Beer, liquor, wine, groceries, milk, and lottery tickets.

West's Package & Variety Stores (413-663-6081; 367 State Rd., N. Adams, MA 01247) and **West's Wines & Spirits** (513-458-5948; 52 Spring St., Williamstown, MA 01267) Bob West is an authority on wine.

Berkshire Food and Beverage Specialties

Nurtured by Berkshire soil or created by Berkshire entrepreneurs, this select group of food and beverage specialties includes condiments and sauces, breads and other baked goods, sweets and sweeteners, and dairy products, spring water, and soft drinks. Some are world famous; all are locally treasured. There's no individual retail outlet for many of these products, but look for them at *Guido's, Bartlett's, The Store at Five Corners, Berkshire Cupboard,* and most other gourmet shops, farm and produce markets, and many supermarkets. In some cases you can also contact the food entrepreneur for more information. Or consider giving—or receiving—a gift basket or box with a selection of these unique items, cleverly packaged by *Gifts of the Berkshires* (800-BERKCTG) through *Berkshire Cottage,* the Great Barrington kitchen and gourmet store.

Beverages

Berkshire Spring Water (413-229-2086, 800-244-3212; 214 Norfolk Rd., Southfield, MA 01259) Bottled daily at the spring, it's sodium-, bacteria-, and additive-free. Or try *Sand Springs Spring Water Co.* (413-458-3412; 160 Sand Springs Rd., Williamstown, MA 01267) The American Indians liked it, why not you? Have either delivered, or buy it in supermarkets. *Gilly's Hot Vanilla* (413-637-1515) was created by Lenox resident Joanne Deutch as a hot-chocolate alternative; just add hot water to the vanilla-flavored powder. And there's no caffeine. Buy it by the bag locally, or have a cup at many local eateries. *Squeeze* beverages originated in Adams and are still available here.

Bread & Baked Goods

Look for some local goods made locally but not sold retail, such as *Berkshire Mountain Bakery.* Its traditional sourdough breads should be sought out at area natural-food stores. The peasant bread and the raisin bread are particular favorites; try their crisp biscotti, too. *Cedars of Lebanon* makes pita bread that's in area supermarkets and groceries. It is pure, simple, and delicious. *Nejaime's* lavasch is deliciously addictive: a Mideast specialty, lavasch is a crusty, crackerlike bread. Nejaime's is made with a variety of flavorings, all good.

Condiments & Sauces

Berkshire Berries (413-23-5779; Rte. 20, Becket, MA 01223), purveyors of jam, jelly, syrup, and honey, sold at numerous local and regional locations, including New York City's Greenmarket.

Dairy Products

Monterey Chèvre is made from the milk of goats at *Rawson Brook Farm* (413-528-2138; Box 426, New Marlboro Rd., Monterey, MA 01245) and from acid starter from France. It's sold deliciously plain, flavored with chives and garlic, or with a particularly tasty combination of wild thyme and olive oil. It is sold younger than imported chèvre and has a milder, more delicate flavor. Milk (with the cream on top) and light or heavy cream from *High Lawn Farm* (413-242-0672) is available at many grocery stores or can still be delivered to the door. The Jersey cows on the farm on Lenox

Road in Lee are the source. **Berkshire Blue Cheese** has in two short years gained a national reputation for cheese made from High Lawn's herd.

Desserts, Sweets, and Sweeteners

Baldwin's Extracts (413-232-7785; Depot St., West Stockbridge, MA 01266) offers "since 1888, the best in vanilla." This manufacturer of flavoring extracts and maple table syrup uses only the best—the Bourbon Vanilla Bean from Madagascar—for their Pure Vanilla Extract. It's made in a copper percolator (the "still") and aged in 100-year-old oak barrels, which can be seen in the small and fascinating retail outlet in a former carriage shop. Inhale essence of vanilla and admire the ranks of extract bottles—including lemon, orange, mint, and more—on the old-fashioned counter. Also available is **Baldwin's Table Syrup**, a blend of maple and cane sugar syrup from a recipe created in the 1920s.

Catherine's Chocolate Shop (413-528-2510; 260 Stockbridge Rd., Great Barrington, MA 01230) makes candies on the premises from century-old family recipes. These smooth and flavorful concoctions include chocolate truffles, a variety of hand-dipped candies, fudges, brittles, and barks. The nonpareils are, in fact, unequaled. Buy 'em by the piece, the pound, or in a boxed gift assortment. **David Rawson's honey** from Richmond is pretty close to nectar for the gods, who get it in 1-pound jars at Bartlett's Orchards (see "Farm, Orchard & Produce Markets").

And . . .

The **Delftree Corporation** (413-664-4907; 234 Union St. North Adams, MA 01247) grows shiitake mushrooms on hardwood logs in a 19th-century textile mill building in North Adams. Shipped all over the world, they are available here.

CHAPTER FIVE
What to See, What to Do
ARTS AND PLEASURES

Judith Monachina

The fine arts of Japanese calligraphy, flower arranging, and cooking are offered at the Japanese Cultural Center in West Stockbridge.

Glorifying God's grandeur by gracefully combining Art and Nature—this was the goal of the Stockbridge Laurel Hill Society, as expressed in 1853. Such thinking joined a new appreciation of the natural setting with a well-developed Berkshire cultural awareness that had roots in Colonial times when the earliest schools, churches, and newspapers were the centers of cultural activity. By the early 19th century, artists came to Berkshire to absorb the beauty and teach its appreciation. By the mid-century, the tradition of a Berkshire cultural bounty had taken hold.

The county's artistic abundance is out of proportion to its size and population. In music, dance, theater, and other art forms, Berkshire has long had a cultural calendar of astonishing excellence and variety—especially for a mountainous area once thought of as remote. There are good reasons for this legacy. Summers in the crowded eastern cities were not only unpleasant but frequently unhealthy. Improvements in transportation opened this area, while other scenic spots some might now find more dramatic were still inaccessible. By the mid-1800s a few families of taste, talent, and money were setting the tone of cultural sophistication still found here today.

Of the intelligentsia that developed around Stockbridge and Lenox in the early 19th century, no single family was more dynamic than the convivial and civic-minded Sedgwicks of Stockbridge. Novelist Catherine Sedgwick shares honors with poet William Cullen Bryant as Berkshire's—and America's—first native-born published writers in their fields. The Sedgwick house and family still grace Stockbridge today.

Other writers like Herman Melville and Nathaniel Hawthorne cross-fertilized their fiction in Berkshire in the 1850s, along with the popular Oliver Wendell Holmes, the doctor/poet who returned to his roots by summering in Pittsfield. Henry David Thoreau beheld a transcendental sunrise on the summit of Mount Greylock. Edith Wharton moved here, creating the kind of opulent European lifestyle that she skewered in her fiction. The list of famous artistic residents is lengthy and impressive. Our bibliography (in Chapter Nine, *Information*) cites several engaging books that tell the story.

When the Berkshires became the "inland Newport" during the late 19th-century Gilded Age, culture rode into Berkshire along with big money: architectural indulgences, furnishings and paintings, musical instruments and people to play them, chefs importing their foreign cuisines, and landscape gardeners. We are the beneficiaries of much inherited culture. Many of the family estates here have become cultural centers, such as Tanglewood for music and the Mount for literature. And yet as if to remind us that beauty need not be ornate or expensive, the Shaker Village at Hancock is also a Berkshire cultural legacy of remarkable value and vitality.

Furthermore, Berkshire families have been patrons of the arts and the landscape. For example, the Crane family of the Crane Paper Company of Dalton started the Berkshire Museum, Francine and Sterling Clark created the Art Institute in Williamstown, and the Tappan family gave Tanglewood to the Boston Symphony Orchestra. We owe them our thanks.

Some of the many of the artists drawn to the Berkshires lived here seasonally, like Wharton; others, year-round like Norman Rockwell. Thousands more have come just to perform or exhibit. Berkshire has left its mark on each. When asked what the Berkshires and Tanglewood mean to him, Seiji Ozawa, former music director of the Boston Symphony Orchestra, replied: "Tanglewood has an absolutely special connotation for me. It was the first place I ever saw in America, since I came to Tanglewood as a student in 1960 at the invitation of Charles Munch. For me and the orchestra, Tanglewood represents an opportunity to appreciate both the beauty of the Berkshires and of the music we make here."

Art combines with nature, from the fine woodwork in colonist John Ashley's study at Ashley Falls to the nation's four founding documents in Williams College's Chapin Library; from dioramas and an Egyptian mummy at the Berkshire Museum in Pittsfield to beautiful flowers and shrubs at the Berkshire Botanical Garden in Stockbridge. In performance halls, museums, libraries, theaters, nightclubs, and historic homes, Berkshire is rich in art and the pleasures it brings.

The following descriptions provide many ideas of where to go and what to do in Berkshire, but they cannot say what's currently playing or showing. Tanglewood issues its summer schedule around March 15; other arts organizations soon follow. For the larger seasonal schedules, such Jacob's Pillow, the museums, theaters, and other concert series, it's best to write, call, or check their Web sites for information. (We provide phone numbers and addresses.) That information helps to customize a personal Berkshire festival. Sold-out performances are not uncommon. Area newspapers provide information on cultural events as they happen. Especially comprehensive is the *Berkshire Eagle*'s Thursday magazine supplement, *Berkshires Week*.

ARCHITECTURE

Those who enjoy roaming through New England in search of handsome buildings will find Berkshire County an inexhaustible delight. They will find styles popular in North America from colonial times to the present. Few counties anywhere can claim this much architectural variety.

Berkshire is justly famous for the scores of mansions built during the opulent Gilded Age. Under "Historic Homes" in this chapter, in the chapters on *Dining* and *Lodging*, and elsewhere in this book, we describe several of the best surviving examples of these great "cottages," as they were called. Yet the saga of the sumptuous cottages isn't half the Berkshire building history.

Humbler examples include one-room schoolhouses or steepled churches, icons of America's simpler past. Still performing as designed in some Berkshire towns, adapted to alternative uses in others, these white-clapboard structures are often handsome and always charming. Some of the best are the ones in Alford, Lenox, Lee, New Ashford, and Washington. A beautiful c.1800 stone church can be found in Lanesborough.

Many Berkshire villages seem architectural set pieces, so artfully coordinated are their building styles and locations. The villages of Alford, New Marlborough, Stockbridge, and Williamstown have this look. Conspicuously absent is neon and plastic commercial clutter. Feelings of space and grace predominate. Yet also in each town arises the clear sense of the heart of a community where religion (churches), education (schoolhouses), government (town hall), domestic life (private homes), and the honor due the dead (cemeteries) all naturally fit together. People who live in cities or suburbs will find the centralization of Berkshire villages intriguing as well as architecturally beautiful. New Marlborough bears all of this out with its archetypal village green surrounded in part by the colonial-style *Old Inn on the Green* (1760), a fine Federal-style house (1824), and a Greek Revival-style *Congregational Church* (1839).

The Congregational Church, Lee, boasts boasts the tallest wooden steeple in the county.

Judith Monachina

Farms have long formed the Berkshire landscape. Almost any country road leads past splendid examples of old farmhouses with numerous outbuildings. Some of the barns date to times earlier than the homes. Good rides for farm viewing include Routes 57 (New Marlborough); 41 (south from South Egremont or north from West Stockbridge); and 7 (north from Lanesborough). Dramatic Tudor-style barns from the Gilded Age are still in use at High Lawn Farm (on Summer St. off Route 7, Lee), but the most famous barn in Berkshire is the round stone barn at *Hancock Shaker Village*, described under "Museums" in this chapter.

South County towns have many impressive buildings, among them several interesting industrial sites. Rising above them all is the Fox Paper Company's *Rising Paper Mill* (c.1875; Route 183 in Housatonic), with its handsome mansard slate roof. A similar mansard slate roof style is pushed to artful extremes on campus buildings at *Simon's Rock College of Bard* (on Alford Road, Great Barrington).

The village of Lee boasts the tallest wood-framed steeple in the county atop its *Congregational Church*. In South Lee *Merrill Tavern* (Route 102), a Federal-period building still functioning as an inn, is exquisitely maintained by the Society for the Preservation of New England Antiquities.

Sheffield, architecturally lovely and filled with antiques shops, appropriately prided itself on having preserved the *oldest covered bridge in Massachusetts* (1837) until it burned in 1994. The Massachusetts Highway Department has erected a duplicate. Otis, a Berkshire hill town, is graced with *St. Paul's Church* (1829), a fine example of the Gothic Revival style.

The simplicity of Shaker design draws thousands each year to the Hancock Shaker Village.

Stockbridge dazzles. Architect Stanford White's turn-of-the-century work appears in impressive diversity here: A casino (now the ***Berkshire Theatre Festival***; at Route 102 and Yale Hill Road); a mansion (***Naumkeag***; on Prospect Hill Road); a former railroad station on Route 7 south of the village; and a church (***St. Paul's Episcopal***; center of town). Two other Stockbridge churches well worth a look are the redbrick ***Congregational Church*** (Main Street, next to Town Hall) and the chapel at the ***Marian Fathers Seminary*** (on Eden Hill, off Prospect Hill Road). Whereas the interior of the Congregational Church has a powerful beauty in its plainness, the Marian fathers' chapel is beautiful for its finely crafted stone, woodwork, painting, and fabrics—much of it done by transplanted European artists. We describe the ***Mission House***, a colonial "Historic Home," later in this chapter.

Three outlying sites in Stockbridge are worth a drive. The district originally called Curtisville, now known as Interlaken (Route 183, north of Route 102), boasts several strikingly pretty 18th- and 19th-century homes and a remarkable former tavern-inn, as well as ***Citizens Hall***, with its Victorian period, Second Empire-style exterior details. Another building of note in rural Stockbridge is at Tanglewood's Lions' Gate (Hawthorne Street, off Route 183), where the replica of Nathaniel Hawthorne's ***"Little Red House"*** overlooks Stockbridge Bowl and the distant mountains. The estate known as ***Linwood*** has opened to the public as the site of the ***Norman Rockwell Museum***, a Robert A. M. Stern-designed New England town hall upscale. Charles E. Butler's unpolished marble cottage, ***Linwood*** (1859), remains the architectural highlight of this delightful Berkshire hilltop.

Finally, in South County, a ride out on the Tyringham Road (off Route 102, south of Lee) and then upland on Jerusalem Rd. will lead to ***"Jerusalem,"*** the remnants of a Shaker settlement dating from 1792. Five buildings remain, none open. Jerusalem Road begins in tiny Tyringham Village. Along the Tyringham Valley Road is the ***Gingerbread House***, a thatched-roof English cottage built by sculptor Henry Kitson in the late 1800s and known currently as *Santarella*; see "Art Galleries" in this chapter.

Central County abounds with notable architecture. In Dalton, a ride along Main Street (Route 9) provides views of the **Crane Paper Mills** (the Old Stone Mill, dating to 1844, is open as a museum in season) and several Crane family estates. In addition to other fine papers, Crane manufactures U.S. currency paper in these venerable mills. In 1816 Zenas Crane, the company founder, built a dignified Federal-style house, which still stands. There are also three 19th-century Richardsonian Romanesque churches on Main Street in Dalton proper.

In the hill town of Hinsdale on Route 8 are some architectural surprises, vestiges of more prosperous, populous times when various mills were alive and well in the Berkshire highlands. The oldest (1798) Federal-style church in Berkshire is here. A Greek-Revival town hall was built in 1848. The public library is in the high Gothic style, designed in 1868 by architect Leopold Eidlitz, who did St. George's Church in New York City and the New York State Capitol in Albany.

The only stone early-Gothic-Revival church in the county is **St. Luke's Chapel**, in Lanesborough (on Route 7). Like many other buildings cited in this book, St. Luke's is on the National Register of Historic Places.

Equal to any other village in Berkshire as an impressive architectural set piece is stately Lenox—especially the historic center of the village, including the **Lenox Academy** (Federal style, 1803), the irresistibly photogenic **Church on the Hill** (1805), and the **Lenox Library** (1815; see "Libraries" in this chapter). All three buildings are on Main Street (Route 7A). The **Curtis Hotel**, dominating the center of town, has been restored and converted to an apartment complex. From the Gilded Age to recent times, the Curtis was one of Berkshire's most fashionable addresses for travelers. Not far from Lenox village, on Route 20 heading toward Lee, is **Cranwell**, once a Jesuit-run school, now a resort, golf club, and condominium complex (see Chapter Three, *Lodging*).

Pittsfield's architectural record is distinguished although problematic. Preservation and restoration nowadays receive good attention, as a walk around Park Square reveals. Several new buildings integrate quite well with the ornate elegance of the old Venetian Gothic Athenaeum, the two churches, the bank buildings, and the courthouse—all dating from the 19th century.

The former *Berkshire Eagle* newspaper building (on Eagle Street, off North Street) is a fine example of the Art Deco style, set on a triangle like a miniature of Chicago's Flatiron Building. Another important business structure in Pittsfield is the General Electric Plastics House, a handsome and interesting experimental display house in the Plastics Division's world headquarters complex. The address? "Plastics Avenue," of course (between Merrill Road and Dalton Avenue).

North County provides stark contrasts in architecture and variety in the stories that buildings tell about social history. The cities of Adams and North

Simplicity was not exactly what drew the "cottagers" to the Berkshires. Bellfontaine is now Canyon Ranch in Lenox.

Courtesy Canyon Ranch

Adams owe their expansion to past industrial times. However, revitalization proceeds, the most spectacular being the conversion of the idle Sprague Electric plant (formerly textile mills) into a mammoth museum of contemporary art (visual and performing), **MASS MoCA**. Although urban renewal hit the downtowns unkindly, Adams and North Adams have recently beautified their main streets. In North Adams, **Western Heritage Gateway State Park** celebrates a 19th-century architectural and engineering wonder, the **Hoosac Tunnel**. (See "Museums" in this chapter.) The spires of North Adams's many churches are a pretty sight when descending into the city from the east on Route 2. In Adams, suffragettes will want to pass the **Susan B. Anthony Birthplace** (1814; a private home near the corner of East Road and East Street) and the **Quaker Meeting House** (1782; near the end of Friends Street), another National Register of Historic Places building.

Williamstown contains homes from colonial to contemporary, a college that has been adding buildings nearly since the country began, quaint shops, and two masterfully designed art museums (the **Clark Art Institute** and the **Williams College Museum of Art**, both described under "Museums"). **West College** (1790), **Griffin Hall** (1828), the oldest (1838) extant college observatory in the U.S. and the 1802 **President's House** at Williams are alone worth touring the campus (via a large map in front of the main administration building, Hopkins Hall, or guided by brochure maps available at the information booth). The much photographed **First Congregational Church** (1869) is the replica of a colonial one that burned in Old Lyme, Connecticut. The **Williamstown Public Library**, which houses the local history museum, faces the **1753 House**, built with authentic methods and materials for the town's bicentennial on Field Park.

In Berkshire, a proud history still stands.

ARTS CLASSES

The world is turning interactive. Art in Berkshire is part of the trend. Not content with simply looking at fine art and craft work in the multitude of galleries and museums in the county, many residents and visitors want to create art, as well. Opportunities grow apace. The Berkshire Museum, the Norman Rockwell Museum, the YMCAs (call for their schedules), and several local institutions have made art education the mainspring of their business.

BERKSHIRE CENTER FOR CONTEMPORARY GLASS
413-232-4666.
www.berkshireweb.com/ bcfcg.
6 Harris St., PO Box 377,W. Stockbridge, MA 01266.
Open: Daily 10–6.

Located just off Main Street opposite Trúc Orient Express and La Bruschetta restaurants, BCCG is a gallery, a glassblowing studio, and a school for glassblowers from beginner through accomplished. Founded and run by artist/sculptors Edward and Judy Bates Merritt, it incorporates the *All Fired Up* gallery, offering fine glass and other art-craft work by local professionals. The glassblowing studio is available to qualified glassblowers and their students. Best of all, the Merritts offer an array of well-structured glassblowing workshops and classes for beginners and intermediates. Paperweight workshops for ages 9 and up, a one-hour course, is usually scheduled with glassblower.

IS183—ART SCHOOL OF THE BERKSHIRES
(Formerly Interlaken School of Art)
413-298-5252.
www.IS183.org.
13 Willard Hill Rd., PO Box 1400, Stockbridge, MA 01262.

Founded in 1992 by eminent hand weaver and visionary Sam Kasten, IS183 has developed into a full-scale, studio-based year-round school of arts. Located with studios on the second floor of MASS MoCA in North Adams as well as in historic Citizens Hall, on Hill Road just off Route 183 (via Trask Lane) in Interlaken Village, it has something for everyone with artistic inclinations. IS183 offers programs for children, teens, and adults, including single classes, semester courses, half-day to weekend workshops, and lectures in painting, drawing, ceramics, printmaking sculpture, metal jewelry, and textiles of several sorts. Classes are offered at MASS MoCA (under "Museums") as well as at the Stockbridge campus. Faculty members are drawn from the local artistic community or are visiting teachers and lecturers. On "Lights & Socks" day in December, faculty art can be previewed for sale; continental breakfast and champagne are served, and discounts are offered for enrollment in winter programs.

CINEMA

THE WILLIAMSTOWN FILM FESTIVAL

Cinephiles should keep their eyes open for the Williamstown Film Festival, begun in a preliminary way in June 1999, now growing and appearing in October. Each festival has honored one of Hollywood's more honorable. Call 413-458-2700.

IMAGES CINEMA
413-458-5612.
www.imagescinema.org.
50 Spring St., PO Box 283, Williamstown, MA 01267.

Eclectic, exciting films—independent first-run flicks as well as the best from camp to classic—are the order of the evening in the only year-round, single-screen, independent movie house in the country. Its survival as North Country's most dynamic movie house is a wonder. In 1989, when it was threatened with closure, local actor and resident Christopher Reeve pulled together support to keep the theater open. In 1998, it became a nonprofit organization under the leadership of energetic managers and support from the community at large. Today, the Images lives on in refurbished modernity. Memberships, printed or e-mailed schedules, and special programs.

LITTLE CINEMA
413-443-7171.
www.berkshiremuseum.
    org.
At the Berkshire Museum.
39 South St., Pittsfield, MA 01201.

This is *the* great little film program in Berkshire, featuring state-of-the-art projection and sound. Films are shown in the summer, with special showings during the year. Fine independent and foreign films, downstairs in the Berkshire Museum auditorium.

OTHER CINEMA

South County

Simon's Rock College of Bard (413-528-0771; www.simons-rock.edu; 84 Alford Rd., Gt. Barrington, MA 01230). Occasional classics and fun films, open to the public.

Triplex Cinema (413-528-8885 info; 413-528-8886 office; fax 413-528-8889; www.thetriplex.com; 70 Railroad St., Gt. Barrington; Mail: PO Box 508, S. Egremont, MA 01258) An art venue as well as cinema with surround sound.

Central County

Regal Berkshire Cinema 10 (413-499-2558; Berkshire Mall, 123 Old State Rd., Lanesborough, MA 01237; off Rte. 8) Dolby stereo, action, adventure, drama, comedy, popcorn.

North County

Regal North Adams Cinemas (413-663-5873; Curran Hwy., N. Adams, MA 01247; Rte. 8) North County's multiplex, with six screens.

Outside the County

Crandall Theatre (518-392-3331; www.crandalltheatre.com; 46-48 Main St., Chatham, NY 12037) One screen in pleasant, old-fashioned movie house showing first-run films with the cheapest popcorn around.
Hollywood Drive-In (518-283-4425; www.hollywooddrivein.com; Averill Park Rd., Averill Park, NY 12018; Rte. 66) Berkshire families are increasingly making the journey over the mountains to this traditional drive-in for an inexpensive evening's entertainment.
Movie House (518-789-3408; Main St., Millerton, NY 12546) The best first-run films, three screens, espresso, and other refinements.

DANCE

ALBANY-BERKSHIRE BALLET
413-445-5382: 800-476-6964.
www.berkshireballet.org.
Mail: 51 North St.,
　Pittsfield, MA 01201
Concerts at various
　theaters.
Season: Intermittently year-round.
Tickets: Discounts for
　seniors, children, and
　groups.

The Albany Berkshire Ballet's summer season (July and August) takes place at Berkshire Community College's Robert Boland Theater, in the Koussevitzky Arts Center. Performances in other seasons are also given at the Consolati Art Center, at the Palace Theater in Albany, and Symphony Hall in Springfield. Lavish productions of *Cinderella* and *Giselle* have highlighted past seasons. Fall and winter concerts are capped with the traditional *Nutcracker*, staged at BCC and throughout New England in November and December.

JACOB'S PILLOW DANCE FESTIVAL
413-243-0745;
　winter 413-637-1322.
www.jacobspillow.org.
358 George Carter Rd.,
　Becket; Mail: Box 287,
　Lee, MA 01238.
Off Rte. 20, 8 mi. E. of Lee
Season: Summer;
　Tues.–Sun.
Tickets: Variety of prices for
　different events.
Special Features: Gift Shop.

Founded in 1933, Jacob's Pillow is America's first and oldest summer dance festival. The Pillow keeps step with the times, presenting the best in classical, modern, postmodern, jazz, and ethnic dance. Its schedule of offerings creates a Who's Who of contemporary dance, featuring over the years Merce Cunningham, Dame Margot Fonteyn, Peter Martins, Alicia Markova, Twyla Tharp, Alexander Gudunov, Martha Graham, Paul Taylor, Alvin Ailey, Phildanceco, the Pilobolus troupe, Jane Comfort and Co., among many others.

　　High on a hillside in Becket is the farm that famed dancer Ted Shawn bought after successfully

The Paul Taylor II company, part of Jacob Pillow's "Inside/Out" series, draws an overflow crowd on a rain-threatened night. In good weather, this series is held outdoors prior to mainstage productions.

touring with his wife, Ruth St. Denis, and the Denishawn troupe in the 1920s. Here Shawn worked to establish dance as a legitimate profession for men, founding a world-class dance-performance center and a school for dance. The school continues to flourish along with the festival, honoring its founder's heartfelt philosophy that the best dancers in the world make the most inspirational dance instructors. In addition to performing here, some of the Pillow's visiting dance luminaries stay on to teach master classes in the compound's rustic studios.

A visit is more memorable for those who drive to the Pillow early to stroll among those studios where works are in progress; dancers are in development. Through a window, lithe figures create choreography. Down at the Pillow's rustic outdoor theater, "Inside/Out," all forms from experimental to ballet are rehearsed and performed—for free. And after savoring that dance hors d'oeuvre, strollers might wish to sup at the Pillow. Happily, here, too, there are several lovely options: the Pillow Café, feasting under a brightly colored tent; or the picnic area, possibly glimpsing a dancer who will be performing later in the Ted Shawn Theatre. The Pillow's Studio/Theatre adds a separate 10-week schedule of new and emerging, offbeat companies, complementing the Ted Shawn Theatre's exciting dance schedule.

Student dancers from around the world come to Jacob's Pillow in the summer to study. Here young men learn the dance that Ted Shawn and his Men Dancers created to depict various sports.

Judith Monachina

OLGA DUNN DANCE COMPANY, INC.
413-528-9674.
321 Main St., PO Box 157, Gt. Barrington, MA 01230.
Season: Year-round.
Tickets: Prices vary.

Since its founding in 1977, the Olga Dunn Dance Company has enjoyed such success that it spawned the Junior Company and the Olga Dunn Dance Ensemble. Performing a free mix of exuberant and witty jazz, modern, and ballet, frequently with live musicians, the company has also toured area schools, exposing children to the creativity of dance and the excitement of movement. Annual performances at its own studio, at the Berkshire Museum, and other theaters in the tri-state area are highlights of the dance year. As Marge Champion—famed dancer and local Berkshire resident—put it: "The Olga Dunn Dance Company has become the radiating center of our experience in appreciating and participating in the art of dance."

OTHER DANCE

With Jacob's Pillow bringing the world's best dancers to the Berkshires, it's not surprising that quality dance troupes would spring up here and there throughout the county.

In **South County**, Great Barrington leads the dance. Many of the most innovative performances take place at the Simon's Rock's *Art Center Theater*, known as "the *ARC*," on Alford Road (413-528-0771), which has been offering student/faculty dance programs in December and May. These feature original music and choreography by members of the school's dance program. *Laurie McLoed* is an award-winning dancer, choreographer, and film maker who with her company, *Victory Girl Productions* (413-298-3006; PO Box 141, Stockbridge, MA 01262), presents innovative works at such places as Jacob's Pillow's and MASS MoCA. She is currently working on short, filmed dance—

under water. Modern dancer and choreographer *Dawn Lane* (413-637-0230; 326 Old Stockbridge Rd., Lenox, MA 01240) teaches for Jacob's Pillow and is well-known for her involvement in the community. She is the program director and choreographer for the Community Access to the Arts (40 Railroad St., Gt. Barrington, MA 01230.) Community Access is a nonprofit organization that brings visual performing arts experiences to the disabled community. There is also a flourishing country and contra dance network in the Berkshires. Check newspapers and bulletin boards for listings.

In *Central County*, *Susan Dibble* (413-637-1199; www.shakespeare.org) is resident choreographer for Shakespeare & Co. She also leads **Dibble Dance**, presenting one or two weekends of dance at Shakespeare & Co.

In *North County*, the *Williams College Dance Department* (413-597-2410) sponsors an ongoing, energetic series with student and faculty choreography, and visiting notables. *Chen & Dancers*, a Chinese company, has been the artists-in-residence; the *Chuck Davis African Dance Collective* has also been seen and heard in Williamstown. Exciting *Kusika,* the college's own African dance company, which accompanies itself with drumming, often performs with the spirited *Zambezi Marimba Band,* usually inviting the audience to join in.

GALLERIES

Since the arrival in Berkshire of nationally recognized early-20th-century sculptors Daniel Chester French (who sculpted *The Minute Man* at Concord) and Sir Henry Hudson Kitson (who did *The Minute Man* at Lexington), the county has been home to an increasing number of talented visual artists.

Much of the art on display in local galleries reflects the uplifting reality of the Berkshire landscape. Many artists focus on the undulating hills and their ever-changing light. Local galleries also show other themes and styles, from traditional still-life sketches to intriguing mixed-media works. Some galleries show Berkshire artists exclusively; others bring in works from artists the world over. Some are only regularly open in warm weather so, it's wise to call ahead. *The Artful Mind* is an attractive, free publication dedicated to the arts and art scene in the Berkshires and neighboring areas of New York and Connecticut. It is a wonderful monthly source for information on what's happening.

South County

GREAT BARRINGTON

Asian Arts (413-528-5091; 199 Stockbridge Rd., Gt. Barrington, MA 01230; Rte. 7) Imported Asian furniture and art.

Berkshire Art Gallery (413-528-2690; Jenifer House Commons, Stockbridge Rd., GT. Barrington, MA 01230; Rte. 7) 19th- and 20th-century and current Berkshire paintings; some sculpture.

Birdhouse (413-528-0984; 280 Main St., Gt. Barrington, MA 01330) Contemporary American folk art and crafts. Open daily 10:30am–5:30pm.

Gallery 304 (413 274-3838; 304 Main St., Gt. Barrington, MA 01330) Art collective.

Habitat Galleries (413-528-9123, winter 561-241-4544; www.habitatgalleries .com; 117 State Rd., Gt. Barrington, MA 01330) The oldest gallery in the U.S. to carry contemporary glass work; national and international artists. Changing exhibitions. Seasonal at this location.

Kaolin & Co. Pottery (413-528-1531; www.kaolinpottery.com; 80 Rte. 71, Gt. Barrington, MA 01330; next to Gt. Barrington airport) Wheel-thrown and hand-built ceramics, including sculptures of animals. Home furnishings to conversation pieces.

Mill River Studio (413-528-9433; 8 Railroad St., Gt. Barrington, MA 01330) Posters, hand-colored engravings, historic maps, and custom framing.

SKH Gallery (413 528-3300; 46 Castle St., Gt. Barrington, MA 01330; at the railroad station, top of Castle St.) Textile arts including the work of world renowned weaver Sam Kasten.

Simon's Rock of Bard College (413-528-7209; www.simons-rock.edu; 84 Alford Rd., Gt. Barrington, MA 01330) Changing exhibits at various venues on campus.

HOUSATONIC

Fox Martin Fine Art Gallery (413 274-1249; 1100 Main St., Housatonic, MA 01236) A new gallery in a town that has become known for its art. This one hosts individual shows representing fine artists in a variety of mediums.

Tokonoma Gallery & Framing Studio (413-274-1166, 402 Park St., Housatonic, MA 01236) A diverse collection of fine art and functional, decorative, contemporary craft. The gallery presents works of such regional artists as Terry Wise along with internationally recognized artists. They also offer a framing service.

LEE

Myles Bradford Collection (413 243-1010; 40 Main St., Lee, MA 01238) A little bit of the Southwest in the Berkshires, along with changing exhibits of artists from near and far. Jewelry, pottery, oils, watercolors and collectibles providing "presents of mind."

MONTEREY

Hayloft Gallery and Studio (413-528-1806; www.berkshire.net/~ckennedy/ weber.html; Montery Stage Rd. Box 11, Gt. Barrington, MA 01330; jct. Rtes. 23 and 57, 4 mi E. of Gt. Barrington) Berkshire prints and watercolors, including popular townscapes, by local artist Leonard Webber.

NEW MARLBOROUGH

Gedney Farm (413-229-3131; www.oldinn.com; Star Rte. 70, New Marlborough, MA 01244; on Rte. 57) Gallery in the beautifully restored barn of an 18th-century inn. Open on exhibit basis.

SHEFFIELD

Butler Sculpture Park (413-229-8924; 481 Shunpike Rd., Sheffield, MA 01257) An outdoor exhibit space for monumental sculpture. Open daily May–October 11am–5pm, winter by appointment.

Fellerman & Raabe Glassworks (413-229-8533; fellerman-raabeglass.com; 534 S. Main St, Sheffield, MA 01257) Glass artists Steve Fellerman and Claire Raabe exhibit blown, sculpted, and cameo-carved glass of their own creation as well as that of other artists.

Loring Gallery (413-229-0110, winter 413-528-1242; www.loringgallery.com; PO Box 938, Sheffield, MA 01257; Rte. 7, diagonally across the road from Bradford's auction house) Fine art, sculpture, and turn-of-the-last-century posters. Open May to October.

SOUTH LEE

House of Earth Studio (413-243-1575; PO Box 145, S. Lee, MA 01260; Rte. 102 E. of town center) Contemporary oil, acrylic, and watercolor landscapes in a rammed-earth studio.

STOCKBRIDGE

Holsten Galleries (413-298-3044; www.holstengalleries.com; 3 Elm St., Stockbridge, MA 01262) Contemporary glass artists, including stunning glass pieces by Dale Chihuly. Daily 11am–5pm.

IS183 (413 298-5252; 13 Willard Hill Rd., Stockbridge, MA 01262) Interlaken School just off Rte. 183 offers classes, shows, a kid's summer camp and weekend workshops in all art mediums. They also have a studio at MASS MoCA in North Adams.

Image Gallery (413-298-5500; Main St., PO Box 111, Stockbridge, MA 01262 Stockbridge, MA 01262) Modern arts and photography—usually by gallery owner and master photographer Clemens Kalisher

Origins Gallery (413-298-0002; 36 Main St., Stockbridge, MA 01262 Stockbridge, MA 01262; the Mews) Tribal and folk art of Africa and Asia, collected by Albert Gordon.

Ronrich (413-298-3556; Rte. 183, Stockbridge, MA 01262; 2 mi. S. of Tanglewood) Works by Ronnie Cutler and others on display. Wednesday through Sunday 11am–6pm or by appointment.

TYRINGHAM

Santarella Museum & Gardens (413-243-3260; 75 Main Rd., PO Box 414, Tyringham, MA 01264) Designed and built by sculptor Sir Henry Hudson Kitson (Lexington *Minute Man*), this structure has a unique rolling thatched roof inspired by the hills; now a museum of his work and others, with contemporary sculpture, for sale, exhibited outside. Artists in residence and museum shop.

Judith Monachina

A beautiful barn in Tyringham, recently converted to the Naoussa Gallery.

Naoussa Gallery (413 243-1812; 8 Main Rd., Tyringham, MA 01264) Featuring Berkshire and regional artists working in a variety of media, including Peggy Braun, Paula Shaun, and Michael Flower.

WEST STOCKBRIDGE

All Fired Up Gallery—Berkshire Center for Contemporary Glass (413-232-4662; 6 Harris St., PO Box 377, W. Stockbridge, MA 01266) Hand-blown contemporary glass, workshops, demonstrations.

Artifacts (413-232-9900; 5 Center St., W. Stockbridge, MA 01266) They specialize in architectural objects and related artworks, including miniatures, wooden items, and intaglio.

Hotchkiss Mobiles (413-232-0200; fax 413-232-0210; www.artmobiles.com; 8 Center St., PO Box 373, W. Stockbridge, MA 01266) Original and colorful mobiles for moving art, both indoors and out. Museum quality at reasonable prices. Another gallery in Lenox.

Train Station Gallery (413 232-7930; 6 Depot St., W. Stockbridge, MA 01266) Bright, open display space in a restored train station featuring a selection of art in various mediums, from a variety of artists including Bruce MacDonald.

Waterside (413-232-7997; 32 Main St., W. Stockbridge, MA 01266) Striking graphics, ceramics, jewelry, and sculpture. Some powerful pieces in many different media.

Central County

BECKET

Becket Arts Center (413-623-6635; www.hidden-hills.com/becketartscenter; Brooker Hill Rd., Becket, MA 01223; Rte. 8) Local shows and programs.

HANCOCK

Beaver Pond (413-738-5895; 2993 Hancock Rd., Hancock, MA 01237; Rte. 43) Paintings by owner Richard Heyer and others; Open daily noon to 5 except Tuesday.

HINSDALE

John Stritch (413-655-8804; 526 Maple St., Hinsdale, MA 01235) A gallery showcasing paintings, prints, and the Tanglewood poster collection by Berkshire artist John Stritch. Studio and sculpture garden open weekend afternoons.

LANESBOROUGH

Stone School Gallery (413-442-0996; www.OldStoneSchool.com; 736 N. Main St., Lanesborough, MA 01237) Photographer Cheryl Sacks exhibits her work and that of others.

LENOX

B. J. Faulkner (413-637-2958; www.bjfaulkner.com; 48 Main St., Lenox, MA 01240) Highlighting the watercolors, oils, and reproductions of the artist/ owner's Berkshire scenes, musical themes, and European dreams.

Charles Steinhacker Editions (800-244-9120; 4 Housatonic St., Lenox, MA 01240) Steinhacker's photographs (some taken while he was a photographer for *National Geographic*) are showcased in this tiny shop, which also sells "the world's best imported chocolate.

Concepts of Art (413-637-4845; fax 413-637-2723; www.lenoxjudaica.com; 65 Church St., Lenox, MA 01240) Crafts—including glass, jewelry, pottery, and wood—concentrating on Judaica.

Ferrin Gallery (413 637-4414; 56 Housatonic St., Lenox, MA 01240) Group shows of well-known artists and sculptors in a stunning new gallery just opened after 20 years in Northampton. Well-deserved reputation for offering the best in ceramic sculpture and studio pottery.

Hado Studio (413-637-1088; 62 Church St., Lenox, MA 01240) Contemporary paintings and sculpture; also furniture and prints. Summer only.

The Hand of Man Gallery (413 637-0632; 5 Walker St., Lenox, MA 01240; in the Curtis Bldg.) A wide range of crafts, photographs, and paintings.

Hoadley Gallery: Contemporary Crafts (413 637-2814; 21 Church St., Lenox, MA 01240 Lenox, MA 01240) Pottery by Tom Hoadley is one of this store's specialties. Functional and decorative objects in all media, including a collection of wearable art.

Hotchkiss Mobile (413 637-4115; www.artmobiles.com; 34 Church St., Lenox, MA 01240) The gallery's Lenox location features mobiles and artwork, jewelry, ceramics, and furniture.

Eziba (413-664-6888; 46 Eagle St., Lenox, MA 01240) An outlet for handcrafted products from around the world found in the stunning Eziba catalog. The merchandise in this shop is discounted.

Inspired Planet (413-637-2836; www.inspiredplanet.com; 36 Pittsfield Rd., Lenox, MA 01240 Lenox, MA 01240; at Brushwood Farms on Rte. 7) Photographs by the owner; paintings, furniture, and artifacts from Asia, Africa, and the Americas.

Lenox Artisans Gallery (413 637-9538; 25 Pittsfield Rd., Lenox, MA 01240; Rte. 7) Eclectic collection of art in a variety of mediums. The playful sculpture on the front lawn sets a whimsical tone. Open daily 10-5, Thurs–Fri. 10–7.

Lenox Gallery of the Fine Art (413-637-2276; 69 Church St., Lenox, MA 01240) Two floors of paintings, watercolors, drawings, and sculpture by major Berkshire artists, including Stephen Filmus. Open daily year-round.

Liliana Gallery (413 637-6964; 38 Church St., Lenox, MA 01240) A shop featuring fine art and custom framing.

Michael Charles Cabinetmakers (413-637-3483; www.michaelcharles.com; 53 Church St., Lenox, MA 01240) Gallery of handmade custom furniture using hardwood and traditional 19th-century joinery.

Ute Stebich (413-637-3566; 69 Church St., Lenox, MA 01240 Lenox, MA 01240) Contemporary art of museum quality, including glass by Tom Patti; international collection of art and primitive African objects.

Wit Gallery (413 637-8808; 27 Church St., Lenox, MA 01240) An acronym for "wonders in time," this gallery offers larger than life sculptures and also features watercolors and oil paintings, all by well-known artists. Open daily 10–4, weekends 10–5.

PITTSFIELD

Berkshire Artisans (413-499-9348; www.berkshireweb.com/artisans; 28 Renne Ave., Pittsfield, MA 01201; 1 block E. of lower North St.) Exhibitions and workshops at the city's nonprofit municipal arts center.

Berkshire Community College, Koussevitzky Arts Center (413-499-4660; www.cc.berkshire.org; 1350 West St., Pittsfield, MA 01201) Changing exhibitions, 9–5 weekdays.

North County

NORTH ADAMS

Contemporary Artists Center (413-663-9555; www.thecac.org;189 Beaver St., N. Adams, MA 01247) A not-for-profit artists' studio facility, with five unique galleries featuring regional and international and CAC artists-in-residence exhibits. Visit their website for more information on their schedule of shows and events.

Dark Ride (413-664-9550; www.darkrideproject.com; 189 Beaver St., N. Adams, MA 01247) Visitors can take a 10-minute ride on the *Sensory Integrator* into creative space. Open Sat. and Sun.1–5 in the Historic Beaver Mill.

Everything Art (413-662-3556; 51 Main St., N. Adams, MA 01247) Fine art (including works by Danny O recently featured in a show at Chesterwoood), gifts, artists' supplies and custom framing.

WILLIAMSTOWN

Harrison Gallery (413 458-1700; 39 Spring St., Williamstown, MA 01267) Wonderful gallery featuring local artists such as Mary Sipp Green's gorgeous landscapes and Jim Schantz's stunning Berkshire scenes along with other well-known painters, potters, and graphic artists.

LiAsia Gallery (413 458-1600; 31 Spring St., Williamstown, MA 01267) A gallery showcasing beautiful oriental handcrafts and antiques.

1/2 Dozen or So (413-458-9582; Mount Greylock Regional High School, 1781 Cold Spring Rd., Williamstown, MA 01267) Changing exhibitions open during school hours.

Plum (413-458-3389; www.plumgallery.com; 112 Water St., Williamstown, MA 01267). Exhibiting the work of painter Mary Natilizia, photographer Nicholas Whitman, and many others. Site of the Art New England Art Faculty Show in 2002.

Wilson Wilde (413-458-8277; Spencer Studio Building, Williams College, Williamstown, MA 01267) Changing student exhibits.

HISTORIC HOMES

ARROWHEAD
413-442-1793.
www.mobydick.org.
780 Holmes Rd., Pittsfield, MA 01201.
About 1.5 mi. E. of Rte. 7.
Season: Open daily Memorial Day Weekend–Oct.31, winter by appointment.
Admission: Adults $6, students 16–25 with ID $4, children 6–15 $2, children 5 and under free.
Special Features: Gift shop.

In 1850, seeking to escape what he later called "the Babylonish brick-kiln of New York," Herman Melville gave in to his yearning "to feel the grass" and moved with his family to the Berkshires. By the time he came here, Melville had already published two tales of his South Sea adventures, *Typee* and *Omoo*, and he had earned a reputation as a man "who had lived among cannibals." Longing to be known as a great writer and fresh from a new "close acquaintance" with the "divine" writings of Shakespeare, here he took off on the grand literary whale hunt that was to become *Moby Dick*.

Arrowhead is home to the Berkshire Historical Society, which offers excellent guided tours through the house. The second-floor study is where Melville wrote his great novel, looking northward at the Mount Greylock range, its rolling form reminiscent of a giant whale. He dedicated his next novel, *Pierre*, to "Greylock's most excellent majesty." The implements of the writer's trade and duplicates of many important books in his library are here.

The other thoroughly "Melville" room is the dining room, dominated by a grand stone hearth. His brother inscribed the mantle with the opening of Melville's story, *I and My Chimney*. The house contains 19th-century period furnishings, fine arts, and textiles with Berkshire origins, several pieces of which belonged to Melville. The Ammi Phillips folk-art portraits are of particular interest. Outside, the piazza is the site of another story. The grounds include an extensive herb garden and a vintage cutting garden. Arrowhead is also a lovely picnic spot.

The barn behind the house is the site of cultural programs such as literary readings and historical talks. A video about Berkshire literary figures and artists takes 20 minutes. Those hungry for more Melville can visit "The Melville Room" at the Berkshire Athenaeum on Wendell Avenue, also in Pittsfield. (See the Berkshire Athenaeum entry under "Libraries" in this chapter.)

COLONEL ASHLEY HOUSE
413-298-3239.
www.thetrustees.org.
Mail: PO Box 792,
  Stockbridge, MA 01262.
Cooper Hill Rd., Ashley
  Falls, off Route 7A.
Season: Memorial
  Day–Oct.14, Sat.–Sun.
  10–5.
Admission: Adults $5,
  children 6–12 $3.

In his military role as a colonel and as a political radical, John Ashley was destined to become as prominent a citizen as Berkshire would produce in the Revolution. He began his Berkshire life as a surveyor, trudging through the woods and swamps of Sheffield and mapping the wilderness with compass and chain.

Ashley loved what he saw. By 1735 he had built a handsome home on the west bank of the Housatonic River, now the oldest extant house in Berkshire County. Framed of well-seasoned oak with chestnut rafters, it was the finest house in Sheffield. Woodworkers from across the colony came to carve paneling and to fashion the gracefully curved staircase. The craftsmanship of Ashley's study, with its broad fireplace and sunburst cupboard, inspires confidence. It was here that Ashley met with a group of his neighbors in early 1773 to draft "The Sheffield Declaration," stating to the world that all people were "equal, free and independent." In Ashley's study, they asserted their independence from Britain, some three years before Thomas Jefferson and associates did so in Philadelphia. One of his slaves, Mumbet, overhearing the conversations, thought she should be free, too, approaching lawyer Theodore Sedgwick, who won her case.

The house was rescued, moved a quarter mile, restored, and turned over to The Trustees of Reservations. TTOR has seen to it that the Ashley House, listed on the National Register, lives on telling the history of the Ashley Family. An herb garden flourishes outside while colonial furnishings, redware, and the original wood paneling survive inside. A visit can complement viewing the extraordinary flowers at Bartholemew's Cobble or antiques hunting in the Sheffield-Ashley Falls area.

The Sheffield Declaration, 1773

Resolved that Mankind in a State of Nature are equal, free and independent of each Other, and have a right to the undisturbed Enjoyment of their lives, their Liberty and Property.

Resolved that it is a well known and undoubted privilege of the British Constitution that every Subject hath . . .a Right to the free and uncontrolled injoyment and Improvement of his estate or property. . . .

Resolved that the late acts of the parlement of Great Breton expres porpos of Rating and regulating the colecting a Revenew in the Colonies: are unconstitutional as thereby the Just earning of our labours and Industry without Any Regard to our own consent are by mere power ravished from us. . . .

THE BIDWELL HOUSE
413-528-6888.
www.bidwellhousemu-
  seum.org
Art School Rd., Monterey,
  MA 01245.
2.5 mi. from town of Mon-
  terey (turn left)
Season: Memorial
  Day–October 15,
  Tues.–Sun., holidays 11–4.
Admission: Adults $5, sen-
  iors/students with ID $4,
  children under 18 $1.

Located at the end of the traveled section of Art School Rd., Bidwell is one of Berkshire's oldest homes, dating to 1750 and listed on the National Register. Because the center of town moved on, Bidwell is now surrounded by 196 acres of pristine Monterey woodland, looking much as it might have back in the 18th century. Two designers from New York discovered the abandoned former home of the Reverend Adonijah Bidwell in the 1960s, brought it back to fine condition, and left instruction in their wills that it continue as a museum.

An active slate of lectures, workshops, and hikes (in the fall along historical Royal Hemlock Road) take place.

**THE WILLIAM CULLEN
  BRYANT HOMESTEAD**
413-634-2244.
www.thetrustees.org.
207 Bryant Rd.,
  Cummington, MA 01026.
Off Rte. 9 on Rte. 112 in
  Cummington.
Open: Grounds open daily
  year-round sunrise–sun-
  set; tours: last weekend in
  June–Labor Day, Fri.–Sun.
  plus Mon. holidays 1–5;
  post-Labor Day–
  Columbus Day, Sat., Sun.
  & Mon. holidays 1–5.
Admission: Adults $5,
  children 6–12 $2.50.

William Cullen Bryant was born in 1794 in a small gambrel-roofed cabin of roughhewn lumber, two miles from the frontier village of Cummington, on a farm of 465 acres. He stayed at Williams College only eight months, shortly thereafter taking up the law. From 1816 on, Cullen, as he was called, practiced law in Great Barrington, where he wrote about 30 well-respected poems on such local themes as Monument Mountain's Indian legend, the Green River, and native waterfowl. With the influence of Catherine Sedgwick's brothers, Bryant became coeditor of the *New York Review* and *Athenaeum Magazine*, then editor at the *New York Evening Post* (one of America's oldest and most influential newspapers), and ultimately America's first popular and widely respected native-born poet.

Bryant returned to and added substantially to his Cummington homestead; today it has 23 rooms. Visitors should read the poems first to capture the tour's fine points. Well managed by The Trustees of Reservations; National Historic Landmark; interpretive trail.

CHESTERWOOD
413-298-3579.
www.chesterwood.org.
Mail: PO Box 827,
  Stockbridge, MA 01262.
Off Rte. 183, Glendale.
Season: May–Oct., daily
  10–5.

At the age of 25 Daniel Chester French was commissioned by his hometown of Concord, Massachusetts, to create his first public monument, *The Minute Man*. Its lifelike pose and exquisite sense of surface modeling won the artist national acclaim, and the statue became an American icon.

Years and scores of sculptures later, French

Through the glass doors at Daniel Chester French's studio at Chesterwood.

Judith Monachina

Admission: Adults $10, seniors $8, college students $7, youths 6–18 $5, children 5 and under free.

Special Features: Gift shop.

sought a permanent country home to augment the New York City studio he maintained. In 1896 he and his wife, Mary, were shown the old Warner Farm and Boys School in the Glendale section of Stockbridge. After taking in the magnificent vista southward, toward Monument Mountain, French pronounced it "the best dry view" he had ever seen and promptly arranged to buy the property. Thereafter, he and Mary spent half of each year in New York City, half at Chesterwood. Glendale "is heaven," he said. "New York is—well, New York."

In Glendale he built a grand residence, studio, and garden complex, which are an enduring and eloquent tableau of his artistry. Here he created his masterpiece, the *Abraham Lincoln* statue that sits in the Lincoln Memorial in Washington. "What I wanted to convey," said French, "was the mental and physical strength of the great President." Visitors are invited to handle sculpting tools in his studio. Centerpieces are his marble *Andromeda*, a surprisingly erotic work; and the "railway" to move his works-in-progress out into the revealing daylight.

French designed magnificent gardens, maintained today after his fashion by the property's managers, the National Trust for Historic Preservation. The grounds host special exhibits during the season.

THE MERWIN HOUSE
413-298-4703.
www.spnea.org.
14 W. Main St., PO Box 72, Stockbridge, MA 01262.

"Tranquility," a bit of 19th-century Berkshire refinement stopped in time, is the former home of Mrs. Vipont Merwin. This charming brick mansion, built about 1825, is filled with antiques (mostly Victorian); both furnishings and col-

Center of town.
Season: June 1–Oct. 15,
    Sat.and Sun. 11–5.
Admission: Fee.

lectibles reflect global travel and domestic dignity. Merwin House is maintained as a property of the Society for the Preservation of New England Antiquities. For Stockbridge strollers, evening views through the multipaned front windows give an inviting glimpse of an elegant world gone by.

The Mission House.

Paul Rocheleau

THE MISSION HOUSE
413-298-3239.
www.thetrustees.org.
Box 792, Stockbridge, MA
    01262.
Corner Main & Sergeant
    Sts.
Season: Memorial Day
    Weekend–Columbus
    Day, daily 10–5
Admission: Adults $5,
    children 6–12 $3.

In 1735, an earnest minister from Yale College came to the Berkshire wilderness to pastor to the Mahican Indians. John Sergeant learned the Indian language in which he preached two sermons every Sunday. In the springtime, he went out with the Indians to tap the maples, writing the first account in English of this sugar production method. He talked with the Indians in the back of his simple log cabin. Under Sergeant's leadership, the Stockbridge Mission flourished.

To please his wife, Abigail, the Reverend Sergeant built what is now called Mission House, high on Prospect Hill. The tall and ornate Connecticut doorway, with beautiful panels, was carved in Westfield, Massachusetts, and dragged by oxen 50 miles over rugged terrain to Stockbridge. This front door and the front rooms were Abigail's domain; in the back, a separate entry and long corridor allowed the Indians access to Sergeant's study.

When he died in 1749, the days of the Stockbridge Mission were numbered, too, although eminent theologian Jonathan Edwards succeeded him. By 1785 the Indians had been displaced from Stockbridge, driven out for the most part by land speculators.

In 1927 Mabel Choate—the art collector and philanthropist who was heir to

Naumkeag—acquired the Mission House. She moved it to its present Main St. location, near the site of John Sergeant's first log cabin. Boston landscape architect Fletcher Steele, who had designed the gardens at Naumkeag, planted an orderly, symmetrical 18th-century herb, flower, and fruit garden beside the restored and relocated Mission House. Today apple and quince trees; herbs such as lamb's ear, rue, and southern wood; bright flowers; a grape arbor; and a "salet garden" filled with garden greens, greet visitors.

The Trustees of Reservations maintains Mission House, which is a National Historic Landmark. Tours of the house capture the 18th century's furnishings, kitchen implements, and the feeling of humble domesticity that gathered around the dominant central hearth. An adjoining museum focuses on Native Americans.

THE MOUNT
413-637-1899, 888-637-1902.
www.edithwharton.org.
2 Plunkett St., Box 974,
Lenox, MA 01240.
Near southern jct. of Rtes. 7 & 7A.
Open: June–Nov., 9–5; grounds 9–6
Admission: Adults $16, students $8, children under 12 free.
Special Features: Book/gift shop; refreshments.

It is amazing what a difference a few million dollars make. With federal money and match, the building has been repaired. Even more spectacular is the restoration of the grounds.

In February 1901 the writer and heiress Edith Wharton arrived at the Curtis Hotel in Lenox for a week in the country. She had summered in the area for the preceding two years and now, having found the "watering place trivialities of Newport" all but intolerable, sought a new site on which to realize the design principles incorporated in her book *The Decoration of Houses.* The Georgian Revival house she built was modeled on Christopher Wren's Belton House in Lincolnshire, England. At first Wharton retained as architect her associate, Ogden Codman. When his design fees grew exorbitant, she called on Francis L.V. Hoppin to complete the job.

Wharton supervised creation of the gardens, orchards, and buildings while finishing her novel *Disintegration,* writing as always in bed and tossing the pages on the floor for the staff to assemble. The Mount, elegant throughout, boasts marble floors and fireplaces and originally required 12 resident servants. Besides the 14 horses in their stables, the Whartons owned one of the earliest motorcars, a convenience that thrilled the visiting Henry James. In the fall of 1904, James and Wharton motored through Berkshire's autumnal splendor every day, enjoying social afternoons and evenings with visiting sophisticates.

"The Mount was to give me country cares and joys," she wrote, "long happy rides, and drives through the wooded lanes of that loveliest region, the companionship of a few dear friends, and the freedom from trivial obligations which was necessary if I was to go on with my writing. The Mount was my first real home . . . and its blessed influence still lives in me."

Happily, its blessed influence lives on for all of us as its physical and spiritual restoration continue. The National Trust for Historic Preservation bought the Mount to save it from commercial exploitation; the house is run today by Edith Wharton Restoration, Inc.

NAUMKEAG
413-298-3239.
www.thetrustees.org.
5 Prospect Hill Rd., Box 792, Stockbridge, MA 01262.
Season: Memorial Day weekend–Columbus Day, daily 10–5.
Admission: House and garden $9 adults $3 children 6–12; garden only $7 adults, $3 children 6–12.
Special Features: Gift shop.

During the Gilded Age of the late 19th century, men and women of power played out their fantasies in Berkshire, dotting the hillsides with dream houses. A most livable example is the mansion of illustrious lawyer Joseph Choate, the summer "cottage" that the Choate family came to call *Naumkeag* (a Native-American name for Salem, where Choate was born.) Here Choate found both a retreat from New York City life as well as an enclave of great legal minds in Supreme Court justices Field, Brewer, and Brown, all Stockbridge contemporaries.

Choate bought the property from David Dudley Field in 1884 and began construction. By the autumn of 1886, the 44-room, shingled, gabled, and dormered Norman-style house was complete, with architectural design by McKim, Mead & White and imaginative gardens by the landscaping pioneer Nathaniel Barrett.

The house eventually came into the hands of Choate's daughter, Mable, who maintained it while adding extensively to the gardens under the direction of landscape architect Fletcher Steele. The Fountain Steps, framed by birches; the Afternoon Garden, an outdoor room; farther southward, the Chinese Pagoda and Linden Walk; uphill, the brick-walled Chinese Garden, mosses and stone Buddhas gathered with carved lions and dogs, all shaded by ginkos; to the north, the topiary of the Evergreen Garden and the fragrance and color of the Rose Garden—all reflect decades of inspired and distinctive garden design.

Now held by The Trustees of Reservations, Naumkeag still includes its gardens, furnishings, and an extraordinary porcelain collection, much of it from the Far East. The tours are excellent.

SEARLES CASTLE
413-528-9800.
389 Main St., Gt. Barrington, MA 01230.
Rte. 7.

When Mark Hopkins, a founder and treasurer of the Central Pacific Railroad, died, his widow, Mary, consoled herself with the creation of a grand home in Great Barrington. Stanford White designed this 40-room castle, which was constructed between 1882 and 1887 of locally cut blue dolomite stone. Upon its completion, Mary Hopkins married her interior decorator, Edward Searles, a man 20 years her junior. Searles had spared no expense on the castle's interior. Many of the major rooms feature massive carved wood or marble fireplaces, each one unique. More than 100 of the world's best artisans and craftsmen were brought on site to work with oak carvings, marble statues, atriums, columns, and pillars. The bills totaled $2.5 million.

The castle now serves as the home of the John Dewey Academy, a residential therapeutic prep school. In 1982 Searles Castle was added to the National Register of Historic Places. Usually closed to the public, the building and grounds are visible to pedestrians walking along Main Street. Several times a year—for an Antiquarian Book Fair, for the Stockbridge Chamber Concerts, and for other special events—Searles Castle is open to the public and well worth a visit.

Touring the Berkshire Mansions

For those who yearn to step back into Berkshire's Gilded Age, visits to Naumkeag, the Mount, and Tanglewood, described in this chapter, will make an excellent start. In the chapters on *Lodging* and *Dining*, other Gilded Age mansions are noted for their original beauty or their contemporary adaptations. In addition, local historical societies and garden clubs arrange visits to some of the best mansions, normally off limits because they remain private homes.

Many Gilded Age "cottages" are visible from the road and are well worth a look. Their owners' privacy should be respected, of course. Carole Owens's book *The Berkshire Cottages* (which is available at most bookstores) tells their stories in lively detail, bringing to life the business magnates, robber barons, philanthropists, architects and designers, artists in residence, and squadrons of domestic servants. Maps to guide the way are included.

VENTFORT HALL
413-637-3206.
www.gildedage.org.
104 Walker St., PO Box 2424, Lenox, MA 01240.
Open: Summer–Oct. 31, daily 10–3; winter by appointment only.
Admission: $8 for tour.
Special Features: Gift shop

This Berkshire cottage's Elizabethan Revival style was already out of date when George and Sarah Morgan built their summer home in 1893, but it is enjoyable today to imagine the kind of life it lead to. For those who need a more visual stimulus, Ventfort served as the set for the orphanage in the 1999 movie *The Cider House Rules*. Unlike the other cottages open for our inspection, Ventfort aims to be more than architecture: a museum of the Gilded Age.

Sarah, sister to J. Pierpont Morgan, kept her last name by marrying a cousin. Their Boston architects, Rotch & Tilden, designed four other homes nearby in Lenox—all different from this one. Placed on the site of a home originally built and named by Ogden Haggerty, "Strong Wind" was for four years home to the Whitneys, who gave the land for October Mountain State Forest. But it paled in comparison to the new Morgan home of "15 bedrooms, 13 bathrooms, and 17 fireplaces." Built perhaps too quickly, the brickwork has sadly decomposed.

Sarah Morgan died soon after it was completed, and the building passed through a number of owners, both private and institutional, until a proposed nursing home threatened "structurecide" by wrecking ball in 1990. Local residents in 1997 joined to form the Ventfort Hall Association and, with a loan from the National Trust for Historic Preservation, purchased the building and the remaining 11.7 acres of grounds. Further state grants and private funds began the daunting preservation work—on the interior, with the skilled assistance of joiner Michael Costerisan, who meticulously pieced together tattered paneling. With none of the original furnishings available, to become a period museum will require a lot more money and a lot more time.

LIBRARIES

BERKSHIRE ATHENAEUM
413-499-9480.
www.berkshire.net/
  PittsfieldLibrary.
1 Wendell Ave. Pittsfield,
  MA 01201.
Open: Sept.–June,
  Mon.–Thurs. 9–9, Fri.
  9–5, Sat. 10–5; July and
  Aug., Mon., Wed., Fri.
  9–5, Tues., Thurs. 9–9,
  Sat. 10–5. Closed
  holidays.

The former Berkshire Athenaeum is a 19th-century specimen of the Venetian Gothic style, constructed next to the courthouse on Pittsfield's handsome Park Square. Built of Berkshire deep-blue dolomite (a limestone) from Great Barrington, along with red sandstone from Longmeadow, Massachusetts, and red granite from Missouri, this Athenaeum, once Berkshire's central library, now serves Pittsfield's courts and registry of deeds.

The new Athenaeum is a three-level brick and glass facility featuring a tall and airy reading room with natural clerestory lighting. An outdoor reading terrace serves adults and another, children.

There is an outstanding dance collection, a Local Authors' Room, and a Local History Room. The jewel of the Athenaeum is its Herman Melville Room: a trove of Melville memorabilia, from carved scrimshaw depicting the terror of the Great White Whale to first editions of the author's works. Here are *Moby-Dick* in Japanese; autograph letters from Melville; photos of his Pittsfield farm, Arrowhead (described under "Historic Homes," in this chapter), and the desk on which he wrote his last, haunting work, *Billy Budd*.

CHAPIN LIBRARY OF RARE BOOKS
413-597-2462.
www.williams.edu./
  resources/chapin.
PO Box 426, Williamstown,
  MA 01267.
On the 2nd fl. of Stetson
  Hall, Williams College.
Open: Mon.–Fri. 10–12 and
  1–5 exc. holidays. Open
  July 4. Call for summer
  hours.

Chapin Library has one of the most well-rounded collections of rare books and manuscripts anywhere. On permanent display are the four founding documents of this country: *The Declaration of Independence*, originally owned by a member of the Continental Congress; *The Articles of Confederation and Perpetual Union; The Constitution of the United States*, annotated by George Mason; and two copies of the *Bill of Rights*. The library also owns General Greene's handwritten order for boats to cross the Delaware, and on loan is George Washington's copy of *The Federalist Papers*. Every July Fourth, actors from the Williamstown Theatre Festival read the Declaration and the British Reply.

In 1923 Alfred Clark Chapin—Williams class of 1869 and mayor of Brooklyn—presented his alma mater with his magnificent library of first editions and manuscripts, specializing in historic literary and artistic master works. Other alumni have subsequently given their collections.

Among other the literary holdings are a Shakespeare First Folio and first editions of Pope, Swift, Fielding, Defoe, Richardson, Sterne, Johnson, Scott, Byron, Burns, Browning, Keats, Shelley, Thackeray, and Dickens. There is also a fine T. S. Eliot collection. Representing American literature are first editions by such writers as Crane, Melville, Whitman, and Faulkner. Scientific endeavor is represented by Tycho Brahe's *Astronomia* (1602), Harvey's *Anatomical Exercitations* (1653), Darwin's *Origins of the Species* (1859), and a double elephant folio of Audubon's *Birds of America*. The Chapin frequently contributes documents to special exhibits at the Williams College Museum of Art and the Clark Art Institute.

LENOX LIBRARY
413-637-0197.
18 Main St., Lenox, MA
01240.
Open: Summer, Mon.–Sat.
10–5; rest of year,
Tues.–Sat. 10–5; Thurs.
until 8.

Built in 1815 as the Berkshire County Courthouse, when Lenox was still the "shire town," this classic Greek-Revival building became the Lenox Library Association in 1873. It is listed on the National Register of Historic Places. Readers there can enjoy the main reading room, with its lofty illuminated ceiling and its amazing array of periodicals, or the outdoor reading park. This is Old World reading at its best. A solid collection of about 75,000 volumes plus a music room are available to the public. There is a closed collection of historical memorabilia, too, including the sled from the incident on which Edith Wharton based her novella *Ethan Frome*.

Current renovations will increase space for young people and computers and reveal the domed ceiling that arched over the original courtroom.

MILNE PUBLIC LIBRARY AND HOUSE OF LOCAL HISTORY
413-458-5369; 413-458-2160
(HLH).
www.milnelibrary.org.
1095 Main St.,
Williamstown, MA 01267
Open: Mon.–Wed. and Fri.
10–5, Thurs. 10–8, Sat.
10–1.

Williamstown is proud that a treasured resource has a roomy home—a former school with ample parking. With strong holdings of children's books, fiction, local history, videos, and popular music, the public library complements the Sawyer Library (below). Comfortable areas for reading and a helpful staff. The House of Local History shares the library's roof, having room enough to display much of its holdings. Both the library and HLH offer frequent programs.

SAWYER LIBRARY
413-597-2501.
www.williams.edu/library.
55 Sawyer Library Dr.,
Williamstown, MA
01267.
Center of Williams College
campus.
Open: Daily except
weekends and holidays
when Williams is not in
session.

At 835,745 volumes, 1,904 periodicals in paper, 2000-plus electronic texts, 488,433 micro texts, 28,620 sound recordings including the Paul Whiteman Collection, 7,579 videos, and 429,833 Federal documents, the Sawyer is a research resource unmatched within the county. Here we find a wide array of the latest periodicals, shelves of newly released books, and a library staff as helpful as they come. The public may use the facility, the stacks are open, and Sawyer is a pleasant place in which to work. The Schow Science Library is state of the art, and there are other departmental libraries, but all titles are included in Francis, the online catalog. The Williams library has recently joined the Boston Library Consortium.

**SIMON'S ROCK
  LIBRARY**
413-528-7370.
www.library.simons-
rock.edu.
Simon's Rock, College of
Bard.
84 Alford Rd., Gt.
Barrington, MA 01230.
Open: Hours vary.

The Simon's Rock Library is one of the best in South County, the staff always attentive to one's research needs. The college it serves may be small, but this library's holdings are exceedingly well chosen. It is open to visitors and to all Berkshire County residents for obtaining a library card. This is a library of half a dozen rooms on two floors in three interconnected pagoda-style buildings—all in a sylvan setting. With large skylights, the reading rooms are highly recommended for naturally lit, wet-weather browsing. And fascinating art exhibits almost always grace the library's skylighted gallery.

**STOCKBRIDGE
  LIBRARY AND
  HISTORICAL ROOM**
413-298-5501.
Mail: PO Box 119,
Stockbridge, MA 01262.
Main St. (Rte. 7).
Open: Mon.–Fri. 9–5, Sat.
9–4; Mon. and Fri. eve.
7–9; closed Sun.; the
Historical Room,
Tues.–Fri. 9–5, Sat. 9–4.

Parts of the Stockbridge Library date to 1864, and the reading room is one the most felicitous anywhere—tall, stately, and obviously from another era. The children's collection is also first-rate.

Called W-nahk-ta-kook ("Great Meadow") by the Mahican Indians who settled there, the town of Stockbridge was incorporated by the English in 1739. The colonial charter made the town Indian property, a mission, and thereafter it was known as "Indian Town." The history of this great meadow and its town is displayed and explained in the Stockbridge Historical Room, a small museum in the basement of the library. Here are Indian artifacts, photos from the mid-1800s onward, memorabilia from many famous residents and visitors to the village, and other intriguing historical bits that illuminate Stockbridge present.

MUSEUMS

THE BERKSHIRE MUSEUM
413-443-7171;
fax 413-443-2135.
www.berkshiremuseum.org.
39 South St., Pittsfield, MA 01201.
Open: Mon–Sat. 10–5, Sun. 12–5.
Admission: Adults $7.50, children 3–18 $4.50, students over 18 with ID and seniors $6, children under 3 free.
Special Features: Gift shop.

Three museums in one, the Berkshire Museum presents strong collections of art, science, and regional history as well as an exciting calendar of lectures, films, concerts, classes, and field trips.

Founded in 1903 by Dalton paper maker and philanthropist Zenas Crane, the museum shows Hudson River School paintings, the Proctor Shell Collection, and the Cohn Collection of Minerals. Also changing exhibits are featured throughout year. The collections are far-ranging: 19th-century glass made in the towns of Berkshire and Cheshire and pre-Christian glass bottles from Egypt; exhibits of shells and aquatic life, fossils, mushrooms, reptiles, and amphibians. The Bird Room has a special section on Berkshire birds; the owl exhibit especially captivates. The Berkshire Backyard presents native mammal specimens. A collection of beautiful dioramas by Louis Paul Jonas Sr. shows the animals of the world in one-tenth scale. An aquarium holds more than 100 species, featuring a hands-on exhibit for children called "Touch of the Sea."

That the museum is committed to families and community is demonstrated by recent exhibits such as action toys, antique toys, and refurbished Alexander Calder toys. The life-sized stegosaurus (named Wally) on the museum's front lawn is a community landmark. The Museum Theater, a 300-seat facility, is site for lectures, plays, concerts, and the Little Cinema's admirable program of feature films.

Upstairs, works of Copley, Stuart, and Peale represent American portraiture. The Hudson River School appears in works by Cole, Inness, and others. A European gallery is devoted to the work of such English portrait painters as West and Reynolds, plus European works by masters spanning the 15th to 18th centuries. In the museum's center is the lofty and skylighted Ellen Crane Memorial Room, devoted to American and European sculpture from the 19th and 20th centuries. An ancient civilizations gallery includes "Pa-hat," the ever-popular Egyptian mummy, who lies resplendent amid a first-rate collection of ancient reliefs and artifacts.

STERLING AND FRANCINE CLARK ART INSTITUTE
413-458-2303, 413-458-9545.
www.clarkart.edu.
225 South St., Williamstown, MA 01267.

Sterling Clark acquired his first Renoir in 1916. By the time he was finished collecting, he owned 36. He and his French wife, Francine, bought what they liked. Thus the basis of this fine collection reflects their personal taste. Included with Impressionists are galleries filled with 19th-

One mi. S of jct. of Rtes. 7 and 2.
Open: Tues.–Sun. 10–5; July and Aug., daily 10–5; closed Thanksgiving, Christmas, New Year's Day.
Admission: June through Oct., adults $10, students and children under 18 free; Nov. through May, free.
Special Features: Gift shop; café.

century American classics—by Winslow Homer, John Singer Sargent, and Frederick Remington—and a small but impressive collection of Old Masters. Traveling exhibits of Renoir, Degas, Millet, and "Painting Quickly in France" have recently attracted large summer crowds. The Clark originated the Vienna Project that united several Berkshire cultural entities in a common theme during the summer of 2002.

The original 1950s building is elegant and efficient, a white Vermont-marble neoclassic structure whose interior is finished in Italian marble, plaster, and natural-finish oak. The large 1973 red-granite addition houses more galleries and a serious art library. Substantial remodeling in 1996 added more galleries, storage, and a café. A new campus and entryway is planned. The museum shop includes an extensive collection of art books.

For most visitors, the centerpiece of the museum's collection is its gathering of French Impressionists, the Clarks' greatest artistic love. Among the standouts, besides Renoir, are works by Monet and Degas, the latter in both his racehorse and ballet dancer series. Almost every gallery has some form of natural light; many galleries offer not only splendid art on the walls but peaceful views of the Berkshire Hills, as well.

The Clark is more than a painting gallery, however. As we walk among its colorful masterworks and their accompanying drawings and prints, we also see some of the collection's antique furniture and silver, masterpieces of craftsmanship. A piano as artwork may be the Clark's most controversial recent acquisition.

An important art education center, as well, the Clark offers a broad spectrum of lectures open to the public, serving as classroom to a graduate program in art history run jointly with Williams College. The Clark also offers major events in connection with its exhibits, chamber music, video film programs, folk music, children's programs, and popular outdoor band concerts in the summer.

FRELINGHUYSEN-MORRIS HOUSE & STUDIO
413-637-0166,
fax 413-637-9790.
www.frelinghuysen.org.
92 Hawthorne St., Lenox, MA 01240
Open: June 28–Labor Day, Thurs.–Sun. 10–4; Sept.–Oct., Thurs.–Sat. 10–4.
Admission: Adults $8, children $3.

Anyone interested in art, architecture, or art history might be intrigued by the home and studio of George L. K. Morris and his wife, Suzy Frelinghuysen, artists and advocates of the avant garde. On exhibit are his and her framed works and murals, along with a smattering of Matisse, Degas, Picasso, Braque, Leger, and Gris. A large earth mother by Gaston Lachaise reclines among the trees on the wooded 46 acres that stretch between Hawthorne Street and Route 183, adjacent to Tanglewood.

The avant-garde stairway at the Freylinghuysen-Morris House.

Judith Monachina

Special Features: Limited items for sale.

Morris built his studio on the grounds in 1930, then added the Le Corbusier-style home in 1940—to the chagrin of Berkshire's traditionally housed residents. Morris, descended from a signer of the Declaration of Independence, died in an automobile accident in 1975. Frelinhuysen, from a line of Dutch-Reform clergymen, college presidents, and politicians, survived the accident, living until 1988.

HANCOCK SHAKER VILLAGE

413-443-0188.
www.hancockshakerv
  illage.org.
Mail: PO Box 927, Pittsfield, MA 01202.
Jct. of Rtes. 20 and 41, 6 mi. W. of Pittsfield.
Open: Memorial Day weekend–late Oct., 9:30–5 daily; Late Oct.–Memorial Day weekend, 10–3; closed Thanksgiving, Christmas, New Year's Day; call ahead in winter.
Admission: Adults $15 summer/fall, $12 winter/spring, children under 18 free.
Special Features: Museum shops, seasonal café; walking-tour brochures available in English, French, German, Spanish, Japanese, and Braille.

The United Society of Believers in Christ's Second Appearing, later called Shakers, were founded in England in 1747 as a small group of religious nonconformists. Ann Lee, a young woman with strong religious convictions, became their spiritual leader. In 1774, a small group joined "Mother Ann" in sailing for the New World. They landed in New York, near Albany, where they later formed the Shaker community of Niskeyuna.

Shaker religion was also a way of life. Members joined into distinct communities isolated from the outside world. Men and women held equal status in daily life and leadership positions, but the genders were separated to support the Shaker commitment to celibacy. Communities were organized into families. Members gave public confession of their sins. Ritual dancing gave rise to their name, originally derisive but later adopted by the sect.

A community was established in 1790 at Hancock. Given the spiritual name of the City of Peace, it prospered for more than 150 years. Residents sought heavenly perfection, resulting in products that came to be known for their beauty. Design of clothing, furniture, implements, and buildings was strictly functional, without addition of deliberate ornamentation. "'Tis a gift to be simple . . ." goes an old Shaker hymn, and such simplicity was a primary aim of both inner and outer life. "Beauty rests on utility," said their credo. Of great beauty, then, is Hancock's symbol, the stunning Round Stone Barn. As splendid as the structure is to the eye, how much more splendid is it that with such an efficient architecture, one farmhand at the center could easily and quickly feed an entire herd of cattle.

When the sect was at its peak, in the mid-19th century, Hancock was one of 18 Shaker communities from Maine to Kentucky and had a population of about 300 members. The agricultural base of the village was augmented by cottage industries, offering such items as cooperware, flat brooms, agricultural seeds and dairy products to sell to the World's People. But as religious ferment ceased, the Shaker population at Hancock declined steadily until 1960, when the last of the Hancock Shakers moved away.

Since then the village and its 1,200 acres of meadows and woodlands have been a living museum to accommodate visitors who want taste of the Shaker ways. The City of Peace now acts as center of re-created Shaker activities, including workshops, candlelit dinners, and evening tours. The second weekend in July is the Americana artists and crafts show.

Visitors can tour 20 original Shaker buildings to see Shaker furniture and tools, some of them attended by craftspeople working in the Shaker way: the chair maker, the blacksmith, basket makers, spinners, and weavers. Hancock's workshops teach how to create Shaker chair seats, oval boxes, natural herb wreaths, and a variety of other crafts. From the gardens, both herbal and vegetable, and from any of the village workers, visitors absorb the power of Shaker simplicity.

Always a destination for families, the replica of a c.1820 schoolhouse—complete with a teacher, in season—the discovery room, and the Center for Shaker Studies, make the museum even more appealing. With a new parking lot and entrance, together with space for rotating exhibits and programs, the village, its original residents departed, nevertheless continues into the future.

For a fee, the village offers its facilities for special events such as weddings.

MASS MoCA (Massachusetts Museum of Contemporary Art)
413-664-4481,
  fax 413-663-8548.
www.massmoca.org.
87 Marshall St., North
  Adams, MA 01247.
Open: June 1–Oct. 31, daily
  10–6; Nov. 1–May 30,
  Wed.–Mon. 11–5; closed

For 12 years the idea of a big museum in an old mill and director Joe Thompson hung on by their fingernails—until the Massachusetts Museum of Contemporary Art, or MASS MoCA as it is universally known, opened as a critical and public success in the summer of 1999. People in numbers beyond expectation streamed into the "supercollider for the best of today's visual, performing, and new media arts," as Thompson defines his 13-acre,

Thanksgiving, Christmas, New Year's Day.
Admission: Adults $7, seniors and students over 16 with ID $5, children 6–16 $2.
Special Features: Museum shop; performances.

27-building factory campus. "Until now," he explains, "large complex art forms—exotic multimedia productions, for example, or monumental installations—have been without a public forum that is striking, properly scaled, and technically wired for cross-disciplinary collaborations."

Although not everyone may take to the art works—gigantic to minimalist by Rauschenberg, Rosenquist, Flavin, Nauman, and Morris—everyone has responded to the gorgeous retrofitting of hangerlike spaces once a textile mill and more recently given over to the manufacture of capacitors. However, it was probably the accompanying variety of special events that made the opening summer and fall such a public success: "Swing Shift Dance Parties," "Film Factory" with outside projection, dance performances by the Paul Taylor Dance Company and others, concerts, and a musical, "Quark Victory," put on by the Williamstown Theatre Festival. With the assistance of Jacob's Pillow, the Clark Art Institute, and WTF, this kind of aggressive programming will continue.

North Adams, done up in banners and flowers, new streetlights, and new signage, looks—improbably as it may seem—like a city being lifted up and uplifted by art. The city itself, with MASS MoCA at its heart, may be the ultimate "large complex art form" on view thousands of visitors from around the world. As the museum changes and evolves, we shall see what they shall see.

NORMAN ROCKWELL MUSEUM
413-298-4100, 800-742-9450; fax 413-298-4142.
www.nrm.org.
Mail: PO Box 308, Stockbridge, MA 01262.
On Rte. 183, 0.6 mi. S. of Rte. 102.
Open: May–Oct., daily 10–5; Nov.–April, Mon.–Fri. 10–4, Sat.–Sun. 10–5. Closed Thanksgiving, Christmas, New Year's Day.
Admission: Adults $12, students over 18 with ID $7, children 18 and under free w/adult.
Special Features: Gift shop; Terrace Café open seasonally.

Norman Rockwell is coming to be seen more as artist than illustrator; the display of his life's work at the Norman Rockwell Museum resonates. A visit to this grand monument to his talent and insight is worth the crush of bus passengers—or go off-season.

Set on a gracious knoll overlooking the Housatonic River in the Glendale section of Stockbridge, the $4.4-million building designed by Robert A. M. Stern has a New England town hall look to it, with slate gables, clapboard siding, and fieldstone terraces. Inside, spacious, well-lit galleries show permanent exhibits of Rockwell's paintings, while exhibits featuring Rockwell and other illustrators change thrice yearly.

At the core is the skylighted gallery where Rockwell's *Four Freedoms* hang on permanent display. Created during the Second World War, they depict what the U.S. was fighting to uphold: *Freedom of Speech; Freedom from Fear; Freedom of Worship; Free-*

Freedom of Worship, *one of the famous "Four Freedoms" paintings by Norman Rockwell.*

dom from Want. These four archetypal American images constitute a shrine to America's progressive image of itself.

Rockwell's 47-year relationship with the *Saturday Evening Post* is well-known; in 1963 it ended, and he signed on with *Look* and *McCall's*. His palette and his cast of characters broadened. Where once he depicted white boys running from a prohibited swimming hole, now federal marshals lead a young black girl to school in Little Rock. From lovers and gossips, he moved on to Peace Corps volunteers and astronauts on the moon.

Outside stands Rockwell's studio, a 19th-century carriage house with a bucolic view of the Housatonic. Inside the studio, which was moved from Stockbridge village to its present site in 1986, we understand the light in which he loved to paint, the curious assemblage of props with which he liked to surround himself, and the modest space he felt was his "best studio yet." The studio is open May through October.

The Rockwell Museum offers a variety of community-oriented programs beyond its public exhibitions, including lectures, performances, special events, and art classes.

WESTERN GATEWAY HERITAGE STATE PARK
413-663-6312.
115 State St., Bldg. 4, N. Adams, MA. 01247-3852.
In freight-yard district.
Open: Daily 10–5; closed Thanksgiving, Christmas, New Year's Day.

Berkshire County, nestled between long ridges, had always been separated from the rest of Massachusetts. In 1851, engineers and construction workers began an assault, drilling and blasting a 4.75-mile-long tunnel through the northeastern ridge. This Hoosac Tunnel was the first major tunneling work in the United States. New methods were devised over the 20-year construction, at a cost of over $20 million and more than 195 lives.

Admission: Free; donations accepted.
Special Features: Gift shop; restaurant.

The building of the tunnel and related railroad development made North Adams the largest city in Berkshire in 1900. "We hold the Western Gateway," says the North Adams seal. At the turn of the 20th century, more than half of Boston's freight came through the tunnel.

Western Gateway Heritage State Park now celebrates the former Boston and Maine Freight House and the Hoosac Tunnel, both of which are on the National Register of Historic Places. Inside, find films, slide shows, and written histories of the railway and tunnel are presented. Outside are shops, the restored freight yard, the Freight Yard Pub restaurant, and the church-spired charm of North Adams.

Heritage State Park is also home to the **North Adams Museum of History & Science** (413-664-4700; www.northadams.com/history; Building 5-A), open Thursday through Sunday from 10 to 4, at no charge. An old-fashioned museum of 25 exhibits, discovery room, and three working train models chronicle the history of and achievements related to N. Adams and Northern Berkshire.

WILLIAMS COLLEGE MUSEUM OF ART
413-597-2429.
www.williams.edu/WCMA.
Main St., Williamstown, MA 01267.
Rte. 2, across from Gothic chapel.
Open: Tues.–Sat. 10–5, Sun. 1–5, inc. Memorial Day, Labor Day, Columbus Day; closed Thanksgiving, Christmas, New Year's.
Admission: Free.
Special Features: Gift shop.

One of the finest college art museums in the country, the Williams College Museum of Art is a 19th-century structure that has been strikingly revisited. Behind the original 1846 building, with its neoclassical octagonal rotunda, is an addition designed by Charles Moore that opened in 1983. Combining wit and sophistication, Moore created a versatile, multileveled exhibition space in both old and new buildings, retaining the brick wall of the former as the stunning backdrop for a multilevel stair well. His design for the building's rear facade is a continuation of his lighthearted approach, featuring his "ironic columns"—their nonfunctionality revealed by the gap near the top. Now the eyes have it in front—as a result of a searching and striking piece commissioned of Louise Bourgeois.

Inside, the museum's permanent collection contains some 11,000 objects. Complementing the Clark's collection of 19th-century European art, WCMA emphasizes early art, 20th-century art, and the art of Asia and other nonwestern civilizations. Thanks to a $32 million gift by the widow of American Impressionist Charles Prendergast, what was once a small, regional museum now houses the finest collection by both Charles and his talented brother, Maurice, and is now the leading center in the world for study of the Prendergasts' work.

A lively education program includes school events and other events for children. Several times a year WCMA hosts popular free "family day," when children can try a range of art projects thematically linked to the collection, guided by enthusiastic Williams students.

Frequent loan exhibitions focus on a wide range of provocative subjects; in the summer of 2002 such an exhibit was influences on Adolf Hitler. Art of Tibet will be shown in 2003. Visitors should expect to be engaged, not soothed.

BERKSHIRE SCENIC RAILWAY MUSEUM
413-637-2210.
www.berkshirescenic
railroad.org.
10 Willow Creek Rd., PO Box 2195, Lenox, MA 01240.
One and a half miles E of Jct. of Rtes. 7 and 20, 5 miles N of Lee exit off the MassPike.
Open: Memorial Day–Oct., weekends and holidays, 10–4.
Tickets: Adults $12, seniors $10, children under 14 $8.
Special Features: Museum; gift shop.

Freed by a major state grant in 2002 and an agreement to use the Housatonic Railroad's tracks, the Berkshire Scenic Railroad will be running again. For the first time in more than a decade, visitors will be able to take a scenic train ride (narrated by a uniformed conductor) along the Housatonic River between Lenox and Stockbridge —a 20-mile round-trip in 1920s-vintage Erie Lackawanna passenger coaches pulled and pushed by a GE diesel locomotive. Afterward, passengers can blow the whistle or ring the bell, check out the model trains in the 1902 Lenox train station, and admire Woods Pond. Also new in 2003: a refurbished 1920s vintage Baltimore and Ohio Railroad coach is being fitted out as a home for a "Gateway to the Gilded Age" exhibit, which interprets the turn-of-the-20th-century era of fabulous summer cottages in the Berkshires.

OTHER MUSEUMS

Besides delving into fine art and rare books, the many museums in Williamstown lead in still other directions. For example, *out* to the **Hopkins Forest Museum** (413-597-2346; *Hopkins Memorial Forest*, the *Rosenberg Center*, and *Buxton Garden*; Northwest Hill Rd.) and such seasonal events as fall harvesting and maple sugaring, while the museum itself exhibits old photographs, farm machinery, and tools. Or *up* to the stars at the 19th-century fieldstone **Hopkins Observatory** (413-597-2188; Main St.) via the projected shows at the **Milham Planetarium** (evenings Tues. and Thurs. summer; Fri. during school year), and out and up to the real pulsars and quasars through the telescopes at Williams College.

Bennington Museum (802-447-1571), 15 miles north of Williamstown on Route 7, west on Route 9 in Vermont; and **Historic Deerfield, Inc.** (413-774-5581), east on Route 2 and south on Route 5, are fine day-trip destinations. Plans are under way to create another major Shaker museum, in New Lebanon, New York.

MUSIC

ASTON MAGNA
413-528-3595, 800-875-7156.
www.astonmagna.org.
St. James Church, PO Box
28, Gt. Barrington, MA
01230.
Just S. of Town Hall.
Season: July and Aug.
Tickets: Call for prices.

Of historic preservation in the Berkshires, none more artistic than the renaissance of Baroque, Classical, and early Romantic chamber music by Aston Magna. Offering unique cross-disciplinary educational programs for professional musicians and superb concerts in the summer and at other times, Aston Magna has specialized in 17th-, 18th-, and early 19th-century music, always played on period instruments or reproductions. In the summer of 2002, Mozart, Haydn, Bach, Handel, Vivaldi, Monteverdi, and Corelli were played as in their own time, with festival artistic director and virtuoso violinist Daniel Stepner leading a distinguished roster of singers and instrumentalists. Participants study the temperament and cultural milieu of the age and then make music that is imbued with the period's sensibility.

Andrew Porter, reviewing this festival in *The New Yorker*, noted that the string players are "probably as good as any in the world. The winds are in tune. The old self-consciousness has been replaced by confidence, by character and, beyond that, by something one might almost describe as a philosophy intelligently and joyfully embraced. For there is more to Aston Magna than authentic instruments, stylistic insights, and technical ability."

BERKSHIRE CHORAL FESTIVAL
413-229-1999 (box office); administration
413-229-8526;
fax 413-229-0109.
www.choralfest.org.
Mail: 245 N.
Undermountain Rd.,
Sheffield, MA 01257.
Performance Venue:
Concert Shed, Berkshire School, Rte. 41, Sheffield.
Season: July and August.
Tickets: Required.

An experiment in mixing amateur, semipro, and professional singers into a chorus culminated in a single concert. Success there has led the Berkshire Choral Festival nearly 20 years later to evolve into a summer-long, professional-quality chorus—changing with each performance—that can be counted on for stirring moments, as in a recent Brahms *Requiem*.

Each summer now brings a five-concert Berkshire celebration featuring 200 adult, amateur voices from all over the world, powerful soloists and conductors, and the Springfield Symphony, at one of the loveliest preparatory schools in New England, The Berkshire School. These performances are also given at other venues around the world.

BERKSHIRE OPERA COMPANY
413-644-9000;
fax: 413-644-9030.

In over a decade, originally under founder-director Rex Hearn, the Berkshire Opera seems stronger than ever. This talented group has won praise from both audiences and serious critics alike

www.berkshireopera.org.
Performance Venue: To be announced.
Season: July and Aug.
Tickets: $20–$60.

for its English-language renditions of chamber opera.

There are discoveries to be made here. Among them was Stockbridge resident Maureen O. Flynn, whom Hearn initially heard singing at the First Congregational Church in Lee and who has since gone from the Berkshire Opera to the Metropolitan and a brilliant international career.

Recent offerings have included an adaptation it and Edith Wharton Restoration commissioned of Wharton's novella *Summer*. While critics' views on the success of the production varied, they united in praising the Berkshire Opera Company for bringing the production into being and filling a needed role in the rich summer life of the region by offering artfully prepared chamber operas.

SHAKER MOUNTAIN PERFORMING ARTS FESTIVAL
800-588-9757.
Performing Venues: Robert Boland Auditorium, Berkshire Community College, Pittsfield; Darrow School, New Lebanon, NY.
Season: Summer.
Tickets: Required for major performances.

In 2001 Denes Stiny opened a music camp for students and newly emerging professional performers at the Darrow School. In 2002 he moved the major performances to the stage at Berkshire Community College, keeping free events at the Darrow amphitheater. Operas and concerts from Shaker Mountain as well as those of the Albany Berkshire Ballet filled the BCC stage that summer. Shaker Mountain put on *Carousel* and selections from opera with the Albany Symphony Orchestra. It aims for nothing less than an abbreviated version of Wagner's *Ring* cycle.

Return to all performances at Darrow? Make BCC the headquarters? Just where the *Götterdämmerung* will take place remains uncertain.

SOUTH MOUNTAIN CONCERTS
413-442-2106.
Mail: PO Box 23, Pittsfield, MA 01202.
On Rtes. 7 & 20 about 1 mi. S. of Pittsfield Country Club.
Season: Sept.–Oct.
Tickets: Prices vary.

South Mountain's colonial-style Temple of Music, built in 1918 and the gift of Mrs. Elizabeth Sprague Coolidge, was intended to house the concerts of the Berkshire String Quartet. The acoustically splendid 500-seat auditorium, listed on the National Register of Historic Places, is set gracefully on its wooded South Mountain slope.

Distinguished performers have always made South Mountain a special place. In recent years string quartets have led the fare—the Guarneri, the Juilliard, the Emerson, and the Tokyo String Quartets have been regular performers. Usually one concert each season features another combination, such as the Kalichstein-Loredo-Robinson Trio.

With a devoted subscription membership, South Mountain Concerts almost always sell out. Nonsubscribers should call early for seats. Fortunately, every seat is good because of the acoustics.

Unlike Tanglewood, where watching the stars or basking in the sunshine may substitute for close listening to the music, South Mountain's more limited season and number of concerts are designed for the serious music lover.

A moving bass passage through Tanglewood's parklike setting.

Boston Symphony Orchestra

TANGLEWOOD
Tickets/information: 413-637-5165; concert line, 413-637-1666; administration, 413-637-1600.
www.bso.org.
297 West St., Lenox, MA 01240.
On Rte. 183.
Off-season: 617-266-1492; 301 Massachusetts Ave., Boston, MA 02115.
Season: June–Sept.
Tickets: $15 lawn on up, rehearsals free.
Special Features: Gift shops; restaurant.

Tanglewood remains *the* summer music festival in New England, an incomparable facility for all the world's musicians and music lovers. Whether you picnic on the lawn or sit closer to the Boston Symphony Orchestra in the Shed, hearing music at Tanglewood is an unparalleled experience. The powerful positive feeling among musicians, students, and concertgoers alike, the sheer fun of seeing and hearing great music made in the great outdoors makes Tanglewood the quintessential Berkshire entertainment—even if some people start repacking their picnic baskets during the Chorale in Beethoven's *Ninth*.

Tanglewood began as the Berkshire Music Festival in the summer of 1934. Members of the New York Philharmonic were bused from Manhattan to the mountains and lodged in the area's hotels for the concert series. A rousing success, it was repeated the following summer. But then the New York orchestra withdrew. As a result, Serge Koussevitzky, the Russian-born conductor of the Boston Symphony Orchestra, was wooed and won. The BSO signed on for a series of three concerts on a single August weekend in 1936.

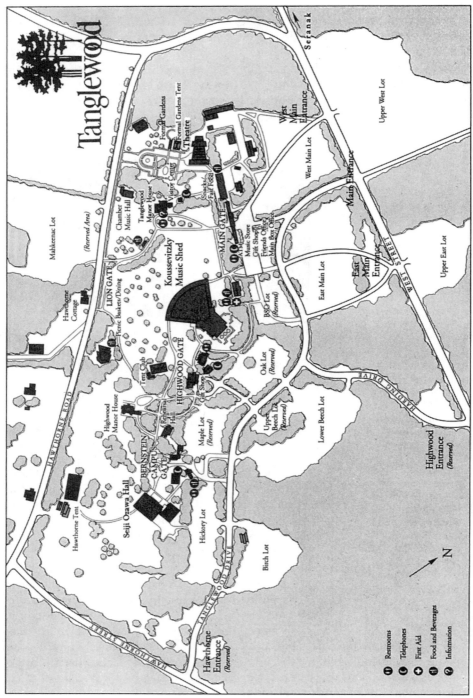

Courtesy Boston Symphony Orchestra

The popularity of this series was immense, with nearly 15,000 people attending. That fall the Tappan family gave their Tanglewood estate on the Stockbridge-Lenox border to the BSO as a permanent summer home in the Berkshires. For the first two summers, concerts were held in a large canvas tent, but during one 1937 program, a torrential thunderstorm drowned out Wagner's "The Ride of the Valkyries" and dampened instruments, musicians, and audience alike. During intermission, an impromptu fund-raising drive raised pledges totaling $30,000 for the creation of a permanent "music pavilion." By the following summer, through the combined efforts of the distinguished architect Eliel Saarinen and Stockbridge engineer Joseph Franz, the Shed was a reality.

Sensing the opportunity and the ideal setting, Koussevitzky and the BSO added the Berkshire Music Center for advanced musicians in 1940, the only such school run by a major symphony orchestra. For the school's opening ceremony, Randall Thompson composed his haunting *Alleluia* for unaccompanied chorus, a work that made such a lasting impression that it has been performed as the school's opening music ever since.

Each summer the Tanglewood Music Center Orchestra is recreated from that year's crop of students; for their weekly concerts, this impressive group is usually led by a student conductor, but sometimes by the likes of Kurt Masur, Zubin Mehta, or André Previn. So significant is this Tanglewood education that upwards of 20 percent of the members of America's major orchestras count themselves among Tanglewood Music Center alumni. Leonard Bernstein was a graduate, as are Seiji Ozawa and Mr. Mehta.

The $10 million arched Ozawa Hall opened in the summer of 1994. Accommodating 1,200 inside and an additional 700 on nearby lawns, the new hall has sides that open, giving it flexibility and versatility as well as excellent acoustics. The hall is located on the Highwood section of Tanglewood, now designated as the Leonard Bernstein campus.

Roberto Abbado is a regular conductor at Tanglewood.

Sylvia Lelli

Where to Sit at Tanglewood

Those planning to picnic at Tanglewood before a performance given in the Shed should arrive an hour or so in advance of concert time. Besides allowing time to eat before listening, arriving early affords a greater choice of spaces on the lawn, an important factor in hearing the music clearly. Although Tanglewood's amplification system is excellent and facilitates good listening from almost any lawn position, places about 25 yards beyond the Shed-mounted speakers provide the best lawn listening.

Inside the Shed, the last series of back rows are good only for saying we were there, allowing only the most distant orchestra views and suffering greatly from much-diminished sound. (In fact, sitting at the optimum sites on the lawn, the sound is far superior.) Those who can afford to indulge should buy their way forward into the good seats, where the sound is rich, sometimes robust and sometimes delicate, and where you can really see classical music in the making. (Food is not allowed in the shed, however.)

The Ozawa Concert Hall has its own lawn with seating for several hundred.

All attendees should allow time for a walk in Tanglewood's beautifully groomed boxwood gardens. As the sun sets on a clear day, the hills range in three states.

The Music Festival has evolved into a performance center of major proportions, with an annual attendance of some 300,000 visitors. Pianists Emanuel Ax and Peter Serkin, violinist Itzhak Perlman, cellist Yo-Yo Ma, and the Juilliard String Quartet return regularly. In addition to the regular BSO concerts, Tanglewood presents weekly chamber music concerts in the smaller sheds, Prelude Concerts on Friday nights, open rehearsals on Saturday mornings, the annual Festival of Contemporary Music, the annual Jazz Festival, and almost daily concerts by gifted young musicians at the Music Center. Some student concerts are free. The Boston Pops comes to play, as well.

A favorite of each season is "Tanglewood on Parade," an amazingly varied musical day lasting some ten hours, climaxing with booming cannon shots and fireworks. But whatever the scale of the offerings, an evening at Tanglewood marks a high point in any summer.

Festivals-within-the-Festival at Tanglewood

Not content to satisfy the classical music lover, Tanglewood offers minifestivals and series featuring contemporary, jazz, and popular music.

Recent offerings in the Contemporary Music Festival have been an appropriately eclectic mix, including a performance by puppets. When our free spirits are being kept too staid by our classicism, we require a dose of Tanglewood's Contemporary Music.

Artistry of an even jazzier sort is showcased during Tanglewood's annual Jazz Festival, with the likes of Branford Marsalis, Dave Brubeck, and the New Black Eagle Jazz band; and songs of a slightly different sort are featured during Tanglewood's Popular Artist Series, frequently including the always-popular James Taylor and a live broadcast of NPR's *A Prairie Home Companion.*

OTHER MUSIC

The winds of the Berkshire Bach Society, in rehearsal for the traditional New Year's Eve performance of the Bach Brandenburg Concertos.

In **South County**, the **Berkshire Bach Society** (413-528-9277; PO Box 553, S. Egremont, MA 01258) offers a fine series of concerts and lectures at various area churches, schools, and colleges. **Berkshire Friends of Music** (413-243-9744; PO Box 2397, Lenox, MA 01240) typically organizes five to seven chamber and orchestral concerts September through June at Seiji Ozawa Hall, Tanglewood, and elsewhere. **Simon's Rock College of Bard** (413-528-0771; Alford Rd., Gt. Barrington, MA 01230) is one of the liveliest promoters of professional music in South County. Under the artistic direction of Hilda Banks Shapiro, **Barrington Performing Arts** (413-528-4454; 81 Egremont Plain Rd., Gt. Barrington, MA 01230) presents several concerts at Simon's Rock's Kellogg Hall. **Close Encounters with Music** (518-392-6677, 800-843-0778; PO Box 34, Gt. Barrington, MA 01230) offers beautiful music and intriguing commentary by artistic director Yehuda Hanani and guests at Great Barrington's St. James Church and elsewhere, with an annual community concert at the Berkshire Athenaeum. The **Curtisville Consortium** (413-698-2618; PO Box 140, W. Stockbridge, MA 01266) takes its name from the hamlet of Interlaken in Stockbridge, which was originally settled as Curtisville. The consortium is a group of Boston Symphony Orchestra musicians and guest artists who present a five-week-long series of concerts each summer at the Trinity Church in Lenox. **Music & More** (413-229-3126; HC 65, Box 123B, New Marlborough, MA 01230) presents later-summer Saturday programs at the Meeting House on New Marlborough Green.

In **_Central County_**, chamber music can also be enjoyed at the **Richmond Performance Series** (413-698-2002; PO Box 199, Richmond, MA 01254). Each of these concerts—performed at the Richmond Congregational Church, Route 41, and other venues—features professional symphony orchestra veterans making intimate music in special settings. **Berkshire Community College** (413-499-4660; www.ccberkshire.org; 1350 West St., Pittsfield, MA 01201) offers concerts year-round. **Stockbridge Summer Music** (413-443-1138; www.baygo.com/ssms) offers concerts on summer Mondays at the Seven Hills Inn, at 40 Plunkett Rd., Lenox. The **Berkshire Lyric Theatre** (413-499-0258; www.berkshirelyric.org; PO Box 347, Pittsfield, MA 01201), plays at Lenox Town Hall and in Central and South County churches. The **Berkshire Concert Choir** (413-443-4758; PO Box. 174, Richmond, MA 01254), under the direction of John Cheney, presents sacred and secular music in two concerts each year, one in December and one in May.

In **_North County_**, **Williams College** alone offers enough music to keep anyone humming, with four classical Thompson visiting performances, a world-music series, and performances by Williams faculty. The **Berkshire Symphony**, part professional and part student, and **Williams Choral Society**, both under the auspices of the Williams Department of Music, generally present three concerts apiece during the academic year. The student **Jazz Ensemble**, **Kusika**, the **Zambezi Marimba Band**, and close harmony groups too numerous to name provide musical saturation of high quality. The **Griffin Hall** series presents harpsichord and organ music. (Concert manager's office: 413-597-2736; 24-hour Concertline: 413-597-3146; Griffin Hall Concerts: 413-597-2428.) In the summer, the **Taubman Piano Festival** brings rising young virtuosi to town to perform at Chapin Hall, Williams.

Elsewhere in Williamstown, the **Clark Art Institute** (413-458-2303; www.clark art.edu, 225 South St., Williamstown, MA 01267) presents free band music outdoors in the summer and a variety of concerts indoors, including those of the **Williamstown Chamber Concerts** (413-458-8273; PO Box 287, Williamstown, MA 01267), which continues its winning ways. **The Northern Berkshire Chorale**, a citizens' group under the direction of Judith Reichert, offers a concert spring and fall. Over in North Adams, **Massachusetts College of Liberal Arts** (413-662-5000) sponsors the **Smith House Concert Series** (413-662-5201), usually professional musicians with local connections. **Opus Berkshire** (413-663-3121, off-season 212-787-6262; 1391 Massachusetts Ave., N. Adams, MA 01247), presents a festival of performances by internationally renowned musicians organized by pianist Daniel Epstein of Blackinton.

Just **_Outside the County_**, in the Berkshire hill town of Charlemont (Rte. 2, Franklin County), the **Mohawk Trail Concerts** (413-625-9511, 888-MTC-MUSE; www.mohawktrail.org; PO Box 75, Shelburne Falls, MA 01370) presents a season of informal classical concerts at the Federated Church. In South Worthington, the Schrade family presents its summer **Sevenars Music Festival** (413-238-5854) at the Academy on Rte. 112.

Just over the state line, in New Lebanon, New York, are the *Tannery Pond Concerts* (tickets 888-846-5848; information 888-820-1696; PO Box 446, New Lebanon, NY 12125). Tannery's season comprises five or six chamber or song recitals between May and October. In adjacent Spencertown, New York, the *Spencertown Academy* (518-392-3693; PO Box 80, Spencertown, NY 12165) puts on concerts that are diverse, compelling, and held in a remarkable elderly former school building that is now a center for the arts.

Two well-regarded chamber music festivals in northwestern Connecticut enrich the greater Berkshire area. One is the *Norfolk Chamber Music Festival* (860-542-3000, fax 860-542-3004; www.yale.edu/norfolk; Ellen Battell Stoeckell Estate, Rtes. 44 & 272; PO Box 545, Norfolk, CT 06058; off season 203-432-1966; PO Box 208246, New Haven, CT 06520). Norfolk presents visiting virtuosi, such as the Tokyo String Quartet and the Vermeer Quartet, mid-June through mid-August, as a byproduct of the Yale Summer School of Music.

In nearby Falls Village is *Music Mountain* (860-824-7126; www.musicmoun tain.org; PO Box 738, Lakeville, CT 06039; Music Mountain Rd., off Rte. 7 opposite Housatonic Valley High School). Here the Manhattan String Quartet and visiting artists perform mid-June to Labor Day. Founded in 1930 by Chicago Symphony Orchestra concertmaster Jacques Gordon, Music Mountain is the oldest continuing chamber music festival in America.

NIGHTLIFE

A lthough the Berkshires may be better known as home to great theater, visual art, and classical music, there is a longstanding tradition of popular nightlife in these parts, including top national and regional performing talent in jazz, folk, rock, and cabaret.

While new venues are always popping up and older ones occasionally fall by the wayside, several well-established nightclubs and restaurants offer after-hours entertainment. Starting in *South County,* Club Helsinki (413-528-3394; 284 Main St., Gt. Barrington, MA 01230) has in the last few years become the shining star of the Berkshire live-music scene, presenting an eclectic array of regional and nationally known performers in an intimate, funky, L-shaped den of brickwork and art-deco objects. The list of artists who have packed the 100-seat club ranges from avant-garde guitarist Marc Ribot to jazz singer Mose Allison to Texas country legend Guy Clark. Reggae, blues, and funk bands often play the club—which boasts a terrific selection of imported vodkas and a bar menu of specialties from the adjoining restaurant, Helsinki Café. The club periodically presents marquee artists like Doc Watson, Pete Seeger, and the Five Blind Boys of Alabama a block away at the Mahaiwe Theatre. Next door to the Mahaiwe, the Castle Street Café's *Celestial Bar* (413-528-5244; 10 Castle St., Gt. Barrington, MA 01230) is a traditional-style piano bar with featured performers on weekend nights, including pianists, guitar-and-vocal trios, and the occasional swing or bluegrass group. Jazz singer Vikki True is resident at *Cheesecake Charlie's* (413-528-7790; 271 Main St., Gt. Barrington, MA 01230), where on most weekends she headlines a jazz cabaret. Over in South Egremont, the *Egremont Inn* (413-528-2111; www.egremontinn.com; 10 Old Sheffield Rd., PO Box 418, S. Egremont, MA 01258; just off Rte. 23) also reliably presents jazz on weekends.

From late spring through foliage season, the *Guthrie Center* (413-528-1955; 4 Van Deusenville Rd., Gt. Barrington, MA 01230) presents weekend concerts featuring regional and national folk talent, including Dar Williams, Christine Lavin, and Bill Morrissey. Located at the historic Trinity Church—best known as the location for the antics immortalized in "Alice's Restaurant," the song and movie—the Guthrie Center also is home base to folksinger Arlo Guthrie, who lives nearby and frequently performs there. In Stockbridge, the *Lion's Den* at the Red Lion Inn (413-298-5545; 30 Main St., Stockbridge, MA 01262; Rte. 7) is a cozy, coffeehouse-style nightclub featuring nightly entertainment—and no cover charge—drawn from the region's top talent, including the ever-popular David Grover. Well-known national performers such as John Hall of Orleans and Jon Pousette-Dart occasionally drop by. During the summer, the *Stockbridge Cabaret* (413-298-4032; DeSisto School, Rte. 183, Stockbridge, MA 01262), just down the road apiece from Tanglewood, is a popular late-night after-concert attraction, boasting top-flight cabaret artists such as Ann Hampton Callaway, Karen Mason, and Jeff Harnar. As its name indicates, the *Berkshire Blues Café* (413-243-0062; Rte. 102, Lee, MA 01238) specializes in presenting local blues-based bands and singers. For years, the *Dream Away Lodge* (413-623-8725; 1342 County Road, Becket, MA 01223) has attracted the bohemian after-hours crowd from Tanglewood and Jacob's Pillow. After a period of hibernation, the rambling, way-off-the-beaten-path roadhouse, which has played host to everyone from Bob Dylan to Liberace, is under a new management that has revived the traditional Wednesday night hootenanny and hosts folk-based performers on weekends. Food's pretty good, too.

In *Central County,* the *Berkshire Museum* (413-443-7171; 39 South St., Pittsfield, MA 01201; Rte. 7), presents monthly concerts in its 300-seat auditorium by nationally known singer-songwriters like Lucy Kaplansky, John Gorka and Cheryl Wheeler. Mexican restaurant *La Cocina* (413-499-6363; 140 Wahconah St., Pittsfield, MA 01201) is ground-zero for the local neo-hippie, jam-band set, and Southwestern restaurant *La Choza* (448-6100; 75 North St., Pittsfield, MA 01201) presents an eclectic array of rock bands, funk groups, and electronic performances. The *Common Grounds Coffee House* (499-0866; 55 Fenn St., Pittsfield, MA 01201), presents troubadour-style folksingers at the First United Methodist Church on a monthly basis.

Sleepy *North County* has awoken over the last few years, in large part due to the opening of the Massachusetts Museum of Contemporary Art (413-662-

---

Festival Frenzy

Music moves outdoors in the summertime, when the Berkshire Hills come alive with the sounds of folk, bluegrass, blues, jazz, and cutting-edge rock music. Neo-hippie jamming is the main theme at the eclectic *Berkshire Mountain Music Festival* (866-BMM-FEST; www.berkfest.com; Rte. 23, Gt. Barrington) typically held in August at Butternut Basin Ski Resort. Past bands at the three-day event with camping include Soulive, Galactic, Moe, and Medeski, Martin, and Wood. Jazz has carved out a niche during the last two weekends of the summer. Working backward from the end of the summer, Labor Day Weekend is reserved for jazz at *Tanglewood* (413-637-5165; Rte. 183) in Lenox, where the august classical music campus turns itself over to a three-day jazz festival featuring the swinging sounds of the likes of Sonny Rollins, Branford Marsalis, and Diana Krall. Jazz fans warm up for Tanglewood the weekend before with the two-day *Berkshire Jazz Festival* (914-674-2005) at Butternut Basin, where Chuck Mangione, Spyro Gyra, and Roy Hargrove have performed in recent years.

Just a short drive over the New York State line gets you to three of the best summer music festivals in the nation. The venerable *Grey Fox Bluegrass Festival* (888-946-8495; www.GreyFoxBluegrass.com) has taken place at the Rothvoss Farm in Ancramdale, New York, for over 20 years. It's a must-stop on the summer bluegrass circuit for fans as well as top performers including Sam Bush, Tony Trischka, Ralph Stanley, Peter Rowan, Bill Keith, and Alison Krauss. The *Falcon Ridge Folk Festival* (ticket info 877-844-7742; www.falconridgefolk.com; mail: 74 Modley Rd., Sharon, CT 06069) at the Long Hill Farm in Hillsdale, New York, rivals the Newport (Rhode Island) Folk Festival for crowds and top contemporary folk acts, including Ani DiFranco, Patty Larkin, Greg Brown, and John Gorka. A week after Falcon Ridge, the *Winterhawk Festival* (ticket info 877-308-5646; www.winterhawk2000.com) takes place on the same site, featuring an eclectic array of old-time string bands, Cajun, Irish, zydeco, western swing, and roots-rock groups. These three festivals are all in July, last for several days, and attract thousands of campers and families as well as day visitors.

2111; 87 Marshall St., N. Adams, MA 01237) in North Adams. *MASS MoCA* itself has become a key venue for nightlife, hosting monthly dance parties featuring live bands playing swing, polka, salsa, African, zydeco, and blues. MASS MoCA also presents several big-name concerts each year—Patti Smith, Dr. John, They Might Be Giants, Suzanne Vega, Nanci Griffith, and Cowboy Junkies are just a handful of the acts who have performed in the museum's state-of-the-art black-box theater or outdoor concert courtyard. The *Railway Café* (413-664-6393; 59 Summer St., N. Adams, MA 01237) is a monthly folk venue at St. John's Episcopal Church hosting top New England singer-songwriters like Cliff Eberhardt. Over in Williamstown, the *Clark Art Institute* (413-458-2303; 225 South St., Williamstown, MA 01267) typically hosts a thematic concert series in the fall and winter, often featuring traditional and experimental folk musicians from around the world. When the Williamstown Theatre Festival is up and running during the summer months, top stars of stage and film occasionally ham it up at the *WTF Cabaret* (413-597-3400) on the Williams College campus. On Friday nights, pianist Howie Levitz accompanies guitarist Jim Bayliss in the tavern at the **Williams Inn** (413-458-9371; 1090 Main St., Williamstown, MA 01267), where the venerable clarinetist Walt Lehman and his jazz ensemble swings the crowd on Saturdays.

Berkshirites think nothing of hopping in the car and driving an hour to nearby Northampton for a fix of that college town's eclectic musical menu at one of several venues, including the recently restored **Calvin Theatre** to see the likes of Lyle Lovett or Sonny Rollins; **Pearl Street** for hot rock, reggae, or hip-hop acts; or the venerable **Iron Horse Music Hall**, where the best in folk, jazz, country and alternative music can be heard most any night of the year. Call the Northampton Box Office (413-586-8686) for schedules or reservations at any of these venues.

THEATER

Barrington Stage Company / Joe Schuyler

Sandy Binion, Jacob Heimer, and Philip Hoffman in Barrington Stage Company's production of Falsettos.

**BARRINGTON STAGE
COMPANY**
413-528-8888;
fax 413-528-8807.

Julianne Boyd, artistic director of the Barrington Stage Company, is a whiz at detecting the enduring in what might seem the old soft shoe, e.g., the 2002 production that took *South Pacific* into the 21st

www.barringtonstageco. org.
Consolati Performing Arts Center, Mt. Everett Regional High School, Box 946, Gt. Barrington, MA 01230.
Season: Summer–Fall
Tickets: Various prices; students half price.

BERKSHIRE THEATRE FESTIVAL
Box office 413-298-5576; administration 413-298-5536.
www.berkshiretheatre.org.
6 E. Main St. PO Box 797, Stockbridge, MA 01262.
On Rte. 102.
Season: Summer.
Tickets: Main Stage, $27–$36; Unicorn Theatre, $18; Children's Theatre, $5-$7.50.
Special Features: Gift shop.

century. Or consider what really got BSC under way in 1995: *Lady Day at Emerson's Bar & Grill*, starring Gail Nelson as blues singer Billie Holiday, playing to sell-outs at restaurants. In between, *Mac and Mabel* had a highly successful run on the main stage, while *St. Nicholas* and *Grease* flourished on Stage II. Barrington runs KidsAct, training 10-to-17-year-olds, summer and fall.

In 1887 architect Stanford White completed his design for the Stockbridge Casino Company, created for the "establishment and maintenance of a place for a reading room, library and social meeting." Forty years later, when the structure had fallen into disuse, Mabel Choate, daughter of Ambassador Joseph H. Choate of Stockbridge, gave the Casino to the Three Arts Society. That group, in turn, moved it to its present site at the foot of Yale Hill, renting it to Alexander Kirkland and F. Cowles Strickland, who opened the Berkshire Playhouse in 1928.

Since that time, the playhouse—later renamed Berkshire Theatre Festival—has been in the forefront of American summer theater. Major works by nearly every American playwright of note have been performed here, including Lillian Hellmann, Tennessee Williams, Eugene O'Neill, and Thornton Wilder. The playhouse produced Wilder's *Our Town* and *The Skin of Our Teeth*, with Wilder himself in featured roles. Yet a production of *Pinafore* was a highlight of the 2001 season.

Leading lights in the theater appear regularly, from a young Katherine Hepburn in 1930 to Joanne Woodward in 1996.

The last two decades have been a period of growth and refocusing for BTF. In the spring of 1976, the building was entered on the National Register of Historic Places. Since then, gradual refurbishment has continued, with a new paint job and, most noticeably, all new seats. The Berkshire Theatre Festival has expanded its educational and rehearsal facilities, principally upon the gift of the Lavan Center, a few miles north of the playhouse. Interns and apprentices live at the center and rehearse there while pursuing a program of classes in acting, voice, movement, and design.

BTF also features performances at its 100-seat Unicorn Theatre, a showcase for younger artists. These are becoming increasingly substantial, recently being highlighted by the painterly *Mississippi Nude*, by John Reaves, one artist's life in living color. The educational aspect, called "The BTF Plays," reaches out to local schools.

**MUSIC-THEATRE
GROUP**
413-298-5504; off season
  212-366-5260.
During season: PO Box 42,
  W. Glendale, MA 01229.
Off season: Suite 1001, 30
  W. 26th St., New York,
  NY 10010.
Season: June and Aug. in
  Berkshire.
Tickets: $15–$20.

For its innovative and penetrating explorations of musical theater, the Music Theatre Group has won 20 Obie Awards in New York. It brings to the Berkshires a world-class adventure for all lovers of music and drama. Under the leadership of producing director Lyn Austin, the group has tackled difficult, esoteric works and created ones that are close to sublime.

"The Music-Theatre Group blazes trails . . ." raved the *Boston Globe*. Theater here is minimally staged; the emphasis is more on script and musical development as many of these works prepare for a New York run.

Said the *New York Times*: "The Music-Theatre Group has produced one of the most innovative and original bodies of work in American theater."

Jason Asprey as MacDuff and Dan McCleary as Macbeth in the Shakespeare & Company production of Macbeth.

Shakespeare & Company/Kevin Sprague

**SHAKESPEARE &
COMPANY**
Box Office 413-637-3353;
  413-637-1197 off season.
70 Kemble St., Lenox, MA
  01240.
Season: Summer, fall.
Tickets: $6.50–$33.50.

Shakespeare is revitalized on stage in Lenox, having moved uptown to Springlawn. Under the powerful artistic guidance of English actor/ director Tina Packer and her artistic associate, Dennis Krausnick, Shakespeare & Company, 25 years old in 2002, has brought new light, feeling, and clarity to Shakespeare, making the works more accessible to many people. Shakespeare & Company works in area schools in the winter, spreading the wonder of the Bard even farther.

Part of the dramatic impact derives from the actors' ability to treat the audience as their alter ego, always privy to secrets of the drama. The plays are staged all around the seating area; intimacy with the action is inevitable, with stage and lighting design creating magical effects.

Wrote the *New York Times* critic Ben Brantley of the company's performance of *A Midsummer Night's Dream*: "The overall result is vulgar, over scaled and loud. And it works. . . . There are few productions of Shakespearean comedy in which the meaning of every joke (whether intended by Shakespeare or not) reads so clearly, and the audience was responsive to each one."

While Shakespeare & Company attends to its namesake, it has also produced Edith Wharton-oriented plays, and contemporary plays. Under the aegis of its Arden Institute, the company has toured, offering free workshops and demonstrations. It also runs programs for young actors. Under construction in Lenox is a replica of the Rose Playhouse, where Shakespeare's *Henry VI* and *Titus Andronicus* were first performed.

Shakespeare & Company is a "must see" for locals and visitors alike.

Richard Feldman

Jessica Stone, Christopher Fitzgerald, and Sara Schmidt in Where's Charlie? *at the Williamstown Theatre Festival.*

WILLIAMSTOWN THEATRE FESTIVAL
413-597-3400;
administration
413-458-3210;
fax 413-458-3147.
www.WTFestival.org.
1000 Main St., PO Box 517,
Williamstown, MA
01267.
Season: Summer.
Tickets: Free–$50.

For Producer Michael Ritchie the challenge is not to be "the best summer theater but the best theater in America." Williamstown Theatre Festival took a giant step in that direction in the summer of 1999, exciting the theater world with Academy Award winner Gwyneth Paltrow in *As You Like It*, followed by an extraordinary production of Arthur Miller's *The Price*. Stellar WTF plays regularly move on to Boston or Broadway. In 2002 WTF received a regional Tony Award for 48 years of sustained excellence, the first summer theater in the nation to be so recognized.

Each summer, in addition to full-scale productions with first-rate sets and costumes on the Main Stage, WTF offers other more intimate theater experiences. There are the four productions mounted at the 100-seat Nikos Stage. Late-night musical cabarets provide surprise cameo appearances by Main Stage celebrities like inveterate songster and raconteur Dick Cavett. Catch Staged Readings; Museum Pieces at the Williams College Museum of Art; Free Theater, usually outdoors at the Buxton School in Williamstown; Act I Performance Projects by the WTF young actor training ensemble, at work in Goodrich Hall on the Williams Campus; and the Greylock Theatre Project, which connects economically disadvantaged young people from North Adams with professional theater artists. Williams College is rebuilding WTF's venue with a larger main stage—and a parking garage.

It's no mistake, then, that *Newsweek* ranked WTF as "the best of all American summer theaters" with "the cream of America's acting crop." The best *theater* in America? It will be worth watching over the next few years.

OTHER THEATER

There are more than a dozen other theater companies in and about Berkshire.

In **South County**, the biggest little theater is **Mixed Company** (413-528-2320; at the Granary, 37 Rosseter St., Gt. Barrington, MA 01230), where fall-off-the-seat comedy alternates with moving drama. Under the direction of playwright Joan Ackermann, Mixed Company has built a solid following, often leading to competition for the theater's few dozen seats. Ackermann's award-winning *Zara Spook and Other Lures* premiered here, as did her droll *Bed and Breakfast*, in which she played an addled Mrs. Digby. The **DeSisto Estate Cabaret** (413-298-4032; DeSisto School, Rte. 183, Stockbridge, MA 01230) hosts dinner theater Tuesday through Thursday evenings in the summer, cabaret performances Friday and Saturday following dinner, and additional cabaret after some Friday and all Saturday Tanglewood concerts.

The **Central County** theater scene has never been livelier. The **Berkshire Community College Players** regularly appear at the Robert Boland Theater at BCC (413-499-0660 when performances are staged; 1350 West St., Pittsfield, MA 01201). *The Town Players* (413-443-9279; www.berkshire.net/townplayers/TOWNPLAYER.HTM; mail: PO Box 765, Pittsfield, MA 01201) occasionally perform at either BCC or the Berkshire Museum. In a recent season, they presented *Into the Woods*, by Stephen Sondheim. *The News in Revue* (888-401-6397; www.newsinrevue.com; mail: PO Box 2336, Westport, CT 06880) performs political satire summers at several locations.

North County is especially theatrical. Besides the Williamstown Theater Festival, in Williamstown, the **Starlight Stage Youth Theatre** (413-458-4246; http://myvanwy.tripod.com/ssyt.html; 57 Linden St., Williamstown, MA 01267), a hands-on theater experience for youth from eight years to 18, performs summers at the First Congregational Church. In the fall and winter slack is picked up by **Williamstheatre**, the Williams College theater group (413-597-2342; www.williams.edu/acad-depts/theater/; Adams Memorial Theatre, 1000 Main St., Williamstown, MA 01267), producing impressive revivals of plays by the likes of Shakespeare, Brecht, and Becket. The drama department at **Massachusetts College of Liberal Arts** (413-662-5000) presents additional performances.

Outside the County, in neighboring Chatham, New York, the **Mac-Haydn Theatre** (518-392-9292; mail: PO Box 204, Chatham, NY 12037; on Rte. 203,) has been offering 15-week-long summer seasons of robust Broadway musicals since 1969. Productions are staged in the round. Their high energy casts are guaranteed to deliver a supercharge of musical theater—less than truly sophisticated, perhaps, but usually a whole lot of fun. In New Lebanon, New York, at the **Theater Barn** (518-794-8989; www.theaterbarn.com; mail: PO Box 39, New Lebanon, NY 12125; on Rte. 20), producers Joan and Abe Phelps zero in on musical comedy, with an occasional murderous dose of Agatha Christie thrown in. **Proctor's Theatre** in Schenectady (518-382-1083; www.proctors.org; 432 State St., Schenectady, NY 12035), and the **Egg** in Albany (518-473-1061; www.theegg.org; mail: PO Box 2065, Albany, NY12220; at the Empire state Plaza), both provide stages for national acts, shows and dramas. Up in Bennington, Vermont, the **Oldcastle Theater Company** (802-447-0564; www.oldcastle.org; mail: PO Box 1555, Bennington, VT 05201; at the Bennington Center for the Arts) can always be counted on for enjoyment, controversy, or both. Back in Massachusetts, the **Miniature Theatre of Chester** (413-354-6565; www.miniaturetheatre.org; mail: PO Box 722, Chester, MA 01011; at Chester Town Hall), hosts large-as-life drama.

SEASONAL EVENTS

A spring street festival in Great Barrington and an impromptu parade of the Berkshire Bateria Scuola de Samba. The Bateria offers free drumming workshops for the public and plays outdoors in Great Barrington throughout the summer.

Judith Monachina

A number of special Berkshire events are tuned to the calendar. Somehow the Berkshire year wouldn't unfold properly without them. Literally leading the parade are Pittsfield's **Home Town Parade** on July 4 and North Adams's **Fall Foliage Parade** on the Sunday before Columbus Day.

Additional information about these and other seasonal events is available from listings under "tourist Information" in Chapter Nine. See also "Festival Frenzy," above.

SPRING

Jazztown, Williamstown's salute to the authentic, takes place all around town in April, with Williams College and the town's chamber of commerce collaborating on a musical blowout. Performing are college big bands from the East, distinguished pros, and alumni groups.

Riverfest is North County's favorite outdoor event every May, celebrating the revitalized Hoosic River, which threads through Adams, North Adams, and Williamstown. Environmental art along the riverbanks, raft rides, food, and music at Cole Field, Williamstown.

SUMMER

Adams Agricultural Fair is the old-fashioned kind, with a midway of rides, noisy big trucks, and judging of produce and animals. For a weekend in August it takes over the fairgrounds off the Curran Highway just south of the Adams-North Adams line. Other notable fairs in the area include those of **Cummington, Schaghticoke, Altamont,** and the **Eastern States Exposition** (the Big E), Springfield.

Berkshire Crafts Fair is a mid-August event, held at Monument Mountain Regional High School (413-528-3346; Rte. 7, between Stockbridge and Gt. Barrington). Top craftspeople offer their extraordinary creations, from handmade paper to hand-blown glass, from handwoven clothing to exotic woodenware.

The Berkshires Summer Arts Festival, held at Butternut Ski Area in early July. American Crafts Marketing, affiliated with American Craftsmen galleries (New York City and Stockbridge) presents a three-day juried crafts show, with music, food, and children's events.

Fireworks over Stockbridge Bowl are spectacular because of echoes from the hills. The biggest bangs and most colorful starbursts come from Tanglewood, on the Fourth of July, and following *The 1812 Overture* at the end of "Tanglewood on Parade," a highlight of the BSO Berkshire season.

The Monument Mountain Author Climb is a literary event commemorating the August day in 1851 when Melville, Hawthorne, Holmes, and friends scaled the Great Barrington peak. They imbibed a good deal of champagne, weathered a thunderstorm, read William Cullen Bryant's poem about the Indian maiden who threw herself in sorrow from the top, and began a lasting friendship. Becoming a fixture is an annual recreation of **Henry David Thoreau's climb up Mount Greylock**, on or about July 20. Watch the *Berkshire Eagle* for announcements.

Susan B. Anthony Celebration & Adams Street Fair is held every July on Park Street, which is closed off for the event. Features are the "Pedal & Plod" bike and foot race, food, and much more. For information, call the Adams Chamber of Commerce (413-743-1881.)

FALL

Great Josh Billings RunAground is Berkshire's great one-day party, an athletic extravaganza that involves thousands of participants and many more admiring, supportive spectators. This late-September biking-canoeing-running triathlon takes its name from Lanesborough's Henry Wheeler Shaw, an inveterate 19th-century prankster-humorist writing under the pen name of Josh Billings. "If a fellow gets to going down hill, it seems as if everything were greased for the occasion," wrote Billings (more or less); and every fall at the RunAground the bike racers, shooting down that last hill on Route183 to Stockbridge Bowl, prove how right old Josh was. After the race, there's a huge party at Tanglewood with food, drink, dancing, and Berkshire camaraderie.

Greylock Ramble. On Columbus Day the Adams chamber celebrates the height of fall foliage. It provides 3,000 or more people of every dimension an opportunity to hike the big hill and certificates for those who do. Other hikes and climbs to and around the lofty top of Mount Greylock in North County are sponsored by the Department of Environmental Management, beginning at Greylock Glen in Adams, the Visitors Center in Lanesborough, the Sperry Road Campground, or Bascom Lodge, often narrated by well-informed guides.

Harvest Festival at the Berkshire Botanical Garden, Stockbridge, is an early-October event packed with cider and doughnuts, apples and pumpkins, hay wagon and fire engine rides, plants and seeds, and mayhem of all sorts appealing to children and grownups. A highlight of the Berkshire calendar, this two-day event includes a live-performance tent featuring the likes of the Bluestars. Besides a great plant sale and flea market, a book sale and second-hand-clothes mart, the festival has also attracted a greater number of crafts-people selling an increasingly refined collection of handcrafts.

Hopkins Forest Fall Festival is the destination on an October Sunday at Hop-kins Memorial Forest, at the top of Bulkley Street, Williamstown, where old-time crafts are practiced, timeless music performed, and tempting cider and applesauce produced.

Lenox Apple Squeeze takes place in the week after the Tub Parade (below). Many shops have major sales; there are craft and food booths; demonstra-tions, live music, and more.

Octoberzest is a fall foliage festival of music and ballet, presented at Simon's Rock by the Barrington Performing Arts. Mixing and matching poets with musicians, dancers with actors into various ensemble pieces really does add a zesty melange to the southern Berkshire fall.

Tub Parade is one of Berkshire's oldest annual events, dating back to the Gilded Age. This late-September parade has been revived with a hitch—that is, with the hitches that attach show ponies to the ornate, flower-decked carts they pull. Under the auspices of the Lenox Village Association and the Colonial Carriage and Driving Society, the Tub Parade gives a glimpse back into turn-of-the-previous-century Berkshire, when dogs with ruffled collars rode next to their masters. Brief but brilliant.

WINTER

Chesterwood holds its Christmas open house from the first weekend in November through Veterans' Day. Tours of the house and studio, shops open, refreshments, demonstrations.

Holiday Walk in Williamstown opens Spring and Water Streets to horses and wagons, which carry spectators to shops where musical and dramatic groups perform, town and gown. Nonprofit organizations present festive exhibits in the Williams College gymnasium, and crafters exhibit in the Towne Field House.

Holly-Days is Lenox's four-day celebration of the holiday season, with the arrival of Santa, a gingerbread house contest, holiday entertainment (such as

the Albany Berkshire Ballet), a pancake breakfast, and an ecumenical candlelight service on Sunday.

Naumkeag at Christmas is extra special because that's when the Choates'
Christmas decorations are taken out, and the house is made to look ever so
festive. Looking in on a quiet turn-of-the-last-century Christmas can make
the viewer's merrier. The historic "cottage" in Stockbridge (described under
"Historic Homes" in this chapter) offers this opportunity to the public on an
irregular basis.

Stockbridge Main Street at Christmas, the first weekend in December, salutes
Christmas and Norman Rockwell. Arts and crafts, readings by actors from
the Berkshire Theater Festival, house tours, luminaria, carolers, a gala concert, and a reenactment of Rockwell's painting *Stockbridge Main Street at
Christmas* (1956) with vintage cars. Information at the Stockbridge Chamber
of Commerce (413-298-5200; www.stockbridgechamber.org; 6 Elm St., PO
Box 224, Stockbridge, MA 01262).

The Tea Ceremony at Great Barrington Pottery is a moving meditation, a
highly stylized form of social communion for both the Tea Mistress and
those she serves. Enter the Chashitsu (Japanese Ceremonial Teahouse and
Formal Garden) at Richard Bennett's Great Barrington Pottery (described in
Chapter Eight, *Shopping*) to return to 14th-century Japan.

VIDEO RENTALS

The following video rental outlets stock the standard Hollywood movies
and a smattering of foreign art titles. There may be other outlets. Public
libraries in the county lend videos.

South County

AVC Video Showcase (413-229-2910; 231 Main St., Sheffield, MA 01257; Rte. 7
next to Sheffield Pub).

Elm Street Market (413-298-3634; 4 Elm St., Stockbridge, MA 01262).

Housatonic Country Market (413-274-3500; 266 Pleasant St., N. Housatonic,
MA 01236).

Impoco's/Alice in Videoland (413-528-9162; 54 State Rd., Great Barrington,
MA 01230; Rte. 7).

Lee Video (413-243-3636; 23 Park Plaza, Lee, MA 01238).

Millennium Video (413-528-5575; 740 Main St., Gt. Barrington, MA 01230; Rte.
7).

North Star Video of Great Barrington (413-528-1067; 224 State Rd., Gt. Barrington, MA 01230; Rte. 23).

West Stockbridge Video (413-232-7851; 20 Main St., W. Stockbridge, MA
01266).

Central County

Dalton Video (413-684-4480; 69 Depot St., Dalton, MA 01226).

East Street Video (413-443-2000; 10 Lyman, Pittsfield, MA 01201).

First Run Video (413-442-6830; 1664 North St., Lanesborough, MA 01237; Rte. 7).

Hollywood Video (413-442-4805; 455 Dalton Ave., Pittsfield, MA 01201).

Melody House (413-442-5724; 307 North St., Pittsfield, MA 01201).

Patrick's Video (413-442-6666; 200 West St., Pittsfield, MA 01201).

Plaza Video (413-443-0943; 444 W. Housatonic St., Pittsfield, MA 01201).

Stop & Shop Video Center (413-443-3548; 660 Merrill Rd., Pittsfield, MA 01201).

Variety Video (413-637-2046; 26 Housatonic St., Lenox, MA 01240).

Video Studio 12 (413-447-7595; 180A Elm St., Pittsfield, MA 01201).

North County

Dox (413-458-4420; 320 Main St., Williamstown, MA 01267).

Video Studio (413-743-7007; 1 Myrtle St., Adams, MA 01220).

Video Studio of North Adams (413-664-7880; N. Adams Plaza, N. Adams, MA 01247).

CHAPTER SIX
Spas & the Spiritual Life
BODY & SPIRIT

The Berkshire landscape has long attracted the traveler in search of beauty. The rolling hills, mountains and farms, open landscapes, and intimate scenes are the backdrop for relaxation and rejuvenation, creativity and renewal.

Sculptor Daniel Chester French called the Berkshires "heaven," and the land is well known for attracting artists and then those who like to be where the artists are. Here there is a long-standing connection of the land to the creative.

But less well known is the even longer attraction of this place to other kinds of seekers—those whose lifelong vocation was spiritual search and, more recently, those looking for new ways, through the disciplines that begin with the body, to rejuvenate the mind

Judith Monachina

A quiet spot for relaxing at Canyon Ranch.

and spirit. The Berkshires, then, is also a place where the physical—the land and the health of the body and mind—is connected to the spiritual.

The area has become a mecca not only for music, dance, and art lovers but also for yoga enthusiasts and macrobiotic and healing arts practitioners of all kinds. In many cases the homes of these organizations started out as "cottages" for wealthy summer residents, later becoming centers for the Jesuits, Franciscans, and other western religious groups. Now they are home to Sufis, virtually all kinds of yoga practitioners, and those who use the Chinese disciplines of Chi Kung and Tai Chi.

A Franciscan monastery has become the Kushi Institute, a well-known macrobiotic center in Becket. The Kripalu Center for Yoga and Health was first a massive 100-room home, then a Jesuit seminary; now people from all over the world come to learn about yoga. Their international network of Kripalu trained yoga teachers includes many countries, and the natural effect of this yoga center in the Berkshires means an abundance of classes in all approaches to yoga. The most luxurious of these health centers, Canyon Ranch of the Berkshires, was first an elegant house (modeled after the Petit Trianon in France), then a seminary; now people come from all over the world to learn to nurture their bodies and spirits.

The newest example is at Cranwell, also one of the former Berkshire cottages that later became a Jesuit school; now it is home to a golf resort and spa.

A WELLNESS CENTER WITH A FOCUS ON YOGA

Yoga at Kripalu.

Judith Monachina

KRIPALU CENTER FOR YOGA AND HEALTH (413-448-3400, 800-741-7353; www.kripalu.org; mail: PO Box 793, Lenox, MA 01240; West St. (Rte. 183) in Stockbridge, south of Tanglewood)

One of the grandest of Berkshire's summer "cottages" was Shadowbrook, a 100-room Tudor mansion built by Anson Phelps Stokes. Later a Jesuit seminary, the original building burned to the ground, and the Jesuit brothers built an equally large but much more modest building to replace it. Though modern and functional, the estate—with its breathtaking views of Stockbridge Bowl and the mountains beyond—continues to move its many guests. It's hard to imagine a more complete line of yoga workshops and classes than can be found at Kripalu. The 70-page catalog includes listings for such classes as Meridian Hatha Yoga, Kundalini Yoga, Bikram Yoga, Restorative, Kripalu and Kitchen Chair Yoga, Kripalu Yoga and Kripalu Yoga Teacher Training, Chakra Yoga, A Kripalu Yoga Retreat, Meditation and Yoga, Raw Juice Fasting, Danskinetics and Haitian Dance, Letting Go of Fear—and that's a small fraction of the offerings at this center, which caters to beginners as well as those well advanced in yoga training. The offerings don't stop with yoga, however, and well-known wellness experts are among those who have offered weekend workshops in their specialties. The topics of workshops include Hand and Foot Reflexilogy, Qigong, the Bhagavad Gita, Healing Retreat for Women, Living with Breast Cancer, Yoga and Buddhism, Yoga and Hiking, Yoga and Cross-Country Skiing. This short list is a small taste of the extensive offerings. Facilities include Danskinetics and yoga studios, saunas and whirlpools, 300 acres of forest, meadows, meditation gardens, miles of woodland trails, a private beach on Stockbridge bowl, a bookstore and gift shop, special health services, and a natural foods kitchen serving tasty, well-balanced vegetarian meals. Health services include various types of bodywork therapies. Kripalu's environment is nurturing. Clients sign on for short-term or longer-term visits. Yoga teacher training and longer term professional training programs are available as well as opportunities for day guests. Prices are quite moderate.

A LUXURY SPA

CANYON RANCH IN THE BERKSHIRES (413-637-4400; www.canyon ranch.com.; 91 Kemble St., Lenox, MA 01240).

Vitality, possibilities, balance: These three words quietly flash on the website screen for Canyon Ranch in the Berkshires, and they sum up the experience of a stay at this luxury spa.

Several years ago health entrepreneurs Mel and Enid Zuckerman took their highly succcessful Tuscon, Arizona, Canyon Ranch formula and transferred it to the sculptured hills of Lenox. Here they transformed and built upon Giraud Foster's splendid "cottage," Bellefontaine, a replica of the French Le Petit Trianon, to create a world-class spa.

It is a spectacular facility, smoothly run by a group of skilled and friendly professionals. Whether used for a short cool out, a vacation, a chance to drop a

Canyon Ranch occupies a former Gilded Age cottage, Bellefontaine.

Judith Monachina

few pounds, an invigorating change of pace, or a whole new start, Canyon Ranch lives up to its billing as "the spa that never leaves you." With over 50 fitness classes to choose from daily, swimming, racquet sports of all kinds and a state-of-the-art gymnasia, the spa complex offers a customized physical workout.

Judith Monachina

The unusual and mature landscape at Canyon Ranch.

In addition, hiking, mountain biking, and cross-country skiing provide indoor outdoor fitness possibilities unimaginable at the average spa. Besides Jacuzzis, steam rooms and saunas, six gyms, and an indoor pool, Canyon Ranch offers inhalation rooms and a range of personal services to pamper guests. Massages, herbal wraps, and various exotic treatments are performed by experts revitalizing inside and out. The healthful opportunities go on and on, from skin and beauty treatments to dietary education and stop-smoking programs. Canyon Ranch visitors—unless they sneak out to nearby Bev's Homemade for locally made ice cream—are on a low-fat, low-cholesterol regime that is as delicious as it is healthy.

Prices vary seasonally but are always substantial. Access to the facility is limited to guests.

A SPA WITHIN A GOLF RESORT

CRANWELL, RESORT SPA & GOLF (413-637-1364; www.cranwell.com, 55 Lee Rd., Lenox, MA 01240; Rte.20)

This new massive spa features 35 treatment rooms, a 60-foot pool, whirlpool and saunas, steam rooms and more saunas. The services list is extensive and includes seaweed, remineralizing and thermal clay therapies, stone therapy, Swedish and deep-tissue massage, reflexology, sport-specific massage, prenatal, duet (for two), and in-room massage.

MACROBIOTICS AND HEALTH

THE KUSHI INSTITUTE (800-975-8744; www.kushiinstitute.org; PO Box 7, Becket, MA 01223)

The quietest of the healthful learning places in the Berkshires lies just outside of the village of Becket, about five miles from Jacob's Pillow Dance Festival. Once a Franciscan monastery, the Kushi Institute now attracts people from all over the world who want to learn about this approach to health.

Michio and Aveline Kushi founded the institute in 1978 in Brookline, Massachusetts, and gradually moved all programs out to Becket by 1990. The internationally known macrobiotic center attracts people who wish to learn more about the macrobiotic way of life. The basic philosophy includes a whole-foods diet and an appreciation of other natural elements for a healthy lifestyle. These include exercise, body care, household products, and livelihood. Macrobiotics has been popularized through books and various media that have detailed its effects on health recovery from debilitating disease. Many people choose the macrobiotic way of life and a natural approach to recovery and optimal health maintenance. The macrobiotic approach can be embraced by people of any philosophy or religion.

The basic institute program, offered year-round, is the weeklong "Way to Health." Kushi also offers a macrobiotic career-training program and annual summer conference. The weeklong programs include cooking classes, lectures, and question-and-answer sessions. Guests can also enjoy the walking trails on this mostly wooded, 600-acre property.

MONASTERIES AND RETREAT CENTERS

MARIAN FATHERS (413-298-3931; Eden Hill, Stockbridge, MA 01262).

Although they do not offer retreat facilities, the Marian Fathers do open their beautiful grounds and chapels to the public. It is a Catholic monastery, but all are invited to use the candle shrines and chapels. The Eden Hill Recreation Center (see below) is owned by the Marians and is open to the public.

SISTERS OF THE VISITATION MONASTERY (413-243-3995; 14 Beach Rd., Tyringham, MA 01264).

In the beautiful Tyringham Valley, this monastery is home to a small group of women who relocated here from Delaware in recent years. They built their monastery at the end of Beach Road on a hill overlooking meadows and fields and cleared walking trails in the meadows. The sisters live in a cloister, and individual retreatants are invited into the cloister for private retreats of meditation and prayer. They are asked therefore to observe the silence of the monastery and the schedule, which includes a great silence after the 8pm service. There is room for two retreatants at any given time.

Retreatants are invited to attend the services at which the sisters sing the hours of the office five times per day. Visitors are not obligated to attend the services or the morning mass but are invited to do so and are given assistance in using the various books for following the prayers and singing. The prayerful voices of the sisters during their services can be appreciated by guests to the nearby chapel, which is not part of the cloister and which is open to the public on most days from the morning mass on. The meadows and fields with walking trails are open to retreatants once inside the cloister.

EAST MOUNTAIN RETREAT CENTER (413-528-6617 phone/fax; www.east retreat.org; 8 Lake Buel Rd., Gt. Barrington, MA 01230).

The center provides facilities and guidance to individuals and groups who wish to visit a quiet place for reflection and meditation. The director will help find teachers or resources needed for a retreat—or just provide a place. The center is open to any serious seeker regardless of faith tradition.

While individual retreats are the primary activity of this center, groups are also welcome. It is expected that individual retreats are primarily silent unless arrangements are made for instrument playing or chanting, for example. The center is located on 90 acres of woodland on the side of East Mountain State Forest in the town of Great Barrington. There are paths, logging trails, and places to walk or sit in quiet contemplation.

A minimum stay is two days; ordinarily two weeks would be the longest stay. Simple meals, bedding, and towels are provided. Kitchen facilities are available for guests to prepare their own breakfast and lunch. A vegetarian hot evening meal, which is provided, is always an option. The director is a United Church of Christ minister, and her advisory board is comprised of people from a variety of religious backgrounds. Fees are very moderate.

THE ABODE OF THE MESSAGE (518-794-8095; www.theabode.net; Abode Rd., New Lebanon, NY 12125).

Just a stone's throw from the Massachusetts border, this former New Lebanon Shaker settlement on 400 acres is now home to a Sufi community. This group invites the public to attend their weekly universal worship services and participate in various programs throughout the year.

While theirs is a community whose members have embraced the ideas of Sufism, all religions are respected, and many of those who participate in programs here come from other paths.

The community puts on events—musical, spiritual, and artistic—throughout the year from various traditions, including Sufi, Buddhist, Zorastrian, and others. It hosts yoga, dance, and musical workshops, as well. Accommodations for those who stay at the Abode include cabins and rooms. Meals are healthy and hearty. Rates are reasonable.

OTHER YOGA, DAY SPAS, & RELATED OUTLETS

Berkshire Mountain Yoga (413-528-5333; 30 Elm Ct., Gt. Barrington, MA 01230) Year-round yoga classes of various kinds, including Ashtanga, Hatha, Flowing Hatha, Yoga Basics, Power Vinyasa Yoga, and classes such as Heartdance.

Body & Soul (413-528-6465; 42 Railroad St., Gt. Barrington, MA 01230) Massage, Dr. Hauschka facials, body treatments, cosmetics, skincare, bath, and body products.

Eden Hill Recreation Center (413-298-1106; Eden Hill, Stockbridge, MA 01262) Various types of recreational programming, including yoga, African dance and drumming, for kids and adults. Classes—as well as a pool for lap swimming—are offered year-round at this Marian monastery overlooking the town. The priests and brothers opened this center to the community years ago. Classes generally begin on a semester schedule.

Essencials Day Spa (413-443-6260; www.BerkshireSpas.com; 439 Pittsfield Rd., Lenox, MA 01240. Offers hair and body treatments, sauna rooms, a fireplace for sipping herbal teas, six treatment rooms, makeup, waxing, and massage.

Kali Ray Tri-Yoga Center (413-229-3389; www.kalirayyoga.com; Rte. 7, Sheffield, MA 01257) This style of flowing Hatha yoga focuses on breath and posture and was founded over 20 years ago by Kali Ray.

Michele's Day Spa (413-528-9999; www.michelessalon.com; 54 Stockbridge Rd., Gt. Barrington, MA 01230. Full day escapes or just one service, including salt glow, massage, dermatological facials, and manicure and pedicure. These services and others by appointment.

Phoenix Rising Yoga Therapy (800-288-9642, www.pryt.com, 5 Albany Rd., W. Stockbridge, MA 01236; at Shaker Mill) Michael Lee, founder of the modality of Phoenix Rising, describes it as a body, mind, and health program based on yoga; thus it is spiritual as well as physical. It offers professional training programs here as well as Phoenix Rising yoga for the general public.

Spanda Holistic Center (413-442-0123; www.spanda.com; 823 North St., Pittsfield, MA 01201) The philosophy of Spanda is: Health comes from the balanced flow of Chi (life force) in the body, mind, and spirit. They offer acupuncture, Chi Quong, Healing the Spirit, Chinese herbs, Energy Psychology, and others.

The Healing Place (413-637-1980; www.thehealingplace.com;1 West St., Lenox, MA 01240) In the center of Lenox, a converted colonial-style house is the site for this total-wellness center featuring massage and facials, yoga and spa treatments, and various classes. Therapies include deep-tissue, Swedish, and pregnancy massage; acupressure and Shiatsu; cranial-sacral bodywork, and Reiki. Treatments include mud body treatments, seaweed body wraps, Dr. Hauschka facials, raindrop therapy, and steam therapy. Yoga and movement therapy are offered on a regular basis.

Frog Lotus Yoga Center (866-664-8686; www.froglotus.com; 189 Beaver St., North Adams, MA 01247; at the Beaver Mill) This new studio features Pilates, Tai Chi, dance, and yoga. Healing arts sessions include Kriya massage, integrative therapy, Swedish, Shiatsu, and Thai yoga bodywork.

YMCAS AND FITNESS CENTERS

Berkshire Nautilus (413-499-1217; 42–56 Summer St., Pittsfield, MA 01201) Stationary bikes, rowing machines, treadmill, StairMaster, whirlpool, sauna, steam, and certified instruction, a rock-climbing wall and free weights.

Berkshire West (413-499-4600; Dan Fox Dr., Pittsfield, MA 01201) Nautilus and free weights, bikes. Also tennis and racquetball facilities, aerobics classes, saunas and steam room and hot tub, pool, and certified instruction. Nursery available. Massage therapy and yoga have also been added to their list of client services.

Lenox Fitness Center (413-637-9893; www.lenoxfitnesscenter.com; 90 Pittsfield Rd., Lenox, MA 01240) Life Fitness training, stationary bikes and rowing machines, StairMasters, aerobics, steam rooms, tanning booths, free weights, yoga, and certified instruction. Senior-citizen and youth packages available. Spa services include manicure, pedicure, massage, facial, waxing. Outdoor programs include hiking and snowshoeing.

Studio 21 Fitness Center (413-528-2148; 329 Stockbridge Rd., Gt. Barrington, MA 01230) Cardiovascular, eliptical trainers, Cybex training. Classes include kickboxing, yoga, spinning, Pilates. Massage and personal training, as well. Various rate schedules to accommodate needs.

Pittsfield YMCA (413-499-7650; 292 North St., Pittsfield, MA 01201) With its North Street facility and **Ponterril Outdoor Recreation Center** (413-499-0640), Pittsfield's YMCA serves more public recreational needs than any facility in the county. At the North Street Y, the range of fitness and sports includes aerobics, swimming, racquetball and squash, Nautilus equipment and programs; special classes for kids. Also saunas and a steam room. From Memorial Day through Labor Day, the Ponterril Outdoor Recreation Center (499-0640) comes to life. On East Acres Road there is an Olympic-sized pool, a wading pool, and a tot's spray pool; swimming lessons are also offered. Down at the lake the Y has a marina with moorings for 50 boats and offers canoe, rowboat, and sailboat rentals; also sailing lessons and tennis (clay courts) and soccer camp, a day camp, and a preschool camp. Other Y memberships are honored with a slight surcharge, and special short-term guest passes can be arranged

Northern Berkshire YMCA (413-663-6529; 22 Brickyard Ct., N. Adams, MA 01247) North County's Y is another center of vitality. There's a six-lane pool, a full gymnasium, weight room, gymnastics room for children, and two handball-racquetball courts, all with programs to match. As with the Pittsfield Y, other Y memberships are honored with a slight surcharge, and short-term guest passes can be arranged.

Kilpatrick Athletic Center (413-528-7777; www.simons-rock.edu, click on athletics; at Simon's Rock College, Gt. Barrington) Open to the public. Full fitness, Nautilus, free weights, cardiovascular, Olympic pool; indoor track; basketball court; squash, racquetball, and tennis; rock wall; and aerobics studio. All kinds of classes: Feldenkrais, water fitness, yoga, Pilates. The center has three, six, and twelve-month memberships.

Health Club at Oak n' Spruce Resort (413-243-3500;190 Meadow St., Lee, MA 01238) Fitness equipment, two indoor pools, one outdoor pool, hot tubs, saunas, and basketball.

Berkshire South Regional Community Center (413-528-2810; www.berkshire-south.org.; Gt. Barrington, MA 01230) Open to the public, both local residents and visitors, who may utilize the facility by buying a membership or paying a general admission. It features a pool, exercise pool, and kids' splash playground, a fitness center, gymnasium, game room and a pre-school, an auditorium with dance floor that includes nightclub lights and sound, two conference rooms, a lounge, kitchen, and a baby-sitting center. Classes are also offered throughout the year.

Please note: New day spas and healing-arts practices open with regularity, making it impossible to give a full listing of the literally hundreds of private practices around the county. Also, many massage therapists, Reiki and other technique practitioners, acupuncturists, and others operate solo businesses and can be found by looking at various brochures and newspapers and the *Yellow Pages*. *The Advocate*, *The Women's Times*, *The Artful Mind*, and the *Shopper's Guide* are excellent sources of information about these professionals.

Cross-country skiing at Canyon Ranch.

Judith Monachina

CHAPTER SEVEN

For the Fun of It

OUTDOOR RECREATION

Berkshire beckons bikers, boaters, hikers, horseback riders, runners, skaters, skiers, swimmers, and nearly every other variety of sportsperson to come outside. Although nature left the area shy of large bodies of water, 19th-century industrialists dammed well, to some degree making up the deficiency. Mountains and trails, lakes and rivers, and Berkshire valley air—which can be breathed without chewing—invigorate. The ski

Judith Monachina

Late afternoon at Stockbridge Bowl.

areas assure groomed winter sport with extensive snowmaking and, in warmer weather, Berkshire's golf courses and tennis courts draw sports lovers from all quarters.

For the spectators among us, school sports teams are competitive and fun in fall, spring, and winter, including downhill and Nordic skiing. The hills are alive with bouncing balls, from youth programs to secondary school teams to college leagues. Three of the four Berkshire colleges—*Berkshire Community* in Pittsfield, *Massachusetts College of Liberal Arts* in North Adams, and *Williams* in Williamstown—field men's and women's teams in soccer, basketball, baseball, and softball. Williams perennially ranks among the best in the nation in NCAA Division III soccer, field hockey, football, cross country, basketball, ice hockey, track, tennis, squash, volleyball, swimming, lacrosse, and crew. In 1996, 1997, and 1999–2002, Williams copped the Sears Cup as the most winning small college in the nation. The athletic departments of the colleges provide schedules.

SPORTING GOODS STORES

The following stores provide sporting goods for a range of activities. Additional listings are provided under individual sports, e.g. bicycling, skiing.

South County

Gerry Cosby & Co. (413-229-6600; fax 413-229-3492; www.cosbysports.com; Under Mountain Rd., Sheffield, MA 01257; Rte. 41)

Housatonic River Outfitters, Inc. (413-528-8811, fax 413-528-5054; www.dry flies.com; 684 S. Main St., Gt. Barrington, MA 01230)

Central County

Arcadian Shop (413-637-3010; fax 413-637-4112; www.arcadian.com; 91 Pittsfield-Lenox Rd., PO Box 1637, Lenox, MA 01240; Rte. 7)

Champ Sports (413-448-2123; www.champsports.com; mail: Old State Rd., Lanesborough, MA 01237; Berkshire Mall, Rte. 8)

Dave's Sporting Goods (413-442-2960; 1164 North St., Pittsfield, MA 01201)

Dick Moon Sporting Goods (413-442-8281; fax 413-448-2718; 114 Fenn St., Pittsfield, MA 01201

Plaine's Bike Snowboard Ski Shop (413-499-0294; 55 W. Housatonic St., Pittsfield, MA 01201; Rte. 20)

North County

Berkshire Outfitters (413-743-5900; fax 413-743-3359; www.berkshireoutfit ters.com; Grove St., Adams, MA 01220; Rte. 8)

Goff's Sports (413-458-3605, 800-424-3747; www.williams-shop.com; 15 Spring St., Williamstown, MA 01267)

The Mountain Goat (413-458-8445; www.themountaingoat.com; 130 Water St., Williamstown, MA 01267)

The Sports Corner (413-664-8654; www.northadams.com; 61 Main St., N. Adams, MA 01247)

BASEBALL & SOFTBALL

The first collegiate baseball game ever was played in Pittsfield, July 1, 1859—Amherst defeated Williams 73–32 in a 26-inning marathon (the rules have since changed). Williams won a companion chess match.

Professional baseball in the Berkshires began later in the 19th century, but it wasn't till the Roaring Twenties that the hardball action was continuous. The Pittsfield Hillies played some admirable ball in the A-level Eastern League, winning a couple of pennants. When the Depression came, baseball went.

Through some of the 1940s, the Pittsfield Electrics played to large home crowds, finally being short-circuited by the advent of televised baseball. Then in 1965 a Red Sox farm club came to play at Pittsfield's Wahconah Park. The Pittsfield-Berkshire Red Sox played in the AA Class of the Eastern League. Starring George "Boomer" Scott and Reggie Smith (both of whom went on to shine with the Sox); the club drew nearly 80,000 fans for the season. The Red Sox farm club moved from the Berkshires in 1976.

Now the Berkshires host two pro teams: The *SteepleCats* of the New England Collegiate Baseball League (www.necbl.com) play at Joe Wolfe Field in North Adams. The *Berkshire Black Bears* of the Northern League perform in Pittsfield at Wahconah Park (105 Wahconah St., Pittsfield, MA 01201). Unlike minor leaguers, neither team's players belong to major-league teams. Chances are the roosters will last the season. The SteepleCats are hotshots in or just graduated from college, playing with wooden bats. They'd like to move up. The Black Bears are guys a bit older who just like to play. The fast balls are wicked, homers are truly belted, and the playing fields are real dirt and grass.

Women's softball is a feature of Berkshire colleges and secondary schools in the spring. Nowhere is the action thicker than at the *Berkshire County Softball Complex* (413-499-1491; 1789 East St., Pittsfield, MA 01201). This three-field park sees at least six games a night during the summer. The complex is also home to the Berkshire County Slow Pitch Softball League, a 30-team men's league sponsored by local businesses. To facilitate matters, the complex has a two-story clubhouse with bar and restaurant.

BICYCLING

How sweet the cycling! For the views, the rolling terrain, and the variety of roadways, Berkshire is made for de rider and derailleur. And now a 5-mile off-road bikeway is open, the Ashuwillticook Trail from Pittsfield to Adams—and later on from there, maybe, North Adams and Williamstown. The Ashuwillticook is good for family biking, walking, and all other manner of person-powered activity. For racers, there's the *Josh Billings Run-Aground* in September, and an annual July race around Brodie Mountain. The Williams College cycling team holds a *Criterion* in the spring. The Greylock Cycling Club sponsors an annual *Greylock Hill Climb*, a 9.2-mile, decidedly uphill race.

For those who are touring, the back roads are tranquil, and some main roads have wide shoulders. The varied terrain intrigues cyclists: stunning views are followed by exhilarating descents that call for *well*-tuned equipment—especially brakes.

Mountain bikers thrive in these hills, 21-speeders rolling through the picturesque landscape, leaving the blacktop behind. Not too steep, not too tortuous, the Berkshire Hills beckon those who have enough brawn, coupled with the

John Hitchcock

Mount Greylock tests a mountain biker's stamina—and gears.

right machine. Mountain bikers frequently gather at the **Mountain Goat** in Williamstown, taking to the hills for some "undulating all-terraining." Mountain bikers should remember that some hiking trails are not open to bikers.

Similarly, cyclists out on the roadways should remember that, until the revolution, motorists in their quaint way still claim the right-of-way. It seems wise to oblige. So: right-hand riding, single file. After dark: a headlight, a red rear reflector, and side and pedal reflectors. In traffic, turns require hand signals with the left hand: extended straight out for left turn, raised 90 degrees for right turn, held down diagonally for stopping. Helmets help, in a crisis, to keep us from losing our heads. Bicycles should be registered at local police departments, so they can help locate a lost one.

The Massachusetts Department of Environmental Management and MassHighway published *Berkshire Bike Touring*, a guide to county routes (available at MassHighway's Lenox office or the DEM South Mountain, Pittsfield, office). A major push is underway to create a north-south bikeway through the county, the first completed segment of which is the Ashuwillticook Rail Trail.

Pittsfield resident Lewis Cuyler, avid bike rider and writer, sums it all up in *Bike Rides in the Berkshire Hills*, available at book and sports stores.

BICYCLE DEALERS

South County

Berkshire Bike and Blade (413-528-5555; fax 413-528-1776; www.bikeand blade.com; 326 Stockbridge Rd., Great Barrington, MA 01230; Rte. 7) Also bike repairs.

Harland B. Foster (413-528-0546; fax 413-528-5474; 15 Bridge St., Gt. Barrington, MA 01230)

Central County

Arcadian Shop (413-637-3010, 800-239-3391; www.arcadian.com; 91 Pittsfield Lenox Rd., PO Box 1637, Lenox, MA 01240)

Mean Wheels (413-637-0644; 57A Housatonic St., Lenox, MA 01240)

Mike's Bike Shop (413-443-1166; www.mikesbikesshop.com: 555 North St., Pittsfield, MA 01201)

Ordinary Cycles (413-442-7225; www.ordinarycycles.com; 247 North St., Pittsfield, MA 01201)

Plaine's Bike Snowboard Ski Shop (413-499-0294; 55 W. Housatonic St., Rte. 20, Pittsfield, MA 01201)

North County

Berkshire Outfitters (413-743-5900, fax 413-743-3359; www.berkshireoutfit ters.com; Grove St., Rte. 8, Adams, MA01220)

The Mountain Goat (413-458-8445; www.themountaingoat.com; 130 Water St., Williamstown, MA 01267)

The Spoke Bicycles (413-458-3456; www.thespoke.com; 279 Main St., Williamstown, MA 01267)

The Sports Corner (413-664-8654; 61 Main St., N. Adams, MA 01247)

BOATING

When Henry Ward Beecher called Berkshire the "American Lake District," he was comparing the number of writers settled here to England's home of the Romantic poets. Nevertheless, while we have nothing the size of Lake Windermere, we have nearly 100 ponds, lakes, and at least one "bowl." Big boats may wish to plow larger seas, but the Otis Reservoir, at 1,056 acres, is the largest recreational freshwater body in the state. Mainly we have water bodies for small craft, from outboards down to inner tubes. Or sculling shells: Spring and fall we can watch the Williams College crews on Lake Onota.

Berkshire Outfitters (see under "Sporting Goods Stores") rents canoes and kayaks. Or one can row. Lew Cuyler founded the *Berkshire Sculling Associa-*

Lew Cuyler sculls on Onota Lake.

Lauren R. Stevens

tion (413-496-9160), which provides rentals, lessons or even purchase at Stockbridge Bowl, by appointment. Lew says: "It takes but an hour to learn the fundamentals. The rest is practice."

South County

Benedict Pond, Beartown State Forest (413-528-0904; Blue Hill Rd., Monterey) Sylvan pond suitable for canoe or rowboat only.

Lake Buel (Rte. 57, Monterey)

Lake Garfield (Kinne's Grove, Rte. 23, Monterey) Boat rentals.

Goose Pond (Tyringham Rd., Lee) Boat rentals.

Laurel Lake (Rte. 20, Lee) Boat rentals.

Otis Reservoir, Tolland State Forest (413-528-0904; Reservoir Rd., off Rte. 8, Otis) The largest of Berkshire's lakes. Small fishing boats, canoes, sunfish, and sailboats for rent and a small family restaurant at *J&D Marina* (413-269-4839; 1367 Reservoir Rd., E. Otis, MA 01029). *Miller Marine* (413-269-6358; Reservoir Rd., E. Otis, MA 01029) provides moorings, sales, and service but no rentals. Summer weekends the water is crowded.

Prospect Lake (413-528-4158; fax 413-528-3666; e-mail prospectlk@aol.com; Prospect Lake Rd., N. Egremont, MA 01252) Canoe, paddleboat, rowboat, and sailboard rental and instruction at a private-access family campground and lake.

Stockbridge Bowl (Rte. 183, Stockbridge) Public launching site on one of the county's prettiest lakes, just below Tanglewood.

York Pond, West Lake, Abbey Lake, Sandisfield State Forest (413-258-4774; New Marlborough and Sandisfield).

Central County

Buckley-Dunton Pond, October Mountain State Forest (Yokum Road, Becket)
An intriguingly remote spot.

Greenwater Pond (Pleasant Point, Becket) Boat rentals.

Lake Onota (Onota Blvd., Pittsfield) Free launching area for motorboats. Good windsurfing. *Onota Boat Livery* (413-442-1724; 455 Pecks Rd., Pittsfield, MA 01201) rents small powerboats.

Pontoosuc Lake (Rte. 7, Pittsfield) The YMCA's *Ponterril* (office: 413-499-0640; East Acres Rd., Pittsfield, MA 01201) offers sailboat and canoe rentals. *U-Drive Boat Rentals* (413-442-7020; 990 Valentine Rd., Pittsfield, MA 01201) on Route 7 features ski boats and jet skis.

Richmond Pond (Swamp Rd., Richmond) Boat rentals.

North County

Mausert's Pond, Clarksburg State Forest (413-664-8345; Middle Rd., Clarksburg)

Cheshire Reservoir (Hoosac Lake) (Rte. 8, Cheshire) Launching site.

North Pond, Savoy Mountain State Forest (413-663-8469, summer only; for camping reservations, call 1-877-I-CAMP-MA; off Rte. 2 in Florida, in Savoy) North Pond and South Pond are two jewels in the hills—quite remote, rarely busy.

CAMPING

See "Walking, Hiking, Camping, and X-C Skiing"

CANOEING AND KAYAKING

Besides all of Berkshire's lovely lakes to canoe and kayak, paddlers have four rivers to choose from, with stretches varying from lazy flat water to rushing rapids. The Housatonic River rises in Washington and the lakes near Pittsfield, flowing southward between the Taconic Range and the Berkshire Plateau, heading for Long Island Sound near Stratford, Connecticut. Four Berkshire trips down the Housatonic are recommended by the Appalachian Mountain Club: Dalton to Lenox (19 miles); Lenox to Stockbridge (12 miles); Stockbridge to Great Barrington (13 miles); and Great Barrington to Falls Village, Connecticut (25 miles). Send for *The AMC River Guide to Massachusetts, Connecticut and Rhode Island* ($9.95, from AMC, 5 Joy St., Boston, MA 02108), or ask local booksellers.

A Canoe Guide to the Housatonic River: Berkshire County, a nifty little booklet published jointly by Housatonic supporters and the Berkshire Regional Planning Commission, contains line drawings, a history of the river and its flora and fauna, and dozens of access points. Highly recommended for Housy paddling; at local booksellers.

In *South County*, the stretch on the Housatonic from Great Barrington to Bartholomew's Cobble in Ashley Falls is classic lazy river paddling. Canoes can be purchased and rented in Sheffield at *Gaffer's Outdoors* (413-229-0063; 216 Main St., Sheffield, MA 01257; on Rte. 7).

For lovely lake paddling, canoes can be rented on *Prospect Lake* (413-528-4158; Prospect Lake Park, 50 Prospect Lake Rd., N. Egremont, MA 01252) and *Lake Garfield* (413-528-5417; www.kinnesgrove.com; Kinne's Grove, Rte. 23, Monterey, MA 01245).

In the fall, when the dam on Otis Reservoir is opened, the West Branch of the Farmington River swells. The stretch south of Route 23, along Route 8 in Otis and Sandisfield, is the site of an annual Olympic kayak-racing event. In early spring, this stretch is a Class III rapids, making for exciting white-water paddling and great viewing. The Westfield offers white-water racing in the spring.

Up in *North County,* the Hoosic River flows northward, and in those parts, *Berkshire Outfitters* (see "Sporting Goods Stores"), canoe and kayak specialists, rents craft and offers sound advice on the best in area boating. The Hoosic River Watershed Association has put out a recreational map of the river to the Hudson, available at sports stores.

CROQUET

In the Berkshires, croquet has had a small but tenacious group of followers, willing to risk the indignity of their ball being sent to the periphery of the lawns at the Lenox Club. The town of Lenox has more courts than any town in the state. Blantyre in Lenox offers resident guests the use of imported equipment and lessons by a certified professional, during a season running from July to September. (See Chapter Three, *Lodging*, for more information on Blantyre.)

The Lenox Club and Blantyre each host a tournament in this wicket sport once a year, duly noted in the newspapers.

CROSS-COUNTRY SKIING

See "Walking, Hiking, Camping, and X-C Skiing"

DOWNHILL SKIING

John Hitchcock

A perfect day to be skiing on the heights at Jiminy.

Berkshire downhill ski areas date back to the 1930s. Evidence suggests that three significant advances in modern skiing had their origins here: The surface ski lift, snowmaking, and the ski bar—referring, of course, to the part of the lift chair that locks in the rider. Berkshire ski areas continue to be innovative, always questing for better and more consistent conditions over a longer season.

But it's not the technology that makes Berkshire skiing so appealing, so popular. The Berkshire Hills are challenging yet picturesque, without being imposing. From the summits of the area's ski mountains, the vistas are splendid—mountains on the horizon (like the Catskills, seen from atop Butternut) and skinny bands of civilization below. With six major ski areas in the region to choose from, skiers in the Berkshires can pick their mountain for a week or tour the hills and ski a different area each day. Each ski mountain has its own character; each caters to a slightly different skier yet welcomes all. Jiminy Peak and Berkshire East have the highest proportion of trails suited to advanced skiers; but Butternut, Catamount, and even Bousquet have dicey runs, demanding enough for many experts. And for the best deal for the dollar, the

Mount Greylock Ski Club shines. Every Berkshire ski area offers instruction; Bousquet with its ski school and Otis Ridge with its ski camp emphasize youth instruction.

Snowboarding is familiar and accepted on Berkshire slopes. Popular especially with younger enthusiasts, snow boards offer both thrilling sport and a challenge to one's skills and coordination. Most Berkshire ski areas can rent or sell a board and follow up with instruction. Some areas segregate snowboarders from skiers; all require courtesy and safety from everyone descending the slopes. Tubing is also growing in popularity; some areas have tubing parks.

BERKSHIRE SKI INFORMATION

From outside Massachusetts: 800-237-5747.

Berkshire Ski Conditions: 413-499-7669. New England Ski Council reports are broadcast twice daily from radio station **WBEC-AM (1420)** and **FM (105.5)** on the dial, Pittsfield.

WHERE TO BUY AND RENT SKI EQUIPMENT

Besides the ski areas themselves, all of which have fully stocked ski shops renting and selling equipment, the following specialty shops sell skis and related paraphernalia. Price-cautious skiers should keep their eyes open in the fall for ski and skate sales of used equipment such as the one at Jiminy Peak that benefits the Hancock Fire Department and the one at Pine Cobble School.

Some of these same stores rent snowshoes, for those who prefer that sport (see "Walking," later in this chapter).

South County

Expeditions (413-528-7737, 276 Main St., Gt. Barrington, Ma 01230)
Kenver Ltd. (413-528-2330; Rte. 23, S. Egremont, MA 01258)
Mechangers Ski & Snowboard Service (413-528-9668; 309 Main St., Gt. Barrington, MA 01230)

Central County

Arcadian Shop (413-637-3010; www.arcadian.com; 91 Pittsfield Rd., PO Box 1637, Lenox, MA 01240)
Klein's All Sports (413-443-3531; Berkshire Mall, Lanesborough, MA 01237; Rte. 8)
Plaine's Bike Snowboard Ski Shop (413-499-0294; 55 W. Housatonic St., Pittsfield, MA 01201)
Ski Fanatics (413-443-3023; 241 North St., Pittsfield, MA 01201; also at Brodie)

North County

Berkshire Outfitters (413-743-5900, fax 413-743-3359; www.berkshireoutfit ters.com; Grove St., Adams, MA 01220 Rte. 8)

Goff's Sports (413-458-3605, 800-4243747; www.williams-shop.com; 15 Spring St., Williamstown, MA 01267)

The Mountain Goat (413-458-8445; www.themountaingoat.com; 130 Water St., Williamstown, MA 01267)

The Sports Corner (413-664-8654; www.northadams.com; 61 Main St., N. Adams, MA 01247)

Bearing in mind that Berkshire areas are less expensive than those in northern Vermont, New Hampshire and Maine, we call our top price category, $35 to $50 for an adult, weekend and holiday pass "Moderate." Below $35 we call "Inexpensive." Skiers should contact ski areas for a more elaborate breakdown, which often includes lower rates for weekdays, for night skiing, for junior and seniors. Bousquet's offers free skiing to those 65 and older.

South County

BUTTERNUT BASIN
413-528-2000.
Ski conditions:
  800-438-SNOW.
www.skibutternut.com.
Rte. 23, Gt. Barrington, MA 01230.
2 mi. E. of town, toward Monterey.
Trails: 22 downhill (20 percent novice, 40 percent intermediate, 30 percent expert); also 8 km of X-C trails.
Lifts: 6 chairlifts (quad; triple, 4 doubles), puma, rope tow.
Vertical Drop: 1,000 ft.
Snowmaking: 100 percent of area.
Tickets: Moderate
Open: Mon.–Fri. 9am–4pm; Sat., Sun. 8:15am–4pm.
Ski School Pro: Einar Aas.

Ski-resort developer Channing Murdoch was lucky. Few entrepreneurs can realize their business dreams in their own backyards as he did. His son, Jeff, now carries on the business.

Murdoch designed and built Butternut Basin Ski Area on a site that has become one of the Berkshires' premier winter recreation meccas. At Butternut, challenging downhill runs, a separate beginner's slope, and extensive cross-country ski trails offer ideal options for every kind of skier—from first timer to serious racer.

But Butternut is more than terrific trails and the welcoming charm of its two lovely lodges. From the top of Warner Mountain extend extraordinary views of the distant Catskills in the west and of Mount Greylock at the northern end of Berkshire County. The mountain's timed slalom course is open to everyone, making a potential Olympic-class racer—at least in fantasy—out of even a beginner. Butternut's personable ski pro, Einar Aas, and his team of expert ski instructors, can aid advanced skiers or those on the slopes for their debuts. Two snowboard parks have been opened.

Plus Butternut's ski shop is one of the most extensive and stylish at any Berkshire mountain.

Butternut's quadruple fixed-grip lift, food facilities at the base—including an area exclusively devoted to their Ski Wee kid's program—and outside "Cruiser" barbecue deck show the resort remains at the skiing edge. From the mogul fields of the expert run, Downspout, to the meandering path of the novice Pied Piper's Trail, Butternut is a delight to the eye as well as a refreshing test of athletic skill.

CATAMOUNT
413-528-1262, 518-325-3200.
www.catamountski.com.
Rte. 23, S. Egremont, MA
  01258.
On NY border.
Trails: 28 downhill (novice
  to expert).
Lifts: 4 chairlifts, T-Bar,
  J-Bar.
Vertical Drop: 1,152 ft.
Snowmaking: 96 percent of
  area.
Tickets: Moderate.
Open: Weekends, holidays
  8:30–4; midweek. 9–4;
  night skiing Wed.–Sat.
  3–10.
Ski School Director: Jen
  Brown.

"On the cutting edge of Berkshire ski country," as *Skiing* magazine put it, Catamount straddles two states and offers magnificent views of four: Massachusetts, New York, Connecticut, and Vermont. The slopes are primarily novice and intermediate, but seasoned skiers can find quite a bit of challenge through the glades near the summit and down on through the Flipper and Dipper trails. For snowboarders there's the Megaplex park.

Called by some a vest-pocket Killington, Catamount is convenient, especially to New Yorkers. Not the trendiest, competition-minded ski resort, although it does offer an extensive race season, it cultivates a pleasant quaintness, right down to the Swiss Hütte restaurant at the mountain's base. Snowmaking equipment at Catamount has been overhauled and expanded, firing state-of-the-art equipment at virtually all trails and slopes. Catamount has installed an additional 22 airless snow makers mounted on towers. Night skiing and an area for kids are attractions.

The Upper and Lower Sidewinder is a new skiing trail a mile long. For borderline skiing in the Berkshires, there's no better.

OTIS RIDGE
413-269-4444.
www.otisridge.com.
Rte. 23, Otis, MA 01253.
Trails: 11 (3 novice, 5 inter-
  mediate, 3 expert).
Lifts: Double chairlift, T-bar,
  pony-bar, 2 rope tows.
Vertical Drop: 400 ft.
Snowmaking: 90 percent.
Tickets: Inexpensive.
Open: Weekends, holidays
  9-4; midweek 9:30-4; night
  skiing Tues.–Sun. 5–10.
Ski School Pros: Dave Day
  and Terri Dunn.

Otis Ridge is the molehill among the mountains, but few slopes do so much to cater to beginners and youngsters, with two ski-school heads. Famous for its winter ski camp, the area takes on a special character on frosty weekends and holiday periods when camp's in session, starting the day after Christmas.

Central County

BOUSQUET
413-442-8316.
www.bousquets.com.
101 Dan Fox Dr., Pittsfield, MA 01201.
Access from South St. (Rte. 7) or Swamp Rd.
Trails: 21 downhill (novice to expert); all-terrain area.
Lifts: 2 chairlifts, 2 rope tows; snowboarding half-pipe; tubing park.
Vertical Drop: 750 ft.
Snowmaking: 98 percent of area.
Tickets: Inexpensive; free tickets for 65 and older.
Open: Weekdays 10am–10pm, weekends 9am–10pm, Sun. 9am–pm, night skiing Mon.–Sat. 4–10pm
Ski and Snowboard School Pro: John Koch.

In 1932 a group of winter enthusiasts approached Clarence Bousquet about using the slopes of his Bousquet Farm for skiing. Three years later the fledgling Bousquet Ski Area put together one of the Berkshires' great travel promotions: Ski trains from New York to Pittsfield (with bus connector to Bousquet) for $2 round-trip.

Now, over 70 years later, the Berkshires' oldest ski area continues to provide friendly slopes, primarily for novice and intermediate skiers. There are, however, several very demanding runs. As a plus, from the summit of Bousquet, a skier has a fine view of Mount Greylock's whalelike profile (nearly the same view that so inspired Herman Melville; see "Arrowhead" in Chapter Four, *Arts & Pleasures*). Bousquet is well known for its effective ski school, a corps of some 50 teachers. The state may purchase this facility.

JIMINY PEAK
413-738-5500.
www.jiminypeak.com.
Corey Rd., Hancock, MA 01237.
Access from Rte. 7, Lanesborough, or Rte. 43, Hancock, via Brodie Mtn. Rd.
Trails: 40 downhill (novice to expert).
Lifts: 8 chairlifts.
Vertical Drop: 1,140 ft.
Snowmaking: 95 percent of area.
Tickets: Moderate.
Open: Weekdays 9am–10:30pm, weekends 8:30am–10:30pm
Ski School Pro: Chuck Seymour.

Jiminy is committed to long seasons of well-groomed slopes. To that end, it goes to extraordinary lengths, frequently opening early in November and staying open well into March, utilizing advanced snowmaking equipment. It has completed a multimillion-dollar expansion program, opening up a new mountain, East Peak, and a cluster of five new buildings called Bentley Brook.

This is one of the area's most demanding mountains, with 40 percent of its trails being suitable for advanced skiers only. Those with such talents will greatly enjoy the North Glade, Upper Lift Line and Whirlaway. For Intermediates, there's the 360, the WestWay and the Ace of Spades. These last two trails reveal a magnificent vista of the Jericho Valley, northward toward Vermont. Two expert glades, an expanded beginners' area with a triple chair, and always and improving snowmaking complete the picture.

In addition to a full calendar of races, clinics, and demonstrations, Jiminy runs a race team just for children, a more serious tri-state race team, a freestyle team, a night adult program, and a ski school. Those who ski at Jiminy spend most of their time skiing: lift lines are carefully monitored so that skiers rarely have to wait more than 12 minutes. Jiminy closes the parking lots when the area nears its capacity.

Jiminy offers facilities and activities to compete with resorts in Vermont. It continues to add more beds (ski-in, ski-out), new lifts, and snowmaking improved to operate at higher temperatures.

North County

BERKSHIRE EAST
413-339-6617.
www.berkshireeast.com.
Rte. 2 Charlemont, MA
01339.
Trails: 45 (12 novice, 14
intermediate, 14 expert).
Lifts: 3 double chairlifts, 1
triple, J-bar, rope tow;
snowboarding half pipe.
Vertical Drop: 1,180 ft.
Snowmaking: 100 percent.
Tickets: Moderate.
Open: Sun.–Tues.
9am–4:30pm, Wed.–Sat.
9am–10pm.

Berkshire East bills itself as "Southern New England's most challenging ski area," and its steep terrain lives up to that claim. With more than 40 percent of its trails suited to experts, this mountain is demanding—especially down the steep Flying Cloud and Lift Line trails, both of which are over 4,000 feet long. For beginners, three separate open slopes around the west lodge provide plenty of room to learn the basics. From the summit of Berkshire East, amid the pines, skiers can get a fine view of the steep-sided Deerfield River valley to the east.

The area offers day and night skiing, accompanied by a rustic lodge with a bar upstairs.

BRODIE MOUNTAIN
413-443-4752.
www.skibrodie.com.
Rte. 7, New Ashford, MA
01237.
Trails: Snow tubing park;
snowshoeing.
Snowmaking: 98 percent of
area.
Tickets: Inexpensive.
Open: Fri. 4:30pm–9pm,
Sat. and holidays
10:30am–9pm, Sun.
10:30am–7:30pm.

At the present time Brodie is closed for skiing but remains open for tubing and snowshoeing. Plans are in the works for resort development.

One of the oldest ski areas in the Berkshires, Brodie Mountain started out under the direction of Gregory Makeroff, acquiring a different flavor under the guidance of the Kelly clan. It became "Kelly's Irish Alps." In the fall of 1999, Jiminy Peak purchased Brodie, to be run as "separate but cooperative corporations." Brodie will continue to be a fun area, and has always had tremendous appeal to singles and younger snow enthusiasts.

After tubing, Brodie keeps the fun going off the slopes with the Blarney Room and Kelly's Irish Pub.

**MOUNT GREYLOCK SKI
CLUB**
413-458-3060; 413-445-7887
(ski conditions).

Mount Greylock Ski Club is a cooperative, which means that in exchange for low rates (family membership is about $100 for a season,

Roaring Brook Rd.,
 Williamstown, MA 01267
In south Williamstown,
 turn east on Roaring
 Brook Rd. beside Rte. 7
 state DPW garage.
 Continue up gravel road
 that, in season, is one
 way until 2:30pm.
Trails: 16 (4 novice, 9
 intermediate, 3 expert).
Lifts: 2 rope tows.
Vertical Drop: 500 ft.
Tickets: Very inexpensive
 membership.
Open: Weekends and
 holidays when snow
 permits (no
 snowmaking).
Features: Lodge, outhouses,
 ski lessons available.

including children up to 21), everyone works. Jobs range from helping to take care of the wood-heated lodge to cutting brush on the trail to running the antique Ford and GMC engines that power the lifts. It is a fine place for a family because the adults look out for all the kids. The very young amuse themselves by the hour, sliding near the lodge while parents ski. Members ski patrol and teach.

The area, which has a base altitude of 1,200 ft, faces north and holds snow well, but if the snow doesn't fall . . . well, then, members get to enjoy the social events and work parties the club sponsors. If the one-way traffic is daunting, the alternative is a pleasant 0.5 mile walk.

FOOTBALL

High-school teams and pick-up touch football games carry on throughout the county, but only in Williamstown can one see collegiate gridiron action, as presented by the Williams College Ephmen (named after their school founder, Ephraim Williams). This is football at its sweetest: No athletic scholarships, studies really do come first, and competition with the likes of Amherst is even and spirited.

Williams College Football (413-597-2344) Weston Field, Williamstown.

The Berkshire Mountaineers, a professional team in the Empire League, can sometimes be located through the sports pages in season.

GOLF

In 1895 Joseph Choate Jr., son of the prominent Stockbridge lawyer, returned from a Canadian trip with three rudimentary golf clubs. Using tomato cans for holes, he made a course in his backyard at Naumkeag, establishing golf in the Berkshires. Three years later, having perfected his swing, Choate won the National Championships with a record low score. (A variation on the tomato can tale cites the Taconic as the first course in the county.)

Nowadays hardy sports folk tee up on 16 courses countywide from March

An autumn drive . . . at Waubeeka.

John Hitchcock

through November. Every course and club runs tournaments. A call or visit will provide exact dates. Long-distance driving options have expanded, too. First there were wood woods, then metal woods, and now—developed from Pittsfield-GE engineered resins—Lexan woods, by Thermo par. And for those who just have to hit some in the dark of night, *Baker's Driving Range & Miniature Golf* (413-443-6102; Rte. 7, Lanesborough, MA 01237) keeps its driving range open from 10am till 10:30pm.

Possibilities in the miniature division: *Par 4 Family Fun Center* (413-499-0051; Rte. 7, Lanesborough, MA 01237), *Jiminy Peak* (413-738-5500; Corey Rd., Hancock, MA 01237), and in South County there's *Rainbow's End Miniature Golf* (413-528-1220; 109 Stockbridge Rd., Gt. Barrington, MA 01230; Rte. 7) inside—yes, inside!—Cove Bowling Lanes.

GOLF CLUBS

Price Code—Greens Fees (weekends; some include cart)
Inexpensive   Under $30
Moderate $30 to $45
Expensive   Over $45

South County

Egremont Country Club (413-528-4222; Rte. 23, S. Egremont, MA 01258) Price: moderate; 18 holes, par 71, 5,900 yards; pro: Marc Levesque.
Greenock Country Club (413-243-3323; 220 W. Park St., Lee, MA 01238 Price: moderate; 9 holes, par 35, 5,990 yards; pro: Michael Bechard.

Stockbridge Golf Club (413-298-3423; Main St., PO Box 223, Stockbridge, MA 01262) Price: expensive; 18 holes, par 71, 6,294 yards; pro: Jim Walker. Must be introduced by a member.

Wyantenuck Country Club (413-528-3229; Sheffield Rd., Gt. Barrington, MA 01230) Price: moderate; 18 holes; par 70; 6,223 yards; pro: Tom Sullivan. Private club.

Central County

Bas-Ridge Golf Course (413-655-2605; Plunkett Ave., Hinsdale, MA 01235) Price: inexpensive; 18 holes, par 70, 5,164 yards.

Berkshire Hills Country Club (413-442-1451; Benedict Rd., Pittsfield, MA 01201) Price: moderate; 18 holes, par 72, 6,606 yards; pro: Bob Meheran. Must be introduced by a member.

Country Club of Pittsfield (413-447-8504; 639 South St., Pittsfield, MA 01201) Price: moderate; 18 holes, par 71, 6,100 yards; pro: Brad Benson. Must be introduced by a member.

Cranwell Golf Course (413-637-1364; www.cranwell.com; 55 Lee Rd., Rte. 20, Lenox, MA 01240) Price: expensive; 18 holes, par 70, 6,387 yards; pro: David Strawn.

General Electric Athletic Association (413-443-5746; 303 Crane Ave., Pittsfield, MA 01201) Price: inexpensive; 9 holes, par 72, 6,205 yards; pro: Jay Aba.

Pontoosuc Lake Country Club (413-445-4217; Ridge Ave., Pittsfield, MA 01201) Price: inexpensive; 18 holes; par 70; 6,305 yards.

Skyline Country Club (413-445-5584; 405 S. Main St., Lanesborough, MA 01237) Price: moderate; 18 holes, par 72, 6,643 yards; pro: Jim Mitus.

Wahconah Country Club (413-684-1333; Orchard Rd., Dalton, MA 01226) Price: expensive; 18 holes, par 71, 6,541 yards; pro: Paul Daniels. Public restricted on weekends.

North County

Forest Park Country Club (413-743-3311; Forest Park Ave., Adams, MA 01220) Price: inexpensive; 9 holes, par 68, 5,100 yards.

North Adams Country Club (413-663-7887; River Rd., PO Box 241,Clarksburg, MA 01247) Price: inexpensive; 9 holes, par 72, 6,070 yards; pro: Jack Tosone.

Taconic Golf Club (413-458-3997; Meacham St., PO Box 193, Williamstown, MA 01267) Price: expensive; 18 holes, par 71, 6,614 yards; pro: Rick Pohle. Open to public Tues.–Fri.

Waubeeka Springs Golf Links (413-458-8355; New Ashford Rd., Rte. 7, Williamstown, MA 01267) Price: moderate; 18 holes, par 72, 6,296 yards; pro: Eric Tiele.

Golfers live in anticipation of a new course, at **Donnybrook** in Lanesborough.

HIKING

S ee "Walking, Hiking, Camping, and X-C Skiing"

HORSEBACK RIDING

Learning to groom at Jeanette Rotondo's Windy Knoll Farm in Lee.

Judith Monachina

O ver meadow and under mountain, there are a slew of riding academies and stables in and around Berkshire County. A quick look in the Yellow Pages under "Riding Academies" or "Stables" opens the barn door to information on horse breeders, dealers, trainers, farriers, and saddle shops. The following is a partial list.

Bonnie Lea Farm (413-458-3149; 511 North St., Williamstown, MA 01267; Rte. 7) Private and group lessons; English and western; indoor and outdoor rings, guided trail rides; year-round.

Horsesense at Golden Hill Farm (413-637-1999; 87 Golden Hill Rd., Lenox, MA 01240) Private and group lessons; English; indoor and outdoor rings; year-round.

Oakhollow (413-458-9278; 651 Henderson Rd., Williamstown, MA 01267) English lessons; trails, indoor and outdoor rings; therapeutic riding program; year-round.

Overmeade School of Horsemanship (413-499-2850; 940 East St., Lenox, MA 01240) Private and group lessons; English; year-round.

Riverbank Farm (413-684-3200; 619 East St., Dalton, MA 01226) Summer riding program; English and western lessons; year-round.

Undermountain Farm (413-637-3365; Under Mountain Rd., Lenox, MA 01240; English lessons; English and western trail rides; spring through fall.

Windy Knoll Farm (413-243-0989; 40 Stringer Ave., Lee, MA 01238) Stable management and riding lessons (weather permitting) for beginners; horse-drawn wagon rides; open May 1–Dec. 1.

HUNTING AND FISHING

The first settlers found Berkshire teeming with fish and game; wildlife is now more plentiful than it has been in 150 years. Deer visit town to devour ornamental shrubbery, wild turkey and beaver have been successfully reintroduced, and bear, pheasant, quail, rabbit, raccoon, fox, coyote, and gray squirrel are sufficient to satisfy nearly every hunter's aim. In Berkshire's waters, large- and small-mouth bass, northern pike, white and yellow perch, horned pout, and trout of all persuasions swim in abundance. Numerous brooks, rivers, ponds, and lakes are stocked with trout each year.

Essential equipment for any hunting or fishing is a pamphlet containing abstracts of the *Massachusetts Fish and Wildlife Laws*, available free at local sporting goods shops; from the *Division of Fisheries and Wildlife* (617-626-1590; www.state.ma.us/dfwele; 251 Causeway, Suite 400, Boston, MA 02114); or from the *Western Wildlife District Manager*, Tom Keefe (413-447-9787; 400 Hubbard Ave., Pittsfield, MA 01201). This pamphlet carefully outlines the rules and regulations of Massachusetts fishing and hunting. Also essential is a license, which can be obtained through either city or town clerks, through the Division of Fisheries and Wildlife at the Boston address above or through many local sporting goods stores (see the list at the beginning of this chapter).

A license permits hunting, fishing, or trapping on property that is not posted, although some towns also require owner permission. State lands are open with a few exceptions, such as a three-quarter-mile radius around the tower on Mount Greylock. No hunting is allowed anywhere on Greylock during the summer and early fall. As deer season varies by a few weeks between Massachusetts and neighboring states, hunters are responsible to know what state they are in.

A LIST OF TROUT-STOCKED BERKSHIRE WATERS
(Bodies of water that are stocked spring and fall are in italics)

South County

Alford: Green River, Seekonk Brook.

Egremont: Green River, Hubbard Brook, Karner Brook.

Great Barrington: Green River, Lake Mansfield, Williams River, West Brook.

Lee: Beartown Brook (W. branch), *Goose Pond*, Greenwater Brook, Hop Brook, Laurel Lake, Washington Mountain Brook.

FISH, EXCLUSIVE OF TROUT, IN BERSKHIRE WATERS

TOWN	WATER	NP	LMB	SMB	CP	WP	YP	BB
South County								
Egremont	Prospect lake				✔		✔	✔
Lee	Goose Pond		✔	✔	✔		✔	✔
Lee	Laurel Lake		✔		✔	✔	✔	✔
Monterey	Benedict Pond		✔				✔	✔
New Marlborough	Thousand Acre Swamp			✔	✔		✔	✔
Otis	Benton Pond			✔	✔	✔	✔	✔
Otis	East Otis Reservoir	✔	✔	✔	✔	✔	✔	✔
Stockbridge	Stockbridge Bowl		✔	✔	✔		✔	✔
Central County								
Becket	Center Pond		✔	✔	✔	✔	✔	✔
Becket	Yokum Pond		✔				✔	✔
Hinsdale	Ashmere Lake		✔	✔			✔	
Pittsfield	Onota Lake	✔	✔		✔		✔	✔
Pittsfield	Pontoosuc Lake		✔		✔		✔	✔
Pittsfield	Richmond Pond		✔	✔	✔		✔	✔
Windsor	Windsor Pond		✔		✔		✔	✔
North County								
Cheshire	Cheshire Reservoir	✔	✔		✔		✔	✔
Clarksburg	Mauserts Pond					✔		✔

Symbols
NP— Northern Pike
LMB— Largemouth Bass
SMB— Smallmouth Bass
CP— Chain Pickerel
WP— White Perch
YP— Yellow Perch
BB— Brown Bullhealds
(Horn Pout)

Monterey: *Lake Buel*, Lake Garfield, Konkapot River.
New Marlborough: Konkapot River, Umpachene Brook, York Pond.
Otis: *Big Benton Pond*, Little Benton Pond, Farmington River, *Otis Reservoir*.
Sandisfield: Buck River, Clam River, Farmington River.
Sheffield: Hubbard Brook, Innworks Brook, Konkapot River.
Stockbridge: Konkapot Brook, Larrywaug Brook, *Stockbridge Bowl*.
Tyringham: *Goose Pond*, Goose Pond Brook, Hop Brook.
West Stockbridge: Cone Brook, Williams River.

Central County

Becket: Greenwater Pond, Shaker Mill Brook, Walker Brook, Westfield River (W. branch), Yokum Brook.
Dalton: Housatonic River (E. branch), Sackett Brook, Wahconah Falls Brook.
Hancock: Berry Pond, Kinderhook Creek.
Hinsdale: Bennet Brook, Housatonic River (E. branch), Plunket Reservoir.
Lanesborough: Sachem Brook, Town Brook.
Lenox: *Laurel Lake*, Yokum Brook.
Peru: Trout Brook.
Pittsfield: Daniels Brook, Housatonic River (S.W. branch), Lulu Cascade Brook, *Lake Onota, Lake Pontoosuc*, Sackett Brook, Smith Brook.
Richmond: Cone Brook, Furnace Brook, *Richmond Pond*.
Washington: Depot Brook.
Windsor: Westfield Brook, Westfield River (E. branch), Windsor Brook, Windsor Jambs Brook, Windsor Pond.

North County

Adams: Hoosic River (S. branch), Tophet Brook.
Cheshire: Dry Brook, Hoosic River (S. branch), Kitchen Brook, South Brook.
Clarksburg: Hoosic River (N. branch), Hudson Brook.
Florida: *Deerfield River, North Pond*, Cold River.
North Adams: Natural Bridge Pond, *Windsor Lake*.
Savoy: Chickley River, Cold River, Westfield River (E. branch).
Williamstown: Broad Brook, Green River, Green River (W. branch), Hemlock Brook, Roaring Brook.

KIDS ONLY

Although the county may be low on video arcades, bumper cars, skating centers, or amusement parks, as far as most kids are concerned, Berkshire is cool. Some do the mall crawl, some hang out on shopping streets. The Ashuwillticook Rail Trail and professional baseball parks are area destinations. Hills and lakes beckon. Besides the dozens of children's camps here, most of

The Stockbridge skateboard park is the most popular spot for kids in town.

Judith Monachina

the ski slopes operate ski schools for kids. In between the summer camping and winter skiing, the Berkshire cultural icons offer a wide range of kid programs, from after school, school to vacation, to summer day camps. Most local libraries have story hours, most of the museums and playgrounds have kids' programs, and many of the local theaters have innovative children's productions. In addition, bulletin boards and signs at all kinds of locations—inns, local stores, libraries, post offices, and the like—keep viewers current. Websites at local museums and other institutions provide the newest news.

South County

In Great Barrington, at the Cove Bowling Lanes on Route 7, is the **Rainbow's End Miniature Golf Course** (413-528-1220, 800-352-4398; fax 413-528-5295), an indoor extravaganza to test even the deftest little putter. Out in New Marlboro, **Four Colors Company** presents theater workshops for kids of all ages at the Flying Cloud Summer Camp (413-528-5614; S. Sandisfield Rd.).

The **Stockbridge Library** (413-298-5501; Main St., Stockbridge; Rte. 7) has a large and cozy children's section, with story hours as a regular event. During the summer, the **Berkshire Theatre Festival** (413-298-5536; 6 East Main St., Stockbridge, MA 01262; Rte. 102, E of jct. Rte. 7) gives Children's Theatre performances of plays written by local kids. It also offers an acting class for students 12 to 14. The **Norman Rockwell Museum** (413-298-4100; PO Box 309, Stockbridge, MA 01262; on Rte. 183, 0.6 mi. S of jct. Rte. 102) offers a variety of activities geared to kids, one the best being its Family Day. Admission prices are lowered, and special guides are provided to inform both parents and kids. The **Berkshire Botanical Garden** (413-298-3926; www.berkshirebotanical.org; PO Box 386, Stockbridge, MA, jct. Rtes. 183 and 102,) holds a wonder-filled day camp for kids in summer, offering children in grades one through six the opportunity to explore the world of nature. Their early October Harvest Festival has lots of kids' activities, too. Art classes are a part of the **IS183** program

(413-298-5252; www.is183.org; 13 Willard Hill Rd., Stockbridge, MA 01262), with special courses for children 8 to 17.

Central County

In Pittsfield, *Buster's Entertainment Center* (413-499-7500; www.bustersfor fun.com; 457 Dalton Ave., Pittsfield, MA 01201) is the place to be. There are more than 100 arcades, plus "Blue Skies & Rainbows" for 1–6 year olds and "Adventure Crawl" for children up to 12 years.

The *Lenox Library* (413-637-0197; 18 Main St., Lenox, MA 01240) has a terrific children's room, which always seems to be brimming with kid energy. *Pleasant Valley Wildlife Sanctuary* (413-637-0320; www.massaudubon.org; 472 W. Mountain Rd., Lenox, MA 01240) runs a History Day Camp, one- and two-week sessions, featuring exciting educational outdoor activities for boys and girls grades 1 through 12.

Central County's other Massachusetts Audubon Society property, *Canoe Meadows Wildlife Sanctuary* (413-637-0320; www.massaudubon.org; mail: 472 W. Mountain Rd., Lenox, MA 01240; on Holmes Rd., Pittsfield), in conjunction with the Berkshire Museum, runs a one-week Native American camp for boys and girls, ages three, four, and five. During the summer, *Hancock Shaker Village* (413-443-0188, 800817-1137; www.hancockshakervillage.org; mail: PO Box 927, Pittsfield, MA 01201; on Rte. 20, Hancock) offers a hands-on experience in its "Discovery Room," where children can try on Shaker-style clothes and participate in such facets of 19th-century life as spinning wool, weaving, or writing with a quill pen at a Shaker desk. Outside, children can see the farm animals and demonstrations of sheep shearing or sheep-herding trials. Hancock Shaker Village also conducts "School Vacation Crafts Workshops" in basket making, cooking, and textiles in February and April.

The *Robbins-Zust Family Marionettes* often perform a full range of "classic tales for children of all ages." Bringing out the heavyweight dramas such as "Three Little Pigs," "Rumpelstiltskin" and "The Emperor's New Clothes," the Robbins-Zust troupe often performs in Lenox and Pittsfield. These are well-crafted marionettes: all their clothes are made by the troupe. For more information, call the Marionettes themselves (413-698-2591; www.berkshireweb .com/zust; East Rd., Richmond, MA 01254). They are "the smallest, established, permanent, floating repertory company in America."

In downtown Pittsfield, the children's library at the *Berkshire Athenaeum'* (413-499-9483; www.berkshire.net/PittsfieldLibrary; 1 Wendell Ave., Pittsfield, MA 01201; at East St.) has a wide range of programs, from story hours to films. The *Berkshire Museum* (413-443-7171; www.berkshiremuseum.org; 39 South St., Pittsfield, MA 01201; Rte. 7) also has an extensive series of educational children's events—theater, dance, and story-telling for the whole family.

At *Dalton Community House* (413-684-0260; 400 Main St., Dalton, MA 01226) kids will find a positive plethora of fun activities. Then there's miniature golf in Lanesborough to keep little hands busy at *Baker's Golf Center*

(413-442-6102; 658 S. Main St., Lanesborough, MA 01237) and the *par-4 Family Fun Center* (413-499-0051; Rte. 7, Lanesborough, MA 01237). Up-county a ways, at *Jiminy Peak* (413-738-5500; Rte. 43, Hancock, MA 01237), the fun goes right into summer with the *Alpine Slide*, a scenic 15-minute ride up, and an exhilarating 5-minute slide down. Jiminy also has a miniature golf course, trout fishing, and a separate tennis program.

North County

Over in North Adams, at the *Heritage Gateway State Park* (413-663-6312; 9 Furnace St. Bypass, N. Adams, MA 01247) a Junior Ranger's program is active. In Williamstown, there's an extensive summer playground program at the public schools, along with swimming lessons and a Nature Program at *Margaret Lindley Park*. Information can be had by calling the *Youth Center* (413-458-5925; Cole Ave., Williamstown, MA 01267). A summer playground program and a score of winter recreational programs are also offered through the Youth Center. The *Massachusetts Department of Environmental Management* (413-442-8928) and Nature's Classroom offer scores of children's programs at several sites on Mount Greylock, including The Glen, in Adams. And treasure hunts, along with children's workshops on various artists, are a few of the offerings for kids at the *Clark Art Institute* (413-458-8109; 225 South St., Williamstown, MA 01267). The *Williams College Museum of Art* frequently has imaginative children's programs. *Kidspace @ MASS MoCA*, a combined effort of the Clark, WCMA, and MASS MoCA to provide a program for children and families who have had little exposure to art. The college's science departments invite children in for imaginative exposure to natural phenomena. The *Williamstown Public Library* offers read-a-louds and a summer reading program. Children's tennis and soccer camps are available on the *Williams College* campus in the summer; call the Conference Office 413-458-2229. The *Williamstown Theatre Festival* (413-458-3200) runs a program for North Adams youth.

CAMPS

There's a colorful list of overnight, resident summer camps in the Berkshires—some specializing in sports, some tuned to the arts, some with other enthusiasms. If youngsters are interested in dance or the theater, hiking or canoeing, tennis or gymnastics, dressmaking, or computers, Berkshire has a camp for them. Most camps take advantage of the beauty of their natural settings, and for many of them that includes lakes and mountains. Warm days and cool nights make for season-long aquatics and sound sleeping. Berkshire cultural life also enriches campers' time here, with Tanglewood and Jacob's Pillow being two of the more popular side trips.

The Indians were the first campers in the Berkshires, and many of its camps bear Indian names. Following is a list of addresses and telephone numbers. "Full program" indicates availability of both arts and sports activities.

South County

Camp Ashmere (413-655-2650 summer, 413-663-3780 winter; Hinsdale, MA 01235) Religious; residential and day; special units.

Camp Danbee (413-655-8115; www.campdanbee.com; Rte. 143, Hinsdale, MA 01235) Girls residential; full program.

Camp Half Moon (413-528-0940; www.camphalfmoon.com; 400 Main St., PO Box 108, Gt. Barrington, MA 01230) Coed day and resident camp; full program.

Camp Hi Rock YMCA (413-528-1227; www.camphirock.com; RD 3 Box 49, Mt. Washington, MA 01258) Sessions for coed groups and adults; full program.

Camp Kingsmont (413-232-8518; www.campkingsmont.com; RFD 2, W. Stockbridge, MA 01266) Coed; nutrition and dietary education program; physical fitness.

Camp Lenox (413-243-2223, summer; 413-269-6036, winter; www.lenox.com; Rte. 8, Otis, MA 01238) Coed day; sports.

Camp Nawaka (413-269-4296; www.abhealthyboston.org/SummerGuide11 .html; Reservoir Rd., Otis, MA 01253) Camp Fire Boys and Girls.

Camp WaWa Segowea (413-229-8613; www.wawasegowea.com; Foley Hill Rd., Southfield, MA 01259) YMCA; coed residential; full program.

Crane Lake Camp (413-232-4257 summer, 212-362-1462 winter; www.eisner camp.org/crane%20lake.htm; State Line Rd., W. Stockbridge, MA 01266) Coed; run by Union of American Hebrew Congregations (UAHC); full program and Jewish education.

Eisner Camp (413-528-1652 summer, 212-650-4130 winter; www.eisnercamp.org /eisner%20camp.htm; Brookside Rd., PO Box 569, Gt. Barrington, MA 01230) Coed children's and adult retreats; run by UAHC; full program and Jewish education.

Madden Open Heart Camp (413-528-2229; www.openheartscamp.org; 250 Monument Valley Rd., Gt. Barrington, MA 01230) Coed for children who have had open-heart surgery or heart transplants; full program.

New England Keswick (413-528-9588; www.nekeswick.com; Chestnut Hill Rd., PO Box 156, Monterey, MA 01245) Evangelical Christian camp and retreat center.

Central County

Belvoir Terrace (413-637-0555; www.belvoirterrace.com; 80 Cliffwood St., Lenox, MA 01240; winter: 212-580-3398, 101 W. 79 St., NY, NY 10024) Girls day; fine and performing arts.

Camp Becket (413-623-8972; www.bccymca.org/camps/becket/CBecket.html; Becket, MA 01223) Boys; full program; operated by Two-State YMCA.

Camp Bonnie Brae (413-269-4481; Algerie Rd., E. Otis, MA 01253) Girls; full program; run by Girl Scouts of the Pioneer Valley.

Camp Chimney Corners (413-623-8991; www.bccymca.org/camps/chimney/ CC.html; Becket, MA 01223) Girls; full program; operated by Two-State YMCA, sister camp to Camp Becket.

Camp Emerson (413-655-8123 summer, 914-779-9406 winter; www.campemer son.com; 212 Longview Ave., PO Box 808, Hinsdale, MA 01235) Coed 7–15; full program.

Camp Greylock (413-623-8921 summer; www.campemerson.com; Rte. 8, Becket, MA 01233; winter, 212-582-1042, 200 W. 57th St., Suite 307, NY, NY. 10019) Boys; full program.

Camp Mah-Kee-Nac (413-637-0781 summer, 201-429-8522 winter; www.campmkn .com; 6 Hawthorne Rd., Lenox, MA 01240) Boys; sports and outdoor-adventure programs.

Camp Mohawk (413-443-9843; www.campmohawk.org; 300 Old Cheshire Rd., Lanesborough, MA 01237) Coed day; run by YMCA.

Camp Romaca (413-655-2715, summer, 800-779-2070, winter; www.romaca.com; Long View Ave., Hinsdale, MA 01235; Girls; full program.

Sports School Day Camp (413-637-3463; Lenox, MA 01240)

Camp Stevenson Witawentin (413-445-5850; http://girlsinc-berkshires.org/ CSW.htm; Churchill Rd., Pittsfield, MA 01201; Girls day; sports; through Girls Inc.

Camp Taconic (413-655-2717 summer, 914-762-2820 winter; www.camptacon ic.com; Hinsdale, MA 01235) Coed sleepaway; full program.

Camp Watitoh (413-623-8951 summer, 914-428-1894 winter; www.campwati toh.com; Center Lake, Becket, MA 01223) Coed; full program.

Camp Winadu (413-447-8900 summer, 407-994-5500 winter; www.camp winadu.com; Churchill St., Pittsfield, MA 01201) Boys; full program.

North County

Manice Education Center (413-663-8463; www.geocities.com/christodora/ page2.html; 68 Savoy Rd., Florida, MA 01247) Coed; full programs; for inner-city youth.

RACQUET SPORTS

RACQUETBALL

There's a lively racquetball scene in Berkshire, with courts in Lenox, Pittsfield, New Ashford, North Adams, and Williams College. The *Northern Berkshire YMCA* (413-663-6529; http://bcn.net/~nbymca; 22 Brickyard Court, N. Adams, MA 02147), has two fine courts. *Pittsfield YMCA* (413-499-7650; 292 North St., Pittsfield, MA 01201) has four; and *Berkshire West* (413-499-4600; www.berkshirewest.com; 100 Dan Fox Dr., PO Box 2188, Pittsfield, MA 01201) has four. Both Pittsfield facilities offer top-flight teaching programs. Williams's is located at the football field.

John Hitchcock

Count 'em, 24 courts, no waiting at Williams.

SQUASH

For the sporting type—as opposed to the garden variety—many squash courts do exist; most are open only to people associated with the private schools maintaining them. Memberships are available at Williams College, which has increased the size of its courts. For travelers: the **Pittsfield YMCA** (see above). Luckily the Y's court is also new, well built, and lively.

TENNIS

In the Gilded Age of the Berkshires at the close of the 19th century, tennis was played on lawns, close cropped and lined with lime. Wheatleigh was an especially favored site. The lawn tennis parties there featured men in white-linen trousers and ladies in ankle-length tennis dresses. Most of the grass courts are front lawns now, and though a few Berkshire connoisseurs still play on turf, tennis—here as elsewhere—is now played principally on clay, composites, and hard courts.

Several tournaments are annual events and can be counted on to test the best skills or provide exciting viewing. A senior tournament in mid-summer honors the fabled Williams College coach Clarance Chaffee and his partner, Billy Hart.

Starting in late summer, tournaments are run by the YMCA's *Ponterril* (413-499-0687, 413-499-0640 Pontoosuc Lake, Pittsfield, MA 01201 Rte. 7,).

Southern Berkshire has traditionally been lacking in public tennis courts, but **Monument Mountain High School** and the **Berkshire Hills Tennis Association** have created seven new hard courts at the school, for both scholastic and community play. The courts are open to the public, with priority given to the school's tennis teams' needs.

TENNIS FACILITIES

South County

Monument Mountain Regional High School (413-528-3346; Rte. 7, Gt. Barrington, MA 01230) 7 hard courts, used by school students on weekdays from 3pm

Monument Mountain Motel (413-528-3272; Rte. 7, Gt. Barrington, MA 01230; opposite Friendly's) Lit all-weather court; fee. Call for reservation.

Greenock Country Club (413-243-3323; W. Park St., Lee, MA 01238) 2 clay courts; fee.

Prospect Lake Park (413-528-4158; prospectlk@aol.com; Prospect Lake Rd., PO 78, N. Egremont, MA 01252) 2 courts; fee.

Simon's Rock College of Bard (413-528-0771; 84 Alford Rd., Gt. Barrington, MA 01230) 4 hard courts plus backboard; summer memberships available.

Stockbridge Golf Club (413-298-3838; Main St., Stockbridge, MA 01262; behind Town Hall) 3 clay, 2 hard-surface courts; nonmembers may arrange for lessons only.

Stockbridge Public Courts for town residents and registered hotel guests; **Pine St.**: 2 hard courts; **The Plain School**, Main St. (Rte. 7); 2 hard courts.

Central County

Berkshire West (413-449-4600; Dan Fox Dr., Pittsfield MA 01201) 6 outdoor courts and 5 indoor hard courts; memberships available.

Cranwell Resort (413-637-1364; 55 Lee Rd., Lenox, MA 01240; Rte. 20) 2 Har-Tru courts. Fee.

Jiminy Peak 413-738-5500; Hancock, MA 01237) 7 outdoor courts; instruction, tournaments. Fee.

Pittsfield Public Courts free to the public when school is not in session; asphalt courts:

Herberg Middle School (Pomeroy Ave.) 4 courts.

Lakewood Park (Newell St.) 2 courts.

Pittsfield High School (East St.) 4 courts.

Taconic High School (Valentine Rd.) 4 courts.

Ponterril/YMCA (413-499-0687; Pontoosuc Lake, Pittsfield, MA 01201; Rte. 7) 6 outdoor clay courts; members have priority, nonmembers may use them for a fee; summer memberships available.

North County

North Adams Public Courts are free; asphalt:
  Greylock Recreation Field (Protection Ave.; off Rte. 2) 2 courts.
  Noel Field (State St. behind Child Care of the Berkshires; Rte. 8A) 2 courts.
Williams College (413-597-3131; Linde Lane, Williamstown; bet. Park St. and
  Cole Ave.) 24 clay and hard-surface courts; summer memberships available:
  Apply to Buildings and Grounds Department.
Williamstown Public Court (off E. Main St. near Colonial Village) first come,
  first serve (ah!).

RUNNING

Runners have run into the right neck of the woods in the Berkshires. With terrain and roadways of all types, clean mountain air, and inspiring vistas, Berkshire draws out the relaxed runner, that meditative runner who can run almost forever. Most back roads and byways have little traffic. Running may be even more pleasant on trails. For the rugged cross-country runner, some of the trails outlined under "Walking" are suitable. Racers or wannabes should check in with the ***Western Massachusetts Athletic Club*** (413-743-5124; www.will.run @snet.net; PO Box 1517, North Adams, MA 01247) for events and society.

SKATING

For ice skaters, the Berkshires offer many smooth and slippery possibilities, most of them framed by hills. Three rinks are open to the public: one at the ***Pittsfield Boys Club*** (448-8258; 16 Melville St., Pittsfield, MA 01201), open Sat. and Sun., 2–3:45; another at Williams College's ***Lansing Chapman Rink*** (413-597-2433; 76 Latham St.) in Williamstown; and the third in North Adams at the ***Vietnam Veterans Memorial Skating Rink*** (413-664-9474; S. Church St.), managed by Massachusetts College of Liberal Arts. All the rinks offer low-priced children's programs. Outdoor skating on flooded fields is a Berkshire tradition. During the colder months, public works crews groom ice at the Common in Pittsfield, by the Dalton Community House, and on the Stockbridge Town Field. Lake and pond skating is exquisite in Berkshire when it freezes before the snow flies.

For those who prefer their skating on wheels, many of the county's smoother back roads make for ideal blacktop cruising. Rollerblading, or in-line skating, has taken off big here, and 'bladers can now be seen skating the hills three seasons a year. In fact, many skiers now tune up during the warmer weather on roller skies. Some towns have developed skateboard parks, while others bother about how to keep skateboarders off the sidewalks. The Ashuwillticook Trail, as smooth as smooth can be, is ideal for wheels of any configuration.

SOARING

Attitude controls speed, which ideally is 51 mph. In this unearthly quiet half a mile up, the Berkshires seem like a Swiss landscape, all rolling patterns of farm and woodland.

The *Mohawk Soaring Club* operates out of Harriman West Airport, North Adams (413-458-8650). Those wishing to soar should hang out with the glider pilots at the far edge of the airstrip on weekends. Those who watch and ask a few questions could end up floating on air.

Should an aircraft seem an encumbrance to soaring, people with wings regularly jump off the top of Mount Greylock in Adams and just as often off the Western Summit of the Mohawk Trail, in Florida, relying on lightweight hang gliders to support their flight. We take no position on such Icarian activity.

SWIMMING

Berkshire is blessed with countless magical swimming spots, some secluded and known only to the likes of otter and some quite public. There are sizable lakes and ponds, rushing green rivers, and deep, chilly quarries. In winter, and for those who prefer their water sports in a more controlled setting, there are numerous swimming pools both indoor and out. Most state and municipal ponds have day use and inexpensive season passes available to residents and nonresidents.

South County

Benedict Pond, Beartown State Forest (413-528-0904; Blue Hill Rd., Monterey; off Rte. 23 E of Gt. Barrington or off Rte. 102, S. Lee) Beach; bath house with showers; picnicking, 12,000-acre state forest. Day fee.

Green River (off Rte. 23, 1 mi. west of Gt. Barrington) Clearest of the clear, greenest of the green, purest of the pure—a summer treat not to be missed. Neighbors deserve consideration, especially in parking.

Lake Garfield, Kinne's Grove (Rte. 23, Monterey).

Lake Mansfield (413-528-6080; off Christian Hill Rd., Gt. Barrington).

Oak n' Spruce Resort (413-243-3500; 190 Meadow St., S. Lee; off Rte. 102) Heated outdoor and indoor pools, saunas, whirlpool bath, physical fitness room. By membership.

Otis Reservoir, Tolland State Forest (413-269-6002, 413-269-7268; Tolland Rd., Otis; off Rte. 23) Swimming, picnicking; 10,000-acre state forest.

Prospect Lake (413-528-4158; Prospect Lake Rd., N. Egremont; 0.75 mi. W of Rte. 71) Camping, day picnics, adult lounge; open daily to 6pm.

Spectacle Pond (Cold Spring Rd., Sandisfield).

York Lake, Sandisfield State Forest (413-258-4774, 413-229-8212; York Lake Rd., Sandisfield; off Rte. 57) Swimming, picnicking, 8,000-acre state forest.

Central County

Ashmere Lake (Ashmere Beach, Rte. 143, Hinsdale).

Berkshire West (413-499-4600; Dan Fox Dr., Pittsfield) Indoor/outdoor pool, bath house, snack bar, showers; memberships available.

Boys & Girls Club (413-448-8258; 16 Melville St., Pittsfield) Under 18; indoor pool open to members only; memberships available. Free swimming early evenings, weekdays; Saturday 1–3pm.

Lake Onota (Onota Blvd., Pittsfield) Free municipal beaches, supervised, 12–8pm daily.

Pontoosuc Lake (Rte. 7, Pittsfield) Free municipal beach.

John Hitchcock

How sweet the summer at North Pond, Savoy Mountain State Forest.

Pittsfield Girls' Club (413-442-5174; 165 East St., Pittsfield) Indoor pool open for recreational swimming evenings, Monday–Friday; Saturday 1–2:15.

Pittsfield State Forest (413-442-8992; Cascade St., Pittsfield) Swimming (lifeguards on duty 10am–6pm), picnicking, 10,000-acre state forest.

Pittsfield YMCA (413-499-7650; 292 North St., Pittsfield).

Plunkett Lake Lion's Club Beach (Church St., Hinsdale).

Ponterril (413-499-0647; Pontoosuc Lake, Rte. 7, N. of Pittsfield) Operated by Pittsfield YMCA; pool open to members only. Season memberships available.

Windsor State Forest (413-684-0948; Windsor; follow signs from Rte. 9 in W. Cummington or Rte. 116 in Savoy) Swimming, picnicking.

North County

Cheshire Reservoir (The Causeway, Farnam's Road, Cheshire).

Clarksburg State Park (Mausert's Pond, Rte. 8, Clarksburg, near Vermont line) Swimming, picnicking, 3,400-acre state park.

Hoosac Valley High School (413-743-5200; Rte 116, Cheshire) Indoor pool open September through June.

Jiminy Peak (413-738-5500; Corey Rd., off Rte. 7, Hancock) Outdoor pool.

Margaret Lindley Park (Rte 7 where Rte. 2 leaves Williamstown) swimming pond open during school summer vacation.

North Pond, Savoy Mountain State Forest (413-663-8459; Central Shaft Rd., Savoy; Follow signs from Rte. 2 in Florida or Rte. 116 in Savoy) Swimming, picnicking, 11,000-acre state forest.

Northern Berkshire YMCA (413-663-6529; Brickyard Ct., N. Adams) Indoor pool.

Sand Springs Pool and Spa (413-458-5205; off Rte. 7, Williamstown; near Vermont line) Mineral pool with year-round temperature of 74 degrees; 2 mineral whirlpools, mineral showers, sauna, shuffleboard, picnic area, beach. Pavilion for private party use.

Windsor Lake (413-662-3047; N. Adams; access via Bradley St. from Mass. College or via Kemp Ave. from E. Main St.) Municipal swimming area; supervised daily.

WALKING, HIKING, CAMPING, X-C SKIING

If you would be happy in Berkshire, you must carry mountains in your brain.

—Oliver Wendell Holmes

It is possible to approximate the opportunities with numbers. Massachusetts may be the sixth smallest state in the union, but its forest and park system is the sixth largest. And of the state's quarter-million protected acres, nearly 150,000 are in Berkshire County. Of the 606,000 total county acres, those owned publicly include 97,000 managed by the Department of Environment Management, Division of Forests and Parks and 12,500 by the Division of Fisheries and Wildlife. The county boasts 21 state parks, all of which have interesting tales and trails. Berkshire nature centers each have scenic paths. In addition, 86 miles of the Appalachian Trail run up through Berkshire County, entering near Bartholomew's Cobble in Ashley Falls and exiting from Clarksburg.

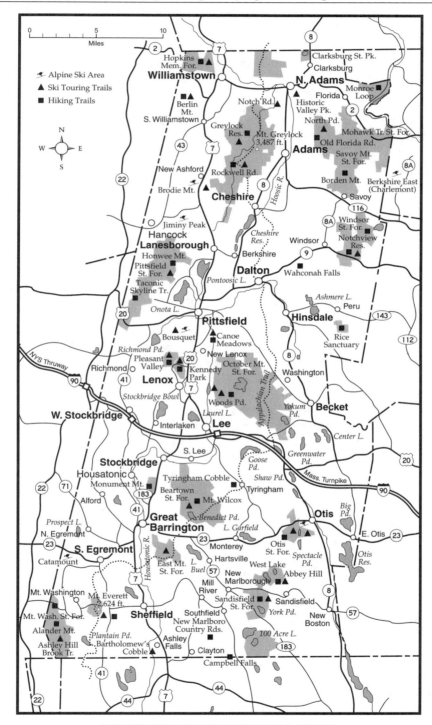

BERKSHIRE RECREATIONAL SITES

A pedestrian bridge (two or four feet) over the Housatonic River in Lenox Dale connects hiking paths.

Judith Monachina

The real pleasures are qualitative, however. With trails along lake and riverside, up hills and steep mountains, the Berkshires offer all types of terrain from an afternoon's jaunt to a full-fledged pack trip.

Now some enthusiasm: No place else exists with the variety of trails from light walks to heavy hikes, suiting any available amount of time, convenient from anywhere in the county, and open to the public. These trails are marked and maintained by volunteers, who give of their time because they love this remarkable place and want visitors to like it, too.

Although a compass and maps are advisable for any deep-woods hiking, it's comforting to know that in Berkshire County, no matter how wild the surroundings, hikers are never more than five miles from a paved road. Nevertheless, for walks of any length, and especially for those taken alone, hikers should notify a friend of plans, including estimated hour of return. Carry water.

Those who want to use snowshoes in winter can rent them at many of the same stores that supply ski equipment. See the list of stores in this chapter under "Downhill Skiing."

PROPERTIES WITH MAINTAINED TRAILS

State properties with campgrounds are marked with an asterisk (*). For camping reservations call 877-I CAMP MA (422-6762) or visit www.park-net.com. Type-1 campgrounds have running water, Type-2 do not. For more properties, see under Trustees of Reservations, below.

South County

STATE OWNED

Beartown State Forest (413-528-0904; Blue Hill Rd., Monterey) 12,000 acres; Benedict Pond; 12 Type-1 campsites; mountain biking, nonmotorized boating,

boat ramp, fishing, hiking, hunting, horseback riding trails, picnicking, x-c skiing, snowmobiling, swimming; beach and restrooms handicap accessible.

Campbell Falls State Park (Campbell Falls Road leaves Norfolk Rd. at the Connecticut line in New Marlborough) A lovely little falls in a two-state park.

*Mount Washington State Forest (413-528-0330; East St., Mt. Washington)
4,169 acres; 15 Type-2 wilderness campsites; mountain biking, canoeing,
fishing, hiking, horseback riding trails, picnicking, hunting, nonmotorized
boating, boat ramp, snowmobiling, x-c skiing. **Bash Bish Falls**, on Bash Bish
Falls Rd., 0.5 mile from the lower parking lot; celebrated by painters of the
Hudson River School and poets, these falls say their name to those who lis-
ten carefully.

Mount Everett State Reservation (413-528-0330; East St., Mt. Washington)
1,356 acres; Guilder Pond, nonmotorized boating, boat ramp, fishing, horseback riding trails, picnicking, hiking, three-state views, Appalachian Trail,
and a road that approaches summit (2,600 feet).

*October Mountain State Forest (413-243-1778, 413-243-9735; Woodland Rd.,
Lee) 16,127 acres; 50 Type-1 campsites, mountain biking, fishing, hiking,
nonmotorized boating, Appalachian Trail, horseback riding trails, hunting,
x-c skiing. Restrooms and some campsites and trails handicap accessible.

Sandisfield and Cookson State Forest 413-258-4774; York Lake Rd., Sandisfield (New Marlboro); 7,785 acres; York Lake, boat ramp, nonmotorized
boating, fishing, hiking, hunting, x-c skiing, snowmobiling, swimming, picnicking.

*Tolland State Forest, 413-269-6002, 413-269-7268; Rte. 8, Otis; 10,305 acres; 93
Type-1 campsites, some overlooking Otis Reservoir; mountain biking, boating, fishing, hiking, hunting, horseback riding trails, picnicking, x-c skiing,
snowmobiling, swimming, picnicking. Handicap-accessible restrooms.

OTHER NATURAL PLACES WITH TRAILS

Bartholomew's Cobble (413-229-8600; www.thetrustees.org; Weatogue Rd.,
Ashley Falls; off Rte. 7, 1.1 mi. S of Sheffield center) Bartholomew's Cobble, a
National Natural Landmark, is a 294-acre sanctuary with limestone outcrop-
pings about 500 million years old. The terrain supports wildflowers, trees
and ferns in great variety and number. Bird flyway. It's a fine place to view
the Housatonic River and its surrounding valley. On the site is the Bailey
Museum of Natural History, open daily 9-5 year-round except holidays.
Grounds open sunrise to sunset year-round. Group tours on request; picnic
privileges available. Adults $4, children 6–12 $1, free to members of The
Trustees of Reservations.

Berkshire Botanical Garden (413-298-3926; www.berkshirebotanical.org; jct.
Rtes. 102 and 183, Stockbridge) The foremost botanical complex in the
county for more than 50 years spreads over 15 acres of gently rolling land.
The magnificent plantings include exotic flowers, primroses, conifers,
daylilies, perennials, and shrubs. A terraced herb garden, a rose garden, and

raised-bed vegetable gardens all delight the eye and other senses. The greenhouses (one of them passive solar) grow seedlings, cuttings, and plants of all sorts. Visitors center, garden gift shop, and herb products shop offer information, practical garden items, and invigorating odors. Berkshire Botanical Garden runs a full schedule of activities year-round, ranging from flower shows and herb symposiums to lectures on flower arranging and English country gardens. The Botanical Garden calendar culminates with its annual Harvest Festival in early October, offering fun and food for both children and adults. Its fine reference library offers books, magazines, and the latest seed catalogs.

Ice Glen (Ice Glen Rd., Stockbridge) Cross the footbridge over the Housatonic River and follow the trail southward to walk a primeval path of glacial boulders. Not recommended for the weak of knee.

Race Brook Falls (Rte. 41, Sheffield) The pullover at the side of the road is marked and usually full of cars. A couple miles of hiking leads to cascades or, farther on, the Appalachian Trail.

Central County

STATE OWNED

*Mount Greylock State Reservation (413-499-4263, 413-499-4262; visitors center: Rockwell Rd., Lanesborough; also accessible from Notch Rd., N. Adams) 12,500 acres. *La crème de la crème* of Berkshire hiking, with state's highest peak (3,491 feet), Appalachian Trail, 100-mile-view from War Memorial Tower. (For **Bascom Lodge**, see *Lodging* chapter.) 35 Type-2 campsites, 45 miles of trails, x-c skiing, hunting, mountain biking, snowmobiling, interpretive programs (wheelchair accessible), picnicking.

*Pittsfield State Forest (413-442-8992; Cascade St., Pittsfield) 10,000 acres. Streams, waterfalls, views. 31 Type-1 and Type-2 campsites. Boating (electric motors only), canoeing, x-c skiing, ski lodge, bicycling, mountain biking, fishing, picnicking, hiking, horseback riding trails, hunting, interpretive programs, snowmobiling, swimming; wheelchair-accessible picnic area and trails, restrooms. Includes **Balance Rock** (Balance Rock Rd.): Of the county's glacial erratics—apparently about to tip off their small bases—this is the most dramatic.

Wahconah Falls (Rte. 9, Dalton) One of the county's largest cascades.

*Windsor State Forest (413-698-0948; winter 413-442-8928; River Rd., Windsor) 1,743 acres. 24 Type-2 campsites; mountain biking, fishing, hiking, horseback riding trails, hunting, picnicking, swimming, x-c skiing, snowmobiling. Includes **Windsor Jambs**, a spectacular gorge.

OTHER NATURAL PLACES WITH TRAILS

Canoe Meadows Wildlife Sanctuary (413-637-0320; www.massaudubon.org; Holmes Rd., Pittsfield) 262-acre preserve of forest, ponds, streams, the

Housatonic River banks and flood plain; owned and managed by the Massachusetts Audubon Society; fee.

Dorothy Francis Rice Sanctuary (South Rd., Peru; off Rte. 143) 300-acre preserve of woodland trails. Owned and managed by the New England Forestry Foundation.

Notchview Reservation 413-684-0148; Rte. 9, Windsor; 3,000 acres of forest, crossed by miles of trails; holds snow for x-c skiing. Owned and managed by The Trustees of Reservations; fee.

Pleasant Valley Wildlife Sanctuary 413-637-0320; www.massaudubon.org; 472 West Mountain Rd., Lenox; off Rte. 7, opposite the Quality Inn) 1,400 acres of forest, field, ponds (beaver dams with real beaver), and streams with 7 miles of trails; educational programs. Owned and managed by the Massachusetts Audubon Society; fee.

Yokum Ridge (off Lenox Rd., Lenox) An assemblage of properties and trails, including Pleasant Valley, mapped by the Berkshire Natural Resources Council, 413-499-0596.

North County

STATE OWNED

*Clarksburg State Park (413-664-8345 summer, 413-442-8928 winter; Middle Rd., Clarksburg) 3,421 acres. Mausert's Pond for swimming. 47 Type-2 campsites; boating (electric motors only), canoeing, x-c skiing, fishing, hiking, hunting, snowmobiling, picnicking. Wheelchair-accessible campsites and restrooms.

Natural Bridge State Park (413-663-6392; Natural Bridge Road, N. Adams; N of downtown on Rte. 8) Waters tumble over a marble dam and then course beneath a natural marble bridge; x-c skiing, too. Newly completed visitors center.

*Savoy Mountain State Forest (413-663-8469; Central Shaft Rd., Savoy; off Rte 2, Florida, and Rte. 116) 11,118 acres; 45 Type-1 campsites and three cabins with fireplaces on South Pond. North Pond for swimming, boating, and fishing. Tannery Falls. Picnicking, mountain biking, canoeing, hiking, x-c skiing, interpretive programs, snowmobiling. Wheelchair-accessible restrooms, campsites, swimming, and trails.

Taconic Trail State Forest (413-499-4263; adjacent to Taconic Trail (Rte. 2), Williamstown) Hiking, hunting, x-c skiing.

OTHER NATURAL PLACES WITH TRAILS

Bear Swamp Hydroelectric Project (413-424-5213 River Rd., Florida) A stop at the visitors center reveals how pumped storage works; a call ahead can result in a tour of the works deep in the mountain.

Duvall Nature Trail (Hoosac Valley High School, Rte. 116, Adams) 2 miles of nature trails overlooking the Greylock Range.

Hopkins Memorial Forest (413-597-2346; www.williams.edu/ces; PO Box 637, Williamstown, MA 01267; Bulkley St., off Rte. 7) 2,500 woodland acres on the slopes of the Taconic Range with miles of hiking trails. Hunting by permit, dogs on leashes. No camping, fires, wheeled vehicles (including bikes). Rare plants, historic relics: barn, sugar shack, carriage house with exhibits on past use of land; Victorian garden. Guided walks by appointment (413-597-4353.)

For more detailed information on the county's state parks, write: *Massachu-setts Department of Environmental Management*, Division of Forests and Parks, (617-727-9800; www.state.ma.us/dem; 100 Cambridge St., Boston, MA 02202) or its Region V office (413-442-8928; Box 1433, Pittsfield, MA 01202).

There are several hiking clubs in the Berkshires. Of these, the *Appalachian Mountain Club* (413-528-6333), *Taconic Hiking Club* (45 Kately St., Albany, NY 12208) and the *Williams (College) Outing Club* (413-597-2317) are the most active. Each organizes hikes through the county. The map on p. 247 shows the entire length of the Appalachian Trail in Berkshire County.

Greylock Discovery Tours (413-637-4442; 800-877-9656; www.greylocktours .com; PO Box 2231, Lenox, MA 01240) will guide *groups* of eight or more along the Appalachian and Taconic Range trails in half- or whole-day hikes, arrang-ing food, lodging, and cultural events, as well.

Cogent books on Berkshire hiking are available: *Hikes & Walks in the Berkshire Hills* by Lauren R. Stevens and, for the Williamstown environs, *The Williams College Outing Club Northern Berkshire Outdoor Guide*, first published in 1927 and completely new in 1999. Stevens's book covers not only a wide variety of challenging hikes for the energetic and ambitious but also a large number of easy strolls for those with less time or gumption. A section outlines walks for the blind and physically handicapped.

In addition to its vast forests, Berkshire is blessed with many interesting out-door sites, each of which shows off natural features, such as waterfalls, unusual geology or plant life. For a description of *Natural Places* in the county, see the book of that name by René Laubach, and *Nature Walks in the Berkshire Hills* by Charles W. G. Smith.

CAMPING

Campsites in *state parks* can be reserved by calling 877-I CAMP MA (877-422-6762) or visiting www.reserveamerica.com. As well, some of the sites at each property are available first come, first serve. For further information but *not* reservations: *Massachusetts Department of Environmental Manage-ment*, Region Five Headquarters, 413-442-8928, Box 1433, Pittsfield, MA 01201.

Fees (depending on amenities) are as follows at all state parks and forests: *Day use:* $5 per car per day; $6 out of state; season pass $35/$45; *Camping:* wilderness free; unimproved $5/$6; flush toilets with showers $10/$12; cabins $25 or $35, depending on size. Public campgrounds (above) are designated with an asterisk (*); private campgrounds follow. All fees subject to change.

Private Campgrounds

South County

Camp Overflow (413-269-4036; Box 645, Otis, MA 01253; on Otis Reservoir, 5 mi. from Rte. 8) 100 sites, electric hookups, dumping station, camp store, fishing, swimming, boating, seasonal rates.

Klondike Campground (413-269-6010; Rte. 8, Otis, MA 01029).

Laurel Ridge Camping Area (413-269-4804; Old Blandford Rd., E. Otis, MA 01029) Electric and water sites.

Maple Glade Campground (413-243-1548; 165 Woodland Rd., Lee, MA 01238; across from October Mountain State Forest) 70 sites; hook-ups available; Small store, swimming pool.

Prospect Lake Park (413-528-4158; Prospect Lake Rd., N. Egremont, MA 01252) 140 sites; Tennis, swimming, boat rentals, basketball court, volleyball; snack bar, playground.

Central County

Bissellville Estate & Campground (413-655-8396; Washington Rd., Hinsdale, MA 01235; Rte. 8) 13 campsites with sewer hookups, 18 with water & electricity, 13 with all three. Closed Labor Day–May 15.

Bonnie Brae Cabins and Campsites (413-442-3754, 108 Broadway St., Pittsfield, MA 01201; 3 mi. N. of downtown Pittsfield, off Rte. 7 at Pontoosuc Lake) Full hookups, free showers, trailer rentals, pool; cabin rentals May 1–Oct. 31. Closed November–April 30.

Bonnie Rigg Campground (413-623-5366; PO Box 14, Chester, MA 01011-0014; corner of Rtes. 8 & 20 in Becket; 200 campsites, by owner/membership only (call for information). Adult lounge, playground, swimming pool, sauna, Jacuzzi.

Fun in the Hills

In the 1860s and 1870s Williams College professor Albert Hopkins organized summer-long Camp Fern at what's now the Sperry Road Campground on Mount Greylock. Borrowing tents from a Methodist meeting and hiring a local Irish girl to cook, families stayed for weeks, with members returning to town as necessary. The boys descended to the Bacon farm in the Hopper early in the morning for milk, eggs, and other perishables. Most of the time Fern campers explored the mountain, but other adventures included organized games, skits, poetry, painting, journal writing, berrying, fishing, singing around the campfire and, oh yes, courting in the hills. Did people know how to have more fun in the nineteenth century?

Bucksteep Manor (413-623-5535; Washington Mountain Rd., Becket, MA 01223; 10 mi. E. of Pittsfield, across from October Mountain State Forest) 15 sites, 9 cabins; showers, swimming pool, tennis, hiking, x-c skiing, weekend restaurant.

Fernwood Forest Campground (413-655-2292; 41 Plunkett Reservoir Rd., Hinsdale 01235; 1 mi. from Appalachian Trail) 30 campsites with water, toilets, showers, electricity; recreation field. Closed mid-October–May 1.

Ponterril (413-499-0640; North St., Pittsfield, MA 01201; Rte. 7, off E. Acres Rd. at Pontoosuc Lake N. of Pittsfield) 12 campsites, swimming pool, tennis, sailing and sailing instructions. Operated by Pittsfield YMCA.

Summit Hill Campground (413-623-5761; Summit Hill Rd., Washington, MA 01235) 110 campsites for tents and trailers, 83 sites with electricity and water; adult lounge, swimming pool, and recreation hall. Closed in winter.

North County

Brodie Campgrounds (413-443-4754; Brodie Mountain Ski Resort, New Ashford, MA 01237; off Rte. 7, just N. of Lanesborough town line) 120 campsites for tents and trailers, rented seasonally; heated swimming pool, tennis, recreation hall.

Historic Valley Park Campground (413-662-3198; Box 751, N. Adams, MA 01247; on Windsor Lake) 100 campsites with electric and water hookups; laundry, camp store, recreation hall, hiking trails; Public and private beaches with lifeguards.

Privacy Campground (413-458-3125; Hancock Rd., Hancock, MA 01267; on Rte. 43, 5 mi. S. of Rte. 7) 475 acres, 35 sites, 4 small cabins; waterfall, pond, 10 miles of hiking trails, paddleboats, volleyball, badminton, horseshoes, tether ball, basketball, campfires, water wheel, windmill, trolley car, playground, sauna.

CROSS-COUNTRY SKIING

Several of the resorts listed under "Downhill Skiing" also offer cross-country skiing.

Berkshire is made for cross-country (also known as Nordic) skiers—from flat runs along the Housatonic to steep trails up Mount Greylock; from tours in town, such as Kennedy Park in Lenox and Historic Valley Campground in North Adams, to wilderness paths like the one around North Pond in Savoy Mountain State Forest.

With no lines, no chair lifts, and (generally) no fees, Berkshire X-C depends only on the whims of the weather. However, since Nordic skiing has gained in popularity, private touring centers have multiplied in the Berkshires. For a small fee, enjoy groomed trails and warm waxing huts at half a dozen such places. Cranwell even offers snowmaking.

History of the Trustees of Reservations

In 1890, before the present national interest in the environment, a young landscape architect returned from study in Europe with a deepening concern for the need to preserve the natural beauty and historic sites of his community.

Charles Eliot (1859–1897), just 31 years old and son of Charles W. Eliot, then president of Harvard University, proposed the establishment of an organization "empowered to hold small and well distributed parcels of land . . . just as the Public Library holds books and the Art Museum pictures for the use and enjoyment of the public."

The Trustees of Reservations was incorporated by the Massachusetts General Court a year later, 1891, the first independent organization in the United States established for the purpose of preserving land.

Many of the properties are listed under "Historic Homes" in the *Arts and Pleasures* chapter. Excellent hiking and x-c skiing opportunities await at the following properties of The Trustees of Reservations in the county or nearby:

Bartholomew's Cobble: Weatogue Rd., (Rte. 7A), Ashley Falls (Sheffield).

Chapelbrook: Williamsburg Rd., Ashfield.

Chesterfield Gorge: River Rd., Chesterfield.

Field Farm: Sloan Rd., off Rte. 7 at the Five Corners in Williamstown.

Glendale Falls: Clark Wright Rd., Middlefield.

McLenan Reservoir: Sun Rd., Tyringham and Otis.

Monument Mountain: Stockbridge Rd. (Rte. 7), Gt. Barrington.

Mountain Meadow Preserve: Mason St. off Rte. 7, or Benedict Rd., Pownal, Vermont, off White Oaks Road, Williamstown.

Notchview Reservation: Rte. 9, Windsor.

Questing,: New Marlborough Hill Rd., New Marlborough.

Tyringham Cobble: 413-298-3239; Jerusalem Rd., Tyringham.

For more information about any of these or any other holdings, write: The Trustees of Reservations, 1 Sargeant St., Stockbridge, MA 01262, call 413-298-3239, or visit their excellent website: www.thetrustees.org.

It's best to ski accompanied, especially in a wilderness area. Those skiing in a state forest should check in at forest headquarters first. Maps and helpful hints are available; besides, it's a good precaution for staff to know that a skier's out there. Along with snacks and water, skiers would be well advised to carry a compass and extra clothes on the trail. The well-prepared also carry a first-aid kit, knife, whistle, flashlight, and space blanket. Hypothermia is the greatest danger; if 20 minutes of exercise doesn't warm the blood, its time to head home.

Although many x-c skiers profess to dislike snowmobiles because of their growl and their tendency to prowl in packs, the going is easier if those creatures have packed the trail. And sometime a cross-country skier in trouble might appreciate a snowmobiler's assistance. We recommend friendly relations with snowmobilers and, on their part, courtesy to skiers.

Most of the properties listed above are available to skiers. A selection of trails are described below, with sufficient directions for a short tour. Skiers should know that if snow is not good in Berkshire, just over the line in Vermont a natural snowbelt provides some of the best cover in the East. *Prospect Mountain* (802-442-2575; Rte. 9, 8 mi. east of Bennington) benefits from nature's largess. Trails are groomed; snowshoeing is available. Rentals and retail. The food offered at the base lodge ranges from vegetarian to burgers. Fee.

Many trails in the *Mount Washington State Forest* offer quintessential Berkshire ski touring. No snowmobiles are allowed, so the whistle of the wind will be the loudest noise. From the forest headquarters on East Street, the Ashley Hill Brook Trail runs south along the brook towards New York State, a four-mile, slightly uphill trip suitable for intermediate skiers. Nearby, from the parking lot just outside the Mount Everett Reservation, skiers can ski up 2,600-foot-high Dome of the Taconics. The climb up the mountain is gentle, passing Guilder Pond; the run down, long and exhilarating with plenty of room to maneuver.

Bartholomew's Cobble in Ashley Falls (Sheffield) has an interesting system of trails, with the runs on the far side of Weatogue Road being the best. Some spots are wet in marginal weather. A map is posted in the parking lot. Donation box: $3 per person.

Beartown State Forest in Monterey has some lovely trails, starting at Benedict Pond and circling through the 12,000-acre forest preserve. Maps are available at the *State Forest Headquarters* (413-528-0904; Blue Hill Rd., off Rte. 23).

Berkshire County Land Trust

The Berkshire County Land Trust and Conservation Fund is an offshoot of Berkshire Natural Resources Council, a private, not-for-profit environmental advocacy group established in 1967. Led by president Tad Ames, this group believes that the wealth of Berkshire lies in its quality of life, natural environment, and cultural heritage. The council works with state and local agencies to ensure that those lands are protected from abuse.

There are about 200 land trusts in America, many of them in New England. By all counts, the BNRC and its offspring in several Berkshire towns are some of the more successful. In Pittsfield the Trust was responsible for increasing the Pittsfield State Forest by 1,800 acres. Along the Housatonic, south of Pittsfield, the Resources Council is coordinating the creation of a 12-mile-long river park, reaching to Woods Pond in Lenox. The BNRC facilitated the preservation of Gould Meadows, that gorgeous 95-acre pasture reaching from Tanglewood to Stockbridge Bowl. The Stockbridge–Yokun Ridge Reserve is another land corridor the trust is assembling to remain forever wild, an 8-mile-long, 6,300-acre spread of Berkshire park.

For more information, contact: Berkshire County Land Trust and Berkshire Natural Resources Council, 20 Bank Row, Pittsfield, MA 01201; 413-499-0596; www.bnrc.com.

Triangular red blazes or wooden markers designate the ski-touring trail in Beartown, with a blue-blazed trail circling Benedict Pond, the white-blazed Appalachian Trail passing through, and the orange-blazed trails for snowmobilers.

The West Lake area of the *Sandisfield State Forest* is a fine site for Nordic skiing. No snowmobiles are allowed on the Abbey Hill Foot Trail (marked with blue blazes). From the state forest headquarters and parking area, just off West Street, a beautiful tour of about two hours circles Abbey Lake, up Abbey Hill (1,810 ft.), and then down past West Lake.

Skiers can follow the Knox Trail in the *Otis State Forest*. Take Route 23 to Nash Road in Otis. Where Nash joins Webb Road is a good place to wax up. Skiers should watch for red *K*s and red blazes marking the trail.

In Great Barrington, *Butternut Basin* (413-528-2000; Rte. 23) has 8 kilometers of groomed novice and intermediate trails, lovely lodges, and a pond-side warming hut. *Otis Ridge* (413-269-4444; Rte. 23, Otis) has over 8 kilometers of packed, but not tracked, trails.

Lenox is graced with beautiful ski-touring areas, the most popular of which is *Kennedy Park*. Its 500 acres were once the site of the grand old Aspinwall Hotel (which burned to the ground in 1931). Now its long rising driveway and bridle paths are used for ski touring. The Main Trail (white blazes) is the widest and simplest, with Lookout Trail (red blazes) being more of a challenge. Stately oaks dot this pretty highland, with access either at the Church on the Hill (Main St., Rte. 7A) or behind the Lenox House Restaurant (north of town on Rte. 7). Equipment available from the Arcadian Shop up the road on Route 7.

Woods Pond area in Lee and Lenox has a pretty, mostly flat trail running along the southern shore of Woods Pond, then north along the eastern bank of the Housatonic River for just over 2 miles. A footbridge spans the Housatonic River. Enter via Woodland Street in Lee. The trail is best skied on weekdays due to weekend snowmobile traffic. *Canoe Meadows*, a Massachusetts Audubon area, also has some lovely trails, open except Monday. A small fee includes a map.

For more advanced Nordic skiers, the *Honwee Mountain–Turner Trail* circuit in Pittsfield State Forest is a challenge. Parking just off Cascade Road in Pittsfield State Forest, skiers should check in at forest headquarters, get oriented, and then start up the Mountain Trail, initially marked in orange, then white. This trail has some great views, tough climbs, and steep descents. Closer to the center of the city, *Sackett Brook Park* (Williams St.), has 4 miles of marked trails.

On Route 9 lies *Notchview Reservation*, in the town of Windsor. Generally the best snow in Berkshire can be found here. Twenty miles of trails are well marked and maintained, with a modest charge for touring. Maps are available for 50 cents. The Budd Visitor Center is open daily as a warming and waxing shelter. Notchview is owned by The Trustees of Reservations. Further information is available at www.thetrustees.org.

South of Lenox on Route 20, *Cranwell*, (413-637-1364; 55 Lee Rd., Lenox) has a network of trails, crisscrossing the golf course, It ventured into snowmaking in the winter of 1996–97. Open to the public; fee charged.

In the hill town of Washington, *Bucksteep Manor* (413-623-5535; Washington Mt. Rd.) operates a long ski-touring season. Set on over 250 acres at 1,900 ft., Bucksteep has 25 kilometers of looped, interconnecting trails. There's a waxing room, a ski shop that sells and rents, and on-site lodging and dining. Nearby in Becket, *Canterbury Farm* (413-623-8765; Fred Snow Rd.) grooms 11 miles of trails for its inn guests and daily cross-country ski guests. There is a ski shop for rentals, and lessons are available. Fee.

Up at 2,000 feet, where the snows come early and stay late, *Savoy State Forest* has miles of cross-country trails, best navigated with a map obtainable at *State Forest Headquarters* (413-663-8469; Florida Rd.). Enter the forest from Route 2 (Florida) or Route 116 (Savoy), and park at North Pond. A 3.1-mile-long trail North Pond Loop makes a challenging circuit up and over a ridge. In North Adams, *Historic Valley Park* offers ski touring quite close to downtown. The trail starts at the parking area next to Windsor Lake and is well marked by blue blazes and signs that even describe the degree of difficulty of the next stretch of trail.

On *Mount Greylock*, many opportunities for fine ski touring exist. Here again, though, it's best to ski during the week because weekends tend to draw heavy snowmobile traffic. (The snowmobiles are supposed to stick to the roads.) Check in at the visitors center on Rockwell Road off Route 7, Lanesborough. Depending on skills and fitness, there's an 8-mile round-trip up Rockwell Road to Jones Nose and back, 15-mile round-trip to Stony Ledge, or 17-mile round-trip to the summit. The views are breathtaking, the skiing sometimes testing, and the weather more dramatic than experienced below. Take extra warm clothing and some snacks.

The area in and around *Williamstown* is striped with trails, ranging from novice or intermediate to demanding, like the *RRR Brooks Trail*. For Brooks, and the *Taconic Crest Trail* attached to it, begin either at Bee Hill Road, west of Route 2, or Petersburgh Pass, at the top of Route 2 west of town. The *Taconic Golf Club* course, which Williams College grooms, and the 4-mile *Stone Hill* Loop in Williamstown are the area's most popular: relatively easy while offering all the splendor of the best ski touring. The golf course trail begins at the clubhouse on Meacham Street. Stone Hill starts and finishes in the Clark Art Museum parking lot (South Street), circling the 1,100-foot Stone Hill, with its wonderful views. At *Hopkins Forest*, Williams College maintains a network of trails just off Northwest Hill Road. The trails are groomed, and maps are available at the forest Carriage House. Many other trails exist, the best of which are described in the *Williams Outing Club's Northern Berkshire Outdoor Guide*. See also the *Mount Greylock Ski Club* under downhill skiing.

CHAPTER EIGHT
Fancy Goods
SHOPPING

Browsing the window at
Farshaws in Great Barrington.

Judith Monachina

Even the shops that were closed offered, through wide expanses of plate-glass, hints of hidden riches. In some, waves of silk and ribbon broke over shores of imitation moss from which ravishing hats rose like tropical orchids. In others, the pink throats of gramophones opened their giant convolutions in a soundless chorus; or bicycles shining in neat ranks seemed to await the signal of an invisible starter; or tiers of fancy-goods in leatherette and paste dangled their insidious graces; and, in one vast bay that seemed to project them into exciting contact with the public, wax ladies in daring dresses chatted elegantly, or, with gestures intimate yet blameless, pointed to their pink corsets and transparent hosiery.

A description of shop windows on the main street of "Nettleton,"
the fictional name for Pittsfield in *Summer*, by Edith Wharton (1917).

Antiques, books, clothing, handcrafts, home furnishings—those shopping for the necessities and the accessories of life will find ample scope in the Berkshires, on still-vital downtown streets and at a variety of retail destinations. They'll find an ever-changing mix of the currently "hot" collectibles along with the genuinely old, and the timeless—sometimes all in one shop. They'll also find imaginative wares designed and made in the Berkshires as well as goods from the farthest corners of the world. There are some chain stores, outlets, and discount centers, too. Note: Many Berkshire shops have been in place for generations; others sprang up last week and will have moved on by next Monday. It's helpful to call ahead before making a special trip and important to keep an eye open for the newest additions to the shopping scene!

ANTIQUES

From formal 18th-century furniture to bold Art Deco tableware, with country primitive carvings and High Victorian accessories in between, antiques in the Berkshires are varied and abundant. Whether we hanker after museum-quality pieces of a specific style and period or whether you simply enjoy exploring unique home furnishings, you'll find plenty to choose from. The antiques scene here includes furniture large and small; vintage clothing, textiles, and jewelry; prints, paper, and other ephemera; trunks and lamps, clocks and rugs, and baskets and wicker; and "kitchenalia" and militaria. European and Asian antiques specialists have also found their way to the Berkshires. A number of antiques shops also include new furnishings and accent pieces that complement their antiques; many offer custom decorating services.

South County in particular is an antiques center, with Route 7 the main artery for an array of multidealer shops, specialists, and generalists. They know their merchandise, and their prices reflect their knowledge. In Central and North County, prices are more flexible, but finding a bargain takes some looking.

Those who extend antiques hunting to auctions or — the sign of the true diehard — to yard sales and flea markets, should check listings in the helpful free weekly shoppers' guides (such as the *Berkshire Penny Saver*), which are stacked up at supermarket entrances and newsstands around the county. The *Berkshire Eagle*, the largest daily paper in the county, also carries classified listings for antiques, tag sales, and auctions. A list of auctioneers is also given below. The annual brochure of the *Berkshire County Antique Dealer's Association* lists dealers and locations, with business hours, telephone numbers, and a brief description of what they offer. Members of this association "take pride in their merchandise and guarantee its authenticity." Their brochure is available in member shops or by mail (send a SASE to: BCADA Directory, PO Box 95, Sheffield MA 01257).

Several rare book specialists also make their home here; they're listed in the following section, "Books."

South County

GREAT BARRINGTON

Asian Antiques (413-528-5091, phone/fax; 199 Stockbridge Rd., Gt. Barrington, MA 01230; Rte 7) High quality Asian, Korean, Japanese, and Indonesian antiques, furniture for home or garden, handcrafts, art, and gifts. For those who have always wanted an opium bed or a temple gong, this is the place to find it.

Berkshire Antiques (413-644-9262; 107 Stockbridge Rd., Gt. Barrington, MA 01230) Lots of space housing an eclectic collection of furnishings, of which 85 percent is imported. Architectural salvage, plumbing fixtures, and an in-house refinishing, painting, and upholstery service make this a perfect one-stop-shopping experience.

Bygone Days (413-528-1870; 969 S. Main St., Gt. Barrington, MA 01230; Rte. 7) Country and formal furniture, large and small, especially for bedrooms and dining rooms; farm tables and chairs, armoires, nightstands, hutches, and china closets and more. Open 12–5 daily.

Carriage House Antiques (413-528-6045; 389 Stockbridge Rd., Gt. Barrington, MA 01230) Tables, chairs, furniture, even sets of doors can be found here. Antique furniture restoration, repair, stripping, refinishing, and custom cabinetry by Eric Schutz are specialties in the newly enlarged quarters.

Chelsea & Co. (413-528-9040: 179 Main St., Gt. Barrington, MA 01230) This large group shop provides a new venue for those seeking an old, unusual, or impressive piece to add ambiance to their decor. Choose the perfect accent piece from the wide assortment of smaller items on offer.

Coffmans' Country Antiques Market (413-528-9282; Stockbridge Rd., Gt. Barrington, MA 01230; at Jenifer House Commons) Two buildings (yellow and red) of high-quality wares, pre-1949, from 200 New England and regional dealers. The large assortment is appealingly arranged in cases and room settings, and includes ephemera and prints, kitchenware, primitives, wood, pottery, furniture, tools, quilts, rugs, baskets, folk art, stoneware, glassware, and tin, brass, and copper.

Corashire Antiques (413-528-0014; Rte. 7 and 23, Gt. Barrington, MA 01230; at Belcher Square) In the red barn: American country furniture and accessories.

Country Dining Room and Tea Garden Antiques (413-528-5050; 178 Main St., Gt. Barrington, MA 01230; Rte. 7) Complete accouterments for dining in style, formal or country. In lavishly coordinated rooms, dining tables boast elaborate place settings of china, silver, glass, crystal, porcelain—down to the matching damask napkins with silk rose napkin rings. Chairs, rugs, paintings, and other furnishings and accessories complete the look. For a less formal but still elegant approach, Tea Garden Antiques, upstairs, offers more place settings, linens, and other accents. Country Dining Room's own Sheila Chafetz wrote two stunning books that show how to put it all together: *Antiques for the Table* and *Modern Antiques for the Table*.

Elise Abrams Antiques (413-528-3201; 11 Stockbridge Rd., Gt. Barrington, MA 01230; Rte. 7) Large selection of 18th-, 19th-, and 20th-century china, porcelain and stemware, plus decorative accessories and fine linens, silver, art and dining room furniture. They even maintain a bridal registry.

Emporium Antique Center (413-528-1660; 319 Main St., Gt. Barrington, MA 01230) A variety of dealers offer estate and costume jewelry, crystal, silver, accessories, furniture, furnishings, and linens. **The Kahns' Antique and Estate Jewelry** is now located here, as well. June–Dec., open daily; Jan.–May, closed Tues., Weds.

Great Barrington Antiques Center (413-644-8848; www.greatbarringtonantiquescenter.com; 964 S. Main St., Gt. Barrington, MA 01230; Rte. 7) A group shop of 50 dealers, featuring realistically priced quality country furniture, oriental rugs and everything in-between displayed in a large (5,000 sq. ft.) open space conducive to browsing.

Le Perigord (413-528-6777; 964 South Main St., Gt. Barrington, MA 01230; Rte. 7) A great source for French furniture, pottery, garden, and architectural accents from the 18th century through the 1960s. Open weekends.

Metropolitain (413-644-8868; 631 S. Main St., Gt. Barrington, MA 01230) A charming shop exhibiting a certain Gallic insouciance specializing in antique furnishings, lighting, garden accessories and decorative objects from France. They also offer interior design services.

Donald McGrory Oriental Rugs (413-528-9594; 24 Railroad St., Gt. Barrington, MA 01230) Antique and decorative Oriental rugs. Open 11–5 daily, closed Tues.

Mullin-Jones Antiquities (413-528-4871; 525 S. Main St., Gt. Barrington, MA 01230; Rte. 7) The fragrance of lavender pervades this importer of 18th- and 19th-century country farmhouse to formal French furniture and accessories. Closed Tues.; call ahead in winter.

Olde—An Antiques Market (413-528-1840; Stockbridge Rd., Gt. Barrington, MA 01230; at Jenifer House Commons) Two floors in the green house are jam-packed with potential treasures. Fifty dealers offer a variety of collectibles. Open 7 days a week, 10–5.

Paul and Susan Kleinwald, Inc. (413-528-4252; 578 S. Main St., Gt. Barrington, MA 01230) The concentration here is on 18th- and 19th-century American and English antique furniture, fine art, accessories; appraisals. Closed Tues.

Phil Watson Antiques & Vintage Lighting (413-644-9150; 2 State Rd., Gt. Barrington, MA 01230 Gt. Barrington, MA 01230; Rte. 7) Interesting collection of 19th- and 20th-century light fixtures and lamps, from funky to fabulous, in a large shop just before the bridge.

Snyder's Store (413-528-1441; 945 Main St., Gt. Barrington, MA 01230) What's inside: Funky furniture and accessories, with rustic pieces, tramp art, jewelry, linens, garden accents, and architectural elements. Open most weekends 12–5; weekdays by whim.

LEE

The Greylock Cottage (413-243-1115; 52 Main St., Lee, MA 01238) Lovely, immaculate shop where while shopping, one can garner lots of wonderful ideas for using and displaying antiques. The emphasis is on cottage and country collectibles. The prices are fair, and the owners are charming. A visit here is a trip down memory lane with something for everyone to enjoy.

Henry B. Holt (413-243-3184; 125 Golden Hill, PO Box 699, Lee, MA 01238) Specialist in 19th- and early-20th-century American paintings. Call for an appointment regarding appraisal, purchase, sale or restoration.

Mrs. V's Attic (413-243-5778; 63 Main St., Lee, MA 01238) Lots of 1950s items interspersed with early-20th-century collectibles, from common to unique, including some furniture. Take time to browse for unexpected treasures.

SHEFFIELD

Village of Ashley Falls

Circa (413-229-2990; Rte. 7A, Ashley Falls, MA 01222) Good collections of Majolica and Canton; 18th- and 19th-century furniture, accessories, and "sophisticated oddments."

Village of Sheffield

Centuryhurst Antiques (413-229-8131, 173 Main St., PO Box 486, Sheffield, MA 01257; Rte. 7) Specializing in antique clocks and Wedgwood; with 18th- and 19th-century furniture, glass, china, paintings, prints, toys, and accessories.

Corner House Antiques (413-229-6627; PO Box 411, Sheffield, MA 01257; Rte. 7 and Old Mill Pond Rd.) Specialists in antique wicker furniture—including whole sets; a variety of styles and finishes. A well-chosen selection of American country furnishings and accessories, as well. Open most days.

Cupboards & Roses Antiques (413-229-3070; fax 412-229-0257; PO Box 426, Sheffield, MA 01257; Rte. 7) Beautifully displayed antique and reproduction paint-decorated 18th- and 19th-century furniture, featuring capacious armoires and chests from Europe and Scandinavia. Decorative accessories, old and new, including wedding baskets, paint decorated bride boxes, textiles, and ceramics. Closed Tues.

Darr Antiques and Interiors (413-229-7773; S. Main St., Sheffield, MA 01257; Rte. 7) Two buildings of elegant room settings displaying formal 18th- and 19th-century American, English, Continental, and Oriental furniture and accessories, with a focus on dining room furnishings. Open June–Oct., Wed.–Mon 10–5.; Nov.–May, Thurs.–Mon. 10–5; or by appointment.

Dovetail Antiques (413-229-2628; 440 Sheffield Plain, Sheffield, MA 01257; Rte.

7) A select collection of American clocks, country furniture, including pieces with original paint or finish, and spongeware, stoneware, and redware. No glass or china. Open daily 11–5; Tues. by chance.

Falcon Antiques (413-229-7745; 176 S. Undermountain Rd., Sheffield, MA 01257; Rte. 41) Country furniture and accessories, with a good selection of brass, copper, pewter, woodworking tools, and treen (small wooden pieces).

Frederick Hatfield Antiques (413-229-7986; 99 S. Main St., Sheffield, MA 01257; Rte. 7) Antiques and collectibles from the 18th through 20th centuries, with country and formal furniture, paintings, silver, paper items, jewelry, architectural elements, and other treasures from New England homes.

Good & Hutchinson Associates, Inc. (413-229-8832, 258-4555; Main St., Sheffield, MA 01257; Rte. 7 on the Green) Specialists in fine antiques and decorative arts from the 18th and 19th century, with American, English, and Continental furniture, Chinese export porcelain, paintings, brass, lamps; for the discriminating buyer. Open June–Oct., Wed.–Sat. 10:30–4, Sun. 11–4; closed Tues. Open Nov.–May by chance.

Kuttner Antiques (413-229-2955; fax 413-229-6000; N. Main St., PO Box 741, Sheffield, MA 01257; Rte. 7) Formal and high country American and English furniture and decorative accessories from the 18th and 19th centuries. Open 10:30–5; closed Tues.

Le Trianon (413-528-3940; trianon@vgernet.net; 1854 N. Main St., Sheffield, MA 01257; Rte. 7) 17th-, 18th- and 19th-century French and Continental furniture, carpets, tapestries, and accessories. Open daily 10:30–5:30.

Lois W. Spring Antiques (413-229-2542; 140 Ashley Falls Rd., Sheffield, MA 01257; Rte. 7A) Eighteenth- and 19th-century furniture and accessories, country and formal. Original painted finishes as far as possible. Open by chance or appointment.

Ole T. J.'s Antique Barn (413-229-8382; 640 S. Main St., Sheffield, MA 01257; Rte. 7) Antiques and collectibles on two floors from all over, some of it gathered by the owners on their travels in the Far East and Africa, also early American and European furniture, jewelry, paintings, rugs, lamps, and other accessories. Thurs.–Mon., by chance, or by appointment.

Painted Porch (413-229-2700; www.paintedporch.com; 102 S. Main St., Sheffield, MA 01257; Rte. 7) Wonderful collection of country antiques displayed in both the Victorian house and out building. The antique furnishings are interspersed with sofas and chairs from Urban Country so one can see how old and new complement one another. Open Thurs.–Mon. 10–5, Tues. and Wed. by appointment.

1750 House Antiques (413-229-6635; S. Main St., Sheffield, MA 01257; Rte. 7) Specialists in the sale and repair of American, French, and European clocks. Also offering music boxes, phonographs, glass, china, and other accessories plus furniture.

Saturday Sweets Antiques and Design (413-229-0026; satsweet@bcn.net; 755A N. Main St., PO Box 814, Sheffield, MA 01257; Rte. 7) Twentieth-century decorative arts with an emphasis on Art Deco, including furniture, accessories, and vintage costume jewelry. Open Fri.–Sun. or by chance or appointment. Call ahead in winter.

Susan Silver Antiques (413-229-8169; N. Main St., PO Box 621, Sheffield, MA 01257; Rte. 7) English furnishings from the 18th and 19th centuries. One specialty is library furniture. Closed Tues.

Vintage Linens (413-229-3549, 229-0003; Main St., Sheffield, MA 01257) Right in the heart of Sheffield, this charming little shop features linens, as one might expect, but also a changing collection of accessories including buttons, dishes, and glassware.

SOUTH EGREMONT

Judith Monachina

It's easy to find just about any kind of antique in Sheffield but also in Egremont, Lenox, Great Barrington, and other towns.

Geffner/Schatzky Antiques and Varieties (413-528-0057; fax 413-644-9406; Rte. 23, S. Egremont, MA 01258; at the sign of the Juggler) Nineteenth century to 1950s furniture and accessories, jewelry, architectural elements. Open May–Aug., daily 10:30–5; Sept.–Apr., Fri.–Sun. 10:30–5, during the week by chance or appointment.

Howard's Antiques (413-528-1232; Rte. 23, PO Box 472, S. Egremont, MA 01258) Specialists in American country furniture and lighting. Antique lighting fixtures from the late 1890s to the 1930s have been wired for present uses. Nineteenth-century dining room tables and chairs are also offered, as well as other country-style antique furniture. Open daily 10–5 except Tues.

Red Barn Antiques (413-528-3230; Main St., Rte. 23, PO Box 25, S. Egremont, MA 01258) Restored antique lighting from the early 19th century and onward, including kerosene, gas, and early electric fixtures. Repair and restoration of antique lamps on site; refinished furniture.

The Splendid Peasant (413-528-5755; Rte. 23, S. Egremont, MA 01258; at Old Sheffield Rd.) 18th- and 19th-century painted country furniture and folk art, all stunningly displayed in a fascinating series of galleries and niches. Original paint a specialty. Open 9:30–5:30 daily.

SOUTHFIELD

The Buggy Whip Factory Antique Market Place (413-229-3576; Main St., Southfield, MA 01259) An antiques market of 95 dealers featuring country to formal furniture, architectural pieces, kitchenware, tools, china, sterling, glassware, jewelry, and books. Closed Tues. and Wed.

Kettering Antiques (413-229-2859; 135 Main St., PO Box 17, Southfield, MA 01259) Formal English and American 18th- and 19th-century furniture and decorative porcelain and brass. Cabinet restoration and polishing available. Winter hours vary.

STOCKBRIDGE

Hillary Beadell (413-298-8102; 6 Elm St., Stockbridge, MA 01262) Tiny shop with great window displays. Lots of interesting pieces here to add a bit of continental flair to one's decor. Pricing is realistic, and the owner is both knowledgeable and friendly.

Nora Martin Antiques (413-298-4840; 8 Elm St., Stockbridge, MA 01262) Formerly a partner in the Bargain Box in Pittsfield, Martin recently started this shop on Church Street. Filled with a variety of items, the shop is a browser's delight. Martin's eye for the unusual, honed in her former shop, is reflected in the wares she offers for sale here. Closed Tues.

WEST STOCKBRIDGE

Sawyer Antiques (413-232-7062; Depot St., W. Stockbridge, MA 01266) In a Shaker-built gristmill, early-American furniture and accessories in a variety of styles: formal, Shaker, country. Open Fri.–Sun. 10–5; other days call ahead.

Ebenezer II Antiques and Gifts (413-232-7017; 2 Main St., W. Stockbridge, MA 01266) Eclectic assortment of antiques and collectibles, also Turkish rugs and copper.

Central County

LENOX

Charles L. Flint Antiques Inc. (413-637-1634; chazma@ugernet.net; 52 Housatonic St., PO Box 971, Lenox, MA 01240) A new home for this shop featuring furniture, painting, accessories, folk art, Shaker items. The owner is a noted local historian who has a genuine knowledge of and enthusiasm for his wares. Mon.–Sat. 9–5 or by appointment.

J. Warner Antique & Wooden Works (413-637-0613; 44A Housatonic St., Lenox, MA 01240) This new addition to the Lenox Antique scene is a group shop with a range of merchandise all tastefully displayed. John Hails, one of the principals, is a charming, knowledgeable guide to the wares he and others have for sale.

La Vie En Rose (413-637-3662; www.lavieenrose.net; 67 Church St., Lenox, MA 01240) Painted furniture (French Canadian), vintage jewelry, contemporary, museum-quality art prints, and gifts in a cottage-like setting. Open daily 10:30–5.

Past and Future (413-637-2225; 63 Church St., Lenox, MA 01240) Nineteenth- and 20th-century silver and small antiques and collectibles; including scales, inkwells, perfumes, sewing items and sporting antiques. Open. Apr.–Jan., daily; Jan.–Mar., weekends and by appointment.

Stone's Throw Antiques (413-637-2733; 57 Church St., Lenox, MA 01240) American, French, English, and Oriental 19th- and early 20th-century furniture, accessories, and collector's items, including china, glass, silver, prints. Open Apr.–Dec., daily 10–5; Jan.–Mar., weekends.

PITTSFIELD

Berkshire Hills Coins and Estate Jewelry (413-499-1400; 222 Elm St., Pittsfield, MA 01201) Specializing in collectible coins, estate gold, and sterling and costume jewelry. Open Mon.–Sat. 10–5:30.

Berkshire Pedlar (413-236-5600; 288 Tyler St., Pittsfield, MA 01201) A huge warehouse full of goodies. The proprietress is delightful, and one can often find unexpected treasures.

Nora's Estate Goods (413-499-0927; 446 Tyler St., Pittsfield, MA 01201) Housed in the former Memory Lane shop and run by the daughter of the owner, Martin, this shop sells used furniture, antiques, and vintage linens. It is the newest outpost of the Bargain Box, Martin's former shop in Pittsfield. Closed Tues. and Sun.

North County

NORTH ADAMS

Mary Ann-tiques & Gifts (413-663-7803: 615 Ashland St., N. Adams, MA

01247) Small but charming shop filled to the rafters with gifts and antiques. Teacups and tea accessories predominate, but there are lots of unexpected treasures, such as vintage hats, lady's slipper chairs, and jewelry.

West End Market (413-663-5050; 437 W. Main St., N. Adams, MA 01247) A funky shop in a building that was once a neighborhood market. Stormy Crandall has collected an eclectic group of antiques and fun stuff. A fun browse and a potential source for just the right accent piece for any home.

CHESHIRE

Winterbrook Farm Antiques (413-743-2177; www.winterbrookfarm.com; 450 N. State Rd., Cheshire, MA 01225; Rte.8) Late 19th and 20th century restored and refinished furniture and accessories. Howard's refinishing products and replacement hardware in stock. Mon.–Fri. 10:30–5; weekends by chance or appointment.

WILLIAMSTOWN

Amber Fox (413-458-8519; 125 Water St., Williamstown, MA 01267; Rte. 43) This shop carries gifts and antiques including candles, quilts, collectibles, boxes, and period lighting.

Collector's Warehouse (413-458-9686; 723 Rte. 7, Williamstown, MA 01267) Antiques; collectibles, including glassware, jewelry, frames, dolls, linen, and furniture. Deborah Elder's Collector's Warehouse was formerly located in the McClelland Building in Williamstown proper; now it has a more deservedly mainstream location. Mon., Wed.–Sat. 10–5, Sun. 12–5, closed Tues.

The Library Antiques (413-458-3436; www.libraryantiques.com; 70 Spring St., Williamstown, MA 01267) Old and new items, artfully displayed in a series of rooms, including jewelry, furniture, writing supplies, housewares, pillows, prints, books, international decor pieces, silver, dishes, pottery, fabrics and textiles. They welcome browsers. A great place for gifts for others or just for ourselves.

Auctioneers

William Bradford Auction Galleries (413-229-6667; Rte. 7, Sheffield, MA 01257)

Roy C. Burdick (413-664-6055; 24 S. County Rd., Florida, MA 01247)

John and Dina Fontaine (413-448-8922, 1485 W. Housatonic St., Pittsfield, MA 01201)

Ralph Fontaine & Heritage Auctions (413-442-2537; 94 Dawes Ave., Pittsfield, MA 01201)

T.A. Gage (413-528-0076, 413-528-4771; Rte. 23, S. Egremont, MA 01258)

LuJohns Auctioneers (800-243-4420; www.lujohns.com; 2130 Cape St., Lee, MA 01238)

Saddleback Antiques (413-458-5852; 1395 Cold Spring Rd., Williamstown, MA 01267, Rte. 7) Furniture, glass, pottery, prints, posters. A group shop in an old schoolhouse with a bell tower. Inventory changes weekly and includes a fine selection of pieces at realistic prices. Mon., Wed.–Sat. 10–5; Sun. 12–5; closed Tues.

BOOKS

The Berkshires' literary traditions are upheld by a number of excellent book stores, new and used, each with its own distinct character. Specialists, rare book, and antique book dealers are also listed.

South County

GREAT BARRINGTON

The Bookloft (413-528-1521; Barrington Plaza, Stockbridge Rd., Gt. Barrington, MA 01230; Rte. 7) A thoughtfully chosen selection of books and tapes, both music and books. It's also a good source for Berkshire-related titles. With its wooden bookcases and pleasant atmosphere, this is one of the nicest places in South County for browsing and consulting with fellow book lovers, particularly owner Eric Wilska.

Farshaw's Books (413-528-1890; www.bibliofind.com; 13 Railroad St., Gt. Barrington, MA 01230) A select offering of antique and used or out-of-print titles for the reader, collector, and bibliophile in a well-organized, browser-friendly shop. The owners, Helen and Michael Selzer, established *Bibliofind* —a large inventory of old, used and rare books, from an international list of booksellers—on the Internet.

Yellow House Books (413-528-8227; 252 Main St., Gt. Barrington, MA 01230) Bob and Bonnie Benson offer a fine selection of used and rare books in three rooms of a house that is more than 100 years old. Specialties include photography, Native American, literature, art, music, children's illustrated books, cooking, and metaphysical.

LEE

Media Merchant (413-243-3359; 50 Water St., Lee, MA 01238; at Prime Outlets) This is a discount book and media outlet. Can be a good source for bargain books. They also have a shop in Prime Outlets dedicated to children's books.

SHEFFIELD

Berkshire Book Co. (413-229-0122, 800-828-5565; 510 S. Main St., Sheffield, MA 01257; Rte. 7) The ideal used-book store for the reader, with an extensive and well-organized collection. Co-proprietor Esther Kininmonth truly knows and loves her stock and its authors, and it's a pleasure to consult with her about various writers and editions. Categories include literature, travel, biography, children's, art, and antiques.

SOUTH EGREMONT

B&S Gventer Books (413-528-2327; PO Box 298, S. Egremont, MA 01258; Tyrrell Rd. and Rte. 23) "Tons of books" from the 15th century to the 19th. Medieval manuscript and Renaissance pages on vellum and various pages from books published from 1300 to 1600; 19th-century hand-colored engravings. Knowledgeable owner Bruce Gventer can tell their stories. June–Oct., Wed.–Sun.; occasional weekends in winter.

Central County

LANESBOROUGH

Waldenbooks (413-499-0115; Berkshire Mall, Lanesborough, MA 01237; off Rte. 8) Berkshire County's entry for this well-known chain, stocking current hardcover and softcover best-sellers as well as representative collections in various categories, including children's books and books of local interest. Books, tapes, magazine section.

LENOX

The Bookstore in Lenox.

Judith Monachina

The Bookstore (413-637-3390; 9 Housatonic St., Lenox, MA 01240) A literate and imaginative selection of new fiction, old fiction, and nonfiction. There are collections of small-press titles and books by local and regional authors, plus well-chosen children's and young-adult titles. The Bookstore is a community center, too, presided over by owner Matt Tannenbaum with grace

---

Book Dealers

These specialist book dealers do business by catalog or appointment:

Howard S. Mott (413-229-2019; Rte. 7, Sheffield, MA 01257) First editions; books from the 16th to the 20th centuries, autographs.

Iron Kettle Books (413-738-5362; Rte. 43, Hancock, MA 01237) By catalog; occasional open houses.

John R. Sanderson Antiquarian Bookseller (413-298-5322; PO Box 844, Stockbridge, MA 01262) Rare and fine books.

North Star Rare Books and Manuscripts (413-644-9595; 684 S. Main St., Gt. Barrington, MA 01230; Rte. 7) Specializing in 18th-, 19th-, and 20th-century historical literary manuscripts and rare volumes. Open seven days a week in a shop located next to "Grape Finds" wine emporium!

---

and humor. Matt and his assistants know their books and are happy to converse with you about them; they organize book-signing parties and special events, too. "The world's oldest, permanent literary establishment, serving the community since last Tuesday."

PITTSFIELD

Barnes & Noble (413-496-9051; 555 Hubbard Ave., Pittsfield, MA 01201; at Berkshire Crossing Mall) This chain "superstore" has a large selection of the most popular titles, along with book CDs and tapes, plus some musical scores. The in-store café features Starbucks coffee and other goodies.

North County

NORTH ADAMS

Papyri Books (413-662-2099; 49 Main St., N. Adams, MA 01247) This shop carries mostly used books, some new; regular programs of music and readings.

WILLIAMSTOWN

Water Street Books (413-458-8071; 26 Water St., Williamstown, MA 01267) A large selection in just about every category displayed on classy architectural shelving. The help is hip and friendly. There are sale books, children's books, and the Williams College bookstore is in the back. A booklover's paradise.

Farther afield but a destination for a good browse: **Librarium** (518-392-5209; 126 Blackbridge Rd., E. Chatham, NY 12060; off Rte. 295, 1 mi. E of E. Chatham) More than 25,000 secondhand, out-of-print books "for all interests and ages." Sept.–June, open most days 10–5 by chance or appointment only. July and Aug., Fri.–Mon 10–6 and by appointment or chance. Browsers particularly welcome.

Especially for Children

Gifted Child (413-637-1191; 80 Church St., Lenox, MA 01240) Children's clothing, newborns to preteens, with a contemporary flair; high-quality toys and gifts. Camp care packages—what a great idea. And don't miss the sale barn. Also in Great Barrington at 23 Railroad St.; (413-528-1395), featuring clothes from newborn to size 6X.

M. Lacey (413-528-5991; 12 Railroad St., Gt. Barrington, MA 01230) A beautiful selection of clothing for infants and children, much of it imported. The whimsical designs are sure to delight both wearer and buyer.

Matruska (413-528-6911; 252 Main St., Gt. Barrington, MA 01230) Toys and books that have been chosen to enhance a child's imagination and sense of beauty. Wonderful dolls from Holland that only absorb a child's love.

Persnickety (413-662-2990; 13 Eagle St., N. Adams, MA 01247) This is a tiny treasure trove of unique gifts for baby and child including delightful outfits, hand-knit cap and sweater sets, along with wonderful finger puppets and toys.

Tom's Toys (413-528-3331; 307 Main St., Gt. Barrington, MA 01230) A happening place for kids that carries all the most popular toys and a great selection of inexpensive trinkets to amuse even the most bored young traveler.

Other spots for clothes, toys, and gifts for children include **Mary Stuart** (413-637-0340; 69 Church St., Lenox, MA 01240), for exquisite clothes designed for grandmothers to give. And several area museums and galleries, particularly the **Berkshire Museum** in Pittsfield, have gift shops with sections devoted to educational items disguised as toys.

CLOTHING & ACCESSORIES

We can outfit ourselves in just about any style of our choice in the Berkshires: classic, traditional, designer, funky, all-natural, English country squire, buckaroo—it's all here. Some boutiques also feature designs and concepts that have been created in the Berkshires, too. For clothing factory outlets, and there are a number of them, check the listings below plus the "Shopping Streets, Mews, & Malls" section.

South County

GREAT BARRINGTON

Barrington Outfitters (413-528-0021; 289 Main St., Gt. Barrington, MA 01230) A good selection of shoes for men, women, and kids along with casual clothes for men and women.

Byzantium (413-528-9496; 32 Railroad St., Gt. Barrington, MA 01230) The sweaters in chenille, wool, and cotton will catch the eye first, but it doesn't stop there. Stylish and easy women's dresses, blouses, skirts, and ensembles, casual to dressy. Lots of lovely lingerie and sleepwear, too, plus jewelry, throws, and other accessories.

Drygoods (413-528-2950; 42 Railroad St., Gt. Barrington, MA 01230) Contemporary women's clothes, hats, jewelry, accessories, and shoes. **Body and Soul** shares space in this cheerful shop, offering a wide variety of body-care products.

Gatsby's (413-528-9455; 25 Railroad St., Gt. Barrington, MA 01230) Useful and funky stuff, including cotton nightgowns, Doc Martins, Teva sandals, Birkenstocks, denim, socks and turtlenecks, and housewares. Gatsby's covers the territory with shops in Williamstown (413-458-5407; 31 Spring St.) and Lee (413-243-3412; 62 Main St.).

Hildi B (413-528-0331; 320 Main St., Gt. Barrington, MA 01230) Natural-fiber clothes, including batik sweaters, skirts, blouses, and dresses. Plus handcrafted jewelry and other crafts, leather items, oils and soaps.

Jack's Country Squire (413-528-1390; 316 Main St., Gt. Barrington, MA 01230) Family clothing and shoes, including Nike, Woolrich, Reebok, Levi.

LEE

Ben's (413-243-0242; 68 Main St., Lee, MA 01238) A friendly store packed with clothing and footwear for the entire family.

A Change of Art (413-243-4800; 61 Center St., Lee, MA 01238) An energetic mix of American designers featuring cotton, linen, and other natural fibers that complement hand-painted and hand-sewn pieces. Under new ownership.

Zabian's Ltd. (413-243-0136; 19 Main St., Lee, MA 01238) Clothing for men with an emphasis on personal service.

Prime Outlets at Lee (413-243-8186; 50 Water St., Lee, MA 01238; exit 2 off the MassPike at Rte. 20) Over 60 discount and factory-outlet stores, featuring women's clothing **(Jones New York, Liz Claiborne),** leather goods **(Coach),** sporting goods, menswear, and shoes **(Johnson & Murphy, Haggar), Polo,** and **Brooks Brothers.**

STOCKBRIDGE

Greystone Gardens (413-298-0113; www.greystonegardens.com; Main St., Stockbridge, MA 01262; in The Mews) Antique clothing for men and women. See the description under "Pittsfield."

Katherine Meagher (413-298-3329; 10 Elm St., Stockbridge, MA 01262) Women's clothing, casual and dressy, classically fashionable; sportswear, separates, dresses, accessories, jewelry.

Sweaters Etc. (413-298-4287; South St., Stockbridge, MA 01262; Rte 7) The third house behind the Red Lion Inn contains a veritable feast of sweaters in wool and cotton. Some are high fashion, while others are more casual. Many are hand knit, and all sweaters are discounted.

Vlada Boutique (413-298-3656; Elm St., Stockbridge, MA 01262) Retail therapy for sure! Selling sophisticated women's clothing with an emphasis on comfort, witty gifts and accessories, lovely and outrageous cards, and clever contemporary jewelry.

WEST STOCKBRIDGE

Out of Vietnam at Truc Orient Express Restaurant (413-232-4204; 3 Harris St., West Stockbridge, MA 01266) The owners of this wonderful Vietnamese restaurant have a shop adjacent that specializes in lacquerware and silk accessories for the home, along with some Asian-inspired clothing and accessories. Open during restaurant hours, 5–9pm daily except Tues., or by appointment.

Central County

LANESBOROUGH

Berkshire Pendleton Store (413-443-6822; 100 Williamstown Rd., Lanesborough, MA 01237; Rte. 7 between Pittsfield and Williamstown) Classic wool clothes and accessories for the complete look. Men's sport shirts and sweaters, too, and a large selection of American Indian trade blankets and robes. They also have an outlet basement.

The Berkshire Mall (413-445-4400; Old State Rd., Lanesborough, MA 01237; off Rte 8) comprises many and varied clothes-shopping options for men, women, teens, and children: **The Gap, Old Navy, American Eagle Outfitters, EMS, Eddie Bauer,** and **Filene's.**

LENOX

Casablanca (413-637-2680; 27 Housatonic St., Lenox, MA 01240) Men's and women's clothes, stylishly displayed in a gallery setting.

Evviva (413-637-9875; 22 Walker St., Lenox, MA 01240) Sophisticated dresses, separates, and accessories by designers "well known and undiscovered." They also have shoes to complete the outfit!

Glad Rags (413-637-0088; 76 Church St., Lenox, MA 01240) Clothes with an emphasis on easy fit and easy care in a variety of fabulous fabrics. Wonderful hats, scarves, and other accessories and jewelry. Also a source for **Berkshire Humane Society** T-shirts and sweatshirts.

Purple Plume (413-637-3442; 35 Church St., Lenox, MA 01240) A large selection of fun and unusual clothing, some batiked or hand-painted, featuring the latest looks and natural fibers. The amazing array of accessories includes jewelry, headbands, and scarves. Gifts and cards, too.

Shooz (413-637-1118; 44 Housatonic St., Lenox, MA 01240) Another shop run by the owners of Casablanca featuring—what else?—shoes to complement today's contemporary look in clothing. They also have great handbags and wonderful jewelry.

Steilmann (413-637-8930; 26-27 Church St., Lenox, MA 01240) This shop features European fashion merchandise for women at discounted prices. Often there are fabulous designer samples offered.

Talbot's (413-637-3576; 46 Walker St., Lenox, MA 01240) Classic women's clothing and accessories, and a special petites section.

Tanglewool, Inc. (413-637-0900; 28 Walker St., Lenox, MA 01240) Sophisticated clothing, shoes, gorgeous sweaters (from Patricia Roberts and other well-known designers) for the fashion conscious.

Weaver's Fancy (413-637-2013; 69 Church St., Lenox, MA 01240) One-of-a kind clothing and hats in hand-created fabrics, along with beautiful hand-painted silks and luscious rayon chenille. The whimsical hats provide both warmth and wit.

PITTSFIELD

Champion Factory Outlet (413-442-1332; 456 W. Housatonic St., Pittsfield, MA 01201; at Pittsfield Plaza) Sweatshirts and turtlenecks at discount prices, plus other athletic apparel.

Color Accents (413-443-0872, 137 North St., Pittsfield, MA 01201) Designer scarves, hats, belts, jewelry, lingerie, and various accessories for the boudoir, including English toiletries and other cosmetics. Instruction in makeup, color analysis, wardrobe planning. Also in North Adams.

The Cottage (413-447-9643; 31 South St., Pittsfield, MA 01201) A popular shop where women's clothing shares space with home and gift items.

Deidre's (413-499-9959; 75 North St., Pittsfield, MA 01201) Women's clothing for any day, especially those special days. Wedding gowns, mother-of-the-bride dresses, bridesmaids dresses, cocktail outfits—even tuxedo rentals for the man in one's life.

Greystone Gardens (413-442-9291; www.greystonegardens.com; 436 North St., Pittsfield, MA 01201) An emporium of timeless treasures. Victorian and vintage clothing, accessories, jewelry, and linens for men and women. The long, high-ceilinged shop has floral carpeting, velvet-curtained dressing rooms with antique mirrors, stacks of old-fashioned hat boxes, swanky fashion prints, and vintage songs being crooned in the background—the perfect setting for '40s evening gowns, sporty rayon dresses, lacy camisoles and wedding gowns, vintage tuxedos, top hats, tweed jackets and coats, bowling shirts, fringed scarves, and more, all eminently wearable. Owner Carla Lund, creator of this outpost of nostalgia, is a genius at putting it all together. Cards, soaps, and other niceties, too. Not to be missed—it or the sister shop in The Mews in Stockbridge.

Steven Valenti (413-443-2569; 157 North St., Pittsfield, MA 01201) Menswear for these times in a well-appointed store, with up-to-date styles by Perry Ellis, Jhane Barnes, and other contemporary designers. Shirts, sweaters, suits, jackets, and coats here feature fine fabrics and colors ranging from traditional to fashion-forward styles. An outstanding collection of silk ties.

Skilled hands and tools of the trade, at Undermountain Weavers, Housatonic.

Jonathan Sternfield

Fabrics and Weavers

For your home or self, two sources of special textiles and fabrics:

Sam Kasten's SKH Gallery (413-528-3300; 46 Castle St., Gt. Barrington, MA 01230; in the Train Station) The old Great Barrington Train Station houses the looms of Sam Kasten's nationally renowned architectural fabrics firm. Wall coverings, upholstery fabrics and carpeting almost too fine to tread upon are the mainstay of his business, but shawls and wraps in exotic and unusual yarns are available, too. Call for hours.

Undermountain Weavers (413-274-6565; 311 Gt. Barrington Rd., W. Stockbridge, MA 01266; Rte. 41) In a restored barn, on century-old hand looms, traditional Shetland Island patterns take shape. Purchase by the yard, or tailoring can be arranged.

North County

NORTH ADAMS

Color Accents and Katie's Korner (413-663-7272; 43 Main St., N. Adams, MA 01247) Mary Shea Knight's North Adams location with a corner of the store devoted to kid's items. She carries April Cornell, Crabtree & Evelyn, and Camille Beckman goods.

WILLIAMSTOWN

The Cottage (413-458-4304; 24 Water St., Williamstown, MA 01267) Specialty fabrics and apparel from designers like April Cornell, Vera Bradley, Putamayo, and Crabtree & Evelyn (nightwear).

Jackie's (413-548-3410; 46 Spring St., Williamstown, MA 01267) Stylish clothing for women, understated but luxurious outfits for everyday or special occasions.

Williams Shop (413-4583605; 15 Spring St., Williamstown, MA 01267) A large selection of items bearing the Williams College logo as well as athletic and sporting goods.

Zanna (413-458-9858; 41 Spring St., Williamstown, MA 01267) Contemporary women's clothes and accessories, featuring natural fibers and up-to-the-minute looks. There is also a selection of sophisticated but comfortable shoes.

GIFT & SPECIALTY SHOPS

South County

GREAT BARRINGTON

Church Street Trading Company (413-528-6120; 4 Railroad St., Gt. Barrington, MA 01230) A trendy mix of antiques, natural-fiber clothes, nature-oriented cosmetics, pottery, crafts, and various lifestyle accessories, attractively arranged.

Crystal Essence (413-528-2595; 39 Railroad St., Gt. Barrington, MA 01230) Geodes, jewelry, gemstones, ceramics, clothes, books, and other items for enhancing a New Age lifestyle.

The Gingham Rabbit (413-528-0048; 389 Stockbridge Rd., Gt. Barrington, MA 01230; Rte. 7) A pastel palate predominates in this two-story shop that sells wonderful cards, pillows, gift items, infant clothing, lingerie, and bath products. They specialize in Berkshire-related gift items.

Herb 'N Country (413-528-0245; 297 Main St., Gt. Barrington, MA 01230) A garden, floral, and gift shop operated in tandem with its sister store Urban Country. The same stylish sensibility pervades both shops. The original store tiling is the perfect background for the shop's eclectic offerings.

La Pace (413-528-1888; 313 Main St., Gt. Barrington, MA 01230) A beautifully conceived and decorated store full of luxurious bath items imported from all over Europe, with an emphasis on Italy. Linen hand towels, chic shower curtains, bath pillow, even rubber duckies for the tub.

Mama's Earth: The Environmental General Store (413-644-8996; 87 Railroad St., Gt. Barrington, MA 01230) A store dedicated to saving the environment by selling recycled, organic, or environmentally friendly products. Clothes from 100 percent organic cotton, toys, books, etc.

Mistral's (413-528-1618; 7 Railroad St., Gt. Barrington, MA 01230) "Provence in the Berkshires" is the way the owners describe their shop. French wire baskets, lamps, and vases as well as jacquard-patterned napkins, Provençal olive oil, faience plates, cutlery, and serving pieces, all guaranteed to win a Francophile's heart. Upstairs are bath and bedroom products.

Nahual (413-528-2423; 9 Railroad St., Gt. Barrington, MA 01230) Handcrafted items from Mexico and Africa. Only open Thurs.–Sun. afternoons.

The Red Door (413-528-1899; 3 Railroad St., Gt. Barrington, MA 01230) Behind the red door is a tiny shop carrying a variety of gift items both old and new.

Sappa (413-528-9592; 308 Main St., Gt. Barrington, MA 01230) An elegant store with style and wit. The very charming young owner has a great sense of design and eye for the unusual. Gifts and accessories from Europe join American antiques and interesting artworks in an ever-changing display of beautiful objects.

Seeds & Co., Inc. (413-528-8122; 34 Railroad St., Gt. Barrington, MA 01230) Simplicity and sophistication of design are the hallmarks of this store. Home and bath accessories with wit and charm share space with those having a 21st-century edge.

T. P. Saddle Blanket and Trading Co. (413-528-6500; 304 Main St., Gt. Barrington, MA 01230) An outpost for the Southwest look, from cowboy-motif pajamas to saddle blankets for your living room, with a colorful abundance of shirts, vests, boots, belts, pillows, books, candles, bedding, dishware, and furniture accents.

LEE

Beartown Gifts (413-243-2008; 87 Main St., Lee, MA 01238) You'll find country-style gifts here, including wonderful Christmas items, hand-painted glass, collectible bears, and lots of charming items for the home.

Pamela Loring Gifts & Interiors (413-243-2689; 151 Main St., Lee MA 01238) Tastefully decorated shop in a renovated Victorian house. Each room is filled with carefully chosen merchandise. There's an emphasis on seasonal gifts and decorations. Besides household decorative items there are candles, bath oils, soaps, potpourris, and charming gifts for children.

SHEFFIELD

Bits and Pieces (413-229-9996; 116 Main St., Sheffield, MA 01257) Rustic country treasures from artisans all across the country.

Campo deFiori (413-528-9180; 1815 N. Main St., Sheffield, MA 01257; Rte. 7) A wonderful source for garden ornaments, pots, botanical prints, interesting soaps, plants, and containers. A very sophisticated touch European country in the Berkshires.

STOCKBRIDGE

Red Lion Inn Gift Shop (413-298-3134; 30 Main St., Stockbridge, MA 01262; at the Red Lion Inn) A lovely shop with gifts, cards, and accessories, featuring Berkshire items.

Seven Arts (413-298-5101; Main St., Stockbridge, MA 01262) A concentration of items with Rockwell motifs, also T- shirts, jewelry, and gifts.

Williams & Son Country Store (413-298-3016; Main St., Stockbridge, MA 01262) A Stockbridge institution, with jams and jellies, soaps, candy, gourmet foods, glassware, gifts, cards, and various nostalgia items. Enjoyable old tins are displayed behind the counter.

Yankee Candle (413-298-3004; Main St., Stockbridge, MA 01262) A huge selection of candles in a variety of shapes, colors, and scents.

WEST STOCKBRIDGE

Charles H. Baldwin & Sons (413-232-7785; 1 Center St., W. Stockbridge, MA 01266) Not only is this an outlet for Baldwin's flavoring extracts along with table and maple syrup, it is also a general store with seasonal gifts, cards, candy and inexpensive toys for children. *Martha Stewart Living* featured this store.

Hotchkiss Mobiles Gallery (413-232-0200; 8 Center St., W. Stockbridge, MA 01266) Open Sat.–Sun.; or call for an appointment. Contemporary mobiles for your home or office.

Central County

LENOX

B. Mango & Bird (413-637-2611; 48 Main St., Lenox, MA 01240) An eclectic mix of home furnishings and accessories in a dramatic, high-ceilinged store, with an outdoor patio where garden gifts and furniture are displayed.

Colorful Stitches (413-637-8207; 48 Main St., Lenox, MA 01240) A rainbow of yarns in wools, silks, cottons, and blends would tempt even a novice knitter. Wonderful patterns, buttons, and all the necessary needles etc. There are even regular weekend instruction sessions.

The Cottage (413-443-5900; 439 Pittsfield-Lenox Rd., Lenox, MA 01240) There are two locations for these "cottages," one in Pittsfield and one in Lenox, offering gifts for home and family along with a lovely selection of women's clothing.

Mary Stuart (413-637-0340; 69 Church St., Lenox, MA 01240) A chic shop carrying accessories for gracious country living, including china, glassware, linen, needlepoint, and toiletries; lingerie and sleepwear; books and cards. A small, but beautiful selection of clothing for infants and toddlers is displayed at the rear of the shop.

Pine Cone Hill (413-496-9700; Rte. 7, Lenox, MA 01240) Housed in the former Lenox Shops compound, this is an outlet store for the Pine Cone Hill brand of bedding and table linens for which local Annie Selke is responsible. These items are sold elsewhere for much higher prices. Styles complement both country and contemporary interiors.

Three Hills and a Cloud (413-637-0461; 11 Housatonic St., Lenox, MA 01240) Dried flowers fill the rafters of this charming shop. There's an assortment of potpourri fragrances and essential oils. Bath blends, massage oil, and floral arrangements also sold here.

Villager Gifts (413-637-9866; 68 Main St, Lenox, MA 01240) An engaging variety of gifts and collectibles, featuring jewelry, pottery, stationery, candles, and cards. This is the largest area dealer for the Cats' Meow Village houses and custom pieces. A Christmas Shop is downstairs.

Yankee Candle (413-499-3626; 639 Pittsfield-Lenox Rd., Lenox, MA 01240; Rte. 7) Candles, gifts, bath accessories. Also on Main St. in Stockbridge.

PITTSFIELD

The Cottage (413-447-9643; 31 South St., Pittsfield, MA 01201) Attractive tableware, including glasses, vases, dinnerware, table linens, baskets, frames, soaps, along with clothes and jewelry.

Museum Facsimiles Outlet Store (413-499-0020; 117 Fourth St., Pittsfield, MA 01201) Open only on Saturday from 10 to 5, this outlet store is worth the wait. Here one can find hand printed greeting cards and stationery sold in the finest museums, along with frames and mirrors to give as gifts or to grace the home.

Pasko Frame & Gift Center (413-442-2680; 243 North St., Pittsfield, MA 01201) The new owner carries on the tradition set by Ann Pasko of offering Berkshire landscapes by Walter Pasko, the Berkshire map, superb custom framing, prints, and posters. They still have a lovely selection of gifts and handcrafts from around the world. Largest area dealer of P. Buckley Moss prints.

Uniques (413-442-8523; 33 Cheshire Rd., Pittsfield, MA 01201; in the Allendale Shopping Center) A sparkling shop filled with fabulous handcrafted items including hummingbird feeders, crystal, pottery, candles, and other truly unique gifts.

North County

ADAMS

The Crafter's Cottage (413-743-2640; 23 Park St., Adams, MA 01220) Unique handcrafted gifts and seasonal offerings in a range of prices. This is an outlet for crafters whose work is often only seen at craft fairs or holiday boutiques.

NORTH ADAMS

Eziba (413-664-6888; 46 Eagle St., N. Adams, MA 01247) An outlet for hand-crafted products from around the world, found in the stunning Eziba cata-log. The merchandise in this shop is discounted.

Moulton's Country Store (413-664-7770; 77 Main St., N. Adams, MA 01247) Large, bright space filled with locally made gifts, baked goods, toys, cards, seasonal items, even an ice cream bar, overseen by a friendly staff, just like in an old-fashioned country store.

Satya's Celestial Emporium (413-663-8900; 34 Eagle St., N. Adams, MA 01247) A New Age shop with crystals, incense, clothing, and jewelry from around the world.

Tala's Quilt Shop (413-664-8200; Heritage State Park, Bldg. #2, N. Adams, MA 01247) From the reports of accomplished quilters, this is a wonderful source for supplies and ideas. Classes available.

WILLIAMSTOWN

The Cottage (413-458-4305; 24 Water St., Williamstown, MA 01267) A variety of gift items including tableware and table linens, cards, children's gifts, photo frames, toiletries from Crabtree & Evelyn, and women's clothes from design-ers like Putumayo. This is an independently owned Cottage store!

Where'd You Get That!? (413-458-2206; www.wygt.com; 20A Spring St., Williamstown, MA 01267) This fun store aims to provide gifts and toys to tickle the brain, the fancy, and the funnybone—and it succeeds.

HANDCRAFTS

See Chaper Five, *Arts & Pleasures, Culture,* for additional listings of galleries with handcrafted art.

South County

GREAT BARRINGTON

Evergreen (413-528-0511; 291 Main St., Gt. Barrington, MA 01230) Contempo-rary American crafts include vases, tableware, pottery, clocks, and hand-crafted jewelry.

Kaolin Pottery (413-528-1531; 80 Rte. 7, Gt. Barrington, MA 01230; near Gt. Barrington airport) Contemporary ceramics from whimsical to elegant at the artists' studio and showroom.

October Mountain Stained Glass (413-528-6681; 343 Main St., Gt. Barrington, MA 01230) A vivid array of lampshades, window panels, and glass acces-sories. Custom design work is a specialty, including commissions for homeowners, builders, and architects. Beveling, sandblasting, repairs, and supplies are also offered. Closed Mon.

Wonderful Things (413-528-2473; 232 Stockbridge Rd., Gt. Barrington, MA 01230) Handcrafted gifts, or make our own with yarn, needlework accessories, beads, feathers, stencils, paint, other craft supplies. Largest needlework store in the county.

HOUSATONIC

The Great Barrington Pottery (413-274-6259; www.gtbarringtonpottery.com; Rte. 41, Housatonic, MA 01236) Potter Richard Bennett uses a Japanese woodburning kiln for firing pottery designs that combine East and West in a beautiful garden setting. Visit the pottery showroom or participate in an ancient tea ceremony. (See "Seasonal Events" in Chapter Five, *Arts & Pleasures*.)

MONTEREY

Joyous Spring Pottery (413-528-4115; 20 Art School Rd., Monterey, MA 01245) Potter Michael Marcus fires his climbing kiln once a year for a 10-day period for his Japanese-inspired unglazed ceramics.

SHEFFIELD

Fellerman & Raabe Glass Works (413-229-8533; www.fellerman-rabe.com; 534 S. Main St., Sheffield, MA 01257; Rte 7) Handblown glass art here includes perfume bottles, jewelry, vases, and paperweights—one of these on a small light box creates a glowing miniature universe. Large glass bowls in organic shapes and glass sculpture, too. Call to find out when to watch glass artists at work. Closed Mon.

Sheffield Pottery (413-229-7700; www.sheffield-pottery.com; PO Box 399, Sheffield, MA 01257; Rte. 7) New England potters' ware, including mugs, teapots, platters, tureens; terra cotta items. Supplies and equipment, too.

STOCKBRIDGE

An American Craftsman (413-298-0175; 36 Main St., Stockbridge, MA 01262) Browse among the unique glass, wood, and jewelry boxes made by some of America's best craftspeople.

WEST STOCKBRIDGE

Berkshire Center for Contemporary Glass (413-232-4666; 6 Harris St., W. Stockbridge, MA 01266) Iridescent bowls, glassware, paperweights, gift items, and clever Christmas tree ornaments. Public viewing area. Glass-blowing instruction, demonstrations, and classes offered.

Hoffman Pottery (232-4646; 103 Rte. 41, Gt. Barrington Rd., W. Stockbridge, MA 01255) Hand-thrown, hand-painted functional works that dance with energy.

Central County

LENOX

Cose D'Argilla (413-637-8886; 93 Church St., Lenox, MA 01240) The owner is Italian with a real flair for picking out the best in contemporary Italian craft pieces including pottery and glass.

Concepts of Art (413-637-4845; 67 Church St., Lenox, MA 01240) Fine crafts and local artisans, with lamps and other glass, wood sculpture, jewelry, throws. There is an emphasis on Judaica.

Inspired Planet (413-637-2836; www.inspiredplanet.com; 36 Pittsfield-Lenox Rd., Lenox, MA 01240; Rte. 7 at Brushwood Farm Shops) This abundant collection of distinctive "cross-cultural art" includes high-quality paintings, jewelry, primitives, rugs, icons, textiles, masks, pottery, carved wooden animals, and other sculpture. These hand-crafted items with symbolic meaning are "gifts that connect." Call ahead for hours.

Lydia Mongiardo Collection (413-637-0809; 51 Church St., Lenox, MA 01240) Furniture by Nicholas Mongiardo, a specialist in 20th-century French designs, plus stunning jewelry and accessories for the home are beautifully displayed in this relatively new addition to the shopping scene in Lenox.

HOUSE AND HOME

South County

GREAT BARRINGTON

Bridlewood Home Furnishing (413-528-5825; 434 Stockbridge Rd., Gt. Barrington, MA 01230) Simple country furniture displayed in a wonderful converted barn. Closed Tues. and Wed.

The Chef's Shop (413-528-0135; 290 Main St., Gt. Barrington, MA 01230) A hardware store for serious cooks, featuring innovative kitchen equipment including top-of-the-line cookware and knives. From garlic peelers to pasta pots, the Chef's Shop has it all. Also pottery serving pieces and cookbooks.

Gatsby's (413-528-9455; 25 Railroad St., Gt. Barrington, MA 01230) In addition to wearables, there are futons, wicker and other furniture, bedclothes, and housewares.

Hammertown Barn (413-528-7766; 325 Stockbridge Rd., Gt. Barrington, MA 01230) Formerly only in Pine Plains, New York, Hammertown Barn's owners have expanded to Great Barrington. Country chic is the theme; comfort is the name of the game. They carry Mitchell Gold furniture, lots of great pillows, rugs, and bedding. One-stop shopping for everything for the home from kitchen to bath.

Out Of Hand (413-528-3791; 81 Main St., Gt. Barrington, MA 01230) Every size, shape, and color of basket you ever needed or imagined—one upstairs room is full of them—plus rugs, throws, pillows, glassware in a rainbow of colors, toys, candlesticks, clothing. A great place for accessorizing the home!

The Lamplighter (413-528-3448; 162 Main St., Gt. Barrington, MA 01230) An exceptional lighting store with a wide selection and knowledgeable staff. Chandeliers, floor and table lamps, and outdoor lighting in all shapes, sizes, and styles, from colonial to art deco to contemporary. Lampshades and other accessories.

Phoebe (413-528-1166; 325 Stockbridge Road, Gt. Barrington, MA 01230) Visit this shop for "luxe" linens, including custom-order bedding, tablecloths, placemats, napkins, and rugs. There are also some great gift items.

Urban Country (413-528-6456; 635 S. Main St., Gt. Barrington, MA 01230) Carrie Herrington is the force and design personality behind this stunning display of country furnishings and accessories. Her eye for style is impeccable. Herrington has recently started designing furniture and offers an interior decorating service.

Wingate Ltd. (413-644-9960; 420 Stockbridge Rd., Gt. Barrington, MA 01230) Importers of antique and reproduction furniture displayed in roomlike settings, with design services offered on the premises.

STOCKBRIDGE

Country Curtains (413-298-5565; 30 Main St., Stockbridge, MA 01262; at the Red Lion Inn) Manufacturer's shop offering curtains and matching bedding from the manufacturer, displayed in charming room vignettes. Select from a variety of styles and fabrics.

WEST STOCKBRIDGE

Anderson & Sons' Shaker Tree (413-232-7072; Main St., W. Stockbridge, MA 01266) Exquisite Shaker reproduction furniture, with quilts, herbs, and other wares. The craftsmanship is so highly regarded that the Andersons were entrusted with permission to measure the Shaker pieces in the noted Andrews' collection at the Metropolitan Museum of Art. The showroom is not always open; call ahead.

Central County

HANCOCK

Hancock Union Store (413-738-5072; Main St, PO Box 1009, Hancock, MA

01237) Fine reproductions of American period furniture—tables, chairs, sofas, and beds. Michael Boulay, cabinetmaker. Call for appointment.

LENOX

Different Drummer's Kitchen (413-637-0606; 568 Pittsfield-Lenox Rd., Lenox, MA 01240; Rte. 7) All manner of equipment and accessories for kitchen and table, from coffeepots to measuring spoons.

Michael Charles Cabinetmakers (413-637-3483; 53 Church St., Lenox, MA 01240) Fine handcrafted furniture in a variety of finishes, all beautiful in their stylish simplicity.

Tassels (413-637-2400, fax 413-637-1836; 36 Pittsfield-Lenox Rd., Lenox, MA 01240; at Brushwood Farm Shops, Rte. 7) Fine furniture and accessories in room settings in a variety of styles. A division of Designers Furniture Showcase, Ltd.

PITTSFIELD

Haddad's Rug Company (413-443-4747; 32 Bank Row, Pittsfield, MA 01201; in Park Square) Specialists in Oriental and Oriental-style rugs, new and antique, plus carpeting and other types of rugs.

Homegoods (413-236-6996; 676 Merrill Rd., Pittsfield, MA 01201) This is a huge discount emporium (a division of TJX), with everything for the home including furniture on occasion.

Paul Rich & Sons Home Furnishings (413-443-6467, 800-723-7424; 242 North St., Pittsfield, MA 01201) A large and well-chosen selection of traditional, contemporary, and country furniture and accent pieces.

Pittsfield Furniture Company (413-499-1106; 2 Brown St., Pittsfield, MA 01201) A move to the space formerly occupied by New England Furniture has given Pittsfield Furniture room to expand. Lots of affordable furniture for all style homes.

North County

ADAMS

Interior Alternative (413-743-1986; 5 Hoosac St., Adams, MA 01220) A home furnishings center with seconds and discontinued famous-brand upholstery and curtain fabric, wallpaper, Oriental carpets, hooked rugs, area rugs, bedspreads, comforters, pillows. Custom sewing available on the second floor of this huge old mill.

NORTH ADAMS

International Outlet (413-664-4580; 115 State St., N. Adams, MA 01247; at Western Gateway Heritage Park) A good source for imported crystal, glassware, dinnerware, kitchen utensils, wicker furniture, rugs, brass, table and kitchen linen, candles, pottery, cookware and terra cotta pots. They advertise "upscale goods at deeply discounted prices."

JEWELRY

For additional jewelry options, check the listings in "Antiques" and "Gifts and Handcrafts."

925 Silver (413-644-6412; in the Barrington House next to Helsinki Café, Gt. Barrington) The owners advertise that this is the finest collection of silver jewelry in the world. They may be right!

Berkshire Classic Leather and Silver (413-637-0727; www.berkshireclassic .com; 74 Main St., Gt. Barrington, MA 01230) The emphasis is on leather goods and silver jewelry. They also carry some Judaica and gift items for both men and women.

Heirlooms Classic Jewelry (413-298-4436; PO Box 515, Stockbridge, MA 01262; in the Mews, off Main St.) A glittering treasure box of a shop, offering an international selection of elegant—and affordable—jewelry.

L'Artisanat (413-232-7187; Main St., W. Stockbridge, MA 01266) Elegant one-of-a-kind custom jewelry pieces; artisan's shop on premises.

McTeigue and McClelland (413-528-6263; 597 S. Main St., Gt. Barrington, MA 01230) This little gem in a tiny, renovated Victorian house emphasizes estate and consignment jewelry but also offers jewelry from prominent contemporary artists.

R. W. Wise Goldsmiths (413-637-1589; 81 Church St., Lenox, MA 01240) Richard Wise finds gemstones from all over the world—traveling recently in Brazil, Africa, and Tahiti—and offers them superbly crafted in contemporary fine art jewelry. Imaginative and unique combinations of gems and precious metals. Custom design service. Closed Mon. in winter.

Sienna Gallery (413-637-8386; 80 Main St., Lenox, MA 01240) A very contemporary decor provides the appropriate for stunning and expensive jewelry from the most talented new designers. The owner's father is a well-known glass artist, and the artistic eye is very much in evidence here.

SHOPPING STREETS, MEWS, & MALLS

Many of the shops described in this chapter are, happily, on Berkshire downtown Main Streets. There, real people actually walk along the sidewalks, go to the hardware store and post offices, get books at libraries, pick up

Downtowns are still shopping places in Berkshire County.

Rich Beaty

groceries, run into friends, and stop for lunch or coffee or ice cream against a backdrop of mostly 19th-century civic architecture, highlighted by a few notable historic buildings. For beyond-the-downtown shopping experiences, short and usually scenic drives lead to clusters of destination shops, some in genuinely venerable buildings, others where the quaintness is of more recent vintage. And, yes, there are even some malls. Following is a roundup of where to find favorite shops and shopping settings. More detailed listings of many of the establishments in these centers may be found in relevant sections of Chapters 4, 5, and 7—*Restaurants & Food Purveyors, Arts & Pleasures,* and *Outdoor Recreation.*

South County

Southfield's **Buggy Whip Factory** (Main St., Rte. 272) Driving there from anywhere is a ride through classic New England scenery. The huge two-centuries-old building houses a large antiques center.

Downtown Great Barrington is a happening place, with a true Main Street atmosphere created by a lively combination of shops and boutiques, antiques stores, bookstores, an outstanding selection of eateries, a first-rate coffee place, and theaters (for movies, opera, and other performances). The action centers around Railroad Street and Main Street and takes in other side streets, too. Great Barrington hosts downtown food and music events throughout the year. There is a fabulous Farmer's Market each Saturday from May to the end of the growing season.

Great Barrington's **Jenifer House Commons** (Rte. 7, Stockbridge Rd.) is just north of the town center. This cluster of multilevel barns and buildings—some old and some new—houses an extensive group of antiques dealers' wares and a restaurant/brewery. Do lunch there or nearby. Open daily.

Recordings, Classical and Jazz

Compact discs, cassette tapes, and even those dinosaurs, records, are available throughout the county, in various chain stores and other retail outlets. Most places here with CDs and tapes have a small classical music selection, but for those looking for more than the Three Tenors or the Four Seasons, visit the **Tanglewood Music Store**, at **Tanglewood** in Lenox, open for Tanglewood audiences, and featuring the music and performing artists of that week, plus much more. The **Berkshire Record Outlet** (413-243-4080; www.berkshirerecordoutlet.com; Rte. 102, Lee, MA 01238) has classical remainders listed in a catalog—send for one for $2—containing thousands of classical CDs, tapes, and LPs, at closeout prices. On Saturdays, customers can also browse through an eclectic selection of recordings in the small retail room, being sure to turn up something they've always wanted.

A well-chosen selection of classical jazz, and blues is available at **Tune St.** (413-528-4999; 294 Main St., Gt. Barrington, MA 01230) along with pop, folk, New Age, and world music recordings. They also sell electronic gear (stereo equipment, etc.) and do custom home installations. A low-key, but vital business since 1979, **White Knight Records** (413-528-9466; 288 Main St., Gt. Barrington, MA 01230) carries a broad range of CDs and tapes. They have been complimented by out-of-towners for their collection of classical music and will do special orders.

Jazz enthusiasts in particular will enjoy **Toonerville Trolley Records** (413-458-5229; 131 Water St., Williamstown, MA 01267) and its array of CDs, tapes, and LPs, out of print and current. In addition to jazz, there's rock, folk, and reggae.

For musically related gift items, including instruments, try **The Music Store** (413-528-2460; Rte. 7, Great Barrington, MA 01230; at Jenifer House Commons).

Main St., Stockbridge still looks like—and is—Norman Rockwell territory, even though the Rockwell Museum has moved (but not far; see *Arts & Pleasures*). The welcoming expanse of the Red Lion Inn shares the scene with the gracious library, an excellent market, and several stores. Connected to Main Street is *The Mews,* a cozy cul-de-sac of shops offering clothes, jewelry, and gifts. Many Stockbridge shops offer Rockwelliana in one form or another, from T-shirts to signed prints. Also around the corner from Main Street is Elm Street, with more shops, eateries, and the post office. Note: Main Street and The Mews can seem overrun during high-season weekends; if possible, weekday visits may be better.

A side trip to the small downtown of *West Stockbridge* will reward with several galleries, good restaurants and cafés, and antiques—not to mention a hardware store and a shop devoted to flavoring extracts. The gallery scene offers outdoor sculptures on display, handcrafted jewelry, mobiles, stained glass, and reproduction Shaker furniture, and many other options for contemporary art and craft work. A vintage depot houses a café and studios; a Shaker mill building is home to antiques. A small concentration of excellent restaurants, including a sophisticated Italian take-out food store, is sure to please.

A relatively new offering on the Berkshire shopping scene is *Lee*'s **Prime**

Outlets. These shops are all stocked with discounted (and, some say, last year's) merchandise. Shoes, clothing, leather goods, cards, gourmet food, and watches are all available from top-of-the-line manufacturers to those more

---

Cultural Shopping

Many Berkshire museums, and other institutions devoted to the arts and culture or to historical preservation, fund and publicize their operations with their own gift and book shops. They are excellent sources for unique Berkshire gifts, books about a wide range of historical subjects and the visual and performing arts, and fun and educational items for children. Institution members often get discounts at the shop.

Berkshire Museum Shop (413-443-7469; 39 South St., Pittsfield, MA 01201) An excellent array of items reflecting the scope of the museum's collections: books, cards, plates (including the reproduction Spode blue and white "Pittsfield" plate) and other home accessories, international crafts, and jewelry. There is a treasure trove of small and creative items for children, from the artistic to the scientific reflecting the Museum's natural history collection. Shop staff, mostly volunteers, are helpful and personable.

The Museum Store at the Clark Art Institute (413-458-9545; www.clarkart.edu; 225 South St., Williamstown, MA 01267) features items based on the Clark's collection and those of museums and art galleries around the world: cards, posters, and prints, matted and framed; fine art books; jewelry; and great toys from basic to upscale. The selection of books has been greatly enlarged in the past few years to include an extensive collection of art books and regional titles.

Ex Libris: The Lenox Library Shop (413-637-0197; 18 Main St., Lenox, MA 01240) This pocket-sized shop offers cards, postcards, toys, T-shirts, bookplates, book- marks, games, tote bags, sealing wax, and various Berkshire-related items.

Hancock Shaker Village Shop (413-443-0188; www.hancockshakervillage.org; Rte. 20, Pittsfield, MA 01201) The spacious gift shop in the new visitors' center offers books, clocks, Shaker reproduction furniture and other items, in kits or assem- bled—even the Shaker cloak. Prints of drawings of the Hancock Shaker commu- nity and of Shaker "spirit drawings," and wonderful children's toys and kits, too.

The Norman Rockwell Museum (413-298-4100, www.nrm.org; Rte. 183, Stock- bridge, MA 01262) A well-designed center for books, prints, and cards; the chil- dren's section has books and toys and art-related things to do. There are limited- edition artist's proofs signed by Rockwell and other items related to current exhibits and programs.

Additional cultural shopping options include the shop at the **Massachusetts Audubon Sanctuary,** *Pleasant Valley;* **Chesterwood,** particularly for their selection of National Trust publications; **Tanglewood**'s gift shop, with lots of Tanglewood- logo wearables and other items; the **Arrowhead Museum** shop, with books about Melville and county history, and cards, gifts; the **Garden Gift Shop** at the **Berkshire Botanical Garden; The Mount** (former home of Edith Wharton and current home of **Shakespeare & Co.**); **Williams College Museum of Art; MASS MoCA;** the Berk- shire Theater Festival; and even the **Berkshire Scenic Railway Museum** (books, toys, T-shirts).

trendy and inexpensive. Conveniently located near exit 2 of MassPike, the shopping village's visibility attracts out-of-town shoppers as well as locals. Local controversy over the design notwithstanding, it is an attractive, well-landscaped area. Shops include **Coach, Liz Claiborne, Jones New York, Tommy Hilfiger, Ralph Lauren, Harry & David, Mikasa, Gap,** and **Carter's** among others.

Central County

Downtown Lenox still maintains a "real" downtown flavor, though the boutique and gallery contingent seems to be in the ascendancy. The appealing variety of architecture—neoclassic and Victorian-cottage predominate—is home to inns and taverns, restaurants, an exceptional library and bookstore, and the aforementioned boutiques and galleries. A number of clothing shops, mostly for women, covers the style territory from fine to funky, from classic to casual; art and handcraft galleries offer Berkshire scenes and world-renowned jewelry and other creations.

Downtown Pittsfield was once the commercial and civic hub of the Berkshires, and though the glory of its main thoroughfare, North Street, has somewhat faded, it still hosts a number of services and shops. The downtown area includes several large churches and buildings that will interest the architecture buff, plus the **Berkshire Museum** and the **Berkshire Athenaeum** (the public library). Besides, occasionally in the summer a free concert downtown is offered.

Berkshire Crossing Mall is the newest addition to the mall scene in the Berkshires. Located off Route 9 between *Pittsfield* and *Dalton,* it has a **Barnes & Noble** store, a **Staples,** a **Pier One,** and the ubiquitous **Home Depot** and **Wal-Mart** along with craft, supermarket, and clothing stores.

Berkshire Mall in *Lanesborough* can supply basic mall needs, with a multi-screen cinema complex, clothing, and shoe stores—among them **Filene's** and **Old Navy**—a food court and sit-down restaurants, a bookstore, and so forth.

North County

Spring Street and **Water Street** in **Williamstown** roughly parallel each other and are across from the main Williams College campus. Both easily walkable, they offer handcrafts, clothing, books, tapes and CDs, places to eat, antiques and accessories, sports gear, and all the Williams memorabilia the most purple shopper could ever need.

Outside the County

A recommended destination just outside the county is *Chatham, New York.* Main Street shops include the **Dakota** for high-end clothes; the **Chatham Bookstore; American Pie**, a contemporary general store; the **Handcrafters** for fine handcrafted gift items as well as art supplies; and the **Warm Ewe** for knitting supplies.

CHAPTER NINE
Practical Matters
INFORMATION

Waiting for a bus near the Lee Information Booth.

Judith Monachina

We offer here a small encyclopedia of useful information to help facilitate everyday life for residents and visitors in the Berkshires.

AMBULANCE, FIRE, POLICE

The general emergency number for all Berkshire communities is **911**. The county-wide set of emergency numbers is:

Ambulance, Fire, Police	911	
Poison Control		800-682-9211
Rape Crisis Hotline:	South County	413-664-9642
	Central County	413-443-0089
	North County	413-663-7459 or -5807

AREA CODES, ZIP CODES, TOWN HALLS/LOCAL GOVERNMENT

AREA CODES

The Area Code for all of Berkshire County is **413**. Area codes for adjacent counties are as follows.

Massachusetts
Franklin (most towns), Hampshire, and Hampden counties: 413.

Connecticut
Litchfield County: 860.

New York
Columbia and Rensselaer Counties: 518.

Vermont
All Vermont: 802.

TOWN HALLS

All Berkshire communities have town or city halls as the seats of local government. Most townships are governed by boards of selectmen; several also have town managers. For general information, call the town offices at the following numbers or write to the Town Clerk, c/o Town Hall.

Town	Zip Code	Town Hall Office
Adams	01220	413-743-8320
Alford	01230	413-528-4536
Ashley Falls	01222	413-229-8752 (Sheffield)
Becket	01223	413-623-8934
Cheshire	01225	413-743-1690
Clarksburg	01247	413-663-5282
Dalton	01226	413-684-6111
Egremont	01258	413-528-0182
Florida	01247	413-662-2448
Glendale	01229	413-298-4714 (Stockbridge)
Gt. Barrington	01230	413-528-3140
Hancock	01237	413-738-5225
Hinsdale	01235	413-655-2301
Housatonic	01236	413-528-3140 (Gt. Barrington)
Lanesborough	01237	413-442-1167

Lee	01238	413-243-5505
Lenox	01240	413-637-5506
Lenoxdale	01242	413-637-5506
		(Lenox)
Middlefield	01243	413-623-8934
		(Becket)
Mill River	01244	413-229-8116
		(New Marlborough)
Monterey	01245	413-528-1443
Mt. Washington	01258	413-528-2839
New Ashford	01267	413-458-5461
New Marlborough	01244	413-229-8116
N. Adams	01247	413-662-3011
N. Egremont	01252	413-528-0182
		(Egremont)
Otis	01253	413-269-0101
Peru	01235	413-655-8027
Pittsfield	01201	413-499-9361
	01202	
	(Post Office Boxes)	
Richmond	01254	413-698-3882
Sandisfield	01255	413-258-4771
Savoy	01256	413-743-4290
Sheffield	01257	413-229-8752
S. Egremont	01258	413-528-0182
		(Egremont)
S. Lee	01260	413-243-5505
		(Lee)
Southfield	01259	413-229-8116
		(New Marlborough)
Stockbridge	01262	413-298-4714
Tyringham	01264	413-243-1749
Washington	01223	413-623-8878
W. Stockbridge	01266	413-232-0300
Williamstown	01267	413-458-9341
Windsor	01270	413-684-3811

BANKS

Several Berkshire County banks are linked electronically to banking systems elsewhere in the United States. Visitors may find these options helpful—especially if they need extra cash or traveler's checks.

Adams Co-operative Bank

93 Park St., Adams; 413-743-0001. Branches: 545 S. Main, Lanesborough, 413-443-4070; 31 Eagle St., N. Adams, 413-664-4571.

Banknorth 800-747-7000

10 Center St., Adams, 413-743-3000; 271 Main St., Gt. Barrington, 413-528-2323; 90 Main St., North Adams, 413-663-6561; 57 Spring St., Williamstown, 413-458-8321.

Berkshire Bank 413-443-5601; 800-773-5601

Pittsfield branches: 66 Allen St., 413-236-3160; 43 East St., 413-499-0150; Allendale Shopping Center, 413-499-1068;165 Elm St., 413-447-1880; 66 West St., 413-445-8365. Great Barrington branches: 244 Main St., 413-644-3520; 255 Stockbridge Rd., 413-528-1664. Other branches: 1 Park St., Lee, 413-243-1800; 37 Main St., N. Adams, 413-644-4061; 103 N. Main St., Sheffield, 413-229-8516; 32 Main St., Stockbridge, 413-298-5526; 2 Depot St., W. Stockbridge 413-232-8542.

Canaan National Bank

51 Main St., Egremont, 413-528-5100.

Greylock Credit Union

Pittsfield branches: 150 West St., 413-256-4000; 75 Kellogg, 413-443-5114; 660 Merrill Rd., 413-445-5555. Other branches: 2 Park St., Adams, 413-743-7333: 312 Main St., Gt. Barrington, 413-528-4567; 47 Main St., Lee, 413-243-2121; 66 Main St., N. Adams, 413-664-4477.

Hoosac Bank

93 Main St, N. Adams, 413-663-5353. Branch: 269 Main St., Williamstown, 413-458-9503.

Lee Bank

75 Park St., Lee; 413-243-2196. Branches: Elm St., Stockbridge, 413-298-3611, 279 Main St., Gt. Barrington, 413-528-5531.

Legacy Banks 800-292-6634

Pittsfield branches: 99 North St., St., 413-443-4421; 436 W. Housatonic St., 413-442-0533; 734 Williams St., 413-442-5611; 609 Merrill Rd., 413-443-3108; 555 Hubbard Ave., 413-499-7898. Lenox branches: 25 Main St., 413-637-0147; 2 Holmes Rd., 413-443-4433. Other branches: 700 Main St., Gt. Barrington, 413-528-4110; 76 Park St., Lee, 413-243-0115; 102 Main St., N. Adams, 413-664-6521; 30 E. Otis Rd., Otis, 413-269-4237.

Lenox National Bank

Lenox branches: 7 Main St., 413-637-0017; 481 Pittsfield Rd., 413-499-0717.

Pittsfield Co-operative Bank 888-447-7304
Pittsfield branches: 70 South St., 413-447-7304; 110 Dalton Ave., 413-395-9626. Other branches: 448 Main St., Dalton, 413-684-1551; 325 Main St., Gt. Barrington, 413-528-2840.

Pittsfield Municipal Federal Credit Union
101 Fenn St., Pittsfield, 413-442-6501.

S. Adams Savings Bank
2 Center St., Adams, 413-743-0040. Branches: State Rd., Cheshire, 413-743-0270; 273 Main St., Williamstown, 413-458-2141.

Williamstown Savings Bank
795 Main St., Williamstown, 413-458-8191.

BIBLIOGRAPHY

Here are two lists of books about the Berkshires, many of which we used in researching this book.

"Available Titles" shows books obtainable either through Berkshire bookshops, bookstores elsewhere, or from the publishers. For information on Berkshire booksellers, see "Bookstores" in Chapter Eight, *Shopping*.

"Harder to Find" suggests a wealth of other reading in publications no longer in print. Some of the more rarefied material on this list does not circulate outside of libraries, and usage may be restricted to those with professional credentials. Several popular items here will especially interest history buffs. The best sources for book borrowing are described under "Libraries" in Chapter Four, *Culture*.

Available Titles

COOKBOOKS

Chase, Suzi Forbes. *The New Red Lion Inn Cookbook.* Lee, MA.: Berkshire House, 2000. 272 pp., photos, $23.95.

Cook, Janey, ed. *Berkshire Victuals.* Stockbridge, MA: Berkshire County Historical Society, 1993. 208 pages, illus., $19.95. Historical and contemporary recipes.

Hopley, Claire. *New England Cooking: Seasons & Celebrations.* Lee, MA: Berkshire House Publishers, 2002. 272 pp., photos, $24.95.

Levitt, Atma Jo Ann. *The Kripalu Cookbook.* Lee, MA: Berkshire House, 1995. 448 pp., $16.95. Recipes featured at the Kripalu Center in Lenox, tailored for home use.

VanderStigchel, Armand, and Robert E. Birkel Jr. *Adirondack Cuisine.* Lee, MA: Berkshire House, 2002. 292 pp., photos, $24.95. Recipes from the region adjacent to—and easily accessible from—the Berkshires.

Williamstown Theatre Festival. *As You Like It.* Williamstown, MA: Williamstown Theatre Festival Guild, 1993. 222 pp., illus, $15.00. Recipes from the festival's stars, directors, writers, and associates.

LITERARY WORKS

The Berkshire Review. Pittsfield, MA: The Berkshire Writers Room. Literary annual devoted to poetry, fiction, plays, and essays by Berkshire authors.

Howard, Walter. *Sisyphus in the Hayfield: Views of A Berkshire Farmer.* Tyringham, MA: Cobble Press, 1988. 128 pp., photos, $14.

Melville, Herman. *Great Short Works of Herman Melville.* New York, NY: Harper & Row, 1969. 507 pp., bibliog. $18.50.

Metcalf, Paul, ed. *October Mountain: An Anthology of Berkshire Writers.* Williamstown, MA: Mountain Press, 1992. 163 pp., $11.95.

Nunley, Richard, ed. *The Berkshire Reader.* Lee, MA: Berkshire House, 1992. 544 pp., illus., $29.95.

Wharton, Edith. *A Backward Glance.* New York, NY: Charles Scribner's Sons, 1985 reprint. 379 pp., index, $13.95.

————. *Ethan Frome.* New York, NY: Scribner's, 1988 reprint. $5.95.

————. *Summer.* New York, NY: Scribner's, 1988 reprint. $10.00.

LOCAL HISTORIES

Babcock, Richard, and Lauren R. Stevens. *Old Barns in the New World.* Lee, MA: Berkshire House, 1996. 192 pp., photos, $21.95.

Burns, Deborah E. *Shaker Cities of Peace, Love, and Union: A History of the Hancock Bishopric.* Hanover, NH: University Press of New England, 1993, 246 pp., $45; $19.95 pap.

Burns, Deborah, E., and Lauren R. Stevens. *Most Excellent Majesty: A History of Mount Greylock.* Lee, MA: Berkshire House, 128 pp., photos, $8.95.

Cahill, Timothy, Mae G. Banner, Richard Nunley, Fred Sokol. *Muses in Arcadia: Cultural Life in the Berkshires.* Lee, MA: Berkshire House, 2000. 272 pp., illus. $19.95.

Chapman, Gerard. *Eminent Berkshire Women.* Gt. Barrington, MA: Attic Revivals Press, 1988. 32 pp., $5.00.

————. *Great Barrington* Gt. Barrington, MA: Gt. Barrington Historic Society, 1999. illus. $49.95.

A History of the Red Lion Inn in Stockbridge, Massachusetts. Stockbridge, MA: Red Lion Inn, 1987. 54 pp., illus., $12.00.

Drew, Bernard A. *Berkshire Further Off the Trail.* Gt. Barrington, MA: Attic Revivals Press, 1992. 56 pp., illus., $7.50.

————. *A History of Notchview Reservation: The Arthur D. Budd Estate in Windsor,*

Massachusetts. Gt. Barrington, MA: Attic Revivals Press, 1986, 48 pp., illus., maps, $5.00.

————. *History of The Mahaiwe Theatre in Great Barrington, Massachusetts*. Gt. Barrington, MA: Attic Revivals Press, 1989, 48 pp., illus., $5.00.

————. *Spanning Berkshire Waterways*. Gt. Barrington, MA: Attic Revivals Press, 1990. 32 pp., photos, maps, $5.00.

————. *William Cullen Bryant's "A Border Tradition."* Gt. Barrington, MA: Attic Revivals Press, 1988, 32 pp., bibliog., $6.50.

Drew, Bernard A., and Donna M. *Mapping the Berkshires*. Gt. Barrington, MA: Attic Revivals Press, 1985. 48 pp., illus. maps, $5.00.

Lee, Laura. *Arlo, Alice & Anglicans: The Lives of a New England Church*. Lee, MA: Berkshire House Publishers, 2000. 240 pp., illus., $16.95.

Miller, Amy Bess. *Hancock Shaker Village/The City of Peace: An Effort to Restore a Vision 1960–1985*. Hancock, MA: Hancock Shaker Village, 1984. 170 pp., illus., photos, appendices, bibliog., index, $19.95.

Murray, Stuart, and James McCabe. *Norman Rockwell's Four Freedoms*. Stockbridge, MA: Berkshire House, Publishers, 1993. 176 pp., illus., $14.95.

Owens, Carole. *The Berkshire Cottages: A Vanishing Era*. Stockbridge, MA: Cottage Press, 1984. 240 pp., photos, illus., index, $29.95.

Pincus, Andrew L. *Scenes from Tanglewood*. Boston, MA: Northeastern University Press, 1989. 287 pp., photos, $14.95.

The Stockbridge Story: 1739–1989. Stockbridge, MA: Town of Stockbridge, 1989. 209 pp., illus., photos, index, $25.00.

PHOTOGRAPHIC STUDIES

Bazan, John. *Rails Across the Berkshire Hills. Railroad Photography, 1890–1984*. Pittsfield, MA: The Author, 1984. Photos, $9.95.

Chefetz, Sheila. *Antiques for the Table*. New York, NY: Viking-Penguin, 1993. 232 pp., 275 color photos, bibliog., Berkshire resource directory, index. Many photographs of Berkshire summer cottages.

Gilder, Cornelia Brooke. *Views of the Valley: Tyringham 1739–1989*. Tyringham, MA: the Hopbrook Community Club, 1989. 142 pp., photos, $15.

Resch, Tyler, ed. *Images of America: Bill Tague's Berkshires*. Dover, NH: Arcadia Publishing, 1996. 128 pp., map, photos, $16.99. A Berkshire photographer's work from 1950s–1980s.

————. *Images of America: Bill Tague's Berkshires, Vol. II*. Dover, NH: Arcadia Publishing, 1998, 128 pp., photos. $16.95.

Scott, Walter. *The Norman Rockwell Bicycle Tours of Stockbridge*. Stockbridge, MA: SnO Publications, 1980. 32 post cards, $10.95.

RECREATION & NATURE

A Canoe Guide to the Housatonic River, Berkshire County. Pittsfield, MA: Berkshire County Regional Planning Commission. Illus., maps. Updated in 1994.

Appalachian Trail Guide to Massachusetts-Connecticut. Harpers Ferry, WV: Appalachian Trail Conference, 1990. 189 pp., maps, $18.95.

Cuyler, Lewis C. *Bike Rides in the Berkshire Hills*. Revised and updated edition. Lee, MA: Berkshire House, 1995. 200 pp., illus., maps, $9.95.

Laubach, Rene. *A Guide to Natural Places in the Berkshire Hills*. Second edition. Lee, MA: Berkshire House, 1997. 288 pp., illus., maps, $12.95.

Lyon, Steve. *Bicyclist's Guide to the Southern Berkshires*. Lenox, MA: Freewheel Publications, 1993. 256 pp., pap., $16.95.

Stevens, Lauren R. *Hikes & Walks in the Berkshire Hills*. Revised edition. Lee, MA: Berkshire House, 1998. 224 pp., maps, $14.95.

Strauch, Joseph G., Jr. *Wildflowers of the Berkshire & Taconic Hills*. Lee, MA: Berkshire House, 1995. 160 pp., maps, illus., $12.95.

Judith Monachina

The River Walk in Great Barrington is evidence of a growing awareness of the natural beauty of the Housatonic. A River Walk garden is devoted to W.E.B. DuBois, Great Barrington native son.

TRAVEL

The Berkshire Hills: A WPA Guide, with a new foreword by Roger Linscott. Boston, MA: Northeastern University Press, 1987. 390 pp., illus., photos, maps, lore, history, $14.95.

Bryan, Clark, W. *The Book of Berkshire*. N. Egremont, MA: Past Perfect Books, 1993 reprint. 304 pp., engravings, index, large color map of county, $24.95. A splendid reprint of the first guide to the Berkshires.

Davenport, John. *Berkshire-Bennington Locator*. Madison, WI: First Impressions, 1988. 112 pp., maps, $10.95.

Whitman, Herbert S. *Exploring the Berkshires*. New York, NY: Hippocrene, 1991. 240 pp., illus., $9.95.

Harder to Find

Annin, Katherine Huntington. *Richmond, Massachusetts: The Story of a Berkshire Town and Its People, 1765–1965*. Richmond, MA: Richmond Civic Association, 1964. 214 pp., photos, illus., index. Only complete, readable history of town.

Birdsall, Richard. *Berkshire County, A Cultural History*. New York, NY: Greenwood Press, 1978 reprint. 401 pp., notes, bibliog., index. Only cultural study of region; emphasis on first half of the 19th century. Chapters cover development of law, newspapers, education, religion. Special attention to the literary heritage.

Bittman, Sam, and Steven A. Satullo, eds. *Berkshire: Seasons of Celebration*. Pittsfield, MA: Either/Or Press, 1982. 112 pp., photos.

Boltwood, Edward. *The History of Pittsfield, Massachusetts from the Year 1876 to the Year 1916*. Pittsfield, MA: The City, 1916. Covers history of most important county communities to early 20th century.

Brooks, Robert R.R., ed. *Williamstown: The First Two Hundred Years* Williamstown, MA: the Town, 1953. 458 pp., 69 illus. A model of its kind.

Bulkley, Morgan. *Mountain Farm: Poems From the Berkshire Hills*. Chester, MA: Hollow Springs Press, 1984. 95 pp., illus.

Collections of the Berkshire Historical and Scientific Society. Pittsfield, MA: Sun Printing Co., 1892–1899. Papers on historical topics read at Society meetings. Often composed by local authorities, subjects range from Berkshire geology to glass manufacture in Berkshire. Often unique and usually reliable.

Consolati, Florence. *See All the People: Or, Life in Lee*. Lee, MA: The Author, 1978. Colorful, quaint history of the town and its citizens. 442 pp., photos, bibliog., index.

Coxey, Willard D. *Ghosts of Old Berkshire*. Gt. Barrington, MA: The Berkshire Courier, 1934. Legends and folk tales of Berkshire people and places.

Drew, Bernard A. *Berkshire Between Covers: A Literary History*. Gt. Barrington, MA: Attic Revivals Press, 1985. 32 pp., illus., bibliog. Brief biographical sketches of deceased fiction writers with significant connections to the Berkshires.

———. *Berkshire Off the Trail*. Gt. Barrington, MA: Attic Revival Press, 1982. 96 pp., illus., index. Informal history of less traditional subjects.

Emblidge, David, ed. *The Third Berkshire Anthology: A Collection of Literature and Art*. Lenox, MA: Berkshire Writers, Inc., 1982. 185 pp., illus.

Field, Stephen, ed. *A History of the County of Berkshire, Massachusetts*. Pittsfield, MA: Samuel W. Bush, 1829. Perhaps the first history of the Berkshires, sponsored by the Berkshire Association of Congregational Ministers. A general history of the county, followed by accounts of individual towns, each written by its minister.

Jones, Electa F. *Stockbridge, Past and Present: Or, Records of an Old Mission Station*. Springfield, MA: Samuel Bowles & Co., 1854. History of Indian mission and Stockbridge Indians.

Kupferberg, Herbert. *Tanglewood*. New York, NY: McGraw-Hill, 1976. 280 pp., photos, bibliog., index. Most thorough history of the Berkshire Music Festival.

Lewis, Joseph W. *Berkshire Men of Worth*. 4 Vols. Scrapbook of newspaper articles. From 1933 until well after Lewis's death in 1938, over 300 columns on Berkshire notables were published in the *Berkshire Evening Eagle*. Series featured penetrating biographical sketches of men whom Lewis regarded as important historical figures. Perhaps the most comprehensive biographical treatment of historical Berkshire figures.

Oakes, Donald, ed. *A Pride of Palaces: Lenox Summer Cottages, 1883–1933*. Lenox, MA: Lenox Library, 1981. 83 pp., illus., photos.

Perry, Arthur L. *Origins in Williamstown*. New York, NY: Charles Scribner's Sons, 1896. Detailed, well-researched history of early Williamstown and other segments of northern Berkshire.

Preiss, Lillian E. *Sheffield, Frontier Town*. Sheffield, MA: Sheffield Bicentennial Comm., 1976. 188 pp., photos, illus., bibliog., index. Good, traditional town history.

Resch, Tyler, ed. *Berkshire, The First Three Hundred Years 1676–1976*. Pittsfield, MA: Eagle Pub. Co., 1976. 163 pp., photos, illus., maps, bibliog., index. Photographs and illustrations of significant and interesting historical events and people, with concise captions.

Sedgwick, Sarah Cabot and Christina Sedgwick Marquand. *Stockbridge, 1739–1939: A Chronicle*. Stockbridge, MA: The Authors, 1939. 306 pp., photos, illus., bibliog. Popular, readable history.

Smith, J.E.A., ed. *History of Berkshire County, Massachusetts, With Biographical Sketches of Its Prominent Men*. 2 vols. New York, NY: J. B. Beers & Co., 1885. Wide-ranging history covering every aspect of Berkshire life. Nine chapters on individual towns. Most comprehensive, reliable history of the first 200 years of Berkshire development.

———. *The History of Pittsfield (Berkshire County), Massachusetts, From the Year 1734 to the Year 1800*. Boston, MA: Lee, Shepard, 1869. *The History of Pittsfield (Berkshire County), Massachusetts, From the Year 1800 to the Year 1876*. Springfield, MA: C.W. Bryan & Co., 1876. The most detailed, thorough town histories for the county. Smith had access to much material since lost; covers surrounding communities, as well.

Taylor, Charles J. *History of Great Barrington (Berkshire), Massachusetts 1676–1882. Part II, Extension 1882-1922* by George Edwin MacLean. Gt. Barrington, MA, 1928. Detailed, accurate history of town, particularly the Taylor segment.

Wood, David H. *Lenox, Massachusetts Shire Town*. Lenox, MA, 1968. Similar to Sedgwick history of Stockbridge but more detailed.

CLIMATE AND WEATHER REPORTS

Judith Monachina

A winter scene in Richmond.

CLIMATE

How the Berkshire climate strikes us depends on what we're used to. People visiting from outside the region may be helped by the following information.

In general, while summers are blessedly mild due to the elevation of the Berkshire Hills, winters can be cold and snowy with tricky driving conditions. Of course, what someone who doesn't ski finds annoying in a New England winter greases the skis for another. Summer visitors should remember that nights can be cool; bring sweaters. And those in search of great snow should note that spring comes to South County well before it does up north and up higher. One morning we cross-country skied on good snow at Notchview in Windsor; that afternoon we rototilled the garden in Great Barrington.

TEMPERATURE AND PRECIPITATION

Average Temperature

October	48.4° F
January	20.4°
April	43.4°
July	68.3°

Average Annual Total Precipitation

Rainfall plus water content of snow	44.15"
Snow	75.7"

For people who are really into statistics or are interested for business or investment purposes, the source for this information and a great deal more, *The Berkshire County Data Book*, is available (for $100) from the Berkshire County Regional Planning Commission (413-442-1521; Dunham Mall, Pittsfield, MA 01201).

WEATHER REPORTS

Great Barrington	413-528-1118
Pittsfield	413-499-2627
North Adams	413-663-6264

GUIDED TOURS

For those wanting to be bused directly to Berkshire's high spots by an informed guide, there are hosts of possibilities, some based here in the hills, some coming from New York and Boston. From the big cities, there are fall-foliage tours, Tanglewood tours, and ski tours, all of which provide transport, tickets, meals, and lodging plus background on the sites. For an individual, these tours offer a taste of the area's delights in a perfectly packaged form. For groups, the tours turn a possible logistical nightmare into a fun-filled holiday.

In New York or Boston, a travel agent may be helpful in choosing the right tour. The best of the commercial tour companies belong to the National Tour Association. The best of the charter bus companies belong to the American Bus Association. Here are a few of the most experienced Berkshire guided-tour companies operating from New York and Boston.

NEW YORK

Parker Tours: 516-349-0575, 800-833-9600; 255 Executive Dr., Plainview, NY 11803.
Tauck Tours: 203-226-6911, 800-468-2825; 276 Post Rd. W., Westport, CT 06880.

BOSTON

Collette Tours: 401-728-3805, 800-752-2655 (in New England exc. Maine), 800-832-4656; 162 Middle St., Pawtucket, RI 02860.

WITHIN THE BERKSHIRES

Within Berkshire, there are also a number of guided-tour options. For something relatively brief and informal, a local cab driver can usually be persuaded to drive around, adding colorful histories that only a cabbie might know. For more organized, detailed tours, consider the following.

Berkshire Tour Company (413-443-5778; 86 Sampson Pkwy., Pittsfield, MA 01201) Berkshire native Nancy C. Hickey provides a wide range of tour services, including group tours of Berkshire County sites (a favorite is the Berkshire Cottages tour), plus walking tours of the Main Streets of Stockbridge, Lenox, and Williamstown. She also provides customized tours including lunch or dinner at local restaurants, excursions to Tanglewood and other music and theater festivals, and combinations of tours for individuals or any size group. Phone for prices and schedules.

Greylock Discovery Tours (413-637-4442; goactive@aol.com; PO Box 2231, Lenox, MA 01240) See "Walking, Hiking, Camping, X-C Skiing" in Chapter Seven, *Outdoor Recreation.*

SERVICES FOR THE DISABLED

Although Berkshire is a region with lots of rough terrain, the disabled will find access quite easy to most cultural sites and events, to many lodgings and restaurants, and to most shops. In Chapter Three, *Lodging*, we specify those places where we know handicapped access is feasible. Elsewhere, to confirm the situation, use the phone numbers we provide to get information.

The **Berkshire Visitors Bureau** (413-443-9186 or 413-237-5747; Berkshire Common, Plaza Level, Pittsfield) publishes an annual guide listing many Berkshire services and attractions, in many cases, specifying access to the disabled. The *AAA Tour Guide*, available through **AAA Berkshire County** (413-445-5635; 703 W. Housatonic St., Pittsfield, MA 01201) also designates restaurants, lodging, etc. with universal access.

As for transportation, the **Berkshire Regional Transit Authority** (413-499-2782 or in county 800-292-2782) runs the public bus system throughout the major towns in the county and has buses equipped with wheelchair lifts. See Chapter Two, *Transportation*, "Getting Around the Berkshires" for more information.

HOSPITALS

GREAT BARRINGTON

Fairview Hospital: 413-528-0790; 29 Lewis Ave.

PITTSFIELD

Berkshire Medical Center: 413-447-2000; 725 North St.
Hillcrest Hospital: 413-443-4761; 165 Tor Ct.

NORTH ADAMS

North Adams Regional Hospital: 413-663-3701; Hospital Ave.

LATE NIGHT FOOD AND FUEL

Convenience Plus (food and fuel) Open all night: 90 Tyler St., Pittsfield, 413-499-1741; 241 Main St., Lee, 413-243-2399; open till 11 p.m.: South St., Stockbridge, 413-298-4036.

Cumberland Farms (food and fuel) Open all night: 70 Ashland St., North Adams, 413-662-2721; 885 Dalton Ave., Pittsfield, 413-496-9774; 154 First St., Pittsfield, 413-443-4478; 707 Main St., Dalton, 413-684-1465.

Dakota Restaurant (food) Open till 11pm, Fri.–Sat.: Pittsfield-Lenox Rd., Pittsfield, 413-499-7900.

Dunkin' Donuts (food) Open all night: 5 Union St., North Adams, 413-662-2274; 18 First St., Pittsfield, 413-499-0371; 200 Housatonic St., Lee, 413-243-1676.

Fillin' Station Too (fuel) Pumps open all night, exc. Fri. till midnight: Lee Travel Plaza, Rte. 102, Lee, 413-243-4411.

Jimmy's (food) Open till midnight Fri.–Sat.: 114 W. Housatonic, Pittsfield, 413-499-1288.

Luau Hale (food) Open till midnight Fri.-Sat.: Pittsfield-Lenox Rd., Lenox, 413-443-4745.

P. J.'s Convenience Store (food) Open till 11:30pm Mon.–Sat.: 139 S. Main, Sheffield, 413-229-6610

Papa Joe's Ristorante & Pizzeria (food) Open till 11pm Fri.–Sat.: 107 Newell St., Pittsfield, 413-499-2151.

Price Chopper Supermarkets (food) Open all night Mon.–Fri., Sat. till midnight: 121 Pittsfield Rd., Rte. 7, Lenox, 413-443-5449; open till midnight Mon.–Sat., till 7 p.m., Sun: 300 Stockbridge Rd., Rte. 7, Great Barrington, 413-528-9262, and 88 W. Park St., Lee, 413-243-2238.

Stop & Shop Supermarket (food) Open all night Mon.–Fri.; Sat. till midnight: 600 Merrill Rd., Pittsfield, 413-499-0745.

MEDIA: NEWSPAPERS AND RADIO STATIONS

MAGAZINES AND NEWSPAPERS

The Advocate (413-664-6900; 111 MASS MoCA Way, N. Adams, MA 01247; Wednesdays) Readable freebie, well-researched articles, mostly on community-related topics, for northern Berkshire and southwestern Vermont.

The Berkshire Eagle (413-447-7311; 75 S. Church St., Pittsfield, MA 01201; daily) The county's newspaper of record, seven days, a Pulitzer Prize-winning publication with extensive world, national, state, and local news, plus features and comics *(Doonesbury!)*. Thursdays for half the year the *Eagle* also publishes *Berkshires Week*, a supplementary magazine-in-newsprint containing a calendar of events and lots of ads from local dining and entertainment places.

Berkshire Penny Saver (413-243-2341; 14 Park Pl., Box 300, Lee, MA 01238; Tuesday) Central County's free shopping guide, including classifieds, TV listings, nightlife, comprehensive business service listings.

The Berkshire Record (413-528-5380; 21 Elm St., Gt. Barrington, MA 01230; weekly) Southern Berkshire weekly features current affairs and articles of historic note.

Berkshire Trade & Commerce (413-447-7700; 137 North St., Pittsfield, MA 01201; monthly) This freebie is Berkshire's answer to the *Wall Street Journal*. Lively up-to-date news of Berkshire business doings.

Country Journal (413-667-3211; 25 Main St., Huntington, Hampshire County; Thursdays) Covers 16 of the central hill towns.

The Paper (518-392-2674; PO Box 336, Chatham, NY 112037; monthly). A features freebie published the first Thursday of the month.

The Pittsfield Gazette (413-443-2010; 141 North St., Pittsfield; Thursday) Lively, even acerbic local Pittsfield news.

Shopper's Guide (413-528-0095; Bridge St., Box 89, Gt. Barrington, MA 01230; weekly) Southern Berkshire's shopping guide, including enticing sections on real estate and automobiles.

The South Advocate (413-637-8840; 27 Church St., Lenox, MA 01240; Wednesdays). *Advocate* replated for Lee and Lenox.

The Transcript (413-663-3741; American Legion Dr., N. Adams, MA 01247; weekday noons, Saturday morning) Local, some state and national news; covers northern Berkshire County and southern Vermont.

Women's Times (413-528-5303; 323 Main St., Box 390, Gt. Barrington, MA 01230; monthly) A classy, well-written magazine-style paper, with articles by, for, and about Berkshire women. Free.

Yankee Shopper (413-684-1373; 839 Main St., Box 96, Dalton, MA 01226; weekly) Central and Northern Berkshire's shopping guide, including scads of used cars, rototillers, computers, vacuum cleaners, and baby bunnies as well as a business/professional services directory.

RADIO STATIONS

National Public Radio. There are five stations receivable in the Berkshires:
WBTN-FM 94.3; 800-639-2192; Vermont Public Radio, Bennington, Vt.
WAMC-FM 90.3; 800-323-9262; Northeast Public Radio, Albany, NY.
WAMQ-FM 105.1; 800-323-9262; Northeast Public Radio, Albany, NY
WFCR-FM 88.5; 413-545-0100; Amherst, MA.
WMHT-FM 89.1; 518-356-1700; Schenectady, NY.
Other Local Radio Stations:
WBEC-AM 1420; 413-499-3333; Pittsfield. General.
WBEC-FM 105.5; 413-499-3333; Pittsfield. Rock music.
WBRK-AM 101; 413-442-1553; Pittsfield. General.
WCFM-FM 91.9; 413-597-2373; Williams College.
WJJW-FM, 91; 413-662-5405; Massachusetts College of Liberal Arts.
WMNB-FM, 100.1; 413-663-6567; North Adams. General.
WNAW-AM, 1230; 413-663-6567; North Adams. General
WNAW-FM, 100.0; 413-663-6567; North Adams. General.
WSBS-AM, 860; 413-528-0860; Great Barrington. General.
WUHN-AM, 1110; 413-499-1100; Pittsfield. General.
WUPE-FM, 96; 413-499-1100; Pittsfield. Rock and other music.

TELEVISION

Local public-access television, run mostly by community volunteers, brings important meetings, events and opinion to listeners who subscribe to cable television.

In addition to live broadcast of town meetings, city council meetings, and other events of civil and local interest, the locally run stations in each region generate other programs such as live viewer call-ins, self-help, and religious programs, along with musical and dramatic entertainments by local performers.

Community-based television channels:
Community Television for the Southern Berkshires (CTSB): Channel 11 (413-243-0676).
Pittsfield Community Television: Warner Cable Channel 5 (413-443-4755).
North Berkshire Community Television: Adelphia Channels 15, 16, and 17 (413-664-4408).
WilliNet (Williamstown): Adelphia Channels 15, 16, and 17 (413-458-0900).
Consult the *Berkshire Eagle* for schedules.

REAL ESTATE

What's our dream house? An isolated cabin deep in the woods? A late 20th-century split-level suburban tract house? A lakeside condo for time-sharing? Or a 40-room Gilded Age mansion that just needs a couple of hundred grand in handyman repairs? Berkshire County has them all.

Those shopping for Berkshire real estate can obtain information as follows.

Lists of realtors: Consult the Yellow Pages of the telephone book or contact any of the three Chambers of Commerce: **Southern Berkshire Chamber of Commerce** (413-528-1510; 362 Main St., Gt. Barrington, MA 01230); **Central Berkshire Chamber of Commerce** (413-499-4000; 66 West St., Pittsfield, MA 01201); **Northern Berkshire Chamber of Commerce** (413-663-3735; 69-1/2 Main St., N. Adams, MA 01247). All three organizations will send a list of their realtor members. The seasonal tourist information brochures from the **Berkshire Hills Conference** (413-443-9186; 50 South St., Pittsfield, MA 01201) also list numerous realtors.

Potential buyers of land or house should check with the local town government about zoning laws, building permits, and the like. Such regulations vary widely from town to town. See: "Town Halls" in this chapter for telephone numbers.

Buyers can also follow the real estate market in the newspapers; see "Media" in this chapter. *The Berkshire Home Buyers Guide* is a free monthly publication, distributed in local shops or available from: 413-243-2500; 80 Run Way, Lee, MA 01238.

RELIGIOUS SERVICES AND ORGANIZATIONS

Berkshire County has an active and unusually diverse religious community. The best source for information about church and synagogue services is the Saturday edition of the *Berkshire Eagle*. The Berkshire County Telephone Directory has a comprehensive list of all mainstream religious organizations, under the headings "Churches" and "Synagogues." Nontraditional groups should keep an eye on community bulletin boards at the area's colleges and in towns such as Great Barrington, Stockbridge, Lenox, Pittsfield, and Williamstown.

ROAD SERVICE

Emergency road service from **AAA,** anywhere in the county, can be obtained by calling 413-443-1635, Pittsfield. For non-AAA drivers, the following is a listing of emergency towing services.

South County
Bachetti's Auto: Sheffield   413-528-5410
Decker's Auto Body: Great Barrington   413-528-1432
John's Garage: Housatonic   413-274-3328
Mac's Garage: Great Barrington   413-528-1234
R W's Inc.: Lee   413-243-0946
Stockbridge Motors: Stockbridge   413-298-4780

Central County
All Hours Towing & Repairs: Pittsfield   413-442-8765
Berkshire County Towing: Pittsfield   413-443-0881
County Auto Wrecking: Pittsfield   413-443-6665
Dickson's Towing Service: Pittsfield   413-442-6188
Sayers' Auto: Pittsfield   413-443-1635
Scratch-A-Ticket Towing: Pittsfield   413-443-1754
Southgate Motors: Pittsfield   413-445-5971
Village Truck Sales: Lanesborough   413-442-0407

North County
Al's Service Center: Adams   413-743-7797
Bator's Service & Sales: Cheshire   413-743-3578
Carpinello's Service Center: Williamstown   413-458-2528
Dean's Quality Auto & Truck Repair: North Adams   413-664-6378
Ernies's Auto Sales: North Adams   413-663-3503
Mohawk Auto Wrecking: North Adams   413-663-6835
North Adams Tire & Service: North Adams   413-664-6362
Ron's Auto Repair: Williamstown   413-458-2238
T&M Auto Sales: North Adams   413-664-6697
West End Auto Body & Glass: North Adams   413-664-6708

SCHOOLS

PUBLIC SCHOOL DISTRICTS

South County
Berkshire Hills Regional School District, Stockbridge; 413-298-3711
Farmington River Regional; 413-269-7105
Lee Public Schools; 413-243-0276
Southern Berkshire Regional School District, Sheffield; 413-229-8778

Central County
Central Berkshire Regional School District, Dalton; 413-684-1330
Lenox Public Schools; 413-637-5550

Monument Mountain High School students decorate Great Barrington stores every Halloween.

Judith Monachina

Richmond Consolidated Schools; 413-698-2207
Pittsfield Public Schools; 413-499-9512

North County
Adams-Cheshire Regional School District; 413-743-2939
Clarksburg School Department; 413-664-8735
Florida School Department; 413-664-6023
Lanesborough Schools; 413-442-2229
Mount Greylock Regional School District; 413-458-9582
New Ashford School Department; 413-458-5461
North Adams Public Schools; 413-662-3225
Northern Berkshire Vocational; 413-663-5383
Savoy School Department; 413-743-1992
Williamstown Public Schools; 413-458-5707

PRIVATE AND RELIGIOUS SCHOOLS

South County
Berkshire School: Sheffield; 413-229-8511
De Sisto School: Stockbridge; 413-298-3776
Great Barrington Rudolf Steiner School: Great Barrington; 413-528-4015
The Kolburne School: New Marlborough; 413-229-8787
St. Mary's School: Lee; 413-243-1079

Central County
Berkshire Country Day School: Lenox; 413-637-0755
Berkshire County Christian School: Pittsfield; 413-442-4014
Hillcrest Educational Centers: Lenox, Great Barrington, Pittsfield, and Hancock.

Miss Hall's School: Pittsfield; 413-443-6401
Sacred Heart School: Pittsfield; 413-443-6379
St. Agnes School: Dalton; 413-684-3143
St. Joseph's High School: Pittsfield; 413-447-9121

North County
Buxton School: Williamstown; 413-458-3919
Pine Cobble School: Williamstown; 413-458-4680
St. Stanislaus: Adams; 413-743-1091

COLLEGES

Berkshire Community College: Pittsfield; 413-499-4660. In Great Barrington: 413-528-4521.
Massachusetts College of Liberal Arts: North Adams; 413-662-5000.
Simon's Rock College of Bard: Great Barrington; 413-528-0771
Williams College: Williamstown; 413-597-3131

TOURIST INFORMATION

Volunteers in several Berkshire towns staff tourist information booths in the summer and early fall. Often information is available at the site even when the volunteers aren't. Year-round tourist information can be obtained from **The Berkshires Visitors Bureau** (413-443-9186, 413-237-5747; Berkshire Common, Plaza Level, Pittsfield). The bureau is open Mon.–Fri., 8:30–4:30. Lodging information can be obtained through **Berkshire Bed & Breakfast Reservation Service** (413-268-7244) and from the **Berkshire Lodgings Association** (413-298-4760, 800-298-4760). Chambers of commerce, listed below, serve the commercial and business needs of the community and can be the source of information on special events.

South County
Chamber of Commerce of South Berkshire: Business office: 248 Main St., Gt. Barrington, MA 01230; 413-528-4284. Information booth: 362 Main St., Gt. Barrington; 413-528-1510. Lodging information: 413-528-4006.
Lee Information Booth: Main St. at the park; 413-243-0852.
Massachusetts Turnpike Information: Eastbound mile marker 8, Lee; 413-243-4929.
Stockbridge Chamber of Commerce: Business office: 7 Elm St.; 413-298-5200; www.stockbridgechamber.org. Information booth: Main St.; 413-298-5200. Lodging information: 413-298-5327.
West Stockbridge Information Booth: Corner Main St. (Rte 102) and Depot St., next to Berkshire Bank.

Central County

Chamber of Commerce of the Berkshires: 66 West St., Pittsfield, MA 01201; 413-499-4000

Lenox Chamber of Commerce: Information office: Lenox Academy, 65 Main St. PO Box 646; 413-637-3646, 800-40-LENOX; www.lenox.org. Summer: 48 Main St.

Pittsfield Information Booth: Bank Row, Park Square.

North County

Adams Chamber of Commerce: at NBCC below; 413-743-1881.

Northern Berkshire Chamber of Commerce: Business office: 57 Main St., N. Adams; 413-663-3735. **Information Booth:** (summer and fall) Union St.

Williamstown Chamber of Commerce: Gatehouse, foot of Spring St., 413-458-9077. Information Booth: Rte. 7 and Main St.; 413-458-4922.

Lee High School Band gets ready for a parade.

Judith Monachina

IF TIME IS SHORT

Berkshire offers so much to the visitor that longer sojourns are most rewarding, but sometimes that isn't possible. Here are some recommendations from the author, the publisher, and the editor from their personal favorites among the multitude of attractions that best exemplify the spirit of Berkshire County and might perfectly suit the visitor with only a weekend or a few days available for a first visit.

LODGING

The Red Lion Inn (413-298-5545; www.redlioninn.com; 30 Main St., Stockbridge) Satisfying meals, an excellent range of lodging options, and endless collections of fine furniture and antiques in a rambling, century-old inn in the old style, pleasing visitors and locals since 1793.

The Orchards (413-458-9611; 222 Adams Rd., Williamstown; off Rte. 2,) A superb small luxury hotel offering a formal clublike atmosphere. Huge rooms, many with bay windows and fireplaces, plus an award-winning restaurant. The service throughout is honed to a fine edge.

RESTAURANTS

Castle Street Café (413 528-5244, 10 Castle St., Gt. Barrington) An American bistro in South County in a charming, brick-walled cafe.

Elm Court Inn (413-528-0325; www.elmcourtinn.com; Rte. 71, N. Egremont) Pleasant inn in South County serving continental cuisine in a cozy traditional setting.

The Mill on the Floss (413-458-9123; Rte. 7, New Ashford) One of the greater gourmet experiences in North County, offering excellent French cuisine in an informal setting.

FOOD PURVEYORS

The Store At Five Corners (413-458-3176; junction of Rtes. 7 & 43, S. Williamstown) A wonderful assortment of gourmet foods, wines, oils, jellies for gift baskets, prepared food for picnics, delicious ice creams and yogurt in a renovated Victorian building. Creative cooks will delight in the myriad offerings, and novice cooks will be inspired to experiment. They can even buy the newest cookbooks to assure culinary success. Devoted noncooks should just stock up on the delicious ready-made salads, casseroles, and baked goods.

CULTURE

MUSEUMS

The Sterling & Francine Clark Art Institute (413-458-9545; www.clark art.edu; 225 South St., Williamstown) Among the museums in the county, the one with the longest-standing national reputation; renowned for its collection of Impressionists, especially Renoir.

Williams College Museum of Art (413-597-2429; www.williams.edu/ WCMA; Main St., Williamstown; Rte. 2) One of the finest college museums in the country and a leading research center. Emphasis on early art and 20th-century American art, to complement the 19th-century collection at the Clark.

MASS MoCA (413-664-4481, www.massmoca.org; 87 Marshall St., N. Adams) The miraculous result of twelve years' work to convert an old mill into a "supercollidor of the best of today's visual, performing, and new media arts" (in director Joe Thompson's words). The 13-acre, 27-building campus houses art from the gigantic to the minimal and is home to performances of every stripe.

Norman Rockwell Museum (413-298-4100; www.nrm.org; Rte. 183, Stock-bridge) Even connoisseurs of fine art find themselves captivated by Rockwell's evocations of America as we always wanted it to be. A guaranteed hit with every member of the family.

Hancock Shaker Village (413-443-0188; www.hancockshakervillage.org; Rte. 20, near Pittsfield-Hancock line) Beautifully restored Shaker village, with numerous exhibits, Shaker buildings, and events for the whole family.

SUMMER MUSIC

Tanglewood (413-637-1666, 413-637-5165; www.bso.org; West St., Lenox; Rte. 183) The obvious choice for the visitor with but one evening or day. Shed concerts Friday and Saturday evenings and Sunday afternoons from early July through late August; Wednesday or Thursday evening recitals in Seiji Ozawa Hall; operas in the newly refitted Concert Hall. In addition to concerts by the Boston Symphony Orchestra and visiting soloists, students of Tanglewood's summer program aspiring professionals give numerous concerts in all venues seven days a week. Popular or jazz artists take the stage at the end of August. The grounds, justly famous for their cultivated beauty, are great for a stroll or a picnic.

South Mountain Concerts (413-442-2106; Rtes. 7 & 20, Pittsfield) Chamber music for the serious listener, primarily string quartets but other combinations, too. Concerts are in a historic building built expressly for small ensembles, in a wooded setting above Pittsfield. Five Sunday afternoon concerts during September and early October.

Tannery Pond Concerts (518-794-7887, or for reservations/tickets call 888-846-5848; Rte. 20, New Lebanon, NY) Five chamber concerts, about one a month between late May and early October. Superb rising stars along with internationally renowned performers, in a former Shaker tannery now converted to a rustic and acoustically excellent hall situated in a beautiful meadow on the grounds of the Darrow School.

SUMMER THEATER

Berkshire Theatre Festival (413-298-5576, 413-298-5536 off season; www.berkshiretheatre.org; E. Main St., Stockbridge; Rte. 102,) and **Williamstown Theatre Festival** (413-597-3400; www.wtfestival.org; Main St., Williamstown) The two granddaddies of American summer stock theater vie with each other to present superior theater in charming settings. Both offer main stage and studio presentations, traditional and new works from mid-June through Labor Day. Call ahead for schedules and reservations.

Shakespeare & Company (413-637-3353 box office, 413-637-1199 off season; www.shakespeare.org; 70 Kemble St., Lenox) Shakespeare's classics and modern plays presented with feeling and clarity by the celebrated company led by Tina Packer and Dennis Krausnick. Longtime resident of the Edith Wharton house, the company now has its own glorious—and growing—campus in downtown Lenox.

RECREATION

Monument Mountain Reservation (413-298-3239; Stockbridge Rd., Gt. Barrington.; Rte. 7) 503 acres. A short but rugged climb up Squaw Peak, the reservation's most prominent feature, offers excellent views of three states from a summit 1,642 feet above sea level.

Mount Greylock State Reservation (413-499-4262; Rockwell Rd., Lanesborough; off Rte. 7, also accessible from Notch Road, N. Adams) 12,000 acres, including the state's highest peak, along with 45 miles of trails.

SHOPPING

ANTIQUES

The Painted Porch (413-229-2700; 102 S. Main St., Sheffield; Rte. 7) A lovely new shop carrying French and English country furniture arranged in vignettes to help one visualize the pieces in one's own home.

Greylock Cottage (413 243-1115; 52 Main St., Lee) A charming shop with lots of collectibles displayed beautifully and priced fairly.

CLOTHING

Evviva! (413-637-9875; 22 Walker St., Lenox) The clever window displays capture the sophistication and variety of clothing and accessories offered. Dresses for special events, romantic hats, unique jewelry, casual country clothes, and hand-painted silks combine to create a feast for the eye. The windows (which change monthly) are fascinating in and of themselves. A recent expansion has added shoes to the mix.

Steven Valenti (413-443-2569; 157 North St., Pittsfield) A men's store with an emphasis on customer satisfaction and stylish yet comfortable clothes for all occasions.

Zanna (413-458-9858; 41 Spring St.) Contemporary women's clothes and accessories, featuring natural fibers and up-to-the-minute looks. Also a selection of sophisticated yet comfortable shoes.

BOOKS

Bookloft (413-528-1521; Barrington Plaza, Stockbridge Rd., Gt. Barrington) a popular source for best-sellers and books about the Berkshires, with a knowledgeable staff in a pleasant setting.

The Bookstore (413-637-3390; 11 Housatonic St., Lenox) A most knowledgeable owner and a slightly 1970s air makes this a great place to browse and chat about books.

GIFTS

Hammertown Barn (413-528-7766; 325 Stockbridge Rd., Gt. Barrington) gifts for decorators, cooks, brides-to-be, or anyone on the list who is an aficionado of what's hot and hip for today country lifestyle.

Mistral's (413-528-1618; 7 Railroad St., Gt. Barrington) A most elegant, sophisticated collection of tableware, linens, and home furnishings from France. The upstairs houses a collection of items for the bed and bath. A beautiful shop to visit for an infusion of French chic.

Pamela Loring Gifts & Interiors (413-243-2689; 40 Main St., Lee) Very attractive shop on Main Street with excellent service, they will wrap packages and provide gift cards. Mostly giftware with an emphasis on floral, pretty gifts for women, and seasonal merchandise.

B. Mango & Bird (413-637-2611; 74 Main St., Lenox) Deep red walls set off an eclectic collection of accessories for home and table. Witty tapes, clever cards, and toys for adults round out the offerings in this shop.

Urban Country (413 528-6456; 635 S. Main St., Gt. Barrington) Stylish shop with an emphasis on country simplicity and sophistication.

FOR FUN . . .

Homegoods (413-236-6996; 676 Merrill Rd., Pittsfield) and **Sappa** (413-528-9592; 308 Main St., Gt. Barrington) are at different ends of the spectrum in relationship to style, but each is fun in its own way for shopping.

Where'd You Get That!? (413-458-2206; www.wygt.com; 20A Spring St., Williamstown) a delightful store with books, toys, and unique gifts to tickle the funnybones of kids 3 to 100!

Index

LODGING BY PRICE CODE

RESTAURANTS BY PRICE CODE

RESTAURANTS BY CUISINE

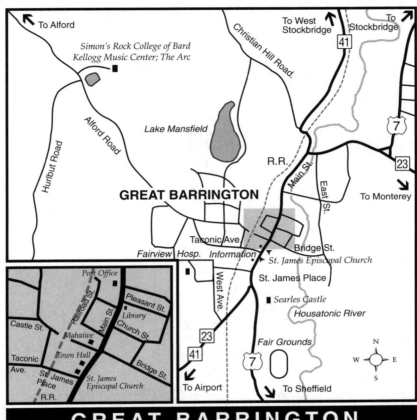

GREAT BARRINGTON

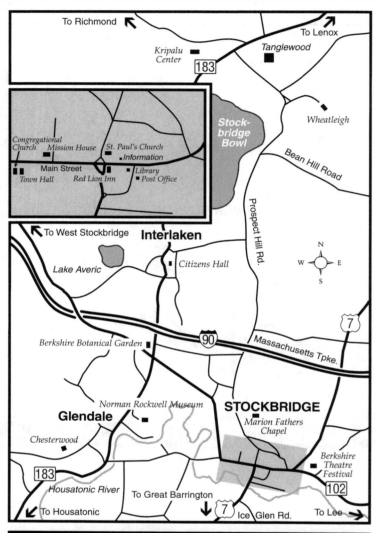

STOCKBRIDGE

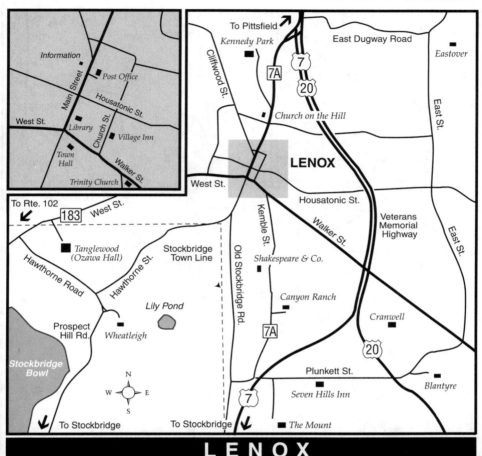

LENOX

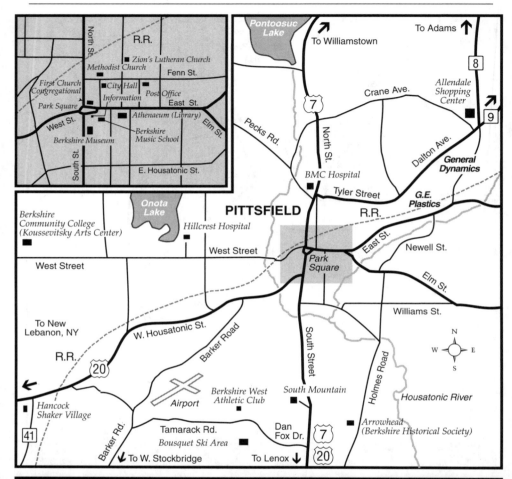

PITTSFIELD

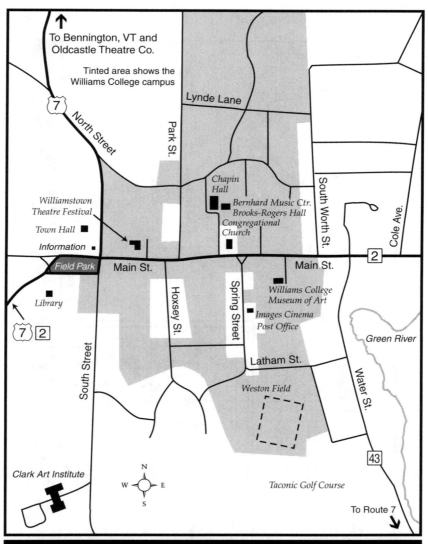

To Bennington, VT and Oldcastle Theatre Co.

Tinted area shows the Williams College campus

Lynde Lane

7

North Street

Park St.

Chapin Hall

Bernhard Music Ctr.
Brooks-Rogers Hall
Congregational Church

South Worth St.

Cole Ave.

Williamstown Theatre Festival

Town Hall

Information

2

Field Park   Main St.   Main St.

Library

7 2

Williams College Museum of Art

Hoxsey St.

Spring Street

Images Cinema
Post Office

Green River

South Street

Latham St.

Water St.

Weston Field

43

Clark Art Institute

N
W   E
S

Taconic Golf Course

To Route 7

WILLIAMSTOWN

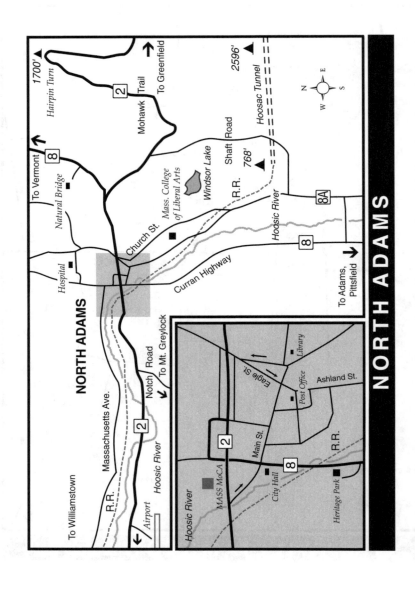

NORTH ADAMS

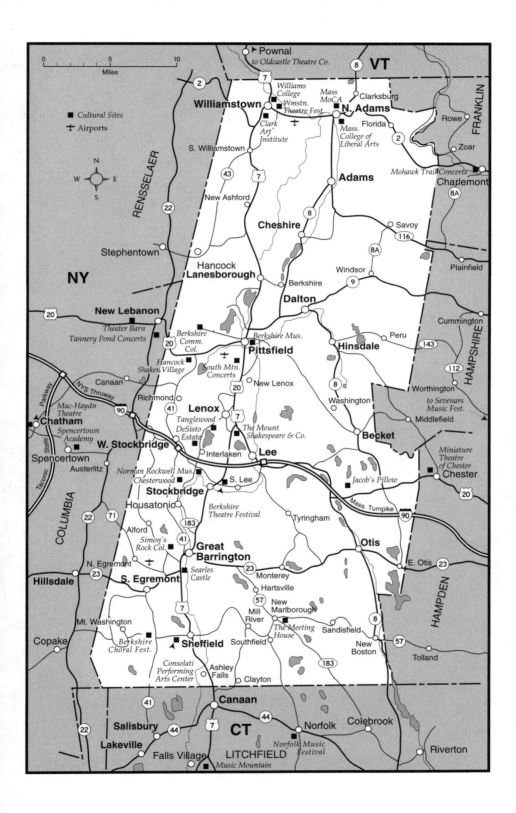

0   5   10
Miles

■ *Cultural Sites*
✚ *Airports*

N
W   E
S

VT

➤ Pownal
to Oldcastle Theatre Co.

RENSSELAER

Williamstown
Williams College
Wmstn. Theatre Fest.
Clark Art Institute

Mass MoCA
○ Clarksburg

N. Adams

Mass. College of Liberal Arts

○ Florida
○ Rowe

FRANKLIN

○ Zoar

Mohawk Trail Concerts
Charlemont

S. Williamstown

○ New Ashford

Adams

Cheshire

○ Savoy

NY

Stephentown ○

Hancock
Lanesborough

○ Berkshire

○ Windsor

Plainfield

Dalton

Peru ○

Cummington ○

HAMPSHIRE

New Lebanon
Theater Barn
Tannery Pond Concerts

Berkshire Comm. Col.

Berkshire Mus.
■ **Pittsfield**

Hinsdale

Worthington ○
to Sevenars Music Fest.

Canaan ○
Hancock Shaker Village

South Mtn. Concerts

○ New Lenox

○ Washington

Middlefield ○

Richmond ○

Lenox
Tanglewood
DeSisto Estate

The Mount Shakespeare & Co.

Becket

Miniature Theatre of Chester
Chester

Mac-Haydn Theatre
Chatham
Spencertown Academy

W. Stockbridge

Interlaken ○

Lee

Norman Rockwell Mus.
Chesterwood

○ S. Lee

Jacob's Pillow

Spencertown ○
Austerlitz ○

Stockbridge
Housatonic ○

Berkshire Theatre Festival

○ Tyringham

Mass. Turnpike

COLUMBIA

Alford ○
Simon's Rock Col.

Great Barrington

Otis

○ E. Otis

Searles Castle

○ Monterey

N. Egremont ○

S. Egremont

Hillsdale

○ Hartsville

Mill River ○
New Marlborough

The Meeting House

○ Sandisfield

New Boston ○

○ Tolland

HAMPDEN

Copake ○

Berkshire Choral Fest.

■ **Sheffield**
Southfield ○

Mt. Washington ○

Consolati Performing Arts Center

Ashley Falls ○
○ Clayton

Canaan

Salisbury

CT

○ Norfolk
Colebrook ○

Lakeville

Falls Village ○

LITCHFIELD
Norfolk Music Festival

Riverton ○

■ *Music Mountain*

About Lauren R. Stevens

Judith Monachina

Lauren R. Stevens is author of *Hikes & Walks in the Berkshire Hills*, *Skiing in the Berkshire Hills*, *Old Barns in the New World* (with Richard Babcock), *Most Excellent Majesty: A History of Mount Greylock* (with Deborah Burns), and a novel, *The Double Axe*. Founder of *The Advocate*, a weekly newspaper for Berkshire County and southern Vermont, he writes on the environment and regional history for several publications. He is a resident of Williamstown and father of three.